Imprecation as Divine Discourse

# Journal of Theological Interpretation Supplements
MURRAY RAE
University of Otago, New Zealand
Editor-in-Chief

1. Thomas Holsinger-Friesen, *Irenaeus and Genesis: A Study of Competition in Early Christian Hermeneutics*
2. Douglas S. Earl, *Reading Joshua as Christian Scripture*
3. Joshua N. Moon, *Jeremiah's New Covenant: An Augustinian Reading*
4. Csilla Saysell, *"According to the Law": Reading Ezra 9–10 as Christian Scripture*
5. Joshua Marshall Strahan, *The Limits of a Text: Luke 23:34a as a Case Study in Theological Interpretation*
6. Seth B. Tarrer, *Reading with the Faithful: Interpretation of True and False Prophecy in the Book of Jeremiah from Ancient Times to Modern*
7. Zoltán S. Schwáb, *Toward an Interpretation of the Book of Proverbs: Selfishness and Secularity Reconsidered*
8. Steven Joe Koskie, Jr., *Reading the Way to Heaven: A Wesleyan Theological Hermeneutic of Scripture*
9. Hubert James Keener, *A Canonical Exegesis of the Eighth Psalm: Y*HWH*'s Maintenance of the Created Order through Divine Intervention*
10. Vincent K. H. Ooi, *Scripture and Its Readers: Readings of Israel's Story in Nehemiah 9, Ezekiel 20, and Acts 7*
11. Andrea D. Saner, *"Too Much to Grasp": Exodus 3:13–15 and the Reality of God*
12. Jonathan Douglas Hicks, *Trinity, Economy, and Scripture: Recovering Didymus the Blind*
13. Dru Johnson, *Knowledge by Ritual: A Biblical Prolegomenon to Sacramental Theology*
14. Ryan S. Peterson, *The* Imago Dei *as Human Identity: A Theological Interpretation*
15. Ron Haydon, *"Seventy Sevens Are Decreed": A Canonical Approach to Daniel 9:24–27*
16. Kit Barker, *Imprecation as Divine Discourse: Speech Act Theory, Dual Authorship, and Theological Interpretation*

# Imprecation as Divine Discourse

*Speech Act Theory, Dual Authorship,
and Theological Interpretation*

KIT BARKER

Winona Lake, Indiana
EISENBRAUNS
2016

Copyright © 2016 Eisenbrauns
All rights reserved.

Printed in the United States of America

www.eisenbrauns.com

---

**Library of Congress Cataloging-in-Publication Data**

Names: Barker, Kit (Lecturer in Old Testament), author.
Title: Imprecation as divine discourse : speech act theory, dual authorship, and theological interpretation / Kit Barker.
Description: Winona Lake, Indiana : Eisenbrauns, 2016. | Series: Journal of theological interpretation supplements ; 16 | Includes bibliographical references and index.
Identifiers: LCCN 2016045033 | ISBN 9781575064444 (pbk. : alk. paper)
Subjects: LCSH: Blessing and cursing in the Bible. | Bible Psalms—Criticism, interpretation, etc. | Speech acts (Linguistics)—Religious aspects—Christianity. | Bible—Criticism, interpretation, etc.
Classification: LCC BS1430.6.B5 B37 2016 | DDC 221.601—dc23
LC record available at https://lccn.loc.gov/2016045033

---

The paper used in this publication meets the minimum requirements of the American National Standard for Information Sciences—Permanence of Paper for Printed Library Materials, ANSI Z39.48-1984.♾™

# Table of Contents

Acknowledgements ................................................................................. ix

Abbreviations ........................................................................................ xi

Introduction .......................................................................................... 1
    Aims ................................................................................................. 1
    Rationale .......................................................................................... 1
    Presuppositions ............................................................................... 5
    Methodology .................................................................................... 7

Part I. In Pursuit of Theological Interpretation ................................... 9

Chapter 1. Speech Act Theory ............................................................ 11
    Introduction ................................................................................... 11
    A Brief History ............................................................................... 12
        John L. Austin ........................................................................... 12
        John R. Searle ........................................................................... 13
    Application to Biblical Studies and Theology ............................... 16
        Speech Act Criticism ................................................................ 17
        Reconceptualising Hermeneutics ............................................ 20
    Conclusion ..................................................................................... 35

Chapter 2. Dual Authorship ............................................................... 36
    Introduction ................................................................................... 36
    Proponents of a *Sensus Plenior* .................................................... 37
        Raymond E. Brown .................................................................. 37
        Evangelical Proponents ........................................................... 38
        Evangelical Modifications of *Sensus Plenior* ........................ 40
    Evangelical Opponents to *Sensus Plenior* .................................. 43
        Walter Kaiser ........................................................................... 43
        Elliot Johnson ......................................................................... 45

Jeannine Brown .................................................................................................. 47
   Challenges to Sensus Plenior ............................................................................. 53
   Speech Act Theorists and Sensus Plenior ....................................................... 55
   Kevin J. Vanhoozer ........................................................................................... 56
   Nicholas Wolterstorff ....................................................................................... 58
   Conclusion ........................................................................................................ 64

Chapter 3. Speech Act Theory, Dual Authorship and
Canonical Hermeneutics .................................................................................... 66

   Introduction ...................................................................................................... 66
   Part A. Speech Act Theory and General Hermeneutics ................................ 66
   Speech Act Theory is Rightly Applied to all Texts ........................................ 66
   Illocution as the Locus of Meaning ................................................................ 69
   Avoiding Romantic Hermeneutics ................................................................ 70
   Summary of Presuppositions .......................................................................... 82
   Literary Levels of Illocution ............................................................................ 82
   Meaning and Thick Descriptions: Primary and Attendant Illocutions .......... 88
   Summary of Part A .......................................................................................... 89
   Part B. Dual Authorship and Canonical Hermeneutics ................................ 90
   Divine Illocutions and Sensus Plenior .......................................................... 91
   Canonical Illocutions ...................................................................................... 95
   Central Illocutions ........................................................................................... 98
   Illocutions—Taxonomy of Levels ................................................................... 99
   Functional Illocutionary Levels .................................................................... 100
   Literary Illocutionary Levels ........................................................................ 100
   Conclusion: Divine Illocutions and the
   Goal of Theological Hermeneutics ............................................................... 101
   Thick Descriptions ........................................................................................ 101
   Identifying Divine Illocutions ...................................................................... 101

Part II. Theological Interpretation and the Psalter ..................................... 105


Chapter 4. The Divine Illocutions of the Psalter in Its
Old Testament Context ..................................................................................... 107

   Introduction .................................................................................................... 107
   The Primary Illocutions of the Psalter ......................................................... 107
   Speech Act Theory and the Psalter ............................................................... 108
   Canonical Inclusion and Primary Illocution ............................................... 109
   Canonical Shaping and Primary Illocution ................................................. 111
   Literary Features and Primary Illocution .................................................... 118
   Yahweh Reigns as a Primary Illocution ....................................................... 120
   Summary of Primary Illocutions of the Psalter in its
   Old Testament Context ................................................................................. 121

Various Conceptions of Dual Authorship in the Psalms .................................. 121
  The Words of God are the Words of the Psalmist
  and the Words of the Pray-er ........................................................................ 122
  The Words of God are No Longer the Words of the Psalmist ..................... 123
  The Words of God in the Presentation of the Psalms ................................. 124
Conclusion: Divine Illocutions and the Psalter ............................................. 125

## Chapter 5. The Theological Interpretation of Imprecatory Psalms .................. 127

Introduction ......................................................................................................... 127
Various Approaches to the Imprecatory Psalms ............................................ 128
Imprecation and the Illocutionary Stance of the Psalter .............................. 132
  Introduction ..................................................................................................... 132
  Imprecation as a Righteous Response .......................................................... 132
  Conclusion: The Divine Illocutions of the Imprecatory Psalms
  in Old Testament Context .............................................................................. 136
Imprecation and the Illocutionary Stance of the New Testament:
Forgive, Bless and Love Your Enemies ............................................................ 136
  Introduction ..................................................................................................... 136
  Forgiveness and Imprecation ......................................................................... 137
  Blessing, Love and Imprecation .................................................................... 150
  The New Testament Invitation to Imprecation ........................................... 154
Conclusion: Imprecatory Psalms and
Contemporary Divine Illocution ...................................................................... 156

## Chapter 6. A Theological Interpretation of Psalm 137 .................................... 158

Introduction ......................................................................................................... 158
Translation ........................................................................................................... 159
Literary and Historical Contexts ...................................................................... 160
  Genre ................................................................................................................. 160
  Sitz im Leben .................................................................................................... 161
  Placement within the Psalter ......................................................................... 162
  Internal Structure ............................................................................................ 163
Exposition ............................................................................................................. 164
The Illocutionary Acts of Psalm 137 ................................................................ 171
  Human Authorial and Editorial Illocutions ................................................ 171
  Primary Illocutions of the Psalter in Psalm 137 .......................................... 174
  Divine Illocutions in the Context of the Hebrew Bible ............................. 174
  Divine Illocutions in the Context of the Christian Canon
  —A Thick Description .................................................................................... 176
Conclusion ............................................................................................................ 178

## Chapter 7. A Theological Interpretation Of Psalm 69 .................................... 180

Introduction ......................................................................................................... 180

Christological Interpretations of Psalm 69 .................................................. 181
　　　Christ is the Speaker of Psalm 69 .................................................................. 181
　　　Christ is the "Consummate Example" of Psalm 69 ......................................... 184
　　　Conclusion ....................................................................................................... 186
　　Exposition of Psalm 69 ................................................................................ 186
　　　Translation of Psalm 69 .................................................................................. 186
　　　Literary and Historical Contexts ..................................................................... 189
　　　Textual Observations ...................................................................................... 193
　　　Summary of Illocutions in the Old Testament Context ................................... 198
　　New Testament Illocutions Regarding Psalm 69 ......................................... 200
　　　Introduction .................................................................................................... 200
　　　Psalm 69 in John ............................................................................................. 200
　　　Psalms 69 and 109 in Acts .............................................................................. 204
　　　Psalm 69 in Romans ........................................................................................ 207
　　　Summary of New Testament Illocutions Regarding Psalm 69 ........................ 209
　　Conclusion: A "Theologically Thick" Description of Psalm 69 ................... 209

Conclusion .................................................................................................................. 212

Bibliography .............................................................................................................. 218

Index of Authors and Subject .................................................................................... 238

Index of Scripture ...................................................................................................... 242

# Acknowledgements

I would like to thank a number of people who have supported me throughout the process of writing this book. First, I would like to thank my doctoral supervisor Andrew Sloane. He has not only provided clear direction and insightful critique, but he has been an enormous source of encouragement over many years. His influence surpasses the role of supervisor. I am continually thankful for his friendship and wise counsel. I would also like to thank Jim Harrison who both encouraged me on this path and made it possible during my initial years of lecturing. I trust that I have been shaped by his academic rigour, pastoral concern and generosity.

I have also enjoyed the support of the faculty, staff, and students at Wesley Institute, Morling College, and Sydney Missionary and Bible College. Their interest in and engagement with my work, both inside and outside the classroom, has been both encouraging and stimulating.

In the final stages of production, my colleague Geoff Harper was the first to read the work without being obligated to do so. I am grateful for his time, keen analysis, and attention to detail. I would also like to thank Anthony Petterson for his critical interaction and Andrew Hope for his technical support in the layout of the document. I am also thankful that Eisenbrauns agreed to publish my work in their series of fine monographs.

Finally, I would like to thank my family—my parents and parents-in-law, who continue to model lives of faithfulness to Christ—my children, who are a constant source of joy—and my wife, Robyn. I am truly thankful to God for her unwavering support and sacrifice.

# Abbreviations

| | |
|---|---|
| AJET | *Africa Journal of Evangelical Theology* |
| ATI | *American Theological Inquiry* |
| BAGD | *A Greek-English Lexicon of the New Testament and Other Early Christian Literature* |
| BDB | *The Brown-Driver-Briggs Hebrew and English Lexicon* |
| BibInt | *Biblical Interpretation* |
| BSac | *Bibliotheca Sacra* |
| BBR | *Bulletin for Biblical Research* |
| CTJ | *Calvin Theological Journal* |
| CBQ | *Catholic Biblical Quarterly* |
| ChrCent | *Christian Century* |
| CSR | *Christian Scholar's Review* |
| Chm | *Churchman* |
| CTR | *Criswell Theological Review* |
| CurBS | *Currents in Research: Biblical Studies* |
| DTIB | *Dictionary for the Theological Interpretation of the Bible* |
| DBI | *Dictionary of Biblical Imagery* |
| DBWC | *Dictionary of the Bible and Western Culture* |
| Dir | *Direction* |
| EvQ | *Evangelical Quarterly* |
| ERT | *Evangelical Review of Theology* |
| ExpT | *Expository Times* |
| HALOT | *The Hebrew & Aramaic Lexicon of the Old Testament* |
| HTR | *Harvard Theological Review* |
| HBT | *Horizons in Biblical Theology* |
| IJPR | *International Journal for Philosophy of Religion* |
| IJST | *International Journal of Systematic Theology* |
| JSNT | *Journal for the Study of the New Testament* |
| JSOT | *Journal for the Study of the Old Testament* |
| JBL | *Journal of Biblical Literature* |
| JHebS | *Journal of Hebrew Scriptures* |
| JNSL | *Journal of Northwest Semitic Languages* |
| JPT | *Journal of Psychology and Theology* |
| JPC | *Journal of Psychology and Christianity* |
| JETS | *Journal of the Evangelical Theological Society* |
| JTI | *Journal of Theological Interpretation* |

| | |
|---|---|
| JTS | *Journal of Theological Studies* |
| LXX | Septuagint |
| ModTheo | *Modern Theology* |
| MT | Masoretic Text |
| PoeTo | *Poetics Today* |
| Presb | *Presbyterian* |
| PSB | *Princeton Seminary Bulletin* |
| ProEccl | *Pro Ecclesia* |
| PEGLMWBS | *Proceedings: Eastern Great Lakes and Midwest Biblical Societies* |
| RTR | *Reformed Theological Review* |
| RelS | *Religious Studies* |
| SBET | *Scottish Bulletin of Evangelical Theology* |
| SJT | *Scottish Journal of Theology* |
| Them | *Themelios* |
| ThTo | *Theology Today* |
| TJ | *Trinity Journal* |
| TynBul | *Tyndale Bulletin* |
| WTJ | *Westminster Theological Journal* |
| ZAW | *Zeitschrift für die Alttestamentilche Wissenshaft* |

# Introduction

## Aims

My desire is to provide clarity to the task of theological interpretation. This will be achieved through the development and application of a speech act theory based hermeneutic that accounts for how Scripture functions as divine discourse. In Part I, I develop the theological hermeneutic and, in Part II, I demonstrate its usefulness for theological interpretation by applying it to a specific set of texts. I have selected the Psalter for this application, and the imprecatory psalms in particular, as they have proved particularly problematic for theological interpretation. I employ the hermeneutic at a number of literary levels within the Psalter: the Psalter as a whole, the imprecatory psalms as a genre, and finally, Psalms 137 and 69 as representative communal and individual imprecations.

## Rationale

The interest in theological interpretation has risen markedly in the last several years with a number of authors providing surveys of the current practice and offering various expressions of it.[1] This interest is related to the shift in

---

1. For an introduction to theological interpretation and a discussion of the emergence of its recent iterance see D. J. Treier, *Introducing Theological Interpretation of Scripture: Recovering a Christian Practice* (Grand Rapids: Baker, 2008). The recently formed *Journal of Theological Interpretation* by Eisenbrauns and the SCM Theological Commentary on the Bible series written by systematic theologians are also products of this renewed interest. This focus is also reflected in both the *Scripture and Hermeneutics* series edited by Craig G. Bartholomew, Scott Hahn, Robin Parry, Christopher Seitz and Al Wolters. The volume of writings has also inspired a dictionary dedicated to the interdisciplinary field: K. J. Vanhoozer et al., *Dictionary for Theological Interpretation of the Bible* (London: SPCK, 2005).

For a survey of this practice throughout Christian history see S. E. Fowl, *The Theological Interpretation of Scripture: Classic and Contemporary Readings* (Cambridge: Blackwell, 1997). For a discussion of theological interpretation in Patristic and contemporary theology see D. Sarisky, *Scriptural Interpretation: A Theological Exploration* (Malden: Wiley-Blackwell, 2013).

general hermeneutics from matters "behind the text" to those "in, and in front of the text", often referred to as the "literary turn."[2] The movement towards a canonical interpretation of Scripture in the second half of the last century is also demonstrative of this influence. This inevitably led to the question, "whose canon is it? " or, more specifically, if the canon is an intentional product, what are its contents, how is it shaped, and who is communicating through it?[3]

While theological interpretation has enjoyed this recent attention, there is little consensus regarding its defining qualities. Beldman and Bartholomew observe that, "this remains a diverse movement, and much work remains to be done in it."[4] They also note that Old Testament scholars are still not trained to think and work in these categories with very few seeing the goal of theological interpretation as the identification of God's voice. Bartholomew comments on his co-edited volume:

> The unique feature of this book is that it makes the telos of reading the Old Testament *listening for God's address*. The bifurcation of theology and biblical studies is well documented, and recent decades have witnessed welcome attempts to overcome this chasm. Nevertheless, the renaissance of theological interpretation of the Bible is still in its early years, and it remains rare to find scholarship on the Old Testament that embodies the kind of integrated theological hermeneutic that retains critical rigor while aiming throughout to hear God's address. This volume aims to fill that gap.[5]

---

Various monographs have also been influential in the past twenty years: R. S. Briggs, *Words in Action: Speech Act Theory and Biblical Interpretation: Toward a Hermeneutic of Self-Involvement* (Edinburgh: T&T Clark, 2001); A. C. Thiselton, *New Horizons in Hermeneutics: The Theory and Practice of Transforming Biblical Reading* (Grand Rapids: Zondervan, 1992); K. J. Vanhoozer, *Is There a Meaning in This Text?: The Bible, the Reader, and the Morality of Literary Knowledge* (Grand Rapids: Zondervan, 1998); K. J. Vanhoozer, *The Drama of Doctrine: A Canonical-Linguistic Approach to Christian Theology* (1st ed.; Louisville: Westminster John Knox Press, 2005); F. Watson, *Text and Truth: Redefining Biblical Theology* (Grand Rapids: Eerdmans, 1997); N. Wolterstorff, *Divine Discourse: Philosophical Reflections on the Claim That God Speaks* (Cambridge: Cambridge University Press, 1995).

2. This interdisciplinary focus is exemplified in a recent collection of essays edited by Firth and Grant: D. G. Firth and J. A. Grant, *Words and the Word: Explorations in Biblical Interpretation and Literary Theory* (Downers Grove: IVP 2008).

3. Brevard Childs championed this shift during the last century and offered the following conclusion regarding the significance of canon, "But irrespective of intentionality, the effect of the canonical process was to render the tradition accessible to the future generation by means of a 'canonical intentionality', which is coextensive with the meaning of the biblical text." B. S. Childs, *Introduction to the Old Testament as Scripture* (Philadelphia: Fortress Press, 1979), 79.

4. C. G. Bartholomew and D. J. H. Beldman, "Preface: The Love of the Old Testament and the Desire for God" in *Hearing the Old Testament: Listening for God's Address* (ed. C. G. Bartholomew and D. J. H. Beldman; Grand Rapids: Eerdmans, 2012), xvi.

5. C. G. Bartholomew, "Listening for God's Address: A Mere Trinitarian Hermeneutic for the Old Testament," in *Hearing the Old Testament: Listening for God's Address* (ed. C. G.

This lacuna in theological hermeneutics, particularly with respect to Old Testament scholarship, inspired my own work. While there are a number of definitions of theological interpretation,[6] I agree with Bartholomew that the definition and the goal of theological interpretation is to explain how a text functions as divine discourse.[7]

This idea, of course, is not new, nor is it without representation in the contemporary expression of theological interpretation.[8] My contribution relies substantially on the work of Nicholas Wolterstorff and Kevin Vanhoozer, who agree that the goal of theological interpretation should be the clarification of how the text functions as divine discourse. Both authors have also employed speech act theory to explain the nature of communication, defend the role of the author in the production of meaning, and highlight the inherent challenges to a hermeneutic of dual authorship. However, the significant contributions of both authors and the subsequent responses to their proposals have not produced a detailed hermeneutic.[9] Consequently, a sustained application of their

---

Bartholomew and D. J. H. Beldman; Grand Rapids: Eerdmans, 2012), 12.

6. Davis and Hays identify nine defining features, one of which may be understood as a reference to divine discourse, "Texts of Scripture do not have a single meaning limited to the intent of the original author. In accord with Jewish and Christian traditions, we affirm that Scripture has multiple complex senses given by God, the author of the whole drama." E. F. Davis and R. B. Hays, *The Art of Reading Scripture* (Grand Rapids: Eerdmans, 2003), 305.

7. For a defence of reading the text as a product of God's prior and continual agency in opposition to Enlightenment epistemology see M. A. Bowald, *Rendering the Word in Theological Hermeneutics: Mapping Divine and Human Agency* (Aldershot: Ashgate, 2007). He comments, "To attempt to remove ourselves from the divine agency in, with and under this text as an instrument of God's gracious judgment, salvation, guidance and comfort is, from this perspective, an act of denial or resistance; even defiance." (Bowald, *Rendering the Word*, 19.) He concludes that the way Scripture is read needs revision: "contemporary frameworks for understanding the act of reading Scripture need a thorough revision. A model that comports with the above analysis and which we suggest offers great potential corrective power is proffered by way of the ancient study of rhetoric. Thus the act of reading will be initially framed by the acknowledgment that the primary author of this text, God is present and "speaking"; as "divine rhetoric." It compels us to not lose track of the priority of God's agency as we consider all the other various aspects of reading that follow." (Bowald, *Rendering the Word*, 174.)

8. Writing 25 years ago Greidanus proposed the same definition and goal: "Theological interpretation seeks to hear *God's* voice in the Scriptures; it seeks to probe beyond mere historical reconstruction and verbal meanings to a discernment of the message of God in the Scriptures; it concentrates on the prophetic, kerygmatic dimension and the theocentric focus." (S. Greidanus, *The Modern Preacher and the Ancient Text: Interpreting and Preaching Biblical Literature* (Grand Rapids: Eerdmans, 1988), 102-103, emphasis original.)

9. Vanhoozer notes the need for further work on his proposed hermeneutic, "Yet God may be doing new things with Jonah and other biblical texts too by virtue of their being gathered together in the canon. Could it be that certain illocutions come to light

proposal to the biblical text is also lacking. Treier comments on both the lack of hermeneutic detail and exegetical application:

> Briggs notes that Wolterstorff does not explain very well how to adjudicate between conflicting interpretations of the divine discourse in a given biblical passage. And Vanhoozer's notion of a "canonical illocution"—happening not in any one text but in terms of the whole Bible, or Scripture serving as the larger context for a particular passage—has not yet offered proof of the pudding in much interpretive eating.[10]

This deficiency is not unique to Wolterstorff and Vanhoozer. Writing in 2009, Moberly comments generally on the project of the theological interpretation:

> There tends to be more discussion about the nature of theological interpretation and theological hermeneutics than there is demonstration in persuasive and memorable readings of the biblical text.[11]

The reasons for this deficiency are undoubtedly many, but I suggest that significant factors are an insufficient comprehension of speech act theory and a confusion regarding its role in theological interpretation. In the following chapter I offer a more detailed survey of its acceptance and appropriation, yet its neglect is notable as Briggs comments:

> Despite a slow trickle of articles over the past 25 years, there have been only a handful of more extensive works making exegetical use of speech act insights. This 'undeserved neglect,' which may be observed not just in biblical studies but in systematic theology as well as the philosophy of religion (Thiselton, 1997: 97), is doubtless

---

only when we describe what God is doing at the canonical level? *More work needs to be done in this area*, but for the moment let me offer the following as possible candidates for the divine canonical illocutions: instructing the believing community, testifying to Christ, and perhaps most obviously, covenanting." (K. J. Vanhoozer, *First Theology: God, Scripture & Hermeneutics* (Downers Grove: IVP, 2002), 194, emphasis mine.)

10. Treier, *Introducing Theological Interpretation*, 145-146. This is despite previous calls for such a project. Scott Blue, writing more than a decade ago, comments on the lack of application in the work of both Francis Watson and Kevin Vanhoozer, "While both Watson and Vanhoozer incorporate speech act theory into their hermeneutical programs, they disregard one important area in their discussions. Neither writer adequately demonstrates how speech act theory can be *practically* included in the process of interpretation. Watson does analyze texts within his biblical theological approach, but does not explicitly show any difference that speech act theory makes in his interpretations. Vanhoozer lays a literalist hermeneutical foundation for interpretation, but, again, fails to demonstrate how speech act principles are to be practiced within that framework." (S. A. Blue, "Meaning, Intention, and Application: Speech Act Theory in the Hermeneutics of Francis Watson and Kevin J Vanhoozer," *TJ*, no. 23 (2002): 161-184.)

11. R. W. L. Moberly, "What Is Theological Interpretation of Scripture?," *JTI* 3, no. 2 (2009): 169.

due in part to the forbidding complexity of much of the philosophical literature, with the inevitable result that biblical critics are sometimes at a loss to say just what exactly constitute the resources of speech-act theory for the task of interpretation. There is confusion over whether speech-act theory is a tool for exegesis as it is already practised, or whether in fact it indicates that exegesis itself needs to be reconceptualized (Buss 1988: 125).[12]

Both Wolterstorff and Vanhoozer believe that theological hermeneutics would benefit from the resources of speech act theory and their proposals rely heavily upon it. Perhaps this pervasive incorporation of speech act theory in their hermeneutics and its relative neglect in theological scholarship has deterred significant development of their thought.

I am convinced that a speech act theory based hermeneutic can offer a significant way forward for theological interpretation. In particular, it can provide a level of terminological clarity previously lacking in descriptions of what it means for Scripture to function as divine discourse, and consequently it can provide both hermeneutic and teleological clarity to the task of theological interpretation. This conviction guides my argument, the results of which, I believe, indicate the value of the approach.

Returning for a moment to the comment by Beldman and Bartholomew regarding the nature of theological interpretation, they noted not only that the goal of theological interpretation should be "listening for God's address", but that such interpretation is necessarily interdisciplinary. They observed that this necessity is not matched by the focus of current Old Testament scholarship, "it remains rare to find scholarship on the Old Testament that embodies the kind of integrated theological hermeneutic that retains critical rigor while aiming throughout to hear God's address."[13] It is into this interdisciplinary void that I hope to make a contribution by both clarifying a theological hermeneutic and demonstrating its application in exegesis.

## Presuppositions

There are a number of presuppositions that shape the aims and methodology of this book. First and foremost is the conviction that all Scripture is, by definition, the continual word of God. As mentioned above, I hold this to be both the basis for and the goal of theological interpretation.[14]

---

12. R. S. Briggs, "The Uses of Speech-Act Theory in Biblical Interpretation," *CurBS* 9 (2001): 230.

13. Bartholomew, "Listening for God's Address," 3, emphasis original.

14. The defence of such a presupposition is beyond the scope of this book. For a discussion of Scripture as divine discourse see: H. N. Wallace, *Words to God, Word from God: The Psalms in the Prayer and Preaching of the Church* (Aldershot: Ashgate, 2005); Bartholomew, "Listening for God's Address; P. Adam, *Hearing God's Words: Exploring Biblical Spirituality* (16; Downers Grove: IVP, 2004); D. A. Carson and J. D. Woodbridge,

A second presupposition concerns the boundaries of Scripture and the identification of canon. I am writing within the Protestant tradition that accepts the Hebrew Bible and the New Testament together as its canon.[15] Therefore, when I refer to canon, this is the reference. While my methodology could conceivably be applied to different conceptions of canon, I am primarily concerned with developing a hermeneutic that is consistent with and useful for my own tradition.[16]

My third presupposition is that speech act theory correctly describes the anatomy of communication and rightly prioritizes the illocutionary act in the construction of meaning. While I will be providing a detailed discussion of speech act theory and its application to theological hermeneutics, I will not offer an explicit defence of it.[17] Implicitly, the theory will be judged in the final

---

*Hermeneutics, Authority and Canon* (Nottingham: IVP, 1986); Vanhoozer, *First Theology*; Wolterstorff, *Divine Discourse*.

15. Exegetical discussion of Old Testament texts will be based on the MT, with reference to the LXX where appropriate. There is continued debate over the nature and content of the Old Testament canon. For a selection of recent essays on the topic see C. A. Evans and E. Tov, *Exploring the Origins of the Bible: Canon Formation in Historical, Literary, and Theological Perspective* (Grand Rapids: Baker, 2008).

For a defence of the priority of a proto-Masoretic text while recognizing the importance of various translations see S. G. Dempster, "Torah, Torah, Torah: The Emergence of the Tripartite Canon," in *Exploring the Origins of the Bible: Canon Formation in Historical, Literary, and Theological Perspective* (ed. C. A. Evans and E. Tov; Grand Rapids: Baker 2008).

For a discussion of the canonicity and authority of the LXX see M. Hengel, R. Deines, and M. E. Biddle, *The Septuagint as Christian Scripture: Its Prehistory and the Problem of Its Canon* (North American paperback ed.; Grand Rapids: Baker 2004). For a recent defence of the priority of the LXX see T. M. Law, *When God Spoke Greek: The Septuagint and the Making of the Christian Bible* (Oxford: Oxford University Press, 2013).

16. For a discussion of the authority of the canon and its place in theological hermeneutics see: Carson and Woodbridge, *Hermeneutics, Authority and Canon*; D. J. Treier, "Canonical Unit and Commensurable Language: On Divine Action and Doctrine," in *Evangelicals & Scripture: Tradition, Authority, and Hermeneutics* (ed. V. Bacote, L. C. Miguélez, and D. L. Okholm; Downers Grove: IVP, 2004); C. R. Seitz, "The Canonical Approach and Theological Interpretation," in *Canon and Biblical Interpretation* (ed. C. Bartholomew, et al.; Grand Rapids: Zondervan, 2006); C. Bartholomew et al., *Canon and Biblical Interpretation* (Grand Rapids: Zondervan, 2006); M. N. A. Bockmuehl and A. J. Torrance, *Scripture's Doctrine and Theology's Bible: How the New Testament Shapes Christian Dogmatics* (Grand Rapids: Baker 2008).

17. Speech act theory has been developed and promoted by philosophers, theologians, and biblical scholars. For its defence see Briggs, *Words in Action*; W. P. Alston, *Illocutionary Acts and Sentence Meaning* (Ithaca: Cornell University Press, 2000); J. R. Searle, F. Kiefer, and M. Bierwisch, *Speech Act Theory and Pragmatics* (10; Dordrecht: D. Reidel, 1980); Vanhoozer, *Is There a Meaning in This Text*; N. Wolterstorff, "The Promise of Speech-Act Theory for Biblical Interpretation," in *After Pentecost: Language and Biblical Interpretation* (ed. C. G. Bartholomew, C. J. D. Greene, and K. Möller; Carlisle: Paternoster

product. If the subsequent theological hermeneutic is cogent and its application to specific texts is beneficial, then the benefits of speech act theory will be evident. So while I assume speech act theory to be correct, this book is a demonstration of its descriptive and explanatory capacity.

The final presupposition is derivative of the above three and is epistemological in nature. Accepting that Scripture is divine discourse and that meaning is a product of illocutionary stance suggests that the meaning of a biblical text is determinate. Therefore, I align myself with hermeneutic realists in my conviction that the task of theological interpretation is to uncover, rather than create, meaning. I am not suggesting that meaning is necessarily *single and determinate*, nor am I suggesting that ancient texts function as divine discourse solely in their original contexts. Rather, I presuppose that all Scripture continues to function as divine discourse, and subsequently, it is the task of theological interpretation to describe this function by attributing illocutionary stance to the divine author.

## Methodology

The methodology is reflected in the structure of the book. In Part I, I develop a theological hermeneutic that accounts for the dual authorship of Scripture and in Part II, I apply the hermeneutic across the various literary levels of the Psalter with a particular focus on imprecatory psalms. I begin Part I with a description of speech act theory and its application in biblical interpretation. This chapter provides the requisite language for investigating the dual authorship of Scripture. Utilizing the descriptive power of speech act theory, I then survey various approaches to dual authorship and *sensus plenior*, offering critique and demonstrating that the issue is more ubiquitous than is often recognized. In the final chapter of Part I, I provide an outline of a theological hermeneutic. In this chapter I use speech act theory to explain the goals of theological interpretation and propose a corresponding hermeneutic. In particular I employ the theory to provide a nuanced explanation of dual authorship and discuss how the canon functions as communicative action.[18]

---

Press, 2001); S. L. Tsohatzidis, "Ways of Doing Things with Words," in *Foundations of Speech Act Theory: Philosophical and Linguistic Perspectives* (ed. S. L. Tsohatzidis; London: Routledge, 1994); V. S. Poythress, "Canon and Speech Act: Limitations in Speech-Act Theory, with Implications for a Putative Theory of Canonical Speech Acts," *WTJ* 70, no. 2 (2008).

18. Dan Treier notes that the affect of the canon is one of the most important contemporary questions for theological interpretation and that the answer to this will have implications for conceptions of biblical authority, "I take it that the way in which divine, canonical speech acts supervene on the Bible's human, particular speech acts remains the most challenging question for evangelicals concerning biblical authority ..." (Treier, "Canonical Unit and Commensurable Language," 223.)

In order to demonstrate and assess the validity and usefulness of the proposed hermeneutic, I apply it to a particular book and to specific texts within it. This is the burden of Part II. Initially, I examine how the Psalter functions as divine discourse in both its original and canonical contexts. Then, after surveying the various approaches to the imprecatory psalms, I explain how they functioned as divine discourse in the context of the Old Testament and how they continue to function as God's contemporary speech acts. Finally, I apply the hermeneutic to individual imprecatory psalms in order to demonstrate its usefulness in exegesis.

The choice of text was, to some degree, arbitrary. I believe that such a hermeneutic could be successfully applied to any text within the canon. However, it was my desire to explore how Old Testament texts continue to function in the context of the canon. The Psalter was, therefore, a natural choice. It is here that the problematic of dual authorship is acute. Furthermore, in order to provide an application with sufficient detail, it was necessary to exegete particular psalms within the Psalter. For this application I chose the imprecatory psalms. Again the choice was natural as these psalms are often rejected in part, or *en masse*, as divine discourse. Psalms 137 and 69 were chosen as representative communal and individual laments respectively. Exegesis of both psalms allowed for an investigation of any differences in how they function as divine discourse. The exegesis of Psalm 137 was required due to its notoriety and its presence in discussions of both imprecation and theological interpretation. Psalm 69 was chosen because of its explicit use in the New Testament. Consequently, it also provided opportunity not only to examine an individual lament but also to engage discussions regarding the Christological interpretation of the psalms.

# Part I

# In Pursuit of Theological Interpretation

# Chapter 1

# Speech Act Theory

## Introduction

The aims of this chapter are to explain the basic features of speech act theory, to provide a survey of its acceptance and utility in both theology and biblical studies, and finally to introduce questions highlighted by speech act theory concerning meaning and the goals of interpretation.

The past century witnessed major changes in philosophy and in linguistics in particular. The "linguistic turn", as this shift in emphasis came to be known, involved structuralist and then poststructuralist philosophies, both of which diminished the importance of the author. Structuralists focused their attention on the text itself and saw all language as a self-referring system. Poststructuralists doubted the existence of such uniform systems and instead were interested in how texts were received in new contexts. Both philosophies considered interpretation based on authorial intention to be unworkable and ultimately uninteresting.[1] Speech act theory represents one line of resistance to this shift in philosophical thought and defends conceptions of reality and language that prioritise the role of the author in determining linguistic meaning.[2]

---

1. For a survey of influential contributors and a discussion of key concepts during this shift in hermeneutics, see Thiselton, *New Horizons in Hermeneutics*.

2. Speech act theory has also been employed by non-realists and these applications will be discussed below. See S. E. Fowl, "The Role of Authorial Intention in the Theological Interpretation of Scripture," in *Between Two Horizons: Spanning New Testament Studies and Systematic Theology* (ed. J. B. Green and M. Turner; Grand Rapids: Eerdmans, 2000); S. J. Grenz and J. R. Franke, *Beyond Foundationalism: Shaping Theology in a Postmodern Context* (Louisville: Westminster John Knox Press, 2001); S. J. Grenz, "The Spirit and the Word: The World-Creating Function of the Text," *ThTo* 57, no. 3 (2000); P. Ricœur, "The Model of the Text: Meaningful Action Considered as a Text," in *From Text to Action: Essays in Hermeneutics II* (Evanston: Northwestern University Press, 2007).

## A Brief History

*John L. Austin*

Speech act theory is a sub-discipline of the philosophy of language and falls under the broader category of pragmatics[3] or "ordinary language" philosophy. Its history has been widely documented and requires only a brief survey here.[4] In 1955 John L. Austin delivered the William James lectures at Harvard, which were subsequently and posthumously published as *How to Do Things with Words*. His central thesis was that speaking is more than simply uttering words or sentences; it also performs an action. While the idea that language accomplished more than just reference or representation was beginning to surface,[5] it was Austin's work that founded speech act theory.[6]

Austin's initial concern was to demonstrate that even "constatives" are "performative." That is, sentences which were held to be simply fact stating or descriptive (i.e., "constatives") are actually still "performances" by an author. Austin developed an anatomy of communication using the terms *locution, illocution,* and *perlocution*. The *locutionary act* is the uttering of the words; the *illocutionary act* is what we do in uttering the words; and the *perlocutionary act* is the effect we bring about by uttering the words. In his own words:

> We first distinguished a group of things we do in saying something, which together we summed up by saying we perform a *locutionary act*, which is roughly equivalent to uttering a certain sentence with a certain sense and reference, which again is roughly equivalent to 'meaning' in the traditional sense. Second, we said that we also perform *illocutionary acts* such as informing, ordering, warning, undertaking, &c. i.e., utterances which have a certain (conventional) force. Thirdly, we may also perform *perlocutionary acts*: what we bring about or achieve *by* saying something, such as convincing, persuading, deterring, and even, say, surprising or misleading.[7]

---

3. In the sense that differentiates semantics, syntactics and pragmatics rather than the philosophy of American "pragmatism."

4. Briggs, *Words in Action*; B. Smith, "Towards a History of Speech Act Theory," in *Speech Acts, Meaning, and Intentions: Critical Approaches to the Philosophy of John R. Searle* (ed. A. Burkhardt; Berlin: de Gruyter, 1990). For a discussion of the usefulness and limitations of speech act theory as a philosophy of language see D. Gorman, "The Use and Abuse of Speech-Act Theory in Criticism," *PoeTo* 20, no. 1 (1999).

5. E.g., L. Wittgenstein, *Philosophical Investigations* (3rd ed.; New York: Macmillan, 1968). For a collection of essays by Paul Grice who adopted speech act theory to develop notions of meaning, see P. Grice, *Studies in the Way of Words* (Cambridge: Harvard University Press, 1989).

6. J. L. Austin, *How to Do Things with Words* (1955; 2nd ed.; Oxford: Clarendon Press, 1975).

7. Austin, *How to Do Things*, 109.

Of the three components identified by Austin, it is the *illocutionary act* that emphasizes the performative nature of language. Austin summarizes:

> I explained the performance of an act in this new and second sense as the performance of an 'illocutionary' act, i.e., performance of an act *in* saying something as opposed to performance of an act *of* saying something; I call the act performed an 'illocution' and shall refer to the doctrine of the different types of function of language here in question as the doctrine of 'illocutionary forces'.[8]

What Austin was attempting to demonstrate is that the primary goal of speaking or communicating is not to convey meaning "in the traditional sense" of "sense and reference" but to elicit understanding of the action (illocution) performed.

*John R. Searle*

While Austin is clearly the initiator of this theory, due to his untimely death, its development was left to others. Among those who continued this work, John R Searle, once a student under Austin, remains prominent. Searle attempted to advance the theory in a number of areas. He proposed clearer distinctions between Austin's three categories, provided a more detailed classification of the various kinds of illocution, elaborated on the "rule governed" nature of illocutionary acts, and focused attention on what he calls "background."[9]

Searle was troubled by Austin's formulation of *locution* which included three separate categories: phonetic, phatic, and rhetic. Austin describes these distinctions in following manner:

> The phonetic act is merely the act of uttering certain noises. The phatic act is the uttering of certain vocables or words, i.e., noises of certain types, belonging to and as belonging to, a certain vocabulary, conforming to and as conforming to a certain grammar. The rhetic act is the performance of an act of using those vocables with a certain more-or-less definite sense and reference.[10]

The distinction that Austin seemed to be making by *phonetic, phatic* and *rhetic* is between uttering: 1) sounds, 2) words and sentences that exist in a language, and 3) words and sentences being used in a specific manner (i.e., with a sense and reference) respectively. Searle's concern was that the illocutionary

---

8. Austin, *How to Do Things*, 99-100.

9. J. R. Searle, *Speech Acts: An Essay in the Philosophy of Language* (London: Cambridge University Press, 1969); J. R. Searle, *Expression and Meaning: Studies in the Theory of Speech Acts* (Cambridge: Cambridge University Press, 1979); J. R. Searle, *Intentionality, an Essay in the Philosophy of Mind* (Cambridge: Cambridge University Press, 1983). Their contributions to the theory have been characterized in the following way: "If Austin is the Luther of speech act philosophy, John Searle may be considered its Melanchthon—its systematic theologian." (Vanhoozer, *Is There a Meaning in This Text?*, 209.)

10. Austin, *How to Do Things*, 95.

act was now being confused with the rhetic act. He proposed the following distinction between speech act components in order to isolate the illocutionary act more accurately:

> (a) Uttering words (morphemes, sentences) = performing *utterance acts*.
> (b) Referring and predicating = performing *propositional acts*.
> (c) Stating, questioning, commanding, promising, etc. = performing *illocutionary acts*." ... Utterance acts consist simply in uttering strings of words. Illocutionary and propositional acts consist characteristically in uttering words in sentences in certain contexts, under certain conditions and with certain intentions, as we shall see later on.[11]

In making this distinction, however, Searle recognized that the propositional act can never occur in isolation. It must occur concurrently with the illocutionary act being performed by the utterer.

> Propositional acts cannot occur alone; that is, one cannot *just* refer and predicate without making an assertion or asking a question or performing some other illocutionary act. The linguistic correlate of this point is that sentences, not words, are used to say things.[12]

One wonders in the end if Searle has actually accomplished anything by this further distinction of *propositional acts*. The same problem that Austin encountered with the *rhetic act* overlapping the illocutionary act seems to have simply changed names. In my opinion, it may be more accurate and helpful to subsume the so-called rhetic and propositional acts into the illocutionary act, acknowledging, as Searle does,[13] that an illocutionary act is not always singular in its force. Thus, the stating and referring component of the sentence would be considered an *attendant* or *secondary* illocutionary act (except in assertives where they are also the *primary* act).[14] Searle's concern at least highlights the need to understand what illocutionary forces are at work in a single sentence and how this relates to its propositional content. This issue will be taken up in later chapters. For the sake of clarity, however, the terms *locution, illocution, and perlocution*

---

11. Searle, *Speech Acts*, 24-25.
12. Searle, *Speech Acts*, 25.
13. Searle, *Expression and Meaning*, 29.
14. Searle of course objects to this collapse, "Stating and asserting are acts, but propositions are not acts. A proposition is what is asserted in the act of asserting, what is stated in the act of stating. The same point in a different way: an assertion is a (very special kind of) commitment to the truth of a proposition. The expression of a proposition is a propositional act, not an illocutionary act ... I am distinguishing between the illocutionary act and the propositional content of the illocutionary act. Of course not all illocutionary acts have a propositional content, for example, and utterance of "Hurrah" does not, nor does "Ouch."" (Searle, *Speech Acts*, 29.)

will be retained for this discussion. These categories seem sufficient and most authors are happy to adopt them.[15]

Further developments of the theory by Searle include a more detailed taxonomy of illocutionary acts and their corresponding "direction of fit" to the world. In response to the possibility that sentences can be used in an indefinite set of "language games" Searle suggests the following:

> If we adopt illocutionary point as the basic notion on which to classify uses of language, then there are a rather limited number of basic things we do with language: we tell people how things are, we try to get them to do things, we commit ourselves to doing things, we express our feelings and attitudes and we bring about changes through our utterances. Often, we do more than one of these at once in the same utterance.[16]

Searle notes the following kinds of illocutionary acts which correspond respectively to descriptions above: assertives, directives, commissives, expressives, and declarations. Additionally, each of these categories relates to the world in a particular way in what he calls its "direction of fit."[17] Assertives attempt to match one's words to the world. Directives and commissives attempt to match the world to one's words. Expressives have no stable direction of fit and declarations go in both directions (word to world and world to word).

His proposal outlined in the quotation above accomplishes at least two things. Firstly, with reference to the challenge of indeterminate meaning, it seeks to limit the discussion to what an author could have been doing with the text. Secondly, it acknowledges the possibility that an author can, and often does, do more than one thing with a sentence. If meaning is connected to illocution, then this results in a corresponding need to sufficiently describe the full range of illocutionary acts performed by an author in order to identify the meaning of the sentence.[18]

A significant contribution to the theory was Searle's discussion of illocutions as "rule governed" behaviour.[19] He argues, "Speaking a language is

---

15. So Alston, *Illocutionary Acts*; Briggs, *Words in Action*; J. K. Brown, *Scripture as Communication: Introducing Biblical Hermeneutics* (Grand Rapids: Baker, 2007); K. J. Vanhoozer, "From Speech Acts to Scripture Acts: The Covenant of Discourse & the Discourse of Covenant," in *First Theology: God, Scripture & Hermeneutics* (ed. K. J. Vanhoozer; Downers Grove: IVP, 2002); T. Ward, *Word and Supplement: SpeechActs, Biblical Texts, and the Sufficiency of Scripture* (Oxford: Oxford University Press, 2002); Wolterstorff, *Divine Discourse*.

16. Searle, *Expression and Meaning*, 29.

17. Searle, *Expression and Meaning*, 3-4.

18. This acknowledges that a sentence itself may not be the primary unit of meaning and may require an understanding of its context.

19. Austin also recognized that communication was governed by such rules and spoke of "appropriate circumstances" and "conventional procedure." However, it was once again Searle who developed these ideas.

engaging in a (highly complex) rule-governed form of behaviour. To learn and master a language is (*inter alia*) to learn and to have mastered these rules."[20] In particular, illocutionary acts are only possible due to the existence of rules inherent in a language:

> ...speaking a language is performing speech acts, acts such as making statements, giving commands, asking questions, making promises, and so on; and more abstractly, acts such as referring and predicating; and, secondly, that these acts are in general made possible by and are performed in accordance with certain rules for the use of linguistic elements.[21]

These public, institutional rules govern the use of language and make communication possible by enabling a hearer to understand the illocutionary acts being performed. Searle's explanation highlights the importance of attending to these rules in order to understand how the language is being used.

While speech act theory continues to be used and developed in various fields of inquiry,[22] the work of Austin and Searle continues to be influential and essentially forms the basis of further discussion.

## Application to Biblical Studies and Theology

The application of speech act theory to biblical and theological studies has also been surveyed elsewhere, yet requires moderate attention here.[23] Broadly speaking, there have been two positive yet different applications of speech act theory to biblical interpretation. The first, and more common, application is to employ speech act theory as a tool for exegesis. This will be referred to as "speech act criticism."[24] The second application, which my work exemplifies, is to employ speech act theory in a more sustained and pervasive manner in order to reconceptualise theological hermeneutics. As each of these applications employs speech act theory in the interpretation of Scripture, they assume its utility is applicable to texts and is not limited to oral communication.[25]

---

20. Searle, *Speech Acts*, 12.
21. Searle, *Speech Acts*, 16. Searle also distinguished between two kinds of rules that operated within a language: regulative rules and constitutive rules. "Regulative rules regulate a pre-existing activity, an activity whose existence is logically independent of the rules. Constitutive rule constitute (and also regulate) an activity the existence of which is logically dependent on the rules." (Searle, *Speech Acts*, 34-35.)
22. E.g., Alston, *Illocutionary Acts*.
23. For such a survey, see Briggs, "The Uses of Speech Act Theory"; Briggs, *Words in Action*.
24. J. G. Du Plessis, "Speech Act Theory and New Testament Interpretation with Special Reference to G.N. Leech's Pragmatic Principles," in *Text and Interpretation: New Approaches in the Criticism of the New Testament* (ed. P. J. Hartin, J. H. Petzer, and B. M. Metzger; Leiden: Brill, 1991).
25. This discussion, however, is outside the scope of the present project and has

*Speech Act Criticism*
Speech act criticism is concerned with the analysis of speech acts recorded within the biblical texts.[26] It does not usually treat the entire text as a speech act, rather it looks for "strong" or significant speech acts being performed by the author or the characters in the text. There are a number of examples of this application, with Dietmar Neufeld's work being representative. In Neufeld's

---

been extensively dealt with elsewhere. While speech act theory was initially developed with respect to verbal communication it also has much to commend itself as an analytical tool for written communication (Briggs, "The Uses of Speech Act Theory," 235.)

There are of course those who debate this point. The infamous exchange between Searle and Derrida is an example of this where Derrida questioned the possibility of a written text being able to communicate the intention of a no longer present author. See J. R. Searle, *The Construction of Social Reality* (New York: Free Press, 1995). The primary objection to employing speech act theory to texts is that the author is no longer present. Paul Ricoeur argues that while speech act theory has effectively described the communicative events between people, it cannot be used as a tool for exegesis or in developing a theological hermeneutic. He states that of the three components, the locutionary act is the easiest to exteriorise, the illocutionary act less so, and the perlocutionary act is the hardest to exteriorise. "The propositional act, the illocutionary force, and the perlocutionary action are susceptible, in a decreasing order, to the intentional exteriorisation that makes inscription in writing possible." (Ricœur, "The Model of the Text," 147.) Ricoeur argues elsewhere that this difficulty of exteriorisation results in the autonomy of the text. It is set free from the authorial intention, the illocutionary acts and what remains is "the sense of the text." He states, "With written discourse ... the author's intention and the meaning of the text cease to coincide ... What the text means now matters more than what the author meant when he wrote it." (P. Ricœur, *Interpretation Theory: Discourse and the Surplus of Meaning* (Fort Worth: Texas Christian University Press, 1976), 29.) According to Ricoeur, dialogue with the author is impossible and the text now engages the reader on its own terms. Ricoeur summarizes his conclusions, ."... what is finally to be understood in a text is not the author or the presumed intention, nor is it the immanent structure or structures of the text, but rather the sort of world intended beyond the text as its reference. (P. Ricœur, "Toward a Hermeneutic of the Idea of Revelation," in *Essays on Biblical Interpretation* (ed. P. Ricœur and L. S. Mudge; Philadelphia: Fortress Press, 1980), 99-100.)

For a defence of speech act theory and, in particular, hermeneutics based on authorial intention in light of Ricoeur's challenge see the following: Alston, *Illocutionary Acts*; Vanhoozer, *Is There a Meaning in This Text*; Vanhoozer, *First Theology*; Wolterstorff, *Divine Discourse*; M. S. Horton, *Covenant and Eschatology: The Divine Drama* (Louisville: Westminster John Knox Press, 2002).

26. The series of articles found in H. C. White (ed.), *Semeia* 41 (1988) represents an attempt at this particular application. See also D. Neufeld, *Reconceiving Texts as Speech Acts: An Analysis of 1 John* (vol. 7; Leiden: Brill, 1994); D. Neufeld, "Acts of Admonition and Rebuke: A Speech Act Approach to 1 Corinthians 6:1-11," *BibInt* 8, no. 4 (2000). Most recently, Anderson has used speech act theory to explore the nature of blessing and cursing in the Old Testament. See J. S Anderson, *The Blessing and the Curse: Trajectories in the Theology of Old Testament* (Eugene: Cascade, 2014).

study of 1 Corinthians 6:1–11 he isolates cases where Paul uses speech acts in order to bring about some change in the Corinthian church. He notes:

> In the ongoing struggle to defend his achieved standing and its public recognition, Paul uses speech acts that function in a setting where institutional roles and situational contexts render them performative speech acts. In other words, "rebuke" becomes performative when the person doing the rebuking has the requisite communal status to do so. In the interminable game of push and shove, the "rebuke" is intended to shame the members of the community (ἐντροπὴν, 1 Cor. 6:5). No doubt, Paul expects that the shame engendered by the rebuke will provoke the Corinthians to accept his challenge and respond to him favourably.[27]

While it is clearly the case that Paul uses the speech act of rebuke in this instance, it is unclear why Neufeld does not discuss *all* of Paul's speech acts. This problem is endemic to speech act criticism, as it does not consider the whole text to be worthy of analysis using speech act theory. In 1988 an entire volume of Semeia was devoted to speech act theory and biblical interpretation.[28] Interestingly, the articles included dealt solely with examples of speech act criticism and not with the text itself as a speech act. It has also been observed that the discussions of these contributors lacked any detail with regards to the application of their own proposals.[29]

A major contributor to the field of hermeneutics who has consistently engaged with speech act theory is Anthony Thiselton. Thiselton has reservations about viewing all texts as speech acts and argues for its limited application. While acknowledging some advantages of a more comprehensive application, in his mind the difficulties of such an approach are too great and his own application of speech act theory engages it as one of many tools for exegesis.[30]

> An increasing number of writers are now viewing *all* texts, including all texts of the New Testament, as speech acts. This offers certain advantages. It ensures that agents "mean" what they wish or will purposively to declare, state, express, promise, convey, or whatever as a temporally conditioned eventful action. It directs attention to speech as a communicative act between a "sender' and a "receiver," or between agents and audiences, and it avoids two problems that

---

27. Neufeld, "Acts of Admonition and Rebuke."
28. H. C. White, "The Value of Speech Act Theory for Old Testament Hermeneutics," *Semeia* 41 (1988).
29. For a critique of the application of speech act theory in these works, see A. C. Thiselton, "Speech-Act Theory and the Claim That God Speaks: Nicholas Wolterstorff's Divine Discourse," *SJT* 50, no. 1 (1997).
30. A. C. Thiselton, "Reader–Response Hermeneutics, Action Models, and the Parables of Jesus," in *The Responsibility of Hermeneutics* (ed. R. Lundin, A. C. Thiselton, and C. Walhout; Grand Rapids: Eerdmans, 1985); Thiselton, *New Horizons in Hermeneutics*; A. C. Thiselton, *The First Epistle to the Corinthians* (Grand Rapids: Eerdmans, 2000).

Wittgenstein identified as generating confusion: the assumption that language always serves to "convey thoughts"; and the mistake of confusing the "physical properties" or *forms* of speech with speech *functions* or constitutive use ... All the same, this "weak" understanding of speech acts threatens to degenerate into the subjective (anything can "count as" anything); worse, speech acts may become so diffused that those important illocutionary acts which (1) *entail serious obligations on the part of the speaker;* (2) *presuppose serious institutional facts* (which in the sense identified by Searle [1995] rest on extralinguistic "brute" facts); and (3) *achieve transformative effects not by causal perlocution but through institutional illocution,* come to *drop from view as paradigmatic or "strong" illocutions.*"[31]

Thiselton's objections seem valid in part. However, I would suggest that his concerns are, at times, overstated. His main concern with viewing the whole text as a speech act is that serious communicative events within it may be marginalised. Yet it would seem possible to recognize serious or "strong" illocutionary acts while still noting and appreciating the presence of "weak" or standard illocutionary acts. If speech act theory does indeed correctly describe the communicative process then it would seem beneficial to employ it at the level of hermeneutics rather than use it selectively as a tool for exegesis. The suggestion by Thiselton that some illocutions are strong enough to warrant description is problematic. Firstly, who decides which speech acts are sufficiently strong? Should we use Thiselton's own criteria? Secondly, while there may indeed be "strong" and "weak" illocutions, is it not the responsibility of the reader to make such a distinction by first considering all of the illocutionary acts present?[32]

Perhaps the resistance to employing speech act theory at the level of a meta-hermeneutic is due to a misunderstanding of what the theory offers. If it is thought that speech act theory should provide a comprehensive hermeneutic then too much is being asked of it. However, if it is recognised that speech act theory can clarify the nature of communication, identify the goals of interpretation and provided an increased level of precision to the language of hermeneutics than perhaps the resistance would be less.[33]

---

31. A. C. Thiselton, "Communicative Action and Promise in Hermeneutics," in *The Promise of Hermeneutics* (ed. R. Lundin, A. C. Thiselton, and C. Walhout; Grand Rapids: Eerdmans, 1999), 237, emphasis original.

32. The significant contributors who defend the reconceptualization of hermeneutics in light of speech act theory are discussed in the following section below. A discussion of weak and strong illocutions will be offered in Chapter 5 with respect to the act of forgiveness.

33. Christopher Seitz also expresses some scepticism regarding the value of speech act theory. In a discussion of whether the canon can display intentionality he comments, "Speech-act theory may be a way to negotiate (or finesse) problems associated with divine and human authorship of scripture, whose last uncomplicated expression may have been that of Calvin ... The problem of speech-act theory at this point is its level of

Speech act criticism fails to utilise speech act theory to its full capacity, either because of a failure to recognize its full potential or because of a concern that the theory claims too much.

*Reconceptualising Hermeneutics*

I suggest that an alternate approach, which considers texts in thir entirety as speech acts, provides greater benefit for hermeneutics.[34] This second appli-cation of speech act theory attempts to reconceptualize exegesis[35] and so reconceptualize hermeneutics.[36] While there have been some attempts to formulate a theological hermeneutic based upon speech act theory, they stop short of providing a detailed description of how this reformulation affects biblical

---

abstraction, by virtue of introducing a philosophical construct to handle the theological problem of divine-human discourse. The problem is also deeply historical, to put it in more concrete terms. It may be possible to say that God commandeers human language toward a specific intended end, but say practically nothing at all about the constitutive, historically real, indeed 'elected and providentially chosen' manner of speaking through Moses and the prophets and Israel as such. Does the commandeering *depend upon prior, genuine, historical inspiration and human electing and acting?* What role does this dimension play? It would be an odd (if rather exalted) form of inspiration (speaking dogmatically) which insisted on divine intention and discourse, but which reduced the agents of that speaking to Origen's plucked instruments—now on the other side of the Enlightenment and with the of a philosophical insight about language and communication." (Seitz, "The Canonical Approach," 97-98.)

Seitz's criticism appears to be based on the possibility that speech act theory could diminish the historical event of inspiration. Such an application of speech act theory is possible, where an ancient text becomes the word of God through subsequent appropriation and diminishes any divine initiative. However, speech act theory does not require any particular understanding of the inspiration process. To criticise a theory because it is possible to use the theory to defend alternative positions is unwarranted.

34. I will argue that texts contain illocutionary forces at a number of levels. Importantly, and contrary to speech act criticism, I suggest that texts of sufficient length and complexity not only contain speech acts (of varying strengths) but are speech acts in their entirety. This will be elucidated in Chapter 3.

35. Briggs, "The Uses of Speech Act Theory," 235.

36. Donald Evans has previously argued for a reconceptualization of theology, or, at least, the supplementation of traditional theological discourse with an appreciation for Scripture's self-involving language, ." . .man does not (or does not merely) assert certain facts about God; he addresses God in the activity of worship, committing himself to God and expressing his attitude to God. In so far as God's self-revelation is a self-involving verbal activity ("His Word is claim and promise, gift and demand") and man's religious language is also a self-involving verbal activity ("obedient, thankful confession and prayer"), theology needs an outline of the various ways in which language is self-involving." (D. Evans, *The Logic of Self-Involvement: A Philosophical Study of Everyday Language with Special Reference to the Christian Use of Language about God as Creator* (London: SCM, 1963) 14).

exegesis.³⁷ Despite the incomplete nature of these works, this second approach appears to offer very significant possibilities. Briggs concurs:

> It may be that the move toward seeing text as communicative action will prove to be one of enduring value when the dust finally settles on the far side of our current paradigm shift; or, to switch metaphors, when we have emerged on the far side of what Ricoeur so memorably called the critical desert.³⁸

Among those attempting a more complete reformulation of theological hermeneutics in light of speech act theory, Kevin Vanhoozer, Francis Watson, Stanley Grenz and Nicholas Wolterstorff have been influential.³⁹ However, within this second group of authors there exists a significance difference between those who are hermeneutic realists and those who, in varying degrees, can be labelled hermeneutic non-realists. On the one hand are authors like Vanhoozer and Wolterstorff who propose that the main goal of interpretation is to understand authorial discourse. To this end, they employ speech act theory as

---

37. See D. Clark, "Beyond Inerrancy: Speech Acts and an Evangelical View of Scripture," in *For Faith and Clarity: Philosophical Contributions to Christian Theology* (ed. J. K. Beilby; Grand Rapids: Baker, 2006), 113-31; P. W. Macky, "The Multiple Purposes of Biblical Speech Acts," *PSB* 8, no. 2 (1987); M. Thompson, *A Clear and Present Word: The Clarity of Scripture* (Nottingham: Apollos, 2006); K. J. Vanhoozer, "The Semantics of Biblical Literature: Truth and Scripture's Diverse Literary Forms," in *Hermeneutics, Authority and Canon* (ed. D. A. Carson and J. D. Woodbridge; Nottingham: IVP, 1986); Vanhoozer, *First Theology*; Wolterstorff, *Divine Discourse*; Watson, *Text and Truth*.

38. Briggs, "The Uses of Speech Act Theory," 265. Interestingly, Briggs' own method is self-confessedly eclectic and draws heavily upon categories of self-involvement. He states, "the direction suggested by Donald Evans remains the most fruitful for utilizing speech act theory in a hermeneutical role in biblical interpretation." (Briggs, *Words in Action*, 5.) Rather than looking for illocutions at every level of the text, Briggs is concerned with only those cases where *strong* illocutions or *strong* construals are found: "I believe that its main insights concerning certain types of strongly self involving language survive these critiques and remain useful for certain purposes. Primary among these purposes are the clarifying of presuppositions, implications and entailments of performative uses of language especially in cases of strong self-involvement. These purposes are sufficient to make speech act theory a worthwhile tool in the field of biblical and theological inquiry." (Briggs, *Words in Action*, 11-12.) Thus, he considers speech act theory to be a helpful tool in the exegesis of texts but does not claim it provides a comprehensive philosophy of language. Speech act theory, according to Briggs, is therefore most useful where it identifies the forces and rules that accompany these strong illocutions (Briggs, *Words in Action*, 294-295). This seems to be an improvement on Thiselton's application yet it remains incomplete as I will demonstrate below.

39. Grenz and Franke, *Beyond Foundationalism*; Vanhoozer, *Is There a Meaning in This Text?*; Vanhoozer, *First Theology*; Wolterstorff, *Divine Discourse*; Watson, *Text and Truth*. See also Poythress, "Canon and Speech Act." For a review of speech act theory in work of Wolterstorff, Grenz and Vanhoozer see C. E. Berry, "Speech-Act Theory as a Corollary for Describing the Communicative Dynamics of Biblical Revelation: Some Recommendations and Reservations," *CTR*, no. 7 (2009).

an analytical tool with a focus on the illocutionary acts mediated by the text. On the other hand, authors like Watson and Grenz prioritise the role of the reader in determining the meaning of the text. Watson should be considered a moderate among those in this category, but the common focus of this group is on the perlocutionary effects of a text in a reader or community.[40]

To date, the hermeneutic realists have provided a more detailed and sustained use of speech act theory. Vanhoozer in particular, has interacted with speech act theory for the past twenty years.[41] These authors recognize texts to be speech acts comprised of illocutionary acts at many levels and attempt a clarification and reformulation of hermeneutics along these lines. Additionally, these authors have also grappled with the dual authorship of Scripture, suggesting that God's illocutions are mediated through the text of Scripture.

*The Hermeneutic Non-Realists.* While many authors have employed speech act theory to defend and practice authorial discourse interpretation, others have employed it to defend a variety of non-realist hermeneutics, particularly reader-response theories.[42] This is a predictable outcome since speech act theory provides an analysis of the full communicative event, including audience reception. While speech act theorists themselves consider the illocutionary act as determinative for meaning, hermeneutic non-realists have adopted the language of speech act theory to support their alternate position that the meaning is located in the perlocution, the effect of a text on an audience.

Francis Watson utilizes speech act theory to promote a community reading of Scripture and call for a hermeneutic that enables readers to both hear and respond to the illocutionary acts performed by it. It may, therefore, seem a little strange to group Watson with the hermeneutic non-realists, especially in light of statements such as this:

> If, as I have argued, the category of the speech act can be extended to include written communications, then current hostility to the concepts of determinate meaning and authorial intention is unjustified. To be understood at all, a series of words must be construed as a communicative action which intends a determinate meaning together with its particular illocutionary and perlocutionary force.[43]

---

40. Watson, *Text and Truth*, 108.

41. See Vanhoozer, *First Theology*; Vanhoozer, *Is There a Meaning in This Text?*; Vanhoozer, *The Drama of Doctrine*. While his earlier works engaged explicitly with the theory in a more detailed and technical manner, his later work focusing on theodrama relies upon speech act theory in a more implicit manner.

42. For further discussion and a summary of current applications see A. B. Caneday, "Is Theological Truth Functional or Propositional? Postconservatism's Use of Language Games and Speech-Act Theory," in *Reclaiming the Center: Confronting Evangelical Accommodation in Postmodern Times* (ed. M. J. Erickson, P. K. Helseth, and J. Taylor; Wheaton: Crossway Books, 2004).

43. Watson, *Text and Truth*, 103.

However, while Watson demonstrates concern to place the intention of the author at the centre of the hermeneutical endeavour, he seems to employ speech act categories in a way that ultimately marginalizes the author. This tension is alluded to in the quote above. Watson suggests that a communicative action contains meaning and also contains illocutionary and perlocutionary force. This seems to imply that the meaning of the text is located in the locution or what he refers to as the "verbal meaning." He makes this more explicit in his summary statement, "To grasp the verbal meaning and the illocutionary and perlocutionary force of a text is to understand the *authorial intention* embodied in it."[44] So initially, Watson locates meaning with locution. This is problematic since a major claim of speech act theory is that the locution, while it contains noematic content, does not have a meaning outside of its employment in authorial discourse. There is no such thing as the meaning of text outside of its illocutionary force.[45]

Furthermore, Watson distinguishes between the verbal meaning (locution) and the entire communicative act, which he labels the "literal sense." The literal sense thus includes all three elements: verbal meaning, illocution, and perlocution:

> The hypothesis of the determinacy of verbal meaning requires an understanding of authorial intention as the presupposition of a text's intelligibility, and implies as its consequence the necessity of an objective interpretative practice. However, establishing the verbal meaning of a text is a necessary but not a sufficient condition for establishing its literal sense. The literal sense is the sense intended by the author in so far as this authorial intention is objectively embodied in the words of the text. But the intention embodied in a communicative action goes beyond the expression of a series of words bearing a certain meaning, as if for its own sake. What is intended in communicative action is that determinate meaning should be the vehicle of illocutionary and perlocutionary force.[46]

In the end, Watson's application of speech act theory argues against determinate meaning being located in the text. This is a predictable outcome since he has understood authorial intention and the literal sense of a text to include not only what the author was doing (illocutionary forces), but also how the audience is effected and responds (perlocution). This seems to be due, in part, to Watson's use of the term, "perlocutionary force", which is an unfortunate confusion of terms.[47] According to speech act theory it is the illocution that carries

---

44. Watson, *Text and Truth*, 123.
45. Of course, Paul Ricoeur would side with Watson on this point in his defence of the "sense of the text" in its autonomous state.
46. Watson, *Text and Truth*, 115-116.
47. Thiselton makes this same mistake when he speaks of the "perlocutionary speech acts" and "perlocutionary force." (A. C. Thiselton, "Authority and Hermeneutics: Some Proposals for a More Creative Agenda," in *A Pathway into the Holy Scripture* (ed. P. E.

the "force" and not the perlocution.⁴⁸ The illocution calls a person to believe, to act, and to respond in any number of ways. The perlocution is the *resulting effect* that occurs in the audience. It itself is not a "force."⁴⁹ Unfortunately for Watson, there is no such thing as a "perlocutionary force" as distinct from the illocutionary force. There are only perlocutionary effects.

Again, this confusion of terms has a predictable result. Because Watson locates the "literal sense" of the text partly in the perlocution, then the reception of the text by the audience would partly determine this sense. This is, in fact, a conclusion that Watson himself embraces:

> As we have seen, a speech act may through writing be indefinitely extended in space and time, so long as the institutional context that gives it its force is maintained. Mark's illocutionary act of proclaiming the gospel in writing may therefore be said to remain in force so long as there is an institutional context in which the intended perlocutionary effect of his speech act continues to be felt. Where an institutional context changes so fundamentally that a text's intended perlocutionary effect ceases to operate, interpreters have the freedom to assess its continuing significance and interest as they will (provided they grasp its verbal meaning). Yet to claim such a freedom in the case of the Gospel of Mark would be an aggressive action directed against the life of the community in which the intended illocutionary and perlocutionary force of this canonical text remains intact. Understood in this light, it can be said the true 'significance' is to be found *in the single, verbal meaning itself*, that is, in its enduring illocutionary and perlocutionary force. The notion of a secondary, ephemeral 'contextual significance' is therefore dependent on and subordinate to the primary, universal significance this text claims by virtue of its role as 'gospel.'⁵⁰

Aside from the problems already discussed above, this comment by Watson justifies locating him among the non-realists. He suggests that the illocutionary act only remains "in force" if there is an existing community within which the institutional conditions are present that allow for that force to be understood and felt. If that community is no longer present then the illocution does not exist. As stated earlier, this has the effect of marginalizing the author. It is

---

Satterthwaite and D. F. Wright; Grand Rapids: Eerdmans, 1994), 132.)

48. Austin will speak of "perlocutionary acts" but only of "illocutionary acts" having an associated "force" (Austin, *How to Do Things*, 109). I will address this in later chapters in the discussion of "strong speech acts."

49. In later chapters I will discuss the category of "strong speech acts" where the relationship between the illocutionary force and the perlocutionary effect is "stronger."

50. Watson, *Text and Truth*, 106. Callahan briefly introduces speech act theory in his defence of a reader-oriented hermeneutic suggesting that the truth of a speech act is dependent on "how well such speech acts function for or among the responsive." (J. P. Callahan, *The Clarity of Scripture: History, Theology & Contemporary Literary Studies* (Downers Grove: IVP, 2001), 230-233.)

true that the communication can "misfire" if there is no audience who is able to understand the illocutionary actions performed by the author due to a lack of common institutional context. However, this does not mean that the author has not and does not continue to perform those actions through the text. It is a curious argument to suggest, taking the example above, that the Gospel of Mark is only relevant or "significant" because a community remains in which the perlocutionary effect is felt. Is a non-Christian community going to grant that the gospel is still significant because a Christian community recognizes it as such? In the absence of such a community, do the illocutions of the Gospel of Mark cease to exist? It is better to recognize that the author of Gospel continues to speak (continues to locute and illocute) through the text and whoever has ears to hear will hear. So while Watson desires to support the place of authorial intention in hermeneutics, his employment of speech act theory appears somewhat confused and ultimately marginalizes the author.

Another author who utilizes speech act theory in defence of a community, reader response hermeneutic is Stanley Grenz. He argues that the goal of interpretation is to hear the Spirit's illocutions as mediated through Scripture:

> Because the Spirit speaks to us through scripture—through the text itself—the ongoing task of the community of Christ is to ask continually, What is the Spirit saying to the church? (Rev. 2:11, etc.). We inquire at every juncture, What illocutionary act is the Spirit performing in our midst on the basis of the reading of this scripture text? What is the Spirit saying to us in appropriating this text? In short, we inquire, What is the biblical message?[51]

However, what Grenz means by the Spirit speaking through Scripture is not what it seems. In his own words, "'the Spirit is speaking in Scripture' refers to the *Spirit's* illocutions, but these are not identical with those of the human authors"[52] Furthermore, he divorces the Spirit's illocutions from the locution of the text of Scripture, "Obviously, when we acknowledge that the Spirit speaks through the Bible, we are referring to an illocutionary, and not a locutionary, act."[53] Unfortunately, it is unclear how an illocutionary act can be accomplished without locution. Furthermore, if the illocutionary act is not identical to the human author's act and yet based on the same locution how are we to discover this illocution? Grenz continues:

> Consequently, we must never conclude that exegesis alone can exhaust the Spirit's speaking to us through the text. Although the Spirit's illocutionary act is to appropriate the text in its internal meaning (i.e., to appropriate what the author said), the Spirit appropriates the text with the goal of communicating to us in our

---

51. Grenz and Franke, *Beyond Foundationalism*, 74.
52. Grenz, "The Spirit and the Word," 358.
53. Grenz, "The Spirit and the Word," 361.

situation, which, while perhaps paralleling in certain respects that of the ancient community, is nevertheless unique.[54]

If exegesis cannot discover this unique illocution, how is the reader able to hear it? Somehow, "The Spirit performs the perlocutionary act of creating a world through the illocutionary act of speaking . . . by appropriating the biblical text as the instrumentality of the divine speaking."[55] In Grenz's description, the Spirit appropriates the text, not the authorial discourse, in order to create a world (the perlocutionary effect) amongst the community of faith. In this relationship, there seems to be very little correspondence between the illocutions in the text and the Spirit's own illocutions, which are, nevertheless, somehow encountered through the text. The result of Grenz's formulation is that the community of faith has direct access to the Spirit's voice, but this may have little or nothing in common with the voice of the human authors of Scripture. What is important is the perlocutionary effect of "world creating", which is accomplished by the Spirit in the community.[56] A number of writers have rightly criticised Grenz for this lack of detail and for locating the goal of interpretation in the community's understanding of the Spirit's voice rather than in the illocutionary acts performed in and through the text of scripture.[57]

Stephen Fowl represents another example of an author who happily adopts speech act categories to discuss theological interpretation, but, like Watson and Grenz, will not equate meaning with illocution.

> It is here in regard to establishing an author's communicative intention that my arguments overlap most closely with those who rely on speech act theory. Like them, I recognize that all utterances are intelligible because they are contextually embedded and that successful communication relies on the knowledge and operation of linguistic and social conventions. . ., however, it will become clear that I do not think that speech act theory can provide either a theory of meaning or the basis for arguing for the interpretive priority of the communicative intention of authors.[58]

Fowl speaks of "successful communication" but does not describe it. He notes, however, that it should not be equated with the "communicative intention of authors." He also argues that due to the perpetual disagreement concerning the meaning of "meaning" we should abandon using the term to define

---

54. Grenz and Franke, *Beyond Foundationalism*, 74-75.
55. Grenz, "The Spirit and the Word," 365.
56. This focus on the ability of the text to create a world is similar to Ricoeur's. See Ricœur, "Toward a Hermeneutic," 99-100.
57. E.g., Caneday, "Is Theological Truth Functional or Propositional?," 154. See also Vanhoozer, "From Speech Acts to Scripture Acts," 194-199.
58. Fowl, "The Role of Authorial Intention," 76-77. Fowl aligns himself with Richard Rorty and Jeffrey Stout who follow a particular interpretation of Austin and distances himself from Thiselton and Vanhoozer who he says follow Searle. (Fowl, "The Role of Authorial Intention," 76.)

the goal of interpretation. He prefers that we use more specific language concerning this goal and not equate it with the "meaning of the text."

> [W]e should eliminate talk of "meaning" in favor of other terms that will suit our interpretive interests and put a stop to futile discussions. Hence, we should be satisfied with being able to articulate an author's communicative intentions, or a text's contextual connections to the clearly laid-out interpretive aim. There is no need to cloud the issue further by calling this or that interpretive activity "the meaning of the text" at the expense of other interpretive activities in which one might engage.[59]

Thus, while Fowl is happy to speak in speech act categories, he is utilizing the theory to simply describe different components of communication and a variety of interpretive activities. He rejects any notion that speech act theory promotes a particular hermeneutic goal and remains committed to a non-realist position.

Terrence Tilley similarly employs speech act theory to defend a theory of communication that prioritises the effects of speech (i.e., the perlocution) upon an audience.[60] He is critical of Searle's explanation of the goal of interpretation:

> Like most speech act theorists, Searle's primary goal is to provide a theoretical explanation of a speaker's intentions and actions. Hence, he has no need to analyze the perlocutionary results of speech acts which are not explicable by a formal theory. For present purposes, this is insufficient. Communicative speech acts affect other people. To understand what concrete acts are being performed and their significance requires understanding the extralinguistic context for and results of those actions. Attending to results can reveal that *results* can change the meaning of the act performed, as the difference between "assault and batter' and "manslaughter" shows. Attending to contexts can reveal that differing *contexts* can also change the significance of an act performed.[61]

In a unique way, Tilley argues that the effects of an act can change its meaning regardless of the meaning the author intended for the act. He uses an example of a man who hit his wife without the intention of hurting her, yet it resulted in her death. That she was hurt, subsequently died, and that he was convicted of manslaughter, demonstrates for Tilley that the action is determined by the effect.

Wolterstorff addresses this by saying that the goal of interpretation is not to uncover what the author intended to do but what the author actually did.[62] In the case above, it does not matter what the man intended at the outset. By

---

59. Fowl, "The Role of Authorial Intention," 80.
60. T. W. Tilley, *The Evils of Theodicy* (Washington: Georgetown University Press, 1991).
61. Tilley, *The Evils of Theodicy*, 20-21.
62. Wolterstorff, *Divine Discourse*, 199.

his actual performance he committed the act of manslaughter. He did this by satisfying the institutional rules that are associated with that act. He was acting irresponsibly (to say the least!) in the sense that his actions were easily understandable in terms of public convention. His actual act, not his intended act, is the meaning of the action. The same applies in both verbal and written communication.[63]

The common ground upon which the authors in this category stand is in their affirmation of the audience as determinative in the communicative event. The audience either determines the goals of interpretation, imports meaning to the text, or simply bypasses the text altogether. In this way, these authors have employed speech act theory to describe and defend a variety of non-realist approaches to hermeneutics. In itself, speech act theory provides the anatomy of communication, and its founders argued that the illocutionary act should be given priority in interpretation. While non-realists have recognized the validity of speech act categories, they have rejected its focus on illocutionary acts.

*The Hermeneutic Realists.* As mentioned, Vanhoozer and Wolterstorff are representative of the hermeneutic realists and their works offer significant contributions to the discussion. They are not entirely alone in their endeavour, yet authors who draw upon their work offer little advancement to their specific program.[64] The contributions of Vanhoozer and Wolterstorff will, therefore, be the focus of discussion in later chapters. For now it will suffice to summarize the reasons for their positive reception of the theory and give a brief overview of their applications.

Vanhoozer argues that speech act theory fits the way Scripture perceives language. He also notes that it provides a defence for hermeneutic realism, and most importantly it enables us to hear more fully the communicative intention in the text and so be transformed by it.

> Why speech acts? First because thinking in terms of speech acts approximates the way the Bible itself treats human speech. Moreover, as Nicholas Wolterstorff has demonstrated, speech act categories have the potential to help us appreciate what it means to call the Scriptures God's Word. For me, however, the most important contribution speech act philosophy makes is to help us break free of

---

63. The establishment of intent may or may not result in further charges being pressed, but the institutionally governed act of manslaughter was committed nonetheless.

64. D. G. Firth, "The Teaching of the Psalms," in *Interpreting the Psalms: Issues and Approaches* (ed. P. S. Johnston and D. G. Firth; Leicester: Apollos, 2005); G. McConville, "Divine Speech and the Book of Jeremiah," in *The Trustworthiness of God: Perspectives on the Nature of Scripture* (ed. P. Helm and C. R. Trueman; Grand Rapids: Eerdmans, 2002); N. Murphy, "Textual Relativism, Philosophy of Language, and the Baptist Vision," in *Theology without Foundations: Religious Practice and the Future of Theological Truth* (ed. N. M. Stanley Hauerwas, Mark Nation; Nashville: Abingdon Press, 1994); Thompson, *A Clear and Present Word*; D. J. Treier, *Virtue and the Voice of God: Toward Theology as Wisdom* (Grand Rapids: Eerdmans, 2006).

the tendency either to reduce meaning to reference or to attend only to the propositional content of Scripture. Viewing texts as doing things other than representing states of affairs opens up possibilities for transformative reading that the modern obsession with information has eclipsed. Finally, speech act philosophy commends itself as perhaps the most effective antidote to certain deconstructive toxins that threaten the very project of textual interpretation and hermeneutics.[65]

Against a reductionistic view of Scripture that sees it as a "storehouse of propositions" to be mined for theological classification, Vanhoozer utilizes speech act theory to draw attention to the diverse actions (illocutionary acts) of the Scriptural authors. Furthermore, his realist position, that meaning is determined by authorial intention, fits with speech act theorists' explanation of the illocutionary act. Vanhoozer summarizes this integration of speech act theory with his realist position in the following statements:

> "Meaning" is the result of communicative action, of what an author has done in tending to certain words at a particular time in a particular manner.
> The literal sense of an utterance or text is the sum total of those illocutionary acts performed by the author intentionally and with self-awareness.[66]

Vanhoozer's "literal sense" is to be identified with "meaning" and is located in the "sum total" of the illocutionary acts performed by an author. In his estimation, the "meaning" of a text therefore requires a "thick" description (i.e., one which considers all of the illocutionary acts present in a text). He comments:

> There are many ways to study discourse, but not all are germane to the task of describing communicative action. Genuine interpretation is a matter of offering appropriately "thick descriptions" of communicative acts, to use Gilbert Ryle's fine phrase. A description is sufficiently thick when it allows us to appreciate everything the author is doing in a text—that is, its illocutions ... Typically, historical-critical commentaries describe either the history and process of a text's composition or "what actually happened." According to the traditional "picture theory" of meaning, the literal sense would be what a word or sentence *referred* to. On my view, however, the literal sense may require a fairly "thick" description in order to bring it to light.[67]

In addition to the above reasons for adopting speech act theory for theological hermeneutics, Vanhoozer also employs it to defend and explain how Scripture can function as God's word. According to Vanhoozer, the goals of interpretation should include the discovery of what God is saying by way of the

---

65. Vanhoozer, "From Speech Acts to Scripture Acts," 163-164.
66. Vanhoozer, "From Speech Acts to Scripture Acts," 177-179.
67. Vanhoozer, "From Speech Acts to Scripture Acts," 179.

canon, particularly through canonical illocutions. He asks whether God's voice is sometimes only fully heard when these canonical illocutions come to light. This suggestion will be discussed in the following chapter so a brief comment by Vanhoozer will suffice:

> There are two complementary senses in which I wish to affirm the canon as God's illocutionary act. First, there is the divine appropriation of the illocutions of the human authors, particularly at the generic level but not exclusively there ... Could it be that certain illocutions come to light only when we describe what God is doing at the canonical level? More work needs to be done in this area ... [68]

Wolterstorff also appeals to speech act theory to define human communication or "what it is to speak", readily adopting Austinian terminology of locution, illocution and perlocution. Of the three concepts, he states that the illocutionary act captures "what it is to speak":

> when I speak of "speaking" (and "discoursing"), I will always have in mind speech actions—that is, actions which can function as what J.L. Austin called *illocutionary* actions. No doubt ordinary English usage is such that in speaking of "speaking," one could also have in mind *locutionary* actions: actions consisting of uttering or inscribing or signing some words. So my usage represents a regimentation of ordinary English.[69]

One of Wolterstorff's main concerns is to defend the morality involved in communication by highlighting the responsibilities of both the speaker and the audience. This represents a significant improvement in speech act theory, particularly with respect to Searle's development, as it recognizes the powerful nature of all illocutionary actions.[70] Wolterstorff suggests that speaking is a public action, open to being interpreted in conventional terms. By this he means that due to the presence of "normative conditions" a speaker is able to acquire a "normative standing" in the public arena:

---

68. Vanhoozer, "From Speech Acts to Scripture Acts," 194.
69. Wolterstorff, *Divine Discourse*, 75.
70. Timothy Ward notes the following, "What Wolterstorff has done is effectively to show the failure of Searle's categories by demonstrating that what Searle describes as unique to 'declarations' is in fact true of every speech act. Even by just asserting something to someone, the speaker (prima facie) changes the status of both himself and his addressee, for his assertion implies a reference to himself as someone who undertakes to be asserting truly and on good grounds, and to the addressee as someone who is obligated to believe the speaker on those grounds. In short, Wolterstorff's concept of speech may be regarded as a rigorous development of the implications of human action in general and speaking in particular of Austin's initial observation that to speak is not to communicate but to act, taking proper account of the fact that speech acts are always performed in a relational and moral environment." (Ward, *Word and Supplement*, 99.) Ward correctly summarizes Wolterstorff's contribution in this regard, however, his final comment that to speak is not to "communicate" but to "act" is an overstatement.

Speech presents us with another, profoundly different, phenomenon: that of acquiring rights and responsibilities of doing so in accord with, or in violation of, obligations ... But speech requires that we be related to material reality and to each other in ways over and above that of causal interchange. It is because normative conditions have been attached to the pronouncing of so innocuous a word as guilty, and because the pronouncing of that word has been invested with normative import, that by pronouncing this word we can speak. By the acquisition of normative standings, we take up the material world into our service.

But even more important for our subsequent purposes is the fact that to speak is not, as such, to express one's inner self but to take up a normative stance in the public domain.[71]

Because a speaker is able to acquire this normative stance, they are also able to assume, in felicitous circumstances, that an audience has the ability to understand their stance. Moreover, Wolterstorff argues persuasively that both the speaker and the audience acquire obligations or moral responsibilities. The obligations of the speaker include the intention of assuming such a normative stance[72] and the obligations of the audience include counting the speaker's action (illocution) as taking up that same stance. Consequently, communication is a matter of "acquiring rights and responsibilities." A speaker is responsible for the normative stance they have attained and so have the right to be understood as having attained it. Likewise, an audience is responsible for properly (normatively) ascribing that stance to the speaker and so granting them the rights and responsibilities of such a stance:

> one's uttering of a sentence may count as one's making a request, it is not necessary that one and one's fellow *actually count it* as that; they may fail or refuse to count it as that even though it is that, and may count it as that even though it is not that. Yet speaker and audience performing the action of counting it as that is indeed intimately related to *its* counting as that. The relation is that speaker and audience *ought to* count it as that—*ought to* acknowledge it as that in their relations with each other. And the standing that thus gets normatively ascribed to one is itself a normative standing—that is to say, it is itself defined in part by (prima facie) mutual duties between speaker and others. To institute an arrangement for the performance of speech actions is to institute a way of acquiring rights and responsibilities.[73]

---

71. Wolterstorff, *Divine Discourse*, 93.
72. Of course, it is often the case that a speaker is being humorous or ironic and is not actually adopting the stance of their statement. In these cases, unless the speaking is being intentionally deceptive, clues to their intended stance are communicated in other ways and enable an audience to understand the actual stance being taken.
73. Wolterstorff, *Divine Discourse*, 84.

For Wolterstorff, this account of communication acts as a defence for authorial discourse interpretation, which locates the meaning of the utterance or text in the intention of the author, specifically in the illocutionary act they have performed. This, in turn, determines the nature of interpretive goals. To interpret an utterance or text is to understand what illocutionary act(s) a speaker has performed. In terms of the moral responsibility of the audience, Wolterstorff defines it in the following manner, "The goal of interpretation, correspondingly, is to discover what counts as what. The discourser takes up a normative stance in the public domain by way of performing some publicly perceptible action."[74]

With this understanding of public actions and normative stance, Wolterstorff avoids the charge of adopting Romantic hermeneutics and its attempt to uncover the mental states and processes of the author. To this possible critique, he responds in the following manner:

> But even more important for our subsequent purposes is the fact that to speak is not, as such, to express one's inner self but to take up a normative stance in the public domain. The myth dies hard that to read a text for authorial discourse is to enter the dark world of the author's psyche. It's nothing of the sort. It is to read to discover what assertings, what promisings, what requestings, what commandings, are rightly to be ascribed to the author on the ground of her having set down the words that she did in the situation in which she set them down. Whatever be the dark demons and bright angels of the author's inner self that led her to take up this stance in public, it is that stance itself that we hope by reading to recover, not the dark demons and bright angels.[75]

The goal of interpretation, then, is not to uncover what the author was thinking or thought they were doing, but to understand what public action an author has committed by convention.

Having adopted a speech act description of communicative action, Wolterstorff's concern is to demonstrate that the locutionary and illocutionary acts of the human authors of Scripture can *count as* illocutionary acts of God. He comments:

> In short, contemporary speech-action theory opens up the possibility of a whole new way of thinking about God speaking: perhaps the attribution of speech to God by Jews, Christians, and Muslims, should be understood as the attribution to God of *illocutionary actions*, leaving it open how God performs those actions—maybe by bringing about the sounds or characters of some natural language, maybe not.[76]

---

74. Wolterstorff, *Divine Discourse*, 183.
75. Wolterstorff, *Divine Discourse*, 93.
76. Wolterstorff, *Divine Discourse*, 13.

Wolterstorff's concern to attribute illocutionary acts to God will be be discussed in more detail in following chapters. For now it is important to note his acceptance of speech act theory as an accurate description of communication and his utilization of it to clarify the goals of interpretation.

Aside from the above two authors who write predominantly in theological and philosophical arenas, a small number of authors in biblical studies have also begun to consider whole texts as speech acts and so deserve a mention under this heading of "reconceptualizing hermeneutics." David Firth, in a recent essay on interpreting the psalms, utilizes speech act theory in order to explain what the psalms are trying to teach their readers.

> In speech-act terms, we can say that each of these psalms is a locution, but the teaching method adopted represents a different illocutionary force, and that the perlocution will thus vary . . . Speech-act theory, with its emphasis on illocutionary force and perlocutions, is a valuable aid to understanding the teaching intent of individual psalms.[77]

Likewise, Hubert Irsigler has provided a sustained application of speech act theory to the interpretation of the psalms. His aim is to explore the question ." . .wie sich Sprechakttheorie als Sprechaktanalyse in eine literature-wissenshaftliche Psalmenexegese interieren läßt."[78] Irsigler's contribution is important as he recognizes the complexity of speech acts that occur at various textual levels.

Gordon McConville has employed speech act theory in his interpretation of the book of Jeremiah. He has recognized that not only are the prophetic speeches within the book examples of speech acts (which God has authorized through deputation), but that the book as a whole is a speech act:[79]

---

77. Firth, "The Teaching of the Psalms," 164.

78. H. Irsigler, "Psalm-Rede als Handlungs-, Wirk- und Aussageprozeß: Sprechaktanalyse und Psalmeninterpretation am Beispiel von Psalm 13", in K. Seybold and E. Zenger, eds., *Neue Wege der PsalmenForschung: Für Walter Beyerlin* (Freiburg: Herder, 1994) 63-104, 63.

79. McConville, "Divine Speech," 29. Andrew Shead also discusses the contribution of speech act theory to an understanding of how God exerts power through the text of Jeremiah. Shead is positive about the role of speech act theory in explaining how speech affects relationships between people, yet his incorporation of the theory is limited. He concludes that speech act theory "tells us what we knew already: that the power of the word of God lies in the power of God and the truth of God . . . what the theory does not address is the means by which words, whether God's or Jeremiah's, exert causal effects, not only on relationships but on the physical universe. Such is the vehemence with which Jeremiah wields language of the word of God that it comes across as a tool, in and of itself, of divine agency in the world. Is this just a manner of speaking, or does it provide us with a unique insight into divine agency?" (A. G. Shead, *A Mouth Full of Fire: The Word of God in the Words of Jeremiah* (Nottingham: Apollos, 2012), 218-219.)

The book of Jeremiah, dependent on underlying speech acts (of God through the prophet), becomes in itself a speech act to the community that hears and preserves it. In turn, it plays its part within the greater communicative event that is Scripture. Its specific contribution to this larger discourse includes the concept of new covenant; its supreme instance of "incarnation" in the OT; its answer to the Old Testament's communal laments generally (in the Psalms and Lamentations) and to other writings that express future hope less definitely (notably Kings).

The original speech acts (spoken and written) belong to their times and settings. Therefore they require the reader to enter their world(s) in order to hear and understand the full force of the communication. It is the world of a Jewish community facing its own world with its startling message of the one unimaged God, who creates, calls, commands, judges, and saves. The force of the communication to new times and settings depends on its meaning within that original Hebraic frame.[80]

McConville calls the interpreter to enter into the world of the text to uncover the original speech acts performed by the author through the text. Understanding how God can be speaking in new ways today is dependent on uncovering the original illocutions. Though he does not refer to them this way, he also alludes to canonical illocutions that arise from Jeremiah forming part of Scripture. As discussed above, Vanhoozer's application of speech act theory also suggests such canonical illocutions.

Both Firth and McConville apply speech act theory in a more comprehensive manner than those engaged in speech act criticism. They acknowledge that the final form of the canonical text is a communicative act and as such contains illocutionary force throughout. This, in my opinion, is a step in the right direction. If speech act theory does indeed describe accurately the anatomy of communication, and if written texts are part of that communication, then speech act theory should be employed in this manner. However, when considering the Scriptures, the speech acts performed by the human authors of the texts are not the only speech acts present. A theological interpretation of Scripture should seek to understand and explain how God communicates through the speech acts of others. On this basis, the works of Vanhoozer and Wolterstorff point us in the right direction. However, neither of these authors have offered sustained, detailed exegetical application of their proposed hermeneutic.[81] While Firth

---

80. McConville, "Divine Speech," 37.
81. Blue, "Meaning, Intention, and Application," 161-184. Wolterstorff does offer an exegetical discussion of Psalm 137 in *Divine Discourse* and I will respond to his conclusions in the chapters below. Vanhoozer has also demonstrated exegetical application, though not in a sustained manner. For a theodramatic interpretation of Philemon assuming speech act theory see Kevin J. Vanhoozer, "Imprisoned or Free? Text, Status, and Theological Interpretation in the Master/Slave Discourse of Philemon" in *Reading Scripture with the Church: Toward a Hermeneutic for Theological Interpretation* (A.K.M Adam,

and McConville have employed speech act categories in exegesis, they have not endeavoured to provide a reformulated hermeneutic. I hope to further this discussion by providing an outline of a theological hermeneutic and demonstrate its usefulness for exegesis.

## Conclusion

I have suggested that speech act theory provides an accurate description of communicative action. It provides terminological clarity for what happens when we speak or write and enables a more precise discussion of the nature of meaning. In particular, it highlights the need for a "thick description" that accounts for the many illocutions an author is performing throughout a text. Consequently, it offers biblical interpreters useful language for describing the nature and goals of theological hermeneutics.

Speech act criticism, with its focus on speech acts made explicitly within texts fails to appreciate that texts themselves are speech acts and thus fails to fully appreciate the potential of speech act theory. In focusing solely on a limited number of speech acts within a text, speech act criticism inherently truncates the meaning of a text.

By its very nature, speech act theory prioritises the illocutionary act in interpretation and so provides added resources to defend and clarify the hermeneutics of authorial intention. For those, such as myself who prioritize authorial discourse, a reformulation of theological hermeneutics using speech act theory is warranted and may yield more than simply a new way of describing traditional hermeneutics. To date, speech act theory has been largely underutilised. While several of its proponents have called for more detail vis-à-vis hermeneutics and exegesis, this detail has not been forthcoming.

---

Stephen E. Fowl, Kevin J. Vanhoozer, Francis Watson, Grand Rapids, Baker, 2006), 51-93.

# Chapter 2

# Dual Authorship

## Introduction

This chapter explores recent discussions concerning the divine and human authorship of Scripture. In the field of theological hermeneutics, scholars who affirm the dual authorship of Scripture are divided over whether it results in any significant implications for biblical interpretation. I suggest that affirming Scripture as divine discourse does present significant hermeneutical challenges. Additionally, when dual authorship is considered in terms of speech act theory these hermeneutical challenges become acute. However, I hope to demonstrate that speech act theory both highlights the problematic of dual authorship and provides necessary resources to overcome it.

The belief that the Scriptures are an instance of divine discourse is not new.[1] The community of faith in both testaments held this basic belief, which, in turn, prompted the formation of their respective canons. Consequently, the church has grappled with the hermeneutical implications of dual authorship, particularly in relation to how the Old Testament functions as divine discourse.[2] It is not surprising that much of the recent discussion occurs within Evangelical Protestantism, as the acceptance of divine discourse, intrinsic to a doctrine of inspiration, is one of its defining presuppositions.[3] For those who believe Scrip-

---

1. This belief is also supported by the self-presentation of the canon. For example, in Matt 19:4–5 Jesus refers to a narrator's comment in Genesis as being the speech of "the Creator." The New Testament writers considered not only the Old Testament Scriptures to be God's communicative action (cf. 2 Tim 3:16) but also understood some of their own writings and the writings of their fellow apostles in the same manner (cf. 2 Pet 3:16).

2. For a brief history of interpretation see A. C. Thiselton, "Hermeneutics," in *Dictionary for Theological Interpretation of the Bible* (ed. K. J. Vanhoozer, et al.; London: SPCK, 2005); G. R. Lewis, "The Human Authorship of Inspired Scripture," in *Inerrancy* (ed. N. L. Geisler; Grand Rapids: Zondervan, 1980).

3. For a summary of various Evangelical approaches to dual authorship see D. L. Bock, "Evangelicals and the Use of the Old Testament in the New," *BSac* 142, no. 567 (1985): 209-223.

ture is divine discourse, understanding the hermeneutical implications of such a belief is vital. The notion of *sensus plenior* is one attempt to account for these issues.

## Proponents of a *Sensus Plenior*

*Raymond E. Brown*

In the last half century a renewed interest in dual authorship was sparked by Raymond Brown's introduction of the term *sensus plenior*,[4] which he defines in the following manner:

> The *sensus plenior* is that additional, deeper meaning, intended by God but not clearly intended by the human author, which is seen to exist in the words of a Biblical text (or group of texts, or even a whole book) when they are studied in the light of further revelation or development in the understanding of revelation.[5]

Brown clarifies this definition by stating that *sensus plenior* is a true sense of Scripture since God is the principle author, and that this sense is "already present or latent in the text."[6] Elsewhere he expands on this idea:

> We would rather phrase it this way: the literal sense answers the question of what this text meant according to its author's intention as that author was inspired to compose it in his particular stage in the history of God's plan of salvation. The sensus plenior answers the question of what the text means in the whole context of God's plan, a meaning which God, who knew the whole plan from the start, intended from the moment He inspired the composition of the text.[7]

A benefit of this proposal is that the meaning of the text is always understood as a product of it. Even though the full meaning is not accessible until the context of the completed canon is available, this full meaning remains, in part, a product of the original text. The further revelation of the canon then assists the interpreter in understanding all that the author (i.e., God) was doing in the text.[8]

---

4. R. E. Brown, *The Sensus Plenior of Sacred Scripture* (Baltimore: St. Mary's University, 1955). William Lasor notes, "The term *sensus plenior* ... is attributed to Andrea Fernandez in an article written in 1925. The subject has been treated most fully by the Catholic scholar, Raymond E. Brown." (W. S. La Sor, "The 'Sensus Plenior' and Biblical Interpretation," in *Scripture, Tradition, and Interpretation: Essays Presented to Everett F. Harrison* (ed. W. W. Gasque and W. S. La Sor; Grand Rapids: Eerdmans, 1978), 273-275.)
5. Brown, *The Sensus Plenior of Sacred Scripture*, 92.
6. Brown, *The Sensus Plenior of Sacred Scripture*, 92.
7. R. E. Brown, "Sensus Plenior in the Last Ten Years," *CBQ* 25, no. 3 (1963): 278.
8. This topic will be treated in detail in Chapter 4.

Of course, at any historical point, legitimate communication occurs through the partial revelation of the canon.[9]

In another clarification of his definition, Brown suggests that *sensus plenior* applies to both the Old and New Testaments. He notes that the key to understanding the Old Testament is the revelation of Jesus Christ who is "the key that unlocked the treasures of the Jewish Scriptures."[10] In regard to the New Testament he writes, "Development in Christian doctrine has enabled us to penetrate more to the core of N.T. texts and understand their *sensus plenior*."[11] It is interesting to note at this point that Brown sees an appropriate application of *sensus plenior* to New Testament texts. His comment, that Christian doctrine enables us to see the fuller meaning, reveals the dual source theology that underpins Catholicism. While the determinative role of tradition is not a presupposition that I share, two points of agreement can be identified. Firstly, in contrast to the prevailing discussion within Evangelicalism, which sees the issue of *sensus plenior* largely with respect to Old Testament prophecy, I will defend its application across the entire canon. Secondly, while I reject the authority of a particular church to determine the correct interpretation of Scripture, I support Brown's suggestion that Christian theology may be of assistance in understanding *sensus plenior* in both testaments.

While the concept of *sensus plenior* enjoys support within various Christian traditions, little work has been done in developing exegetical procedures that account for it. This is despite a number of calls for such work. In his 1963 article, Brown quotes R. Murphy as saying, "The primary task that remains to be done is the working out of the *sensus plenior* in actual exegesis."[12] Over 50 years later, this assessment remains largely unchanged.

*Proponents of* Sensus Plenior

A number of Evangelical writers have accepted the concept of the *sensus plenior* to describe their own hermeneutic.[13] Others have attempted various modifications. All of these writers, however, recognize the existence of this category of meaning.[14] Firstly, they argue that much of the prophetic literature of

---

9. I am aware that this raises questions regarding the canon of Scripture. In particular, which form of the canon is authoritative and functions as divine discourse. As I stated in the introduction, I am assuming an authoritative canon and that the final form of the Protestant canon is given priority (as opposed to Brown himself who adopts the wider canon of the Roman Catholic tradition).
10. Brown, *The Sensus Plenior of Sacred Scripture*, 93.
11. Brown, *The Sensus Plenior of Sacred Scripture*, 93.
12. Brown, "Sensus Plenior in the Last Ten Years," 281.
13. Evangelical opponents to this concept will be discussed below.
14. D. L. Bock, "Evangelicals and the Use of the Old Testament in the New," *BSac* 142, no. 568 (1985); J. Goldingay, *Models for Interpretation of Scripture* (Grand Rapids: Eerdmans, 1995); W. S. La Sor, "Prophecy, Inspiration, and Sensus Plenior," *TynBul* 29 (1978); D. J. Moo, "The Problem of Sensus Plenior," in *Hermeneutics, Authority, and Canon* (ed. D. A. Carson and J. D. Woodbridge; Eugene: Wipf & Stock, 1986); V. S. Poythress,

the Old Testament cannot be understood solely in terms of its human authorial meaning in its original context. Johnson comments:

> the 'authorial will' we are seeking as interpreters is God's intended sense... we should not be surprised to find that the authorial will of God goes beyond human authorial will, particularly in those sections of the Word of God that belong to the earlier states in the historical process of special revelation.[15]

Secondly, explanations of inspiration, which understand the whole of the Scripture as divine discourse, warrant such a concept. If God is the author of the canon as a unified document, rather than as a collection of separate works by the same author, then it seems likely that the meaning of the initial (i.e., earlier) part of the work can only be fully understood in light of the whole. This level of meaning necessarily transcends that of a human author. Darrell Bock states the following:

> The reason this writer rejects a "total" identification between the divine intent and the human author's intent is that in certain psalms, as well as in other Old Testament passages, theological revelation had not yet developed to the point where the full thrust of God's intention was capable of being understood by the human author.[16]

Thirdly, the presupposition that God continues to communicate with people in every subsequent generation suggests that the human author's intention may not be sufficient for this task. Vern Poythress notes the strength of any approach which accounts for "God Speaking Now":

> First, it has the advantage of vividly emphasizing the presence of God, his intimacy with you here and now, and therefore also the necessity of application.
> Second, the present-time model can emphasize the universal and intimate claims of God and of Christ on you...
> Third, the present-time model can emphasize the centrality of the gospel...
> Fourth, like the once-for-all model, the present-time model makes more explicit the spiral character of hermeneutics. A central commitment to Christ, growing in strength, depth, and purity, controls the entire hermeneutical process, and is in turn nourished by the word that God speaks.[17]

---

"Divine Meaning of Scripture," *WTJ* 48, no. 2 (1986); Thompson, *A Clear and Present Word*; Vanhoozer, *Is There a Meaning in This Text*; Wolterstorff, *Divine Discourse*.

15. S. L. Johnson, *The Old Testament in the New: An Argument for Biblical Inspiration* (Grand Rapids: Zondervan, 1980), 50.
16. Bock, "Evangelicals," 308.
17. Poythress, "Divine Meaning," 210.

Poythress argues for a combination of approaches, the last of which can be described as a *sensus plenior* approach.[18] While other models of Scripture attempt to explain how God continues to communicate through it, I suggest that an approach which embraces *sensus plenior* is the most convincing. It remains, therefore, to elucidate a respective hermeneutic and demonstrate how such a hermeneutic affects exegesis.

*Evangelical Modifications of* Sensus Plenior

While many Evangelicals are comfortable with adopting *sensus plenior* terminology, others desire to replace it with what they describe as a "Canonical Approach."[19] These authors, however, have not sufficiently addressed the issues raised by *sensus plenior* and in most cases resort to a form of *sensus plenior* hermeneutics. Representative of this group is Douglas Moo, who defines his approach as follows:

> The meaning intended by the human author of a particular text can take on a "fuller" meaning, legitimately developed from his meaning, in light of the text's ultimate canonical context. Without necessarily appealing to the divine author as intending a meaning separate from, and hidden from, the human author at the point of inspiration, we would appeal to the divine author as providing the larger context of the developing canon as the framework within which the New Testament writers read the Old Testament. What is involved is not just the ultimate significance of a text, or its valid manifold applications, but the meaning of the text, not fully understood by the human author.[20]

Moo is correct that the question at hand is one of meaning rather than significance or application. He is concerned that the meaning formed by canonical influence is one that is legitimately connected with the human author's original meaning. He objects to the idea that God intended a different meaning from the human author at the time of writing and that God also kept this meaning hidden. Rather, Moo suggests that God created the canonical context that allowed the New Testament writers to interpret the Old Testament. It is hard to see how this differs markedly from a *sensus plenior* description. Even though Moo argues that the fuller meaning is "legitimately developed from [the human author's] meaning", this fuller meaning was undiscoverable and unknowable in its Old Testament context. Any "fuller meaning" embedded in the text that the human authors did not intend or know of can only be attributed to the divine author. This fuller meaning is an instance of *sensus plenior*. Moo clarifies his position in a statement that highlights what he sees as its strengths.

---

18. Poythress, "Divine Meaning," 267-268.
19. Moo, "The Problem of Sensus Plenior."; B. K. Waltke, "Canonical Process Approach to the Psalms," in *Tradition and Testament: Essays in Honor of Charles Lee Feinberg* (ed. J. S. Feinberg, and P. D. Feinberg; Chicago: Moody Press, 1981).
20. Moo, "The Problem of Sensus Plenior," 210.

... the questionable division between the intention of the human author and that of the divine author in a given text is decreased, if not avoided altogether, in this approach. Appeal is made not to a meaning of the divine author that somehow is deliberately concealed from the human author in the process of inspiration—a *"sensus occultus"*—but to the meaning of the text itself that takes on deeper significance as God's plan unfolds—a *"sensus praegnans."* To be sure, God knows, as He inspires the human authors to write, what the ultimate meaning of their words will be; but it is not as if He has deliberately created a *double entendre* or hidden meaning in the words that can only be uncovered through a special revelation. The "added meaning" that the text takes on is the product of the ultimate canonical shape—though, to be sure, often clearly perceived only on a revelatory basis.[21]

Moo's hesitation to isolate the human author's meaning from the divine author's meaning is understandable, but his own model fails to avoid the same outcome. He states that he would rather appeal to the "meaning of the text itself that takes on deeper significance as God's plan unfolds—a '*sensus praegnans*.'" Unfortunately, this explanation is flawed since the "text itself" cannot communicate, unless Moo is suggesting that a text can mean something other than what the author intended it to mean.[22] Authorial intention must be present in order to understand the text, a point which Moo himself belabours. This then begs the question of which author is communicating through the canon and leaves Moo's position much closer to that of *sensus plenior* than he concedes.

A partial solution could be found in an appeal to editors of the Old Testament who were involved, to some degree, in its canonical shaping. For example, both the Psalms and books within the Twelve appear to intentionally communicate something greater by their inclusion and location in the Psalter and the book of the Twelve respectively. This acknowledges an editorial intention that may surpass the intention of the human authors of the individual psalms or books.[23] However, to suggest that there is a human editorial intention that spans the entire Old Testament is a claim too difficult to sustain. Any intention at this level would belong to the divine author and constitute *sensus plenior*.[24]

---

21. Moo, "The Problem of Sensus Plenior," 211.

22. It is clear that Moo does not wish to adopt such a position, but the lack of precision in his discussion leads to such suggestions. For a thorough critique of "the text itself" having an intention see Wolterstorff's critique of Ricoeur in *Divine Discourse*, Ch. 8.

23. This level of editorial intention could arguably represent another form of *sensus plenior*.

24. For a discussion of the canonical shape of the Twelve see C. R. Seitz, *Prophecy and Hermeneutics: Toward a New Introduction to the Prophets* (Grand Rapids: Baker, 2007). For a recent discussion of the canonical shape of the Psalms see G. J. Wenham, "Towards a Canonical Reading of the Psalms," in *Canon and Biblical Interpretation* (ed. C. Bartholomew, et al.; Grand Rapids: Zondervan, 2006).

Ultimately Moo, while attempting to avoid *sensus plenior*, or *sensus occultus* as he describes it, must appeal to a form of *sensus plenior* in his last comment, "The "added meaning" that the text takes on is the product of the ultimate canonical shape—though, to be sure, often clearly perceived only on a revelatory basis." Even if "added meaning" is related to the original meaning it is still "added" and not part of the communication of the original author. This justifies it as an instance of *sensus plenior*. Part of the problem that Moo encounters in his attempt at a solution is his lack of precision when discussing "meaning", a ubiquitous problem which I hope to clarify with the aid of speech act theory.

Bruce Waltke suggests an approach similar to the above and calls it a "canonical process approach."[25] He states that it bears similarities to *sensus plenior*, but that it also differs on key aspects:

> the canonical process approach holds that the original authorial intention was not changed in the progressive development of the canon but deepened and clarified... The canonical process approach is similar to the approach known as *sensus plenior* in that it recognizes that further revelation brought to light a text's fuller or deeper significance, but it differs from that approach in several ways.[26]

Waltke notes three ways in which his proposal differs from a *sensus plenior* approach. The first is that "the canonical process approach does not divorce the human authorial intention from the divine intention." This alleged separation is a common objection to *sensus plenior* hermeneutics. Waltke attempts to avoid it by suggesting that the original authors spoke in "ideal forms" which were "fleshed out" by progressive revelation. Secondly, he argues that *sensus plenior* tends toward an allegorical hermeneutic, whereas, his approach "underscores the continuity of the text's meaning throughout sacred history along with recognizing that further revelation won for the earlier text a deeper and clearer meaning." Third, his approach emphasizes distinct stages in the progress of revelation which inform the "clearer and deeper significance of older texts."[27]

Like Moo's proposal, this one resists the conclusion that the divine meaning can differ from the meaning intended by the human author. Waltke's proposal, however, lacks the terminological precision required to provide a tenable alternative. His suggestion that "ideal forms" are "fleshed out" and that the "deeper significance" of the older texts is uncovered avoids the critical question... is the canon an intentional work, and if so, whose work is it? Waltke states, "By the canonical process approach I mean the recognition that the text's intention became deeper and clearer as the parameters of the canon were expanded."[28]

Waltke equates meaning with the "text's intention" and this meaning is clarified as the canon expands. Thus, the answer to the above question is that

---

25. Waltke, "Canonical Process Approach."
26. Waltke, "Canonical Process Approach," 8.
27. Waltke, "Canonical Process Approach," 8.
28. Waltke, "Canonical Process Approach," 7.

the canon has its own intention. This solution suffers from the same problem that Moo encountered: the "text" does not have an intention. As soon as one speaks of meaning in relation to intention, then an author is necessary. Waltke has not come to terms with how the canonical text can "intend" anything without God being the author who is communicating through it in a way that the human authors cannot. These alternatives to *sensus plenior* do not ultimately provide a better description of the phenomena nor do they avoid the hermeneutic challenges inherent to it.

## Evangelical Opponents to *Sensus Plenior*

While the above writers all affirm that the meaning of Scripture can transcend the intention of the human author in certain cases, the following writers all contend that this is not the case. This latter group argues that the meaning of a text is single, determinate, and based upon the original intention of the human author. Even though they affirm the divine inspiration of Scripture, they maintain that God's intention is coterminous with the intention of the human author. This section will highlight some significant contributions from this group of writers.

*Walter Kaiser*
One of the most vigorous opponents to any formulation of *sensus plenior* is Walter Kaiser. His proposal sets out to prove that all of the cases in which the New Testament writers interpret the Old Testament can be explained without resorting to a *sensus plenior* based hermeneutic. He writes:

> But some will contend that is it God who speaks in the Bible and not men (sic); the men who wrote the Scriptures were the mere receptacles of what God wanted to say through them. Revelation, in this view, is perhaps concealed as much from the authors as it made known to them. Therefore the normal rules of interpretation do not apply. The answer to this charge is easy. What God spoke, He spoke in human, not heavenly, language! . . . It is not as if there were two logics and two hermeneutics in the world, one natural and the other spiritual.[29]

Kaiser is concerned that the adoption of a "spiritual" *sensus plenior* hermeneutic will result in the marginalisation of the human author. Therefore, he will not allow for "a wedge between God and the writer—unless he cares nothing for the writer's own meanings, these meanings were received from God."[30] If this wedge is forced, Kaiser believes that the subsequent hermeneutic will lack a definitive method and a determinate result, ultimately relying on the

---

29. W. C. Kaiser, "Legitimate Hermeneutics," in *Inerrancy* (ed. N. L. Geisler; Grand Rapids: Zondervan, 1980), 122-123.
30. Kaiser, "Legitimate Hermeneutics," 145.

Church for authentication.[31] This concern is evident in his response to Childs's approach:

> While evangelicals can only applaud the courage of Childs' bold new program which takes the Scripture on its own terms as canon, we regret that this must be a canon severed from the original writer's intention in all of its historical particularity ... Childs allows that the canon will confront each new generation as a new Word from God by virtue of its transhistorical capacity, but he pays a high price for this. Ultimately, the tradition will need to be authorized in some way—only the Church is left to do the job. It seems that Childs would ultimately be led back to Rome for authentication of the canon—or are there other options available to authenticate it? We would, instead, point out most vigorously that the writers themselves as well as the early Church insisted that the normativeness of the text was prior to and the very basis for the Church itself.[32]

Kaiser's concerns warrant careful consideration and he offers the following list of hermeneutical errors that should be avoided:

> (1) using the New Testament as a proving ground to identify possible predictions in earlier texts (2) using the New Testament to set the meaning that an Old Testament text may have (3) allowing New Testament argumentative quotation of the Old Testament to reinterpret or to supersede the original meaning and sense of the Old Testament writer and (4) separating the doctrinal sense of a New Testament argumentative use of the Old Testament from the doctrinal sense of the Old Testament writer and thereby breaking continuity in the progress of God's revelation.[33]

While Kaiser certainly avoids the problems associated with *sensus plenior* approaches, his own proposal creates insurmountable obstacles to interpretation. Additionally, Kaiser's suggestion that the prophets were only ignorant of the timing of their prophecy but that they understood the rest of the revelation seems to be unfounded. There are many Old Testament texts which are applied in the New Testament in ways that the human author of the Old Testament text could not have anticipated. The command to keep the Sabbath is one such example. Not only is the original primary illocution commanding observance of

---

31. Kaiser's anxiety appears to be a product of modernist foundationalist epistemology where his desire for certitude in belief does not allow for the provisional and contextual nature of human knowledge. Cf. A. Sloane, *On Being a Christian in the Academy: Nicholas Wolterstorff and the Practice of Christian Scholarship* (Carlisle: Paternoster, 2003), Chapter 1.

32. W. C. Kaiser, *Toward an Old Testament Theology* (Grand Rapids: Baker, 1981), 81.

33. Kaiser, *Toward an Old Testament Theology*, 123-124. For a discussion of how prophecy is fulfilled in a variety of ways displaying different levels of "transparency" and "translucence" see D. B. Sandy, *Plowshares & Pruning Hooks: Rethinking the Language of Biblical Prophecy and Apocalyptic* (Downers Grove: IVP, 2002), 129-154.

the Sabbath no longer in play, but it is also used to speak of an eschatological rest in which the reader is invited to enter in the present (cf. Heb. 4).[34]

Kaiser's unwavering commitment to single determinate meaning based upon human intention in the original setting leaves a disconnect in the communicative power of Scripture. If the text only means one thing and that meaning is never supplemented, then Kaiser needs to explain how texts related to the Old Covenant function in the contemporary church. Kaiser's response to this is to appeal to the text's continuing "significance":

> We certainly recognize that a passage may have a fuller *significance* than what was realized by the writer. We also wholeheartedly agree that the subject to which the Old Testament prophets made individual contributions was wider by miles than what they ever dreamed of. But the whole revelation of God as revelation hangs in jeopardy if we, an apostle, or an angel from heaven try to add to, delete, rearrange, or reassign the sense or meaning that a prophet himself received.[35]

It is clear that Kaiser has a deep respect for the Scriptures and is concerned that its message is preserved. It is, therefore, unfortunate and ironic that his proposal silences much of Scripture by marginalising its relevance vis-à-vis a contemporary community. His suggestion that the text has a "fuller significance" is an attempt to avoid this marginalisation, but the essential question remains unanswered: How is "significance" related to meaning? More broadly, how can the entire canon continually function as God's communication? If the meaning of the text is singular as he suggests, and if meaning is defined in terms of authorial intention, then the burden of proof remains on Kaiser (and others who hold this view) to demonstrate how the text can authoritatively speak to a contemporary community when the human author was speaking in a singular way in a very different context and under a different covenant.

*Elliot Johnson*

Elliot Johnson, who rejects both *sensus plenior* and single determinate meaning, suggests a solution based on distinguishing between sense and reference:

> The *defining* sense of the passage is to be identified as the author's/writer's intention. This meaning is shared by God and the human writer of the text. Reference is first of all a question of meaning and then the question of truth-value can be judged ... The nature of the divine reference, in His omniscience, will be fuller than the human reference in the shared meaning. The human author truly refers to the reality but not fully. The distinction between sense and reference is not the same as the distinction between meaning and significance.

---

34. Cf. D. A. Carson, *From Sabbath to Lord's Day: A Biblical, Historical and Theological Investigation* (Grand Rapids: Zondervan, 1982); W. L. Lane, *Hebrews 1-8* (Dallas: Word, 1991).

35. Kaiser, *Toward an Old Testament Theology*, 134-135.

Reference concerns implications of meaning that are apparent when the sense is related to the historical stance.[36]

Johnson is suggesting that while both God and the human author share the sense of the passage, only God has full understanding of the references. In his words, "The single sense is capable of implying a fullness of reference. This is not *sensus plenior* but *sensus singular* as expressed in the affirmations of the text ... The full references are only divine and only fully recognized by the interpreter in the progress of revelation." [37] Consequently, he uses the term "*references plenior*" to describe God's full understanding of the text.

This distinction, however, is ineffective. It does not solve the problem of separate authorial intentions. God is still able to do more with the text than the human author. Johnson may be correct to say that the sense of the text is shared by both, but this avoids the larger issue of meaning which he himself acknowledges is connected to reference. An analysis of sense and reference in terms of speech act theory reveals the weaknesses of such a distinction. God is able to do more (even if He merely expands the referents) and so *mean* more than the human author can do or mean.[38]

In a later work, Johnson addresses the issue of divergent divine and human intentions in relation to the meaning of the text. His thesis is that both authors share a common meaning, but God also intends an unspecified number of submeanings that are only able to be uncovered when the intended referent consequently appears.

> The divine and human authors shared the textually expressed meanings. How many additional unstated submeanings the human author consciously knew is unnecessary to determine. At the same time God, since He is omniscient, intended all the submeanings necessary to this expressed type of meaning ... such recognition of submeanings is a not "consequent" sense. Nor are they "separate" in the sense of *unrelated*. They are separate only in the sense of being *unstated*. Nor are they "different" in the sense of being *conflicting*. They are different only in the sense of being *unexpressed* ... Marshall exhibits the same concept. He imagines the Apostle John responding, "I hadn't consciously thought of the story like that, but now that you suggest it to me, I would agree that you could also understand it in that way." This approach also helps clarify passages that are difficult to interpret.[39]

---

36. E. Johnson, "Author's Intention and Biblical Interpretation," in *Hermeneutics, Inerrancy, and the Bible* (ed. E. D. Radmacher and R. D. Preus; Grand Rapids: Academie Books, 1984), 416-417.

37. Johnson, "Author's Intention," 427-428.

38. This will be discussed in greater detail in Chapter 4.

39. E. E. Johnson, "Dual Authorship and the Single Intended Meaning of Scripture," *BSac* 143, no. 571 (1986).

This proposal also suffers from significant problems. Firstly, it reduces the issue of dual authorship to prophetic or typological texts.[40] Secondly, it fails to avoid a *sensus plenior* approach by effectively substituting "full meaning" with "submeanings." Thirdly, it is unclear how submeanings are congruent with the human author's meaning when they are both "unstated" and "unexpressed" in the original text. Lastly, while it is convenient to appeal to Apostolic approval, unfortunately how we imagine the Apostles might respond to our interpretation is not a convincing method of verification.

*Jeannine Brown*

Jeannine Brown has recently defended meaning as a result of human authorial intent in contrast to a *sensus plenior* approach. Her work represents a sustained and sophisticated argument using resources from both theology and communication theory.[41] Brown employs speech act theory to clarify the nature of communication and the goals of interpretation.[42] Through this she is able to advance the discussion by providing a level of precision that was previously lacking.

Brown describes her communication model of interpretation in the following way, "Scripture's meaning can be understood as the communicative act of the author that has been inscribed in the text and addressed to the intended audience for purposes of engagement."[43] In relation to dual authorship, Brown contends that God's intention is always equated with the human author's intention:

> When interpreting Scripture, readers believed they were hearing from the human or the divine author. It was not uncommon for those listening for the human author to hear something distinct from those listening for the divine author.[44]

> I will be arguing that we should not try to separate the two—what the human author was communicating stands in for God's communicative intent.[45]

Her objection to the *sensus plenior*, which receives only brief attention, is the standard objection that it lacks hermeneutical controls.

---

40. This issue will be addressed in due course.

41. Brown, *Scripture as Communication*. For a similar but brief treatment of the issue of God speaking that also employs speech act theory see W. J. Houston, "What Did the Prophets Think They Were Doing? Speech Acts and Prophetic Discourse in the Old Testament," *BibInt* 1, no. 2 (1993).

42. In this way, her work mirrors my own. Though, as it will soon become clear, her presuppositions and conclusions are markedly different.

43. Brown, *Scripture as Communication*, 14.

44. Brown, *Scripture as Communication*, 27.

45. Brown, *Scripture as Communication*, 27.

Problematic for the *sensus plenior* view as applied to contemporary "fuller meaning" is the lack of any adequate controls for what might be part of this new, fuller sense. For "it is difficult to tell the difference between [the *sensus plenior*] and the projection onto the text of a theological idea or belief acquired by some other means. If one appeals to the 'literal sense' as the control, has one really learnt anything new from a passage by the *plenior* method?"[46]

Brown recognizes that in rejecting any form of *sensus plenior* she must account for Scripture's ability to function as God's word in new contexts. Relying on Wright and Hirsch, Brown argues for *transhistorical intentions* in order to explain how a text can continue to mean something in new contexts:

> ... how can we affirm the newness of continuing meaning (its futurity) while still binding it to the author's communicative intention? I believe we can most adequately address this tension by understanding continuing meaning as an author's "transhistorical intentions." Hirsch introduces this term to express an author's unforeseen intentions for future readers. As Hirsch notes elsewhere, "Different applications do not necessarily lie outside the boundaries of meaning ... so long as [they belong] to the true extension of meaning, part of what does not change—that is, part of meaning itself." (Hirsch, "Meaning and Significance", 210) In a similar vein, Vanhoozer speaks of the author's communicative intention as the author's "intended meaning" and refers to its application as the author's "extended meaning." (Vanhoozer, *Meaning*, 262).[47]

This appeal to transhistorical intentions, however, is unconvincing. It is obvious that in some cases an author intends that their text be used in a variety of contexts, even in future generations.[48] However, when we consider the particular case of Scripture it is brave to suggest that the human authors would understand the entire influence of later canonical writings or how their text continues to communicate under the new covenant. The problems are far greater than her solution suggests.

Additionally, Brown's appeal to Vanhoozer in this particular context is misleading. She suggests that his comments support the concept of transhistorical intention and the extension of meaning, but Vanhoozer is happy to equate this with the intention of the divine author and a *sensus plenior*.[49]

Still aware of the need to clarify if texts take on new meaning in new contexts, Brown offers a number of qualifications:

---

46. Brown, *Scripture as Communication*, 115. Brown is quoting from N. T. Wright, *The New Testament and the People of God* (Minneapolis: Fortress Press, 1992), 58-59.
47. Brown, *Scripture as Communication*, 116.
48. E.g., The Psalms and Deuteronomy explicitly anticipate future generations of readers.
49. Which he does in the next couple of pages. (Vanhoozer, *Is There a Meaning in This Text?*, 262-265.)

> First, it is true that at least some authors foresee future readers, and so inevitably some kind of future "application" or "contextualization" of their meaning...
> Second, although continuing meaning is in some ways "new" (it is not simply an identical linguistic expression of communicative intention), its tie to original meaning need not be conceived of as a slim one... Understanding well the distinction between meaning and contexualization can also assist in affirming meaning as stable and unchanging. Contextualization occurs at the intersection of meaning and the reader's context, so, while contextualiztion is tied to meaning, it is not coterminous with meaning. Therefore, meaning has not necessarily changed when it is contextualized. Meaning contextualized in different settings explains its perceived "newness." But the newness arises from meaning's intersection with a new context, not from meaning itself evolving. In fact, the very stability of meaning is what leads us to sense the importance of a strong connection between meaning and its contextualized expressions.[50]

The problem with this solution is that Brown seems to have abandoned her use of speech act categories. Given that she associates meaning, at least in part, with locution and illocution (and even "perlocutionary intent"),[51] does she now really want to affirm that these illocutions continue to function directly in new contexts? If Brown had explained this "newness" of meaning in speech act terms, it would have highlighted some of the inherent problems with her solution. In the subsequent discussion of "Scripture's shaping influence", she returns to speech act categories and the results are as anticipated:

> The connection between speech act theory and Scripture's shaping influence is a natural one. As we have just discussed, we can envision the Bible at its canonical level in terms of divine locutions, illocutions, and perlocutionary intentions. How might these conceptual categories assist us in the contextualization process of specific biblical texts? One contribution of speech act theory is its attention to the intentions of an author for reader enactment. In other words, authors, including God as author, have intentions for how readers respond to their messages. These intended effects, the author's perlocutionary intentions, are an extension of meaning. This construct encourages us in our quest to contextualize its message to ask the question of the intended effect of any particular text. If a particular locution, that is, a set of words, does not bring about an effect in a new setting that is consistent with the intended effect for the original audience, we may need to hear a recontextualized locution for the new setting.[52]

---

50. Brown, *Scripture as Communication*, 116-117.
51. Brown, *Scripture as Communication*, 47-48. I will address the concept of perlocutionary intent in later chapters.
52. Brown, *Scripture as Communication*, 268.

This proposal raises several key questions: What if the intended effect in the original audience is incompatible with the new community and further revelation? Why should we want to bring about the same effect or even an effect consistent with the original one? And who decides what's consistent? What is missing from this account is a canonical sensitivity that allows for God to perform different illocutions based on the original locutions. Furthermore, as discussed below and despite claims to the contrary, Brown cannot accommodate canonical illocutions within her model since it counts God's speech acts as coterminous with the human speech acts and no human speech act can be identified at this higher literary level. Most importantly, the relationship between meaning and contextualization requires clarification in order to determine how one moves from the former to the latter. Brown argues that the distinction she makes avoids the problem of normative meaning and non-normative applications. I am not convinced that it does:

> This formulation of meaning and contextualiztion avoids the critique levelled at certain views of application "that a text can have only one normative meaning but many possible applications, which can never become normative." In my formulation, Scripture's meaning, understood in all its complexity, is normatively addressed to its particular context yet normatively addresses other contexts as well...Thus, if we are serious about contextualizing the biblical message in our settings, we will pursue this as a normative task...This formulation preserves meaning as distinct from contextualization and prior to it. It also emphasizes the importance of a strong cord of continuity between exegesis—the search for original meaning—and contextualization.[53]

It is not clear that these distinctions avoid the problem in the way Brown suggests. Her definition of contextualization is "the task of bringing a biblical author's meaning to bear in other times and cultures ... to contextualize is to hear Scripture's meaning speak in new contexts."[54] This sounds very much like "application" and the original problem remains: how is contextualization related to meaning and how should we move from one to the other. Brown has not explained how the original speech acts function in a new context.

Furthermore, Brown argues that contextualization is distinct from meaning and that meaning is normative (i.e., unchanging). However, if meaning is understood as distinct from contextualization then there is a breach in the communicative activity. This is one of the benefits of speech act theory to which Brown herself appeals. Speech act theory highlights the performative and interpersonal character of communication. Authors perform actions through texts (illocutions), which enable the readers to understand what course of action

---

53. Brown, *Scripture as Communication*, 118. Quoting J. Zimmermann, *Recovering Theological Hermeneutics: An Incarnational-Trinitarian Theory of Interpretation* (Grand Rapids: Baker, 2004), 22.

54. Brown, *Scripture as Communication*, 25.

(perlocution) is being requested of them. If meaning (illocution)[55] is not directly connected to contextualization, then contextualization suffers from the subjectivity she was attempting to avoid. If Brown had maintained the use of speech act theory in her discussion of contextualization, she may have avoided such inconsistencies and her model would likely have been stronger.

This resulting breach in the communicative activity is due to the marginalisation of the author who, in Brown's model, spoke only into their original context. The author is no longer present in the contemporary setting (i.e., they do not perform contemporary speech acts). What remains in her model is a text that reveals historically bound speech acts, and these ancient speech acts require continual contextualization. This unfortunately undermines the communicative nature of Scripture. God's speech acts are understood as performed solely in the original context of the book or canon, so it remains unclear how God continues to speak to a contemporary audience. This raises a significant problem for Brown's model as she herself argues strongly for the personal nature of communication:

> ... a communication model adequately attends to the interpersonal nature of texts. An understanding of meaning that attends to texts as expressions of personal interfacing rather than impersonal objects will help us adequately attend to authors, texts, and readers, while keeping each in proper focus.[56]

Brown offers the following implications of the divine nature of Scripture:

> Here, I would simply point out two ramifications for contextualization, if Scripture is indeed divine discourse. First, because the analogy of incarnation allows us to affirm that Scripture is truly God's word to us, we can approach the Bible with a hermeneutic of engagement. We can expect God to speak as we open the Bible. We can come ready to hear from God and be engaged by God. Walter Brueggemann speaks of this engagement as the proper work of the text ... This means our response to Scripture will encompass more than just our head. A hermeneutic of engagement will involve a readiness to respond with all we are to the call of God to us through Scripture. Second, understanding the Bible as divine discourse also encourages us to come to the Bible from a stance of trust.[57]

This description suffers from a lack of terminological precision due again to her unfortunate abandonment of speech act categories. Brown suggests that we can hear from God and so be engaged by God. However, she also states that God

---

55. As I discuss earlier, Brown also locates meaning in "perlocutionary intention" which also contradicts her desire to remove subjectivity from the process of interpretation.
56. Brown, *Scripture as Communication*, 71–72.
57. Brown, *Scripture as Communication*, 234.

can only mean what the human author meant.[58] In speech act terms, God can only perform the illocutions of the human author. This means the end result of what can be counted as God speaking is greatly reduced. Original commands and promises, for example, which can no longer apply to new covenant communities in a direct manner (through the same illocution) must be discounted. Brown has not explained how we hear from God or dealt in any detail with how the words of human authors can count as the words of God. Concluding her discussion of the divine nature of Scripture, Brown states:

> What difference does it make to read and interpret the Bible with the conviction that it is divine discourse? First, if it is divine discourse we can assume the unity of the Bible, although without muting the diversity of the voices of its individual human authors.
> Second, reading the Bible as divine discourse means we will expect the Bible to impact readers. We can affirm the cultural locatedness of the biblical text without downplaying its power to speak into new contexts, because it is the Holy Spirit who empowers its message. "The role of the Spirit is to enable us to take the biblical texts in the sense they were intended, and to apply or follow that sense in the way we live." (fn. Vanhoozer, First theology, 228) The empowered message will be likely to "hit home" in both familiar and unexpected ways. Often it will reaffirm its truth when we need to be encouraged. Yet it may also come to us as a surprisingly new and fresh word from God.[59]

With respect to the implications of divine discourse, an affirmation of canonical unity is a clear starting point. However, Brown's model limits this unity to an agreement between the various human authors, rather than any direct communicative activity at the higher levels of testament or canon. The human writers were not the authors at these levels[60] and therefore cannot perform illocutionary acts through them. By implication, according to Brown, neither can God. This assertion of unity is limited in comparison to *sensus plenior* approaches.

Additionally, Brown again takes Vanhoozer out of context. Vanhoozer is affirming that the Holy Spirit enables us to understand the intended meaning and corresponding application, but in Vanhoozer's proposal the intended sense is God's intention.[61] Brown is taking a line of argument similar to that of Stanley Grenz.[62] While arguing strongly for determinate meaning based on the human

---

58. Brown, *Scripture as Communication*, 254.
59. Brown, *Scripture as Communication*, 256-257. Quoting Vanhoozer, *First Theology*, 228.
60. Though editors may certainly have communicated their intent at various levels within the canon.
61. According to Vanhoozer it is the Holy Spirit who enables one to understand the illocutionary acts and then prompts an appropriate perlocution. See the discussion below.
62. See Grenz and Franke, *Beyond Foundationalism*.

intent, Brown introduces indeterminacy to the communicative act at the level of Holy Spirit empowerment. Can the Holy Spirit use a text to mean anything? Which illocutions is the Holy Spirit likely to make? Her appeal to determinate meaning is less consequential than initially suggested.

Brown's concluding comments reveal the subjectivity and indeterminacy of her own model. This is a natural consequence of attempting to prove the contemporary relevance of historical text within a hermeneutic based on a single determinate meaning and human authorial intent:

> I listen to the text, in all its otherness, as if my life depends on it. I am passionate about discovering what the author's message might mean for my own contexts, for me and for us these many years later. I listen to hear from God, who has authored Scripture as much as its human authors did. I listen in continuity with the people of God in all other times and places. I read and listen, aware of both the distance and nearness of the Bible. This distance and nearness arise from the incarnational nature of Scripture ... [63]

Brown's advice to interpreters who are seeking to "recontextualize" the Scriptures is that they be sensitive to the fact that "mere reproduction of an utterance from one context into a different context may very well produce a meaning that is foreign to an author's communicative intention." In order to avoid this *faux pas*, her conclusion is that "we will want to consider carefully how a locution originally uttered in one context might be "transferred" into another setting in order to be true to communicative intention." The call to "consider carefully" is sage advice, yet offers little assistance to the interpreter in making this critical move from ancient text to contemporary context. Part of the problem lies in Brown's focus on locution rather than illocution. The question that needs to be addressed, and the one which is highlighted by the limitations of her proposal, is whether the illocutions performed in the original context remain in play and whether new illocutions exist due to the expanded canonical context.[64]

*Challenges to* Sensus Plenior

Despite the weaknesses of models that reject *sensus plenior*, it is evident that *sensus plenior* models of interpretation also face significant challenges. A major objection to this kind of hermeneutic is that the interpretive controls are ill-defined or exterior to Scripture. Kaiser's retort that such a proposal results in tradition being granted a higher authority than Scripture reflects this sentiment.[65]

---

63. Brown, *Scripture as Communication*, 251.
64. For a review of Brown's work in *Scripture as Communication*, see R. S. Briggs, "Scripture as Communication: Introducing Biblical Hermeneutics," *EvQ* 80, no. 1 (2008).
65. Kaiser, "Legitimate Hermeneutics," 134-135.

Robert Stein has critiqued the *sensus plenior* hermeneutic on a number of levels.[66] He believes the *sensus plenior* hermeneutic was developed by considering only a small portion of Scripture and should not be determinative. He states:

> I do not believe that one's basic hermeneutical approach to the interpretation of Scripture should be developed based on the predictive prophecies of Scripture. The vast majority of Scripture involves other genres (narrative, teaching, proverbs, poetry, laws, parables, etc.). Even in the prophetic books predictive prophecy makes up only a portion of the contents of these books. We should derive a hermeneutical system based upon the most frequently used genres and then see how predictive prophecy fits the system of hermeneutics that has been developed.[67]

Stein continues by saying that his preferred method for constructing a biblical hermeneutic would be to base it on the "simpler and more common passages" and then see how it applies elsewhere. Stein's objection is a valid one. Too often *sensus plenior* has been discussed only in relation to Old Testament prophecy or New Testament usage of Old Testament texts. However, Stein's alternative, to form a hermeneutic based on majority genre, does not sufficiently address his own objection. Would it not be better still to formulate a hermeneutic that is able to account for the entire canon and each genre contained within it? Obviously, the different genres require specific treatment, but a meta-hermeneutic that accounts for the canon would no doubt be superior.

Stein's second objection to *sensus plenior* is less insightful. He argues that there is no access to God's use of language and no way of understanding what God means except through the language of the human author:

> We have no way of understanding what God means except through what his apostles and prophets wrote in Scripture, and in seeking to understand God's apostles and prophets, we want to know what these human, inspired authors meant by their words. We simply have no access to a separate divine meaning.[68]

On the one hand, this is simply the question of hermeneutical controls raised by other authors. As stated, this is a valid critique. However, his main line of argument does not allow for the canon to play a significant role in developing our understanding of God's language. The charge that there is no access to God's meaning begs the question of why God cannot communicate at higher literary levels.

---

66. R. H. Stein, "The Benefits of an Author-Oriented Approach to Hermeneutics," *JETS* 44, no. 3 (2001).
67. Stein, "The Benefits of an Aurthor-Oriented Approach," 464.
68. Stein, "The Benefits of an Aurthor-Oriented Approach," 464-465.

The third objection to *sensus plenior* is that it takes prophecy too literally. Stein argues that if one claims that the prophets understood their own work to be metaphorical and figurative then the need for *sensus plenior* disappears:

> Frequently those scholars who seek to interpret prophecy more literalistically argue that these passages must be interpreted as possessing a *sensus plenior*, so that there is both an author-related meaning and a separate divine meaning. Yet, once we accept that these prophecies were understood by the prophets as referring to events in their own time, the need for a *sensus plenior* disappears. Once we acknowledge that the Biblical authors understood this imagery metaphorically and figuratively, we have no need for a *sensus plenior*.[69]

This suggestion, like others discussed previously, does not address the issue with enough precision. The question that needs to be considered is whether God can mean (i.e., intend and perform) something that the human author did not mean. Can God perform illocutions divergent from those of the human author? While the human author may well have spoken figuratively, the increased referent produced by subsequent canonical revelation results in new illocutions and so, new meanings. Furthermore, if Stein's first objection (that the *sensus plenior* was based upon a minority of texts) is answered by demonstrating that a *sensus plenior* approach is also necessary in non-prophetic texts and even across the entire canon, then this last objection is mute.

## Speech Act Theorists and *Sensus Plenior*

Most of the discussion of dual authorship and *sensus plenior* has been undertaken without the resources of communication theory. However, there are notable exceptions that have entered the discussion in recent years. As discussed, both Vanhoozer and Wolterstorff employ speech act theory in the development of theological hermeneutics.[70] Whereas Jeannine Brown has used speech act theory to defend a single intention hermeneutic,[71] both Vanhoozer and Wolterstorff have employed speech act theory to explicate *sensus plenior* type hermeneutics. Interestingly, through their application of speech act theory both authors conclude that the entire canon should be interpreted in light of something akin to *sensus plenior*.[72]

---

69. Stein, "The Benefits of an Aurthor-Oriented Approach," 466.

70. Other writers have made contributions to the discussion, but their contributions are limited in comparison and in substance. See also Horton, *Covenant and Eschatology*; McConville, "Divine Speech"; Treier, *Virtue and the Voice of God*; Ward, *Word and Supplement*. These works will be discussed in some detail in the following chapter. See also Poythress, "Canon and Speech Act."

71. By "single intention" I am referring to approaches which understand the meaning of human and divine authors as coterminous.

72. Wolterstorff comments, "The particular practice of biblical interpretation on which I am focusing my attention, in these discussions on interpretation, is that practice

*Kevin J. Vanhoozer*

With respect to the dual authorship of Scripture, Vanhoozer utilizes speech act categories to explain how both the human author and God can communicate through the one text. His main thesis is that divine illocutions are present at the canonical level,[73] yet this is not the only way in which Scripture can be affirmed as God's word. As I cited above, Vanhoozer contends that:

> There are two complementary senses in which I wish to affirm the canon as God's illocutionary act. First, there is the divine appropriation of the illocutions of the human authors, particularly at the generic level but not exclusively there. For example, God still uses the book of Jonah to satirize religious ethnocentrism. (Indeed the message of Jonah is as relevant today as ever.) Yet God may be doing new things with Jonah and other biblical texts too by virtue of their being gathered together in the canon. Could it be that certain illocutions come to light only when we describe what God is doing at the canonical level? More work needs to be done in this area, but for the moment let me offer the following as possible candidates for the divine canonical illocutions: instructing the believing community, testifying to Christ, and perhaps most obviously, covenanting.[74]

Vanhoozer suggests that God's illocutionary acts occur at a variety of levels. Within the canonical books and especially at the level of the book as a whole, he believes that God appropriates the illocutions of the human authors. Additionally, he argues that God may be "doing new things" with the text in its canonical and contemporary context, noting that "more work needs to be done in this area." Elsewhere, he specifically affirms the concept of *sensus plenior* in explaining his hermeneutic:

> My thesis is that the "fuller meaning" of Scripture—the meaning associated with divine authorship—emerges only at the level of the whole canon...
> How then shall we address the problem of *Sensus Plenior*? Does the meaning of the biblical text go beyond what the human authors could have intended? The answer, I believe, depends on what—or rather, whose—intended act we are interpreting. A text must be read in light of its intentional context, that is, against the background that best allows us to answer the question of what the author is doing. For it is in relation to its intentional context that a text yields its maximal

---

which takes the Christian Bible as a whole to be an instrument of divine discourse..." (Wolterstorff, *Divine Discourse*, 186.) So also LaSor who writes, "Something like a *sensus plenior* is required by many portions of Scripture, possibly by all of Scripture." (La Sor, "Prophecy," 59.)

73. Christopher Seitz argues similarly in a discussion of the book of Amos, where he suggests that the "entire book" should be treated "as an intentional speech-act." (Seitz, *Prophecy and Hermeneutics*, 227-229.) See also C. R. Seitz, *The Goodly Fellowship of the Prophets: The Achievement of Association in Canon Formation* (Grand Rapids: Baker 2009).

74. Vanhoozer, *First Theology*, 194.

sense, its fullest meaning. *If we are reading the Bible as the Word of God, therefore, I suggest that the context that yields this maximal sense is the canon, taken as a unified communicative act...The divine intention does not contravene the intention of the human author but rather supervenes on it.*[75]

What Vanhoozer seems to be suggesting is that God performs illocutionary acts by appropriating the illocutionary acts of the human author. Additionally, God performs illocutionary acts at a level that is impossible for the human author, namely, the canonical level.[76] These divine illocutionary acts at the canonical level "supervene" rather than "contravene" the illocutionary acts at lower levels. It is the sum of these illocutionary acts that Vanhoozer would label *sensus plenior*. In relation to these canonical illocutions being "new" Vanhoozer responds that they were always present in that God had always intended that these texts would function canonically:

> The latent potential of a text is really there, buried in the cumulative wisdom carried by a literary form. What this means is that the literal sense—the sense of the literary act—may, at times, be indeterminate or open-ended. However—and this is crucial—the indeterminacy we are considering is intended; moreover, it is a definite feature of the meaning of the text. If there is a *sensus plenior*, then, it is on the level of God's gathering together the various partial and progressive communicative acts and purposes of the human authors into one 'great canonical Design.'[77]

Vanhoozer offers good candidates for what these canonical illocutions may be: "instructing the believing community, testifying to Christ, and perhaps most obviously, covenanting." However, the proposed existence of illocutions at this literary and theological level raises a number of significant questions.

Firstly, canonical illocutions must be based upon canonical locutions. The connection between the locutions/illocutions of books within the canon and the locutions/illocutions at the canonical level is unclear and needs further discussion. A related issue is whether there are any levels of locution/illocution that occur between the levels of book and canon (e.g., at the level of testament or partially complete testament).[78]

Another question this proposal raises is often asked of *sensus plenior* advocates: how do we interpret for the divine intention at the canonical level?

---

75. Vanhoozer, *Is There a Meaning in This Text?*, 264-265, italics original.

76. He states, "Perhaps the most important question we can ask of the canon is: whose act is it? If interpretation is a matter of ascribing and inferring communicative intentions, to whom do we ascribe the illocutions?" (Vanhoozer, *First Theology*, 196.)

77. Vanhoozer, *Is There a Meaning in This Text?*, 313-314.

78. Once again, this raises the question of which canon is authoritative. I presuppose the authority of the final form of the Protestant canon. For a discussion of the canonical differences between the Hebrew and Greek Old Testaments see G. Goswell, "The Order of the Books in the Hebrew Bible," *JETS* 51, no. 4 (2008); G. Goswell, "The Order of the Books in the Greek Old Testament," *JETS* 52, no. 3 (2009).

Unfortunately, Vanhoozer does not address these particulars of the hermeneutic.

Furthermore, Vanhoozer speaks of God's appropriation of human illocutions at the whole book or generic level, yet there was little detail offered regarding the nature of this appropriation. Additionally, the question of whether God could do something with the text at that level that the human author did not do (i.e., perform new and different illocutions through the appropriation of that text in new contexts) was not addressed. Possibly, Vanhoozer means to address this by his discussion of canonical illocutions, but due to the lack of detail in that discussion it is hard to determine. Overall, Vanhoozer's intuition and suggestions appear cogent and much of the following discussion will build upon his proposal.

*Nicholas Wolterstorff*

Wolterstorff's discussion of dual authorship leads him to conclude that two separate but related hermeneutics are required.[79] He too employs speech act theory to describe not only the phenomena of God communicating but how it is that human discourse can be counted as God's. Wolterstorff notes two ways a person's discourse can count as another person's discourse: deputation and appropriation. He argues that "appropriation" is the best way to explain God's relationship to the human discourse "given the extraordinary diversity of the biblical text." He also notes, "on this way of thinking of the matter, a doctrine of inspiration really is a supplement. However these books came about, the crucial fact is that God appropriates that discourse in such a way that those speakings now mediate God's speaking."[80] On the relationship between the two requisite hermeneutics, Wolterstorff provides the following description:

> Interpreting Scripture for divine discourse requires a double hermeneutic: first one interprets these writings so as to discern the human discourse of which they are the trace; then, and only then, does one move on to interpret for what God said by way of this human discourse. If you make a point by way of approvingly citing what someone else has said, then for me to discern the point you are making I must first discern what the writer you quoted was saying ... If there's to be divine-discourse interpretation of Scripture, that practice will have to be employed in pretty much the way it is presently employed by its best practitioners. It's only when we move to the second hermeneutic that explicit use of the theological conviction that Scripture is God's book comes into play.[81]

---

79. He labels them the "first" and "second" hermeneutic referring to discovering the human and divine intentions respectively (Wolterstorff, *Divine Discourse*, Chapters 11 and 12).

80. Wolterstorff, *Divine Discourse*, 185-187.

81. Wolterstorff, "The Promise of Speech-Act Theory," 87.

Wolterstorff suggests that there are a number of ways in which God appropriates the human discourse, allowing him to do something different with the text than was originally performed by the human author. He comments: "at those points where we have found ourselves forced to depart from the baseline of construing the stance and content of God's discourse to be that of the human discourse, how is God's discourse related to the locutions and discourse of the human authors which mediated it?"[82] This is the critical question.

Wolterstorff offers five general patterns that emerge. The first is that it might be necessary to change the "rhetorico-conceptual structure" to move from the human to divine discourse. He cites the example of Paul declaring, "God, whom I serve ... ", and notes that this declaration makes no sense if it is attributed by appropriation to God.

The second pattern occurs in cases where God appropriates the main point but not all the points that the human author was making. He suggests that there are times when we can discard the way the point was made by the human author but understand that the "main point" is appropriated as divine discourse. He cites Psalm 93 as an example where God could not possibly be affirming what Wolterstorff believes reflects "geocentric cosmology widely shared among the people of antiquity."[83] Therefore he concludes:

> God can't be saying here that the earth is immobile. But the main point of the discourse of this Psalm, once we make the appropriate alteration of rhetorical structure, is that God is worthy of being hymned for majesty, strength, and steadfastness. So we attribute that main point to God, and discard the psalmist's particular way of making the point as of purely human significance.[84]

The third pattern is that God may speak "tropically" (i.e., metaphorically) when the human writer speaks "literally." Psalm 137 is apparently an example of this situation and will be discussed below in detail.

In the fourth pattern, Wolterstorff suggests that some cases can be explained by what he calls "transitive discourse." He defines this as the "phenomenon of one act of discourse on the part of a person counting as another act of discourse on the part of that same person."[85] The two acts of discourse can be labeled *discourse-generating* discourse and *discourse-generated* discourse respectively. Parables and allegories are examples of transitive discourse. He describes this in speech act terms, "it also happens rather often that by performing one illocutionary action we perform another illocutionary action—that by saying one thing, we say another thing, that one of our acts of discourse counts as another of our acts of discourse."[86] In relation to dual authorship, Wolterstorff

---

82. Wolterstorff, *Divine Discourse*, 208.
83. Wolterstorff, *Divine Discourse*, 209.
84. Wolterstorff, *Divine Discourse*, 210.
85. Wolterstorff, *Divine Discourse*, 213.
86. Wolterstorff, *Divine Discourse*, 212-213.

is suggesting that there may be cases of divine discourse where God appropriates the human discourse in transitive manner, in contrast to the way it originally functioned (i.e., God is doing something different with the text to what the human author was doing).

Lastly, Wolterstorff makes a distinction between specificity and generality. This distinction is used to explain cases where it might happen that God is speaking specifically to a particular people on a particular subject that does not directly apply to all people in all times and places. Wolterstorff uses the example of Paul requiring women to be silent and suggests this might be a case where God is not commanding this generally.[87]

In discussing how interpreters know which of these five patterns to apply to a particular situation, Wolterstorff argues that it will be obvious that some methods will not work in various texts. He concludes his comparison of "tropical" and "main point" patterns with the following:

> it often turns out, when one looks into the details of the passage to be interpreted, that the choice between these two patterns of interpretation is easy. One can't even think of how one of the two patterns might go; it doesn't prove viable. There will be other cases in which, though both are viable, one of the two proves very implausible as a construal of what God is likely to have intended to say by appropriating this particular passage. That probably leaves us with a few cases where close scrutiny of the passage, coupled with reflection on what God might have intended to say by appropriating the passage, leaves us with equally viable and plausible alternatives. I judge that then one should prefer the tropic interpretation over the main point/ancillary point interpretation, for the reason cited above.[88]

A number of comments are warranted vis-à-vis Wolterstorff's five patterns of communication.[89] The first suggestion to change the "rhetorical-conceptual structure" might make some sense, but the instances where this applies are better accounted for by recognizing illocutions at higher levels in the text.[90] Wisse has rightly noted that changing the rhetorico-conceptual structure produces a change in illocution. The result is that the text now "means" something

---

87. Wolterstorff, *Divine Discourse*, 215-216.

88. The "reason cited above" is that Wolterstorff "would prefer that—on the ground that a plausible metaphorical interpretation of an appropriated passage is more honouring of the passage and its appropriation than an interpretation which just leaves that passage behind as making an ancillary point." (Wolterstorff, *Divine Discourse*, 217-218.)

89. I have previously critiqued Wolterstorff's 'second hermeneutic' in K. Barker, "Divine Illocutions in Psalm 137: A Critique of Nicholas Wolterstorff's 'Second Hermeneutic'," *TynBul* 60, no. 1 (2009). See also M. Wisse, "From Cover to Cover? A Critique of Wolterstorff's Theory of the Bible as Divine Discourse," *IJPR* 52, no. 3 (2002).

90. I will offer a detailed discussion of such levels in the chapters below.

other than it did and Wolterstorff's method has not maintained a link between the two hermeneutics.[91]

The second suggestion of a metaphorical appropriation appears to justify allegorical interpretation. This is something that Wolterstorff sees as occasionally unavoidable, but which seems to undermine his entire project. On the one hand he offers these patterns in an attempt to avoid a "wax nose" of Scripture that can be turned in any direction in the hands of the reader. On the other hand, to offer a metaphorical appropriation with no controls allows the reader to "turn the nose" at their discretion.

The third suggestion, that interpreters can choose the main point of a text and jettison the ancillary points, is entirely unsatisfying. Who decides which points are the main points? On what basis do we reject the various speech acts that comprise a text?

The fourth suggestion that some discourse is transitive merely describes the problem at hand. A *sensus plenior* approach deems it likely that God will do something with the text that the human author did not intend. Without adequate clarification this suggestion again undermines interpreting for authorial intent. The fifth pattern may well be true. Some illocutions may not have universal force, but how do we know? How is the reader to determine which illocutions remain in play in their own context? Again, this suggestion merely highlights the problem.

Wolterstorff is aware that he hasn't solved the issue. He speaks of the "anxiety" interpreters have of distorting what God is saying because their theological presuppositions affect their judgment. In the end, he is cautions against too great a certitude regarding what God says in Scripture:

> I conclude that there is no way to avoid employing our convictions as to what is true and loving in the process of interpreting for divine discourse—no way to circumvent doing that which evokes the wax-nose anxiety, the anxiety, namely, that the convictions with which we approach the process of interpretation may lead us to miss discerning what God said and to conclude that God said what God did not say. The anxiety is appropriate, eminently appropriate, and will always be appropriate. Only with awe and apprehension, sometimes even fear and trembling, and only after prayer and fasting, is it appropriate to interpret a text so as to discern what God said and is saying thereby. The risks cannot be evaded.[92]

When it comes to diminishing the risks and lowering this anxiety, Wolterstorff offers the following principles for refining this hermeneutic. The first is that "the appropriator says what the person whose discourse is appropriated said. The appropriated discourse anchors the appropriating discourse."[93] Wolterstorff recognizes that this does not account for all the phenomena of

---

91. Wisse, "From Cover to Cover?," 160.
92. Wolterstorff, *Divine Discourse*, 236.
93. Wolterstorff, *Divine Discourse*, 236.

Scripture. He concludes that at times it is necessary to depart from this first principle as long as there is "good reason":

> There may well be good reason for departing at certain points from the results of applying that principle; but that, then, is what we must be attentive for, good reason for departing. Absent such good reason, we interpret the appropriator or deputizer as saying what the person whose discourse is appropriated or deputized said ... And let it be added that having good reason to depart is also not license for unbridled play of the imagination.[94]

The second principle is that the interpreter needs to remain open to the possibility that their hermeneutical presuppositions might be wrong, "one minimizes the risk by doing one's best to remain genuinely open to the possibility that the beliefs with which one approached the enterprise of interpreting for divine discourse are mistaken".[95]

Thirdly, he suggests we minimize the risks by growing in knowledge of ourselves and of the world. He argues that our scientific knowledge for example, enables us to conclude that God could not be saying what the psalmist is saying in Psalm 93 about the stability of the earth.[96]

Wolterstorff's rejection of the psalmist's illocution at this point is unnecessary. An appreciation of the various illocutions being performed through the psalm offers a solution. The psalmist's main *assertion* is not about the fixedness of the earth in relation to the sun, but about the stability of the world as something set by Yahweh. Using the language and cosmology of the day (and, in fact, we use the same language even in our post-Copernican context), the psalmist is meditating on Yahweh's power, *asserting* Yahweh's rule and *inviting* a response of worship. Having understood what the psalmist was doing in that verse (the illocutions being performed) allows for greater precision in understanding what God could be doing with that same verse.

The fourth and, in his mind, the most important principle is that we grow in our knowledge of God since, "Interpretation of a person's discourse occurs, and can only occur, in the context of knowledge of that person ... A hermeneutics of divine discourse requires supplementation with discussions of other ways of knowing God, and of ways of knowing God better."[97]

Wolterstorff has offered sound advice, but unfortunately it is of little assistance in explicating a hermeneutic of dual authorship. The first principle, that one should count the illocutionary stance of God as congruous with the illocutionary stance of the human author is a good place to begin. However, the main issue is whether God does things with the text that the human author does not do and whether there are procedures to uncover this divine action. Wolterstorff

---

94. Wolterstorff, *Divine Discourse*, 237.
95. Wolterstorff, *Divine Discourse*, 238.
96. Wolterstorff, *Divine Discourse*, 238-239.
97. Wolterstorff, *Divine Discourse*, 239.

suggests that we can depart from this first principle if there is "good reason", which once again begs the question—what constitutes good reason?

The second principle is similarly unhelpful. It states that one's hermeneutic may be flawed and one must be willing to recognize the fact. This is certainly true, yet Wolterstorff offers no clarification of how to determine this or what constitutes a correct hermeneutic.

The third and fourth principles are helpful, if limited. Knowledge of oneself and of God is critical, but how do we gain such knowledge? Wolterstorff speaks of "engaging simultaneously in whatever practices might yield a better knowledge of God."[98] Scripture is the primary means through which we gain such knowledge, thus making his argument either circular or one that prioritizes other forms of revelation. In the end, Wolterstorff offers good advice, but it falls short of addressing the challenges raised in proposing a hermeneutic of dual authorship. Wolterstorff's contribution, however, should not be underestimated. His description of the communicative event and his employment of speech act theory as a descriptive tool that shapes the goals of interpretation offer significant advances for biblical interpretation and my discussion that follows is heavily indebted to his work.[99]

---

98. Wolterstorff, *Divine Discourse*, 239.

99. Wolterstoff's work has been influential and although it is incomplete and does not offer a clear hermeneutic, I believe it should shape the task of theological interpretation. The influence of his work is represented in the collection of essays responding to his work in the Symposium on Divine Discourse in 2001. The essays contained a range of responses. Paul Helm is largely positive but argues that Wolterstorff's distinction between speaking and revealing is too sharp. He also notes that Wolterstorff does not discuss that illocutions such as commanding, asserting and requesting also reveal, P. Helm, "Speaking and Revealing," *RelS* 37, no. 3 (2001). I discuss this issue in subsequent chapters noting that a thick description of a text will affirm a primary illocution and recognize the presence of various attendant illocutions.

The other two responders, Quinn and Westphal are less positive with Quinn asserting that Wolterstorff has failed to "provide strong grounds for accepting" the claim that God can and does speak, P. L. Quinn, "Can God Speak? Does God Speak?," *RelS* 37, no. 3 (2001). Westphal questions whether or not anything more basic than the canonical process can be offered regarding how God appropriates the text, M. Westphal, "On Reading God the Author," *RelS* 37, no. 3 (2001). See also C. Libolt, "God Speech: A Conversation with Nicholas Wolterstorff's Divine Discourse," *Crux* 43, no. 3 (2007). While the defence of God's speech is a crucial element of Wolterstorff's thesis, whether or not Wolterstorff is able to sustain his argument is not critical to my own. Wolterstorrf's defence of authorial discourse using speech act theory lays a strong foundation for my own work and his exploration of how to move from the first to the second hermeneutic offers a helpful platform. However, a failure to prove that God speaks does not undermine my argument as I (and my tradition) presuppose that God does speak and my aim is to aim to develop a hermeneutic that accounts for such a presupposition.

For a favourable reception of his thesis see S. N. Craigo-Snell, "Command Performance: Rethinking Performance Interpretation in the Context of Divine Discourse," *ModTheo* 16, no. 4 (2000). See also Lindbeck who argues that Wolterstorff's work is a significant

Responding to the works of Vanhoozer and Wolterstorff, other writers have appealed to the Spirit as the guide to hearing divine discourse, a point with which Vanhoozer in a particular would agree. Daniel Treier, arguing for a sapiental hermeneutic concludes the following:

> Thus we must develop and deploy a doctrine of Scripture in terms of the Trinitarian economy of salvation. As the Word of God by which the Spirit bears witness to God's final Word, Jesus Christ, Scripture is divine and human somewhat analogously (Scripture is not a person) to the duophysite Christ. Just as in Christ God's self-disclosure comes by way of Spirit-led human faithfulness, so Scripture "makes us wise unto salvation' as divine speech that comes by way of and elicits Spirit-led human faithfulness. Such an emphasis is compatible with the "wisdom" model of the present work: Scripture as divine discourse establishes a locus of communication, with integrity of textual illocutionary action, but properly transitive and timely hearing of its propositional content and perlocutionary force requires Spirit discernment. Moreover, to use a different emphasis, in its Spirit-led humanity Scripture is an instrument of both the *embodiment and the enablement* of the wisdom found in Christ, God's final Word. That is, in different genres and various ways Scripture communicates both theological judgments and patterns for theological judgment as an ongoing practice. Bluntly put, we read Scripture for how God says that we may or should speak about God.[100]

It is certainly the case that the Spirit can both guide the interpreter in understanding the meaning of the text (the sum of its illocutions), and direct them into the appropriate response (perlocution). Treier has, therefore, identified the kind of person for which this endeavour could be successful. He also encourages confidence in God's desire and ability to communicate clearly and meaningfully. What remains is the development of a hermeneutic that aids the interpreter in their search for divine discourse.

## Conclusion

The concept of dual authorship has been largely accepted throughout church history. The last decade has witnessed a resurgence in discussions of its relevance to theological interpretation. Those who offer a hermeneutic convinced that the divine illocutions are coterminous with the human author's

---

contribution that requires both attention and future work in order to demonstrate its usefulness in exegesis, G. Lindbeck, "Postcritical Canonical Interpretation: Three Modes of Retrieval," in *Theological Exegesis: Essays in Honor of Brevard S. Childs* (ed. B. S. Childs, C. R. Seitz, and K. Greene-McCreight; Grand Rapids: Eerdmans, 1999), 50.

Various other weaknesses in Wolterstorff's proposal have been noted. See Horton, *Covenant and Eschatology*, 157-158; M. I. Wallace, "Divine Discourse: Philosophical Reflections on the Claim That God Speaks," *ProEccl* 7, no. 2 (1998): 242-243.

100. Treier, *Virtue and the Voice of God*, 148. See also Ward, *Word and Supplement*, 301.

illocutions have not grappled significantly with the implications of such a stance. To relegate the illocutionary stance of God to history does not account for the living and active nature of the God's word. It fails to explain how God continues to speak to His people in subsequent generations without marginalising large portions of the canon. An appeal to transhistorical intentions merely highlights the problem as it is untenable to hold that the Old Testament authors understood how their text would function in the light of the canon and in particular in light of the New Testament revelation of Jesus Christ. If one relegates God's communicative action to history in this manner, in effect very few of those illocutions will be declared "in play" under the new covenant. This has the result of marginalizing large portions of Scripture as being at best, informative (assertive illocutions) and, at worst, irrelevant. Subsequently, God's voice in the text is diminished and much of the communicative event is undermined. A theological hermeneutic that is founded upon the presupposition of inspiration must account for how the entire canon continues to function as God's speech acts.

Proponents of *sensus plenior* have recognized the weaknesses of the above approach and have sought to integrate the doctrine of inspiration in a more consistent manner. However, the weakness in much of the *sensus plenior* discussion to date is that it is reductionistic. Most of its proponents and opponents have limited its application to either Old Testament prophetic texts or to cases of New Testament interpretation of Old Testament texts. This is an unfortunate reductionism as the issue of *sensus plenior* is much larger than this discussion has indicated.

Writers who have employed speech act theory in an attempt to defend a type of *sensus plenior* hermeneutic have made significant advances to the discussion by the recognition that all of Scripture continually functions as divine discourse. They have also provided the conceptual tools needed to clarify the goals and challenges of a hermeneutic of dual authorship. However, to date their contributions are largely suggestive and lack exegetical detail. I aim to contribute to this discussion by also employing speech act theory to explicate a *sensus plenior* hermeneutic of dual authorship, providing both a clarification its goals and a demonstration of application in exegesis.

# Chapter 3

# Speech Act Theory, Dual Authorship and Canonical Hermeneutics[1]

## Introduction

Chapter 1 introduced speech act theory and its appropriation in biblical studies. Chapter 2 surveyed contemporary hermeneutics vis-à-vis dual authorship. In this chapter I intend to connect these two lines of inquiry in the formation of a theological hermeneutic. This chapter is structured in two parts. Part A will outline my particular application of speech act theory for general hermeneutics and an associated understanding of "meaning." Part B will expand the hermeneutic to account for both the human and divine authorship of Scripture and so outline my proposed "theological hermeneutic."

### Part A—Speech Act Theory and General Hermeneutics

*Speech Act Theory is Rightly Applied to all Texts*
I have argued that speech act theory, as outlined by Austin and discussed above, correctly identifies the constitutive elements of interpersonal communication. When applied to textual hermeneutics, speech act theory provides a level of precision that was previously lacking. It accomplishes this by specifying not only the nature of communication, but by identifying what it means for a reader to understand a text.

When compared with real-time speech, textual interpretation poses additional challenges due to the diminished presence of the author. While these

---

1. The title of this chapter is borrowed from my previous paper: K. Barker, "Speech Act Theory, Dual Authorship, and Canonical Hermeneutics: Making Sense of Sensus Plenior," *JTI* 3, no. 2 (2009). Content found in the latter sections of this chapter is a development of this work.

challenges are significant, they do not undermine the application of speech act theory to this task. I will address this further in the discussion below.

Not only does speech act theory apply to textual communication, it applies to texts in their entirety. However, as mentioned in Chapter 1, various writers have employed speech act theory to identify particular speech acts recorded within texts. This application has been described as "speech act criticism." Employing speech act theory in this way is appropriate. However, to limit its application to this specific task is reductionistic and fails to understand the very nature of the theory. Speech act theory suggests that all texts and utterances of sufficient size and complexity are both collections of speech acts and speech acts as a whole. Speech acts not only occur in texts. Texts themselves are speech acts. It is this realization that shapes the current project and several others previously mentioned.[2]

Some writers have argued that while speech act theory does apply to texts in their entirety, it is inappropriate to apply it to all genres. Philip Esler suggests that it only applies to non-literary genres. His two theses are as follows:

> a. Nonliterary texts are predominantly performative, illocutionary, and perlocutionary in character; and
> b. Literary texts are predominantly nonperformative and locutionary in character.[3]

Esler claims that novels and poems, as examples of literary texts, are not vehicles for illocutionary acts. He is critical of Searle who has a "worrying tendency to discover illocutionary acts in every utterance."[4] This, however, is a gross misunderstanding of speech act theory and reveals an overly simplistic view of communication in fictional works. It is hardly controversial to suggest that novels have "a point" and that an author of a novel desires to communicate something to his audience.[5] However, Esler attacks Searle on this very issue:

---

2. Wolterstorff, *Divine Discourse*; Vanhoozer, *Is There a Meaning in This Text?*; Vanhoozer, *The Drama of Doctrine*; Poythress, "Canon and Speech Act."

3. P. F. Esler, *New Testament Theology: Communion and Community* (Minneapolis: Fortress Press, 2005), 102.

4. Esler, *New Testament Theology*, 103.

5. Osborne comments, "Every text is the product of a world view and attempts to control readers and draw them into that social world. Interpreters need to be aware of this on the part of both the text and themselves, then, in the words of Habermas, must free the text from 'systematically distorted communication' via a 'scenic understanding' that analyses the forces behind a particular language game in terms of competence and viability. At first glance, this seems a challenge to our theory, but in reality it recognizes the viability of not only detecting the intended meaning of a text but also of discerning the ideological purposes of the text, that is, its illocutionary and perlocutionary purposes. This is indeed the case." (G. R. Osborne, "Literary Theory and Biblical Interpretation," in *Words and the Word: Explorations in Biblical Interpretation and Literary Theory* (ed. D. G. Firth and J. A. Grant; Downers Grove: IVP 2008), 28.) See also M. L. Pratt, *Toward a Speech Act Theory of Literary Discourse* (Bloomington: Indiana University Press, 1977).

Accordingly, when [Searle] confronts the question of fictional discourse, he simply assumes that it, too, is illocutionary. He then seeks to find some way of resolving the 'paradox' that although we usually accept the truth of statements about how things are ("assertives"), in fiction such statements are not 'true' because the characters they refer to are nonexistent. His answer, largely accepted by Richard Freadman and Seamus Miller, is that these statements are just *pretend* and not *actually asserted*. Yet Searle's theory really rests on a false premise, namely, that a work of fiction is itself illocutionary. This would mean that a novelist writing a novel was setting out to achieve one or more of the illocutionary acts that Searle has helpfully taxonomized. Yet the only plausible candidate is an assertive, consisting of a statement about how things actually are, that is either true or false. But fiction, by definition, cannot have such a quality. It is a work of imagination, not a description of the real world. That is to say, fiction, of its very nature is constative and locutionary. The novelist is not seeking to *do* something by writing a novel; like a poem, a novel *is*. Thus Searle has been led into an entirely false dilemma and is concerned with a paradox that does not exist.[6]

Esler's critique of Searle is far from convincing. According to speech act theory, intelligible discourse of any form caries illocutionary force. If a novel were simply locution, it must either be a collection of disparate phrases that miraculously tell a story, or the author spoke real words in a gibberish (nonconventional) fashion with no intention of communicating anything. Either way, it is unlikely to produce a novel. Fiction is illocutionary in nature as the author is, at the very least, performing the illocutionary act of "inviting the reader to imagine."[7] Esler has not only misunderstood the broad nature of communication, but has not recognized that illocutionary acts are embedded in genre. That the characters in a story perform illocutions is not the issue. Their illocutions are not necessarily the author's illocutions (e.g., Samson's speech acts are not necessarily those of the author of Judges). The author may be using the text to do any number of things. He may be promoting a particular ideology, critiquing culture, or simply asking the reader to identify (and/or be horrified) with a particular character. These are just a few of the numerous illocutions that a novel may perform. To suggest that fiction is limited in its illocutionary force to the act of assertion, and that these assertions are coterminous with

---

6. Esler, *New Testament Theology*, 103-104.
7. For a defence of the illocutionary nature of literature see Pratt, "The real lesson speech act theory has to offer is that *literature is a context, too*, not the absence of one." Pratt, *Toward a Speech Act Theory*, 99. See also Briggs, *Words in Action*, 95. Paul Grice, who utilises speech act theory to explain "an utterer's meaning" notes that even "utterers can be said to have meant something when "there is no actual person or set of persons whom the utterer is addressing and in whom he intends to induce a response", citing examples such as signage or diaries (Grice, *Studies in the Way of Words*, 112-116).

those of the characters in the narrative, and that they are "untrue" and therefore non-existent is to misunderstand the very nature of literature.

Not only does Esler marginalize the novel to a non-communicative (non-illocutionary) event, poetry suffers the same fate. He appeals to Austin in his explanation: "Austin argues that the words in performative statements must be spoken seriously and taken seriously. Thus someone who utters one 'must not be joking, for example, nor writing a poem.' Residing in this observation is the recognition that poems are, by nature, nonperformative."[8] This reference to Austin is misleading and obscures the point that he was making. Austin was not suggesting that poetry is non-communicative; rather, he was noting that poetry, like humour, is governed by rules not common to other forms of communication. To reduce poetry to non-performative language is highly problematic. If poetry is non-performative (non-illocutionary) then it communicates nothing at all. Another problem with Esler's theory is that poetry is notoriously difficult to define. Furthermore, in religious writings, many creedal and hymnic texts are poetic, but to suggest they communicate nothing is to abandon any attempt to understand the conventions employed in their production. Finally, what are we to do with large portions of Scripture that are written in poetic form?[9] Esler's argument is poorly structured and does not address the obvious questions raised.

In contrast, I side with those who accept the employment of a genre is a communicative act. As such it is governed by rules that assist readers to recognise and interpret the illocutionary acts performed by its employment. Therefore, every text of Scripture, precisely because it employs genre, is a communicative act with corresponding illocutionary force.[10]

*Illocution as the Locus of Meaning*

Since I am locating textual meaning in the illocutions performed through it, I accept that texts can have determinative meaning.[11] This is not to be confused with the affirmation of *single* determinate meaning[12] nor does it discount the possibility of indeterminate meaning in texts where authors have intentionally allowed for such a surplus. As mentioned in Chapter 1, hermeneutic realists

---

8. Esler, *New Testament Theology*, 99-100.

9. The illocutionary nature of poetry and of the psalms in particular will be addressed in the following chapters.

10. Our ability to recognize and understand genre in all its subtleties constitutes part of the hermeneutic challenge. This will be discussed further in the second part of the chapter.

11. There are of course exceptions to this rule. If an author is being deliberately obtuse to the point of intentionally attempting to confuse a reader, or if they are using the language in an incompetent manner, or if they are just randomly inscribing words then the text *may not have* a determinate meaning. An absence of meaning occurs when the linguistic conventions (language games) are not being applied. The resulting locutions may carry no illocutionary force.

12. This topic forms part of the discussion below.

and non-realists alike adopt speech act theory to defend and clarify their ideologies and hermeneutics. The originators of speech act theory, however, were arguing from a realist position and understood the theory to inherently support this perspective, as it anchored the text to a cultural and conventional context wherein an action becomes intelligible. I too suggest that the meaning of a text is defined by the illocutionary acts performed in the text by the author.

Vanhoozer's definitions, quoted previously in Chapter 1, helpfully summarize this position:

> "Meaning" is the result of communicative action, of what an author has done in tending to certain words at a particular time in a particular manner.

> The literal sense of an utterance or text is the sum total of those illocutionary acts performed by the author intentionally and with self-awareness.[13]

The assertion that textual meaning is defined by the illocutions performed in a text by an author has not been universally, or even largely, accepted. On the one hand, it is objected that such a definition suffers from problems associated with the so-called "intentional fallacy" of "Romantic hermeneutics" where the goal of interpretation is to uncover the mental processes of the author. On the other hand, it has been suggested that this definition is simply another form of structuralism. I propose that upon closer inspection the definition offered is not only the best way to understanding meaning, but that it can also avoid both the Scylla of Romanticism and the Charybdis of structuralism.

*Avoiding Romantic Hermeneutics*

*Embodied Actions Versus Motives.* The distinction between the current project and one where the goal is to uncover the mental life of the author has been briefly mentioned in Chapter 1 where I agreed with Wolterstorff that speaking and writing are public actions. Thus, to speak is to take up a normative stance in the public domain, and to understand a speaker is to correctly ascribe to them the stance they have taken.[14] Vanhoozer argues similarly when he speaks of meaning as "enacted" and "embodied" actions:

---

13. Vanhoozer, "From Speech Acts to Scripture Acts," 177-179. Savas L. Tsohatzidis also notes the importance of illocutionary acts for the construction of meaning (Tsohatzidis, "Ways of Doing Things," 1-2). For further discussion see Alston, *Illocutionary Acts*.

14. Wolterstorff, *Divine Discourse*, 93. Those who are interested in interpreting for authorial intent have offered a number of explanations that defend their project in light of the intentional fallacy. For some of the most cogent responses see: M. Levering, *Participatory Biblical Exegesis: A Theology of Biblical Interpretation* (Notre Dame: University of Notre Dame Press, 2008), 86; R. S. Briggs, "Speech-Act Theory," in *Words and the Word: Explorations in Biblical Interpretation and Literary Theory* (ed. D. G. Firth and J. A. Grant; Downers Grove: IVP 2008), 181-182; N. C. Murphy, "Textual Relativism, Philosophy of

To sum up: the meaning of a text emerges only against the backdrop of the author's intended action and the background of the author's context.

(1) *Every text is the result of an enacted intention...* I have argued that there is more to meaning than signs relating to other signs. The "more" is the author's intention, but this does not refer to hidden mental states so much as to the directedness of the text as a meaningful act. Intention is not something that can be reduced to simpler non-intentional events; it is rather an emergent property that is required to explain what illocutionary act has been performed in a text. What we see in the text is the author's intentional action...

(2) *Every text is an embodied intention.* Writing fixes the author's enacted intention in a stable verbal structure. It is only fallacious to appeal to intention when the appeal is to some mental, pre-textual event, rather than to the intention embodied in the text. According to Nathan Scott, "verbal meaning is constituted of those intentions of the author which are *embodied* in his text and which, under the prevailing conventions that control linguistic usage, are *shareable* by his readers."[15]

In this account, the intention of the author is not discovered by knowing their mind or of having access to the thought process that led to the production of the text. In fact, it is not even *necessary* to know the identity of the author. Their intention is not something beyond the text but is an "emergent property" of their action. Furthermore, these actions are public and "shareable" so that any audience privy to the prevailing conventions at the time of writing can gain access to these intentions through the text.

In order to avoid the intentional fallacy, Stephen Fowl offers a slightly different explanation when he makes the distinction between the "motives" of an author and the "intentions" of an author. Drawing upon the work of Mark Brett[16] he concludes:

> The best way to do this is to reshape a notion of intention so that it does not presume problematic notions of selfhood. One way to do this is to try to distinguish authorial motives from an author's communicative intentions. "That is to say, one ought to distinguish between *what* an author is trying to say (which might be called a 'communicative intention') and *why* it is being said (which might be called motive)." An author might write from any number of motives. She might have a desire for fame and fortune, or failing that, tenure. She might have a deep psychological need to share her thoughts with a wider public. There might be (and probably are) motives at work of

---

Language, and the Baptist Vision," in *Theology without Foundations: Religious Practice and the Future of Theological Truth* (ed. S. Hauerwas, N. C. Murphy, and M. Nation; Nashville: Abingdon Press, 1994).

15. Vanhoozer, *Is There a Meaning in This Text?*, 252-253.
16. M. G. Brett, "Motives and Intentions in Genesis I," *JTS*, no. 42 (1991).

which an author is not fully conscious. Alternatively, in the case of lying, an author may be conscious of her motives but wish to conceal them from others ... A desire to discover an author's motives will be quite hard to fulfil in almost all cases. Moreover, in the case of ancient authors an interest in motives will tend to be frustrated by our comprehensive lack of knowledge about these characters.
Alternatively, to render an account of an author's communicative intention one need not attend to an author's motives. Rather, such an account requires attention to matters of semantics, linguistic conventions operative at the time, and matters of implication and inference, to name only three. In the case of dealing with the biblical writers, attention to these matters is inescapably historical.[17]

I will argue below that the hermeneutical task is "inescapably historical" and that it requires attention to semantics and linguistic conventions. To claim, however, that the best way to overcome the intentional fallacy is to make a clear distinction between motives and intentions concedes too much. While it may be impossible (and uninteresting) to uncover every motive for an author's intentional action, in many cases their intention is to communicate their motives. Speech act theory inherently recognizes this phenomenon when it draws a strong connection between illocution and perlocution: an author locutes in order to illocute in order to encourage a particular perlocution.[18] Their motivation is, in part, to encourage a particular response from the audience or, in the case of strong speech acts, to produce a particular effect. Therefore, the illocution reveals something of the motivation. To suggest that an intention never communicates the motivation of the author, either explicitly or implicitly is naïve, and again concedes too much in terms of hermeneutic goals. To adopt this position would mean that an audience, once they have understood the illocutionary act(s) performed by the author would necessarily need to guess how to respond. A good communicator, however, will make it clear to the audience, either implicitly or explicitly, what they desire from them. Granted, it is unlikely that all of the authorial motivations are revealed or can be uncovered, but felicitous communication means that some of them are necessarily embedded in the text in intelligible ways. Fowl's position is ultimately too reductionistic by not allowing the intention to communicate any level of motivation.

In summary, the goal of interpretation is not to uncover the motives of an author by attending to realities that lie behind and beyond the text. Rather, the goal is to attend to those actions that are publically performed by way of the text. In the case of Scripture, these public illocutions will reveal the intention of the author(s) and this intention will, at times and in limited ways, reveal something of the motivation for the production of the text.

*Perlocutionary Intention and The Meaning of the Text.* One of the most common areas of confusion in speech act theory is the relationship between illocution

---

17. Fowl, "The Role of Authorial Intention," 74.
18. I am not suggesting that any of these actions is necessarily singular.

and perlocution. A number of authors, speaking from non-realist perspectives, suggest that meaning should be understood in terms of perlocution. This formulation is consistent with such an ideology.[19] Confusion occurs, however, in cases where the author is arguing from a realist position and proceeds to define the goal of hermeneutics in terms of "perlocutionary intent."[20] This concept of perlocution differs from the classic speech act definition which describes it as the effect upon the reader, thus any so called "perlocutionary intent" is a characteristic of the author.

Jeannine Brown argues for this understanding of meaning in a section entitled "Probing Meaning: Perlocutionary Intention." She provides the following example and explanation:

> If I say, "Pass the butter, please" (a locution) as a request (the illocution), your act of passing the butter to me does not count as part of my communicative act. So far, so good. Now, in requesting the butter, I want to get you to perform the action of passing the butter to me. This intent can be termed my "perlocutionary intention."
> Notice that perlocutionary intention is a mediating concept between what speakers and hearers do in the act of communication, what we have termed the actualized communicative event. A perlocutionary intention is the speaker's intention for hearer response. In this example, my intention is that you pass the butter in response to my request. Is this perlocutionary intention part of speaker meaning? This is an important question because of the mediating position this concept holds between speakers and hearers. In our definition of meaning in Chapter 2, we have defined meaning, in part, as locution plus illocution. What about a speaker's intention for a perlocution? There are a number of factors to consider as we attempt to answer this question.[21]

This warrants a number of responses. First, to define meaning as locution plus illocution is tautologous and confusing. Illocutions cannot occur without locutions. If meaning is located in the illocution then a locution is inherently present. Meaning is attributed to the locution by means of its use to perform the illocution. The locution does not have a meaning outside of its use.[22]

---

19. See Chapter 1.
20. Unfortunately, Adams' evaluation of the current state of the discussion is correct. "Speech act theory is laden with a host of complex and intricate concepts found in a vast amount of dense material that does not lend itself to a casual perusal. A number of inherent ambiguities along with differing opinions exist in the philosophical literature. Due to this, misunderstanding and misapplication typically mark the non-specialists' use of speech act theory, specifically in biblical studies. In addition, very little dialogue has occurred among biblical interpreters who have utilized speech act theory." (J. W. Adams, *The Performative Nature and Function of Isaiah 40-55* (448; New York: T&T Clark, 2006), 3.)
21. Brown, *Scripture as Communication*, 111.
22. My response to Brown contradicts both Wolterstorff's explanation of meaning

Second, to identify meaning in terms of perlocutionary intention is unnecessary. The example given above is a good place to start. There is little difference between the illocution requesting the butter and the perlocutionary intent that the hearer passes the butter. If the meaning is located in the illocution, as I am suggesting, successful communication occurs when the hearer understands the illocution requesting that they, the hearer, pass the butter. *Any perlocutionary intent that may be present is bound to the illocutionary act.* Any other perlocutionary intent (i.e., not communicated in the illocution) is hidden in the mind of the author and any claim that it is a necessary part of interpretation is subject to the intentional fallacy. If the speaker requests the butter (and that is the total illocutionary act being performed) and the hearer understands this request, the hearer is not required to discern any other perlocutionary intentions.[23] The intent is that they pass the butter! Admittedly, Brown does not think that perlocutionary intent is the locus of meaning but rather it lies at the edges of meaning or is "an extension of meaning." This is a better understanding, but still fails to appreciate the embedded nature of any perlocutionary intention within the illocutionary act and the necessity to attend to the later.

Third, the communication can be successful irrespective of any perlocutionary intent being satisfied.[24] If the hearer refuses to pass the butter even though they understood the illocution of request, the communication was successful, but the perlocutionary intent was not satisfied. It was communicated in the illocution, but it was not satisfied. This is important in terms of

---

in terms of noematic content and Altson's explanation of illocutionary act potential. Extended discussion occurs below.

23. Assuming of course that there are no extenuating circumstances that provide a context for understanding the words metaphorically or as code for some other illocution.

24. Tim Meadowcroft argues that a significant flaw in speech act theory is its inability to explain the progression from illocution to perlocution. He comments, "But a speech-act based search for meaning in interpretation exhibits a yet more serious deficiency. Despite the care with which the practitioners of speech act have differentiated categories of illocution and perlocution, they do not provide a convincing explanation of how the progression from illocution to perlocution works. How is it that a text's perlocutionary effect may end up at least for some readers at odds with the illocutionary intent? Or, what has happened to a text when it functions in, or is able to be used in, a way never intended?" (T. Meadowcroft, *Haggai* (Sheffield: Sheffield Phoenix, 2006), 17.)

Meadowcroft's objection, however, does not appear to undermine the theory in any significant manner. The progression from illocution to perlocution is dependent upon the type of illocution. As I will discuss in later chapters, "strong" illocutions can produce a perlocution without the consent of the audience. It just happens *to* them in the act of the illocution. Other illocutions require both understanding of the illocution and an appropriate response (perlocution) on the part of the hearer for the progression to "work." When the hearer's perlocution is at odds with the illocution, this should be considered either an interpretive "misfire" or deliberate non-acquiescence. Either way, a perlocution that is not commensurate with the illocution is not a problem with speech act theory, but a problem inherent to interpersonal communication.

understanding felicitous communication and the attribution of meaning. Vanhoozer comments:

> Perlocutionary intents fail regularly, but this does not threaten the possibility of communication, for perlocutionary intents pertain not to the act, but to the effects of meaning. If, on the other hand, I fail in my illocutionary intent, then the communicative act itself is defective ... Illocutionary intent is thus constitutive of communicative action and of meaning in a way that perlocutionary intent is not.[25]

Perlocutionary intent is best understood as part of the reason for the illocutionary act. As Vanhoozer notes, it relates to the effects and not the acts of communication. An illocution is performed because the speaker desires an effect to occur. To locate meaning in the perlocutionary intent is unnecessary. It is only by means of the illocution(s) that the hearer gains access to any perlocutionary intent. Furthermore, to suggest that the goal of interpretation is to understand why an author performed the illocutionary actions (i.e., the perlocutionary intention) is to delve back into their psyche and tends towards Romantic hermeneutics. Ironically, this utilization of speech act theory ignores its foundational beliefs, that language is a public and shared phenomenon used to perform actions according to conventional rules. Alston concludes:

> Perlocutionary intent is, therefore, an unnecessary category. Any perlocutionary intent is communicated in the illocution. *To understand the illocution is to understand the perlocutionary intent.* What it does contribute is recognition that illocutionary acts are directed at an audience and usually require a response. There is a further situation, however, where any perlocutionary intent is a moot point for interpretation. Sometimes it is necessary for the hearer to understand and respond to the illocution for the perlocutionary intent to be realized in a perlocution. At other times an illocution is so strong that it accomplishes its perlocutionary intent by its very performance, irrespective of the hearer's understanding or acceptance of it. For example, when a judge pronounces a defendant "guilty" the perlocution (intent and effect) is automatically realized. To understand the statement in this case is to understand the illocutionary act. A "secondary" perlocutionary intention may be that you recognize the illocutionary act as having occurred, but in these cases the perlocutionary intent is actualised in the performance of the illocution.[26] Overall, those who focus hermeneutics on perlocution or perlocutionary intent have either misunderstood the function of illocution or prioritise the reader in the construction of meaning.

---

25. Vanhoozer, *Is There a Meaning in This Text?*, 261.

26. Alston argues persuasively that perlocutionary intention is not always present with an illocution and is therefore a deficient way to understand illocutionary acts (Alston, *Illocutionary Acts*, 45–49.).

*Avoiding the Structuralism of the New Criticism.* While some claim that speech act theory falls prey to the intentional fallacy, others conversely suggest that it closely resembles the structuralism of the New Criticism in its treatment of the text as an artifact. Tim Meadowcroft is concerned that speech act theory, in effect, marginalizes the author and effectively displaces the text from its context:

> The achievement of speech-act (*sic*) is that it has made both the intention and response, author and reader, indispensable to the understanding of a text. At the same time, the concept of locution allows the reader to be aware of intent within the text rather than understanding it as an external agent ... The danger with that position, though, is that a speech-act approach can be simply another manifestation of New Criticism's focus on the text as artefact.[27]

While I do not believe that speech act theory suffers from this problem, Meadowcroft could be forgiven for this assessment when statements like those made by Wolterstorff resemble Ricoeur more than Austin:[28]

> I hold that literality and metaphoricity are a matter of *use* rather than of *meaning*. Thus I side with Searle and Davidson in my understanding of tropes, against the majority. A well-formed sentence of a language has a meaning, or perhaps several. Not a literal meaning, not a metaphorical meaning, not an ironic meaning; just a meaning. Nor does a sentence have one meaning relative to one context and another meaning relative to another context—with perhaps one of those literal and the other, metaphorical. It always has just the meaning that it has *per se*. What differs from occasion to occasion is not the meaning of the sentence but the noematic content of what is said by using the sentence. We can use it literally, strictly, and directly; we do so when, by uttering it in a certain circumstance, we perform an illocutionary act whose noematic content is the meaning (or one of the meanings) of the sentence. But we can also use it metaphorically. For me to use it metaphorically, it must have a meaning and I must know that meaning; the metaphoricity of my use inheres in a certain relationship between the meaning of the sentence and the noematic content of what I say. To explain that relationship is the central challenge which a theory of metaphor tries to meet and overcome. Such theory, on my view, would take as its underlying

---

27. Meadowcroft, *Haggai*, 17. On the early applications of speech act theory to the analysis of narrative, see R. W. Gibbs, *Intentions in the Experience of Meaning* (Cambridge: Cambridge University Press, 1999), 206; G. Genette, *Narrative Discourse Revisited* (Ithaca: Cornell University Press, 1988); and S. S. Lanser, *The Narrative Act: Point of View in Prose Fiction* (Princeton: Princeton University Press, 1981).

28. It should be noted that Ricoeur's own desire was to distance himself from the structuralism of the New Criticism while at the same time accepting the structuralist claim that the text itself has "a sense."

framework, that sentences do not acquire metaphorical meanings but are put to metaphorical uses.[29]

In this paragraph, Wolterstorff suggests that meaning is not connected to usage. Rather, sentences have meanings that can be used in different contexts (e.g., literally or metaphorically). He identifies the locus of meaning in the noematic content of the illocution rather than in the illocution itself. The result of this identification is that one is justified in locating the meaning of a text independent from how an author is using it. Thus, the text has inherent meaning(s) that can be utilized in any number of ways. In the example above, a sentence has a meaning that Wolterstorff suggests can be used literally or metaphorically.[30]

Perhaps a better explanation of metaphor is that the author has acknowledged a previous use of this language but is intentionally drawing a parallel not envisaged by the previous usage. Thus, there are two different meanings based on different contexts and usage. The metaphorical meaning is derivative and assumes that the audience is able to remember the previous usage and recognize the derivative nature of the metaphor.[31]

Wolterstorff's evaluation of metaphor strangely resembles Ricoeur's "sense of the text" with some qualification. With respect to textual communication, Ricoeur will say that text has a "sense" and that this "sense" is not necessarily connected to what an author meant when they wrote it. The language is freed from its original context through the process of textualization and from that moment onwards, the text portrays a world and invites the reader to enter into it. The sense of the text is all that remains:

> To mean is what the speaker does. But it is also what the sentence does. The utterance meaning—in the sense of propositional content—is the "objective" side of this meaning. The utterer's meaning—in the threefold sense of the self-reference of the sentence, the illocutionary dimension of the speech act, and the intention of recognition by the hearer—is the "subjective" side of meaning.
> This subjective-objective dialectic does not exhaust the meaning of meaning and therefore does not exhaust the structure of discourse.[32]

This account of textual interpretation obviously differs markedly with that of Wolterstorff's who spends an entire chapter distancing himself from

---

29. Wolterstorff, *Divine Discourse*, 193.

30. A further problem is that it seems to prioritize the sentence as the fundamental unit of communication. This may not always be the case in larger texts where various literary levels produce illocutions that affect those at the lower-level. See the discussion in Chapter 4 regarding Psalms for further anaylsis.

31. For a discussion of the function of metaphor in biblical prophecy see Sandy, *Plowshares & Pruning Hooks*, 58-74. See also P. Ricœur, *The Rule of Metaphor: Multi-Disciplinary Studies of the Creation of Meaning in Language* (37; Toronto: University of Toronto Press, 1977).

32. Ricœur, *Interpretation Theory*, 19-20.

Ricoeur's position and arguing against his "sense of the text."[33] Wolterstorff does not believe that textuality eliminates the intentional activity of the author. Convergence with Ricoeur's proposal occurs, however, when Wolterstorff argues that the noematic content of a sentence is identical with the meaning of the sentence. More specifically, the noematic content could be construed to mean a number of different things, but it is here that the meaning(s) of the text reside. Consequently, in this description, the illocutionary action of the author is not to be identified with the meaning of the text (contra Vanhoozer).

The problem with this construal is that it undermines, if only in a subtle manner, the very project that Wolterstorff has undertaken. His suggestion that "meaning" is not to be associated with illocution (and so historical or linguistic context) has the effect of marginalizing the author. Certainly Wolterstorff speaks of the goal of interpretation in terms of the illocutionary stance of the author when he says, "The goal of interpretation, correspondingly, is to discover what counts as what. The discourser takes up a normative stance in the public domain by way of performing some publicly perceptible action."[34] However, the combination of his two theses creates a disjunction between the meaning of the text and the goal of interpretation. Summarized, the goal of interpretation is to identify the illocutions, but the meaning of the text is a stable, conventionally governed entity. The meaning of the text and what the author was doing with the text are consequently separated. Thus, one could use Wolterstorff's explanation to side formally with Ricoeur by saying that they are still attending to the meaning of the text (its "sense") even though they are no longer interested in what the author was doing historically. It is clear that Wolterstorff would be unhappy with such a move, but it is made possible by his separation of the "meaning" of the text from the illocutionary acts performed through it.

In a similar fashion to Wolterstorff, William P. Alston also identifies sentential meaning, not with the illocutionary act (IA) of the author, but with the illocutionary act potential of the sentence itself:

> Why should we identify sentence meaning with *usability* to do so-and-so, rather than with *being used* to do so-and-so? Why is it IA [Illocutionary Act] *potential* rather than IA *performance* that is constitutive of meaning? The shortest and best answer to this question is found in the generative force of language. No limit can be put on the number or complexity of sentences in a language. No matter how large a set we construct, we can enlarge it by combining members of the set into more complex sentences. Therefore, there will be many sentences of a language that are never employed to perform illocutionary acts. Hence meaning must be construed as something potential rather than as something actual. Moreover, even with sentences that are put to use, their meaning is not exhausted by their actual track record. By virtue of meaning what they do, they retain a

---

33. Wolterstorff, *Divine Discourse*, Chapter 8.
34. Wolterstorff, *Divine Discourse*, 183.

potential to be used an indefinite number of further times to perform matching IA's. Meaning cannot be tied down to a set of actual speech episodes.[35]

There seem to be a number of problems with this formulation of meaning. First, just because sentences could be constructed to produce illocutionary acts and yet are never so constructed does not mean that they exist somewhere and carry that meaning intrinsically. In other words, potential is just that, potential. It is not actualised. This leads to the second problem, which Alston uses to strangely support his thesis. He argues that sentences could be used in an "indefinite number of further times to perform matching IA's." However, if the illocutionary act potential of a sentence is indefinite then its meaning is also infinite. Illocutionary act potential is thus a moot category. If meaning is to be identified with illocutionary act potential and illocutionary act potential is infinite, then the meaning of a sentence is infinitely indeterminate and unknowable. Infinite potential is an unworkable definition. In other words, if every sentence has infinite potential, then every sentence has the same potential. Illocutionary act potential is, therefore, an unhelpful category. To claim it is the locus of meaning merely suggests a sentence can mean anything and does not assist the interpreter in any way.

I side with Vanhoozer and identify the meaning of a text with the illocutionary acts performed in the text by the author.[36] Contrary to Wolterstorff's account, the noematic content of a sentence can be explained in terms of embedded or attendant illocutions.[37] Contrary to Alston's account, meaning is a product of usage. There are an infinite number of rules that can be constructed in order to produce an infinite number of meanings. Unless we remove the understanding of "meaning" from the goal of hermeneutics then these alternatives are deficient. Neither Wolterstorff nor Alston falls prey to structuralism as they both recognize the need to understand the public action of the author in historical and cultural contexts. However, in similar ways, their definitions of meaning divorce it from the goal of interpretation and open up the possibility of discovering meaning without attending to the author's usage of a sentence.[38]

*Illocution is Public and Conventional.* This section began by suggesting that it was possible to avoid both Romantic hermeneutics and the structuralism of the New Criticism. A form of Romantic hermeneutics is avoided in the proper utility of speech act theory with its emphasis upon public and conventional action

---

35. Alston, *Illocutionary Acts*, 281.
36. I do agree with Wolterstorff in terms of his goal of interpretation, even though I reject his explanation of meaning.
37. Briefly, the noematic content of the sentence is simply comprised of lower-level illocutions (assertions) that make possible higher-level illocutions. Thus the meaning of the sentence is the sum total of the illocutions being performed.
38. Alston too formally separates "meaning" from the goal of hermeneutics when he suggests that illocutionary acts go beyond sentence meaning (Alston, *Illocutionary Acts*, 188).

granting the reader access to the intention of the author. Therefore, "the mind of the author" is present in the text as far as the author has revealed this to the reader. In the words of Wolterstorff:

> So our interest as authorial-discourse interpreters is indeed in what the speaker said—not in what he intended to say, but in what he did say, if anything. But saying is an intentional action. And more importantly, we have to know how he was operating, or trying to operate, the system ... [39]

The intention of the author is mediated by the text, if they intended something other than what they *did* with the text, they have failed to properly utilize the conventions and the communication has misfired.

Alternatively, Meadowcroft was concerned that speech act theory tends toward structuralism.[40] In part this is true, and reflects the belief that authors are at times only accessible through the conventions they employ.[41] Yet with a number of qualifications there are very significant differences between the two in terms of both ideology and hermeneutics. His concerns, though important, only apply to deficient articulations of speech act theory as discussed above. If the conventional nature of the language, upon which speech act theory is based, is taken to mean that the author is irrelevant to hermeneutics, then his concerns are well founded. However, the application of speech act theory in this project recognizes some important qualifications that distance it from a strictly structuralist approach. First, the conventional nature of language is culturally and historically located. This means that an author uses language in their context to perform particular actions. To interpret the text is to attend to how the author utilized the available conventions (at that time and in that culture) in order to communicate. Once the text leaves the original context and new, later or unforeseen audiences read the text, speech act theory argues for a careful historical, cultural, linguistic investigation that enables the reader to appreciate the language games being played at the time. Paul Noble labels this the "intentional context" and succinctly explains the approach, though he does not employ speech act terminology:

> What I am arguing, then, is that author's intention is a 'Regulative Principle' for correct interpretation. A text is an instantiation of some particular language -system, with reference to which the author made certain choices in producing his or her text—the author selects from among the options that are available in that language, arranging its components in such a way as to express the desired meaning. It will therefore be through interpreting a text in relation

---

39. Wolterstorff, *Divine Discourse*, 199.
40. Granted, both Wolterstorff and Alston define meaning in ways that support a structuralist theory as discussed above.
41. For a summary and cogent critique of structuralism see J. Barton, *Reading the Old Testament: Method in Biblical Study* (Rev. and enlarged. ed.; Louisville: Westminster John Knox, 1996), 135-136.

to the milieu of its production that the most worthwhile meanings will be found in it—alternative contexts are inherently inferior because they will yield inferior meanings.

The preceding discussion can be summed up and generalized a little by introducing the idea of a text's 'intentional context'—i.e., the linguistic, social, and cultural context in relation to which the author's intentions were exercised in producing that text.[42]

The second qualification that distances this current project from a structuralist approach is that it allows the author to be as present as they desire to be. At the very least, the author is present in their use of the conventions in play at the time of the composition of the text. As mentioned above, this grants the reader access to the author's intention with potentially no other information regarding the author being offered. There are many examples in both secular literature (e.g., pseudonymous writings or those of an unknown author) and in Christian Scripture (e.g., various psalms or the letter to the Hebrews) where little to nothing is known about the author's identity or their specific context at the time of writing.

In these cases, a focus on the text is enhanced, since it is the text alone that grants us access to the enacted intention. Moreover, it should be realized that in many cases the author has desired to remain anonymous. The reasons for this are undoubtedly varied, yet in each case the author is convinced that their "absence" from the text will not undermine the interpretive endeavour. In fact, in some cases, revealing their identity may distract the audience and result in reductionistic interpretations that do not appreciate the broadness of scope intended by the author (i.e., the full range of illocutions and the relevance of these illocutions to wider audiences).[43]

The relative absence of the author in these texts is compensated for by their clear use of convention. The readers are able to discern what the author was likely to do with the text or likely not to do with the text because they are familiar with the conventions available to the author. In particular, genre now plays an even more significant role in interpretation as it allows the author to utilize the basic rules that govern these decisions.[44] Vanhoozer notes that even when the historical author masks their identity or replaces their identity with another, this is still an intentional decision to aid the reader. He says:

> The historical author, I submit, must be inferred from the work itself, including its "created" or implied author. Booth rightly urges caution in identifying any one particular voice in the text as the historical author's. *Everything* we read is the product of the author's decisions: "We must never forget that though the author can to some extent

---

42. P. R. Noble, *The Canonical Approach: A Critical Reconstruction of the Hermeneutics of Brevard S. Childs* (Leiden: Brill, 1995), 197.

43. I will argue that this phenomenon does, in fact, occur within the Psalter.

44. Of course, they may choose to manipulate these rules depending upon their desired effect.

choose his disguises, he can never choose to disappear." The device of the implied author, therefore, need not exclude the notion of the historical author as communicative agent.[45]

While the hermeneutic offered here will encourage a sustained focus upon the text, it distances itself from structuralist hermeneutics in two main ways: first by its attention to the intention of the author accessed by the cultural and linguistic conventions in play at the time of writing; second, by realizing that the relative absence or presence of the author is by design, that is, it is an intentional act which does not diminish, and in some cases even enhances, the force of their communication.

*Summary of Presuppositions*

In light of these points of clarification, the related presuppositions of this project can be summarized as follows:
1. Speech act theory correctly describes the communicative event.
   a. It should be applied to texts in their entirety.
   b. It should be applied to all genres.
2. The meaning of a text is the illocutionary act(s) performed by the author.
   a. This is a public, rule-governed activity that enables the reader to access the author's intention.
   b. The relative absence or presence of the author in a particular text or genre is an intentional activity that does not undermine the communicative process, but in fact enables a reader to appreciate the full range of illocutionary acts.

*Literary Levels of Illocution*

Many texts are complex phenomena and it is the responsibility of the interpreter to adequately account for this complexity. Various authors have suggested the need for what has been described previously as a "thick description."[46] Vern Poythress' response to Searle's conscious decision to focus on "atomic propositions" as opposed to "molecular structure" acknowledges the need for such a thick description:

> Speech-act theory focuses primarily on the contrastive-identificational features that characterize particular kinds of behavioreme. But what becomes of the distributional aspect of these behavioremes? Small speech acts are embedded ("distributed") within

---

45. Vanhoozer, *Is There a Meaning in This Text?*, 239; cf. W. C. Booth, *The Rhetoric of Fiction* (Chicago: University of Chicago Press, 1961), 20.

46. Vanhoozer, *Is There a Meaning in This Text*; Treier, *Virtue and the Voice of God*; Poythress, "Canon and Speech Act," 340. Irsigler argues for the same concept when he suggests the presence of illocutionary acts throughout a text at its various levels including that of the text as a whole (Irsigler, "Sprechaktanalyse und Psalmeninterpretation am Beispiel von Psalm 13", 69).

larger groupings of human behavior. Speech-act theory does encourage reflection about contextual conditions that may be necessary for the happy execution of a speech act. The condition of being an umpire is necessary in order to call a strike in a baseball game. But because of the focus on atomic propositions, there is little attention to the way in which behavioremes can be embedded in larger behavioremes in a hierarchical array, and how several smaller purposeful human actions may together accomplish a larger purpose.[47]

A thick description of the text is one that sufficiently explains the sum of its illocutionary acts. In order to accomplish this, illocutions at various levels within and over the text need to be identified and assessed.

*Sentential and Sub-Sentential Illocutions.* Illocutions occur at a number of literary levels, the most basic being sentential and sub-sentential. Even simple sentences often contain a number of illocutions depending on their context. For example, assertions may be used to perform a command or warning (e.g., "I smell smoke"). In cases of compound sentences, a number of attendant illocutions can be identified at the sub-sentential level. This "embedded" nature of speech acts is a critical consideration for the interpretation of texts, yet as noted by Poythress, this issue is largely absent from the discussion. For example, Alston discusses meaning at the sentential level but does not discuss illocutions occurring at lower literary levels: "the sentence is the minimum linguistic vehicle for a complete autonomous act of communication ... Hence our first task is to understand what complete communicative jobs are such that usability to perform them constitutes sentence meaning."[48] In discussing lower-level components of a sentence he says, "subsentential acts are ancillary to the illocutionary act to which they contribute. The former has to be construed in terms of the latter, and not vice versa."[49] While the above statement correctly identifies the function of the "subsentential acts" as ancillary, Alston does not discuss these "subsentential acts" as possibly performing attendant or ancillary illocutions. Long sentences surely contain more than one ancillary illocution. For example, the statement, "I am leaving now and driving to the beach" is a compound sentence that makes multiple assertions. Depending on the context, this might be used as a command to one's children to hurry up and leave the house, or it might be a single assertion made on the phone to let one's friend know that they'll be there shortly. The sub-sentential illocutions are attendant to the primary illocution. They are embedded within it and enable its enactment. The meaning of the sentence or its "primary illocution" is only fully appreciated if its embedded illocutions are recognized.

*Super-Sentential Illocutions.* While it is necessary to recognize sentential and sub-sentential illocutions as basic to the performance of textual speech

---

47. Poythress, "Canon and Speech Act," 340.
48. Alston, *Illocutionary Acts*, 157.
49. Alston, *Illocutionary Acts*, 158.

acts, recognition of higher-level illocutions (super-sentential) is just as critical. An assertion made at the sentential level may not be functioning as an assertion when understood as part of the larger text. For example, this would occur when a character in a narrative makes an assertion but the narrator depicts this person as foolish and does not adopt their stance. The assertion made by the character is limited to them and actually functions in the broader text as a critique of such beliefs. This kind of effect upon a text by its literary context is widely recognized. However, it is important to clarify the relationships in terms of speech act terminology. This will enable the reader to identify the illocutions at each level and then consider how they function within the whole. Various authors have noted the importance of such a task and this is Poythress' observation above.[50] He continues with specific reference to illocutionary levels:

> Even within a monologue we find complexities in human purpose, partly because of hierarchical relationships. A political speaker makes a request (a speech act) as part of an apology (a larger speech act?—but it is no longer "atomic"), as part of an explanation (a behavioreme) as part of a political speech (a larger behavioreme). The speech as a whole rhetorically has several purposes, to praise his party, to justify its policies, to rally and encourage the faithful, to raise funds, and to promote his own election. The embedded request represents not just a speech act of making a request, but also a verbal behavioreme that serves the several larger purposes. Description in terms of speech acts may sometimes stop with saying, "He is making a request." That is technically correct. But it focuses on only one aspect (the contrastive-identificational aspect of a particular verbal behavioreme).[51]

This is a fine description of both the complexity of communication and the inherent dangers of reductionism. That the speech has several purposes: "to praise his party, to justify its policies, to rally and encourage the faithful, to raise funds, and to promote his own election", suggests that the interpretation of the speech requires a sufficiently thick description (i.e., rather than simply observing that "He is making a request"). Poythress is concerned that even though speech act theory is a useful tool, many of the discussions in which it is utilized do not account for this complexity and could promote a reductionistic view of the text. He continues:

> ... it is easy for less sophisticated users of the theory to overlook this possibility of complexity. And it is easy to think that such complexity is exceptional. But Jakobson's classification of multiple dimensions

---

50. See also C. J. Scalise, *Hermeneutics as Theological Prolegomena: A Canonical Approach* (Macon: Mercer University Press, 1994). Here Scalise discusses Ricoeur's explanation of reading as a "dialectical process" that moves from "the level of the word" to "the level of the sentence" to the "level of discourse." (Scalise, *Hermeneutics as Theological Prologomena*, 29-30.)

51. Poythress, "Canon and Speech Act," 341.

of communication suggests that it is pervasive. Let me put it another way. Speech-act theory, if used simplistically, tends to make people think that each sentence-level act makes a single, simple speech commitment, defined as its "illocutionary force": it either asserts, promises, commands, wishes, or the like. But a sentence in the Bible may often have, in addition to one more obvious and direct commitment, multiple, interlocking purposes, related in multiple ways to its literary context and its addressees.[52]

The concerns that Poythress raises are certainly valid. However, it is not the fault of the theory that it can be misapplied. It may be that casual readers of the literature do not grasp the wider application of the theory and do not see comments like Searle's, quoted above, as necessary qualifications. This in no way limits the descriptive or analytic power of the theory. Carefully nuanced applications, like those offered by Poythress, not only avoid a reductionistic understanding of illocution, but will also combat the reductionism inherent to many hermeneutics that neglect speech act theory altogether.

To summarize, the category of super-sentential illocution recognizes that texts not only contain speech acts at the sentential level, but that texts themselves are speech acts. For example, a letter, a narrative, or a psalm will have an illocutionary force in its entirety. Those texts that are sufficiently long will also have various illocutionary forces produced at levels between that of the sentence and of the text as a whole (i.e., paragraphs, chapters, or stanzas produce distinct illocutions). Wardlaw recognizes that illocutions occur at these intermediate literary levels when he comments on the illocutionary force of Exodus 15:22-27, offering both "teaching Israel" and "enjoining" Israel as examples in this case:

> What is the illocutionary force of Exodus 15:22-27? Or in other words, what is the author trying to do by including this narrative and reciting the events in this way? First, within the narrative world of Exodus and the Pentateuch, the author is teaching Israel that God may be trusted to work miraculous deliverance regardless of Israel's dire circumstances. Therefore, Israel is enjoined to trust the Lord in similar situations in the future.[53]

This complexity suggests that a thick description of any text will attend to the various literary levels and account for the illocutions at these levels and at the level of the text as a whole.

*Generic Illocutions.* A particularly important species of "super-sentential" illocution occurs at the level of genre. The significance of genre for textual

---

52. Poythress, "Canon and Speech Act," 344.
53. T. R. J. Wardlaw, "Discourse Analysis," in *Words and the Word: Explorations in Biblical Interpretation and Literary Theory* (ed. D. G. Firth and J. A. Grant; Downers Grove: IVP 2008), 288-289.

communication has been widely discussed,⁵⁴ and those employing speech act theory have also sought to explain its significance accordingly. Vanhoozer has already used the phrase "generic illocution" to describe the meaning of a text produced in this way.⁵⁵ Similarly Adams, while he does not identify genre with illocution, does speak of the possibility of an "overarching illocution." ⁵⁶ Furthermore, he suggests that genre is both informed by the illocutions within the text and that genre exerts its own force upon the text, which assists readers in understanding the illocutionary acts performed through it:

> Searle notes how genre can impact the function of a particular illocutionary act, but illocutions are never equated with genre as envisioned by form critics. With this adjustment in mind, determining a particular genre does include the analysis of language and imagery employed. The terminology used may express an overarching illocution and thus could impact how one conceives and categorizes a unit's genre. Conversely, genre can also provide clues for identifying types of illocutions expressed within a particular unit. In addition, genre does possess a certain force or overall aim and in this way the two ideas can be related.⁵⁷

Vanhoozer's discussion of genre and "generic illocution" in particular is an important advancement in addressing the complexity of communication and levels of meaning. Genre enables readers to understand the wider game being played with the language and properly identify the lower-level illocutions. He summarizes the importance of genre in the following statement:

> Certain things that authors do only become visible at the level of literary genre. Like speech-acts, literary genres—speech-acts of a higher order—have both propositional matter and illocutionary energy. The *generic* illocution describes what an author is doing at the level of the whole text. Narratives, for example, have the unique ability to *display human action in a temporal world*. Displaying a world is the illocutionary force of narrative; the world displayed, its propositional content. We can generalize the point: every genre in Scripture, not only narrative, does more than convey information; each performs its distinct illocutionary act (or acts).⁵⁸

---

54. For a recent treatment of the topic see J. K. Brown, "Genre Criticism and the Bible," in *Words and the Word: Explorations in Biblical Interpretation and Literary Theory* (ed. D. G. Firth and J. A. Grant; Downers Grove: IVP 2008). Although Brown is familiar with speech act theory and discusses it at length in previous work, she does not refer to it explicitly in this essay.

55. See Vanhoozer, *Is there a Meaning*; *The Drama of Doctrine*. See also Adams, *The Performative Nature*; Treier, *Virtue and the Voice of God*.

56. Adams, *The Performative Nature*, 6.

57. Adams, *The Performative Nature*, 6.

58. Vanhoozer, *The Drama of Doctrine*, 283.

Acknowledging the presence of generic illocutions is critical to textual interpretation. As Vanhoozer states above, understanding the genre being utilized enables the reader to understand the "rules of the game" and so attribute the correct stance that the author is taking to the literature. To correctly interpret a text, therefore, requires that a reader is competent in both recognizing genre and understanding how the genre both performs its own illocutions and supervenes on the lower-levels of the text to shape the illocutions embedded therein. Vanhoozer comments on the necessity of such competence:

> It follows that the biblical interpreter must be competent in more than one literary form, for it is precisely the canonical forms that mediate to the reader the capacity to see, taste, and feel *biblically*. A certain generic competence may well be a necessary condition for conceptualizing and participating in various aspects of covenantal life.[59]

Furthermore, it needs to be recognized that one of the ways in which genre is employed and then identified is through the type of illocutions found within the text. For example, hyperbolic assertions might be one of the clues that leads the reader to correctly identify the text as proverbial. This is only part of the process of identifying genre, but the point to be noted is that the illocutions embedded at lower-levels of the text are not only supervened by higher-level illocutions, but that they can also contribute to the production of higher-level illocutions. Vanhoozer comments, "These levels are arranged in a hierarchy of complexity, where the higher (literary) levels emerge out of or supervene on the lower (linguistic) ones."[60]

The ability to recognize genre and attribute illocutionary action is due to the fact that genre is a relatively stabilizing force that enables interpretation across contexts. The commonality of human experience and thought forms aids this process, as the reader is able to recognize similarities between the text and their own context.[61] Dan Treier comments on this quality of genre:

> The added complication [to texts entering new contexts] is that authors of texts cannot presume the same stability of context (and thus of "background" which relates to the pragmatic component of "relevant" understanding) that speakers can. Genres provide a crucial element of relative contextual stability, but the stability is relative: genres therefore serve as a source of meaning potential. Thus we may not ignore the tie between text genres and institutions. The communicative practices involved with genres are those of people and groups, and their relative stability occurs as the story of traditions engaged in maintaining, yet always defining, their identity.[62]

---

59. Vanhoozer, *The Drama of Doctrine*, 285.
60. Vanhoozer, *Is There a Meaning in This Text?*, 331.
61. Vanhoozer, *Is There a Meaning in This Text?*, 214. This focus on the function of a text was, of course, recognized by form critics who sought to understand the function of the text in light of its *Sitz im Leben*.
62. Treier, *Virtue and the Voice of God*, 134.

Examples of generic illocutions are offered by a number of authors writing in biblical studies and theological hermeneutics. As noted above, Vanhoozer suggests narrative texts in general "display a world" and adds, "They also establish a point of view: the stance of the narrator."[63] As a specific example of narrative he states that an apocalyptic text "displays the *end* of the world, and perhaps "exhorts" and "comforts" as well."[64] With respect to a particular book, Vanhoozer offers "satirizing religiosity" as a generic illocution of the book of Jonah.[65] David Firth comments on the teaching function of the Psalms[66] and notes, "At the most basic level, the majority of the psalms offer instruction on how to pray, simply because they are examples of prayer in action."[67]

*Whole-Text Illocutions.* An important distinction needs to be made between illocutions performed at the level of the text as a whole and those performed at the level of genre. Illocutions occurring at the level of text as a whole (i.e., "whole-text" illocutions) can also be described functionally as the primary illocutions of the text. This may or may not be the case vis-à-vis generic illocutions as they can occur at number of literary levels since a number of generic illocutions can occur throughout a text when the text employs a diversity of genres.

For example, and this will be explained in detail in later chapters, a psalm of lament will perform various generic illocutions by nature of it being a lament psalm. Yet, due to a diversity of content (lower-level illocutions) each psalm of lament will additionally perform its own unique set of illocutions, including those at the level of the psalm as a whole. Furthermore, the psalm of lament will also perform illocutions by way of its inclusion in the Psalter. Therefore, the generic illocutions performed by virtue of being a psalm of lament is not the sum total of the illocutions performed by any particular lament psalm at this level. Unfortunately, Vanhoozer's discussion, while very helpful, does not clarify this distinction and, in fact, creates some confusion when he says that the generic illocution "describes what an author is doing at the level of the whole text."[68] At times this is true, the generic illocutions can function at this level. However, as just discussed, it is preferable to describe these as whole-text illocutions, acknowledging that generic illocutions occur at a variety of literary levels and not exclusively at the whole-text level.

*Meaning and Thick Descriptions: Primary and Attendant Illocutions*
Having addressed the various levels at which illocutions may occur, it is now important to revisit the definition of meaning. Vanhoozer's definition,

---

63. Vanhoozer, *The Drama of Doctrine*, 283-284..
64. Vanhoozer, *The Drama of Doctrine*, 283.
65. Vanhoozer, *Is There a Meaning in This Text?*, 331.
66. In the following chapters, I will provide a more detailed discussion of generic illocutions in the Psalms.
67. Firth, "The Teaching of the Psalms," 163. Again, Firth does not use the term "generic illocution" but the concept is clearly implied.
68. Vanhoozer, *The Drama of Doctrine*, 283.

previously quoted, acknowledges the need for a "thick" description of text, "*The literal sense of an utterance or text is the sum total of those illocutionary acts performed by the author intentionally and with self-awareness.*"[69] Again, in light of the complexity of communication and the various levels of illocution, it is necessary to define meaning in a way that accounts for this. A few points of clarification can now be offered.

If we examine a paragraph of text there will be a number of illocutions that the author is performing. Take Psalm 1 as an example. It makes assertions about the righteous, assertions about the wicked and assertions about how God relates to both. However, it could be argued that the primary illocution is not an assertion but a call to be the righteous person and simultaneously a warning against following the wicked or surrounding oneself with wicked people. Furthermore, the psalm is also influenced by its function as introduction in the Psalter, its connection with Psalm 2, and its inclusion in the canon.[70] Through these relationships the psalm is used to perform additional illocutions.

Various types of illocution can now be identified. The "main point" of the text is the primary illocution and the sub-points, attendant illocutions.[71] The attendant illocutions are no less important, but they are not the primary function of the text, rather they support that function. Additionally, there may be several primary illocutions communicated through the text when it is considered as part of the whole.[72] In the case of Psalm 1, its relationship with Psalm 2 and the Psalter provide possible levels at which a primary illocution might be functioning. Furthermore, both attendant and primary illocutions occur from the sentential to whole-text levels. Assessing the various levels of illocution and their hierarchical relationships is therefore essential to understanding the text in the "thickest" possible manner. In other words, it is not simply a manner of listing all the illocutions performed through a text, but of identifying the relationships between the illocutions.

*Summary of Part A*

In light of the preceding discussion regarding the complexity of communication, the original definition of meaning can now be adjusted and the implications for hermeneutics can be outlined.

---

69. Vanhoozer, "From Speech Acts to Scripture Acts," 177-179.

70. The canonical level will be discussed extensively in the section below.

71. Irsigler has called for a similar differentiation suggestion "primary" and "secondary" illocutions. He comments, "*Die Gewichtung von Sprechakten in ihrem Verhältnis zueinander betrifft ihren leitenden oder begleitenden bzw. nur vermittelnden Status. Er sei mit den termini dominant oder primär) eigentlich und hauptsächlich intendiert) gegenüber subsidiär oder sekundär) untergeordnet, als Mittel zum eigentlichen Zweck eingesetzt, mitgemeint) bezeichnet* (Irsigler, "Sprechaktanalyse und Psalmeninterpretation am Beispiel von Psalm 13", 72), emphasis original.

72. Adams speaks of the "central illocution" of Isa 40-55. He is, however, not using the term "central" in any technical manner and it corresponds with what I have described above as a "primary illocution." (Adams, *The Performative Nature*, 16.)

1. The meaning of a text is the sum total of the illocutionary acts performed through it.
   a. This requires a recognition of the various literary levels at which illocution occurs.
   b. This also requires an understanding of the relationships between these illocutions since certain illocutions will be formed by other supervenient illocutions.
   c. The resulting understanding of meaning is thus determinate but not single. A "thick" description is required.
2. The goal of interpretation is, therefore, to understand the sum of illocutionary acts being performed throughout the entire text.

## Part B—Dual Authorship and Canonical Hermeneutics

In the remainder of this chapter I provide a synthesis of the insights of Part A (i.e., levels and kinds of illocution and meaning as "thick") with the presupposition that Scripture is an instance of continual divine discourse. This presupposition raises a number of interpretive issues regarding levels of illocution. If the divine author is communicating through each book contained in the Scriptures and also through the canon as a whole, then illocutions occurring at the canonical level should be investigated when attempting a thick description. Furthermore, it is necessary to explain how the illocutions performed through the text by the human authors are related to any divine illocutions performed through the same text. It may be that the illocutions performed by the divine author are identical with those performed by the human author, yet there are instances and levels where this is not possible. Therefore, I presuppose and defend the necessity of a *sensus plenior* hermeneutic. Such a hermeneutic explains the continuing relevance of the biblical text by accounting for how its divine illocutions remain in play.

The valid criticisms of *sensus plenior* approaches, previously discussed, primarily focused on its apparent subjectivity. Yet those who reject any form of *sensus plenior* are alternatively faced with the following challenges:
   a. The manner in which Jesus and the New Testament authors interpret the Old Testament.
   b. How the Old Testament can function as God's current word to the new covenant community.
   c. How there could be any communicative intent at the canonical level.
   d. Whether God can be understood to share the communicative intent of the human author in every case.

To date, *sensus plenior* proponents have not adequately responded to its detractors, yet its detractors have not sufficiently explained how the entire canon continues to function as God's ongoing communicative act. Describing *sensus plenior* in speech act categories both clarifies its problems and offers a pathway to a solution.

*Divine Illocutions and* Sensus Plenior
Sensus plenior should be recognized as such wherever it can be demonstrated that God is performing an illocution by means of a particular text that cannot be attributed to the human author of that text. With this in mind, speech act theory not only clarifies the problem but also demonstrates that this occurs more frequently than the discussion to date has realized. While most writers employ *sensus plenior* to explain diachronic divergences in illocution, the application of speech act theory not only reveals greater incidence of this phenomenon but also presents incidents of synchronic illocutionary divergence that should similarly be considered part of the text's *sensus plenior*.

*Synchronic Illocutionary Divergence.* "Synchronic illocutionary divergence" will be used to refer to instances where the divine illocutions differ in some way from the human illocutions performed through the same text in a particular canonical context. In many instances the divine illocutions can be identified with the human authorial illocutions. This occurs, for example, when God appropriates the stance of the narrator.[73] More specifically, it can occur when the narrator reports the content of God's communication to the people. In these cases God appropriates the stance of the narrator in calling the people to remember or be aware of what God has communicated.[74] At the same time this example includes instances of synchronic illocutionary divergence. While the divine illocution is identical to the human author's illocution in terms of the stance taken toward the report, there is often an inherent divergence in the illocutions *of the report*. God is performing illocutions at various levels within the report that cannot be attributed to the human author. In other words, the human author is taking a stance toward the report as a whole and is not necessarily adopting the illocutions within it.[75] For example, it is nonsensical to suggest the human author performs the illocutionary act declaring, "I am the LORD your God, who brought you out of Egypt, out of the land of slavery" (Exod. 20:2). At this point the narrator is both reporting the event and calling the people to covenant loyalty. However, while God is similarly calling the people to covenant loyalty, his appropriation of the text includes the first person claims of this verse. Their illocutionary acts do converge, however, at a higher literary level where both authors assert that the LORD did in fact make this declaration.[76]

---

73. I assume a level of inspiration that guarantees that the stance of the human authors is always authorized, if not appropriated, by God.

74. There would undoubtedly be many more illocutions performed through the inclusion of such a report. The example given is a broad illocution.

75. It is possible that the human author could appropriate God's discourse (e.g., God calls the people to repent, or warns them of impending judgment and the human author uses this report to do the same). However, due to the relationship between the human author and God, it makes little sense to suggest that the human author thought that God was speaking for them.

76. Both authors assert that God made the declaration and also use this to perform other illocutions throughout the text.

Thus, the divine illocutions are not always coterminous with the human illocutions even in texts that are functioning in the contexts that the human author envisaged.

The reverse situation is also true. Just as God performs illocutions that cannot be attributed to the human author, the human author performs illocutions that cannot be attributed to God. It should be noted that the specific act of *appropriation* is the issue at hand since to appropriate an illocution is to adopt its stance. In some cases God does not appropriate the illocutions of the human author, as it is nonsensical for Him to do so. How the text functions as divine discourse in these instances requires further explanation.

A consideration of the psalms may be helpful as an example of this kind of synchronic divergence. While it seems likely that many of the illocutions within the psalms could be echoed by God (e.g., Blessed is the man who...; Kiss the Son . . . ; etc.), there are many examples of illocutions which are nonsensical if attributed to Him (e.g., David's request for a clean heart in Psalm 51; any of the requests made to God for salvation from one's enemies; any time a psalmist questions God's presence or purposes, etc.). It makes sense that since the psalms are directed to God then God is not performing some of the illocutions of the psalmist.

This creates a little-recognized tension for those who presuppose that all Scripture is God's communicative act: If God is not performing the illocution of the human author how can He be communicating through the text? More pointedly, how can this be considered God's word?[77] This tension highlights the need for a speech act theory informed hermeneutic which recognizes the various levels at which illocutions can occur. In cases such as these, it is best to understand God as authorizing rather than appropriating the illocutions of the human author at this level. In other words, God is taking a particular stance towards the illocution of the human author. More specifically, God is performing an illocution at a higher literary level that incorporates this lower-level text. General illocutions of authorization might include: "I authorize this kind of response to this kind of situation" or "I affirm the attitude expressed by the human author." While God authorizes the illocutions at this level, it is likely that both He and the human author are using these illocutions to perform higher-level illocutions through the text. Both the authorizing illocution and the presence of higher-level illocutions allow for the text to continue to be counted as God's communicative act even if He does not perform all of the illocutionary acts of the human author.[78]

---

77. For a fuller discussion of the issues see Wolterstorff, *Divine Discourse*, chapters 12 and 13.

78. It should be repeated that the understanding of inspiration presupposed in this project is one that ensures that the human authors always speak in ways that honour God such that God either appropriates their illocutions or, alternatively, authorizes or affirms their illocutions. This will form the discussion of later chapters vis-à-vis the psalms and imprecation where the psalmist even questions the fidelity of God.

Synchronic divergence, and therefore a *sensus plenior*, not only occurs in Old Testament texts, but also in New Testament texts. As discussed earlier, Wolterstorff's application of speech act theory to exegesis suffers from his attempt to explain God's illocutions at the sentential level in every case. An example previously cited where Paul states, "God, whom I serve . . ." (Romans 1:9), leads Wolterstorff to change the rhetorico-conceptual structure of the text to explain what God is saying at that level. He proposes the following: "So whatever we take God to be saying by way of this passage, its noematic content will have a different rhetorico-conceptual structure from the noematic content of what Paul said. The point holds for a great deal of the Bible, and is obvious and noncontroversial."[79] It is clear that God is not appropriating the declaration of Paul in this verse of Romans. Wolterstorff's use of speech act theory has demonstrated that the issue of God speaking through the text is more complicated than is typically recognized. However, his solution that reshapes the rhetorico-conceptual structure is overly reductionistic.[80]

I suggest that a better solution is to accept that God performs illocutions at higher literary levels than that of a particular phrase or sentence. God's speech through Paul might be at the level of a paragraph or larger literary unit where God appropriates Paul's illocutions directly, yet at the lower sentential levels, like the one in question, God might be performing the illocution of affirming Paul's stance or authorizing Paul's response (i.e., "I accept/agree with Paul's declaration of faith" etc.). Both the Psalter and Paul's declaration in Romans function as God's word, but this does not require that God perform every illocution of the human author. I have previously commented:

> It needs to be recognized that across genres and within genres God's illocutions might be identical with the human author's, yet they might be necessarily different. It is not a simple divine appropriation of every human speech act and it is not a simple appropriation of only higher-level speech acts. Each genre and text requires individual analysis to determine exactly how God is speaking through it. Again, a sensus plenior approach that utilizes speech act theory recognizes the complexity of God's speech in Scripture and allows for greater precision in discussing how and, in particular, at what level, God is communicating.[81]

The result of the above discussion reveals that traditional approaches to *sensus plenior* have been deficient in their recognition of its scope. *Sensus plenior* should be recognized whenever the divine author performs an illocution other than the illocutions of the human author. In the examples given from both Testaments, it is clear that a *sensus plenior* is required to account for the thickest meaning of the text in its original context. Most *sensus plenior* approaches to date have only recognized its application to "diachronic divergence" (i.e., how

---

79. Wolterstorff, *Divine Discourse*, 209.
80. For further discussion, see Barker, "Divine Illocutions."
81. Barker, "Speech Act Theory," 234.

the Old Testament needs to read in light of the New Testament). This deficiency is ameliorated once it is recognized that "synchronic illocutionary divergence" is also present; a reality that speech act theory helps to elucidate. This situation is clearly seen in the psalms where God appropriates the text yet does not perform *all* of the original illocutions of the human author. In other words, the thick description of what God is doing with the text differs from the thick description of what the human author is doing. This formal change in the illocutionary content by definition is a change in the meaning of the text and justifies a *sensus plenior* application.

*Diachronic Illocutionary Divergence.* As mentioned earlier, *sensus plenior* proponents have argued that such a category is necessary in order to explain how particular Old Testament texts are fulfilled in ways that were unexpected by their human authors. In these cases, the human author of the Old Testament text did not intend this "fuller meaning" and a *sensus plenior* hermeneutic is applied to account for the diachronic divergence of the Divine and human illocutions. This seems justified. However, if it is assumed that God continues to speak through the entire canon, then according to speech act theory this means that God continues to perform illocutions across the entire Old Testament. When this is examined in detail a *sensus plenior* is a reality in more instances than are traditionally recognized. For example, unless one adopts a theonomist position, many commands within the Pentateuch are clearly not functioning in the same way today as they did in their original context (e.g., laws pertaining to ritual cleanliness).[82] In speech act terminology, many of the original primary illocutions are no longer being performed by either God or the human author. If it is believed that God is still communicating through the text, then God must now be performing new illocutions through the same text and a *sensus plenior* hermeneutic is justified.[83] There are a variety of ways in which God may use these texts in new covenant communities. Most of these involve dissolution of the primary illocution and its replacement with either attendant illocutions embedded in the original communication or with entirely new illocutions that occur by virtue of the text's relationship with the New Testament. This will be discussed below in greater detail. For now, it is important to recognize that either of these changes the "meaning" of the text and thus constitute an instance of *sensus plenior*.[84]

---

82. For further discussion, see A. Sloane, *At Home in a Strange Land: Using the Old Testament in Christian Ethics* (Peabody: Hendrickson, 2008), 113-127. See also C. J. H. Wright, *Old Testament Ethics for the People of God* (Downers Grove: IVP, 2004).

83. I presuppose that the entire canon remains relevant as a continual divine communicative act.

84. Admittedly, the change in meaning where the primary illocution is dissolved and an attendant illocution is promoted is a "weaker" form of *sensus plenior* as the human author performed the illocution in the original setting. The meaning of the text, however, has formally changed in a way that they did not envisage.

If, however, a *sensus plenior* approach is rejected with respect to the Pentateuch and the Old Testament, then the illocutions of God are necessarily taken as coterminous with the illocutions of the human author (both synchronically and diachronically). The result of this hermeneutic is that much of the Old Testament continues to function merely as the reporting of history and it is unclear how God communicates through it today. An example from the Pentateuch clarifies the point. The command of Yahweh that His people observe the sabbath in particular ways is clearly a case of divine illocution. The author of the Pentateuch is likewise asserting that this is Yahweh's command. How does this text function diachronically? Unless a contemporary illocutionary act can be attributed to God, then all that remains for the reader to uncover are the original illocutions of the human author (which are taken as coterminous with those of God). This results in the Old Testament functioning in a very limited way, more limited than the New Testament writers suggest.[85]

Diachronic divergence occurs due to changes in the normative conditions within which the original illocutions were performed. This results in the dissolution of some of these original illocutions. If the peculiar nature of Scripture as continuing divine discourse is to be sustained, then new illocutions must be performed, and these cannot be attributed to the original author. This is explained by the original locutions being used under new and different normative conditions that enable the performance of new, contemporary divine illocutions. This change in conditions requires its own explanation and to accomplish this it is necessary to consider the function of the canon.

*Canonical Illocutions*

As discussed earlier, Vanhoozer has provided the clearest explanation of how God communicates through the canon. It was noted, however, that his proposal is self-confessedly not overly detailed and lacks exegetical application. My proposed hermeneutic hopes to supplement his work and to clarify the issues that it has raised.

Vanhoozer speaks of canonical illocutions, which he says supervene upon Scripture. As mentioned, his thesis is that divine illocutions are present at this canonical level, yet this is not the only way in which Scripture can be affirmed as God's word. At this stage, it is worthwhile repeating the full quotation:

> There are two complementary senses in which I wish to affirm the canon as God's illocutionary act. First, there is the divine appropriation of the illocutions of the human authors, particularly at the generic level but not exclusively there. For example, God still uses the book of Jonah to satirize religious ethnocentrism... Yet God may

---

85. There may be many attendant illocutions that could remain in play such as those concerning God's holiness and the need for His people to repent and purify themselves. But the broader issue is whether God can perform new illocutions on the basis of the canon. These illocutions are not anticipated by the human author and cannot be understood as embedded within their original illocutionary structure.

be doing new things with Jonah and other biblical texts too by virtue of their being gathered together in the canon. Could it be that certain illocutions come to light only when we describe what God is doing at the canonical level? More work needs to be done in this area, but for the moment let me offer the following as possible candidates for the divine canonical illocutions: instructing the believing community, testifying to Christ, and perhaps most obviously, covenanting.[86]

Vanhoozer suggests that God firstly performs illocutions by appropriating the illocutions of the human author. Additionally, God performs illocutions at the canonical level, which are impossible for the human author.[87] These divine illocutions at the canonical level "supervene" rather than "contravene" lower-level illocutions.[88] It is the sum of these canonical illocutions that Vanhoozer labels the *sensus plenior*.

In my opinion, Vanhoozer's work has been the most helpful contribution to understanding *sensus plenior* in terms of speech act theory. He recognizes that all texts are communicative acts, that meaning is a function of the sum of illocutions which an author performs by the text, that God appropriates human illocutions, and that God performs different illocutions as the author of the canon. Yet, his explanation is not comprehensive and at various points merely highlights the inherent difficulties with *sensus plenior* approaches.[89] For example, Vanhoozer has not addressed the cases where it is nonsensical for God to be appropriating the illocutions of the human author at the sentential level, a point that Wolterstorff's work has highlighted and the discussion above regarding synchronic illocutionary divergence has explained.

Furthermore, it is not clear how "canonical illocutions" can exist. Illocutions must be based upon locutions; likewise, canonical illocutions must be based upon canonical locutions. This raises the question—which locutions form the basis of the canonical illocutions? The connection between the locutions/illocutions of books within the canon and the locutions/illocutions at the canonical level is left unclear.[90] To address the issue of "canonical illocutions" a number of clarifying comments are required.

While Vanhoozer did not specify how canonical illocutions are related to locutions, he does discuss the presence of canonical genre. As I explained above, generic illocutions occur by convention and through lower-level illocutions

---

86. Vanhoozer, *First Theology*, 194.
87. He states, "Perhaps the most important question we can ask of the canon is: whose act is it? If interpretation is a matter of ascribing and inferring communicative intentions, to whom do we ascribe the illocutions?" (Vanhoozer, *First Theology*, 196.)
88. Vanhoozer, *Is There a Meaning in This Text?*, 264-265.
89. These issues were initially raised in Chapter 2 and are repeated here for further discussion.
90. A related issue is if there are any levels of locution/illocution that occur between the levels of book and canon (e.g., at the level of testament or at partially complete testament).

that either function at a higher-level or allow the reader to identify the genre of the text.

The challenge in suggesting canonical illocutions based on generic convention is that the canon is not one kind of literature that follows specific conventions in order to make these extra-textual judgments. Vanhoozer offers a number of genres that apply to Scripture as a whole ("confessing faith" and "testifying to Christ"), and notes that more work is needed is this area:[91]

> Genre theory is especially important for interpretation. For the Bible is not one book but many books of different kinds, with a wide repertoire of illocutions. The illocutionary force of Paul's letters, for instance, is not so much "displaying the story of Jesus" as "explaining the story of Jesus." ... Other literary forms may have their own characteristic illocutionary forces: wisdom ("commending a way"), apocalyptic ("displaying the *end* of the word," "exhorting"), psalm ("celebrating a created world," "addressing God"). And the various literary forms, taken together as Scripture, may on the canonical level have yet another illocutionary force: "proclaiming God's salvation"; "testifying to Christ." These are only approximations, for genres too have rough edges. Much work needs to be done on this level of discourse, a level that, I believe, has great potential in aiding the recovery of biblical theology.[92]

> In the context of Scripture, each of the literary genres of the Bible has an additional illocutionary force, namely, "confessing faith" or "testifying to Christ." Being part of the canon, in other words, allows yet another level of complexity to emerge: the level of 'bearing witness.' The genres of the Bible, though diverse in form, overlap in content and function.[93]

These canonical genres and their associated illocutionary forces are essential to understanding the meaning of Scripture and of providing the thickest possible description of individual texts. How one might identify these canonical genres is another issue. I offer two brief comments in this regard. First, since it is presumed that Scripture is divinely authored and is subsequently a unified whole, various internal statements can be understood as genre informing.[94] Second, a canonical competence will lead to both an intuitive understanding of the illocutions present in the text and the possibility of inferring canonical illocutions through a synthesis of lower-level illocution. Vanhoozer comments in this regard:

---

91. In these two statements below, Vanhoozer argues for generic, canonical illocutions.
92. Vanhoozer, *Is There a Meaning in This Text?*, 341-342.
93. Vanhoozer, *Is There a Meaning in This Text?*, 349.
94. For example 2 Timothy 3:16 is an obvious candidate for explaining, in part, the function of the Old Testament (and arguably the New Testament as well).

It follows that the biblical interpreter must be competent in more than one literary form, for it is precisely the canonical forms that mediate to the reader the capacity to see, taste, and feel *biblically*. A certain generic competence may well be a necessary condition for conceptualizing and participating in various aspects of covenantal life.[95]

*Central Illocutions*

In addition to the preceding types of canonical illocutions, I propose the concept of central illocutions as an essential category that provides additional clarification not only regarding the presence of canonical illocutions but also regarding the nature of theological hermeneutics. *Central illocutions are those that either create or reveal realities that affect the extra-textual context in which other illocutions may be performed.*

These central illocutions could occur at any level of the canon, but, by definition, have influence at the canonical level. This is one difference between central illocutions and Vanhoozer's canonical illocutions—central illocutions can occur at any level of the text, sentential to canonical. At times, they may also be canonical illocutions, but regardless of the literary level in which they occur, they function "centrally" and thus have a canonical and supervening impact. They "supervene" upon the rest of Scripture so that all other illocutions are formed in the context of, and are consistent with, these central illocutions. The recognition that central illocutions can occur at any level also provides greater clarity regarding the connection between locution and illocution. This is a weakness in Vanhoozer's formulation which seems to only allow canonical illocutions to supervene over the canon. Canonical illocutions, while an important category, are more difficult to demonstrate as they require greater synthesis of lower-level illocutions. Recognizing that central illocutions occur at a lower literary levels means that these illocutions can be more easily connected to their corresponding locutions.

Central illocutions are reality creating and/or revealing. They either create the reality through the illocution (the notion of a "strong" illocution) or they reveal a reality that already exists. For example, a letter from the Sheriff's department stating that you have been summoned for jury duty alters the extra-linguistic background. Any further imperatives directed towards you are then binding and have legal consequences if an appropriate response is not offered. You cannot discount the imperatives of the letter since the central illocution has changed your relationship with this division of the government. Additionally, until a future letter releases you from service through the performance of another central illocution, you are bound to understand any future requests as binding.

Biblical examples of central illocutions include God's covenantal promises. The presence of these promises shapes the normative conditions for whatever

---

95. Vanhoozer, *The Drama of Doctrine*, 285.

else is said in the context of the books in which they occur and in the later canon as well. They do this by creating a new relationship between God and his people. This is the key feature of a central illocution. It affects the way in which previous and future texts need to be read, and it achieves this by effecting extra-linguistic realities. It alters or reveals realities that become part of the context in which locutions become illocutions. Unless future central illocutions alter these conditions then whatever central illocutions remain in play are determinative for the contextual reality. Theological interpretation should therefore not only identify central illocutions in the Christian canon, but also demonstrate how later central illocutions affect earlier (central) illocutions.

The existence and presence of central illocutions in Scripture explains the diachronic illocutionary divergence discussed in the section above and so provides further clarification of *sensus plenior* hermeneutics. In particular, it accounts for why some primary illocutions in the Old Testament no longer remain in play and how these texts can be used in the newly created context to perform different illocutions.

In many cases, central illocutions that occur in the New Testament have altered the conditions necessary for the primary illocution of the Old Testament text to remain in play. These new conditions could affect the original locutions and corresponding illocutions in a number of ways. Where it is no longer possible that God is performing the primary illocution of the original Old Testament text, it may be the case that one of the attendant illocutions now becomes primary. In the Pentateuchal examples mentioned above, this could be any number of assertions concerning God's character, the sinfulness of humanity, or the need for justice and atonement, to name just a few. In this case the *sensus plenior* is simply that the primary illocution of the Old Testament text ceases to be performed and an attendant illocution becomes primary for the new covenant community. Alternatively or additionally, the central illocution may supervene in such a way that it creates an entirely "new" illocution that the human author could never have understood or intended. This would be a more traditional understanding of the *sensus plenior*.

*Illocutions—Taxonomy of Levels*
The following table is a summary of the various illocutionary levels discussed above. These illocutionary levels can be categorized as either functional levels or literary levels. Functional illocutionary levels include: attendant, primary, and central illocutions. These functional illocutions can occur at any literary level. Literary illocutionary levels include: sub-sentential, sentential, super-sentential, generic and canonical.

## Functional Illocutionary Levels

| | |
|---|---|
| Primary Illocutions | The main actions being performed. |
| Attendant Illocutions | Illocutions performed in the performance of a primary illocution. They are not the main action, but they support and enable the performance of primary illocutions. |
| Central Illocutions | These may or may not be the primary illocution. However, since they effect extra-linguistic reality, their performance supervenes in such a way that they affect all other illocutions being performed in that same text. They may also affect the reality and background of other texts. |

## Literary Illocutionary Levels

| | |
|---|---|
| Sub-sentential Illocutions | Occur within a sentence and are by definition, attendant rather than primary. |
| Sentential Illocutions | Are performed by the sentence in its entirety and are by definition primary at this level. |
| Super-sentential Illocutions | Occur at various intermediate levels between that of the sentence and that of the text as a whole. These occur at levels of pericope, paragraph, chapter, stanza, etc. They may be primary or attendant. |
| Generic Illocutions | Produced by the employment of a genre and are common to texts of that genre. |
| Whole-Text Illocutions | Occur at the level of a text as a whole. These include, but are not limited to, the generic illocutions |
| Canonical Illocutions | Produced by intertextuality throughout the canon. |

## Conclusion: Divine Illocutions and the Goal of Theological Hermeneutics

*Thick Descriptions*
In light of the preceding discussion of canonical and central illocutions, a return to the discussion of thick descriptions is needed. In Part A it was suggested that a thick description is the goal of hermeneutics. To achieve this thickness an account of the various illocutionary levels is required. The levels discussed spanned sub-sentential illocutions through to the level of the text as a whole and its genres. Applying these insights to Scripture necessitates the inclusion of both literary and functional illocutions, namely, canonical and central illocutions. In order to provide the thickest description of a text, illocutions at these higher-levels must be understood. In particular, central illocutions (whether canonical or sub-canonical) are essential to the overall task as they shape the contemporary use of all other locutions in the performance of contemporary illocutions.

Consequently, a thick description is only possible if a hermeneutic is employed that accounts for *sensus plenior* since many of the illocutions within the canon cannot be attributed to the human author. Both synchronic and diachronic illocutionary divergence demonstrated the need for this approach. Some illocutions are nonsensical if attributed to the human author and other illocutions are nonsensical if attributed to God. Furthermore, at the level of canon it is necessary to appeal to *sensus plenior* as the human author cannot perform illocutions at this level.

A thick description of any text of Scripture therefore accounts for all of the illocutions being performed in the text. This includes both human illocutions and divine illocutions. Ultimately, the goal of theological interpretation is to attribute an illocutionary stance to God. To do this, however, necessitates a prior understanding of the human illocutions. This is critical for a number of reasons. First, many of the human illocutions are identical with the divine illocutions. Second, where there is synchronic illocutionary divergence, an understanding of the divine illocutions is only possible if one first understands the illocutionary stance of the human writer. Once this is accomplished it is possible to investigate God's stance towards their illocution. Third, the divine illocution often directs the reader back to the human illocution by authorizing their stance.

*Identifying Divine Illocutions*
The recognition of divine illocutions is central to the task of biblical interpretation, yet the method through which we determine these receives little discussion.[96] The content of this chapter provided some direction and clarification

---

96. See the discussion in Chapter 2, particularly with respect to Wolterstorff.

in this regard by utilizing the resources of speech act theory and suggested that attending to the human illocutions was indispensable to the task.

*The Importance of the Human Illocutions in Scripture.* Wolterstorff suggests that the illocution of the human author should be counted as the illocution of God unless there was "good reason" to think otherwise. This is a fine place to start. As mentioned above, I affirm that a focus on human illocutions is necessary. The question remains, however, why the illocutions of the human author should be taken as the illocutions of God. This part of the hermeneutic is simply a function of the presupposition that the Scriptures are inspired and therefore count as God's word. The illocutionary stance of the author, particularly at the generic level of the text, is to be identified with the illocutionary stance of God. At lower levels this may not make any sense as the discussion of synchronic divergence explained. So the first step in identifying the divine illocutions is to understand the human illocutions and determine whether it makes sense for God top adopt this stance. This is not a theological decision based on whether or not God would take such a stance; rather it is a logical decision that asks whether or not God *could* take this stance (i.e., whether or not it is formally possible for God to perform the speech acts of the human author at any particular point.) A clear example of this is the request of the psalmist that he be delivered from his enemies, since it is illogical to suggest that God performs this particular speech act at this level of the text.

*The Role of Canonical and Central Illocutions*  So far, the method has avoided the "wax nose" by only identifying God's illocutions with those of the human author. The next move is more risky.[97] Diachronic illocutionary divergence assumes that God can perform illocutions through the text that the human author did not perform. It requires an understanding of both canonical illocutions and central illocutions. Canonical illocutions are inferred either through a synthesis of lower-level illocutions or by a recognition of canonical genre (which is also a product of lower-level illocutions). Central illocutions are those portrayed in the text as reality creating or reality revealing and can either occur at or below the canonical level. These are either directly performed at sub-canonical levels or, like all canonical illocutions, require either inference or generic convention in order to be identified.

At this point, I have not provided the specific means by which either canonical or central illocutions can be identified. This task is the joint responsibility of both biblical scholars and systematic theologians. A speech act theory based hermeneutic will not provide a direct answer to the question of which illocutions in Scripture are central or which are canonical. This requires all the resources of the above two fields of specialization. However, a speech act theory

---

97. Bowald notes that hermeneutics which prioritise divine agency ["type three" in his model] are prone to eisegesis (Bowald, *Rendering the Word*, 162.) This is a caution that I affirm and it is fundamental to my goals that the processes of determining the divine speech acts are given greater clarity.

based hermeneutic that recognizes the need to identify both canonical and central illocutions is a step forward.

While this hermeneutic will not provide those answers, it does avoid some of the anxiety of the "wax nose" syndrome. Canonical and central illocutions provide boundaries within which the discussion of divine illocutions may occur. Any suggestion that God is using a text to perform illocutions other than those of the human author now requires that the supervening illocutions be identified and the manner of their supervention explained.

*The Presence of God.* Earlier in Part A, the issue of authorial presence was discussed in response to charges of structuralism. It was noted that authorial presence in a text is not uniform and occurs along a continuum accros genres. At times the author does not reveal their identity, intentionally remaining anonymous. In the case of Scripture, this variation in the level of authorial presence is intentional. A presupposition of this project is that the entire Christian canon is divinely superintended and functions as divine discourse. A corollary to this belief is that all of the illocutionary acts performed in the text, including those which reveal the level of authorial presence, have been divinely authorized. Therefore, when an author remains anonymous, knowledge of the author is assumed to be unnecessary and a "text immanent" approach is justified. However, even though the human author may remain anonymous in some cases, the above presupposition regarding divine discourse means that the divine author is always assumed and, in the context of the canon, always present. In this canonical context, God sufficiently reveals Himself in order to attain a personal relationship with humanity. Therefore, we can expect that the canon effectively communicates His identity.[98] Individually, the books in the canon do not equally reveal the identity of God. However, since the reader has access to the divine author through various other parts of the canon, the divine author is equally present in every text.[99]

The identity of the divine author both forms part of the goal of theological interpretation, and is also its hermeneutical key. Knowing "who the author is" and "what the author is like" is essential to deciding whether or not the author should be understood to take up a particular stance. This is, in part, a circular argument as the text itself gives us access to the author through its illocutions. Yet the presupposition that God desires to be known and knows how to communicate to his creatures should give the interpreter confidence in this task.

Again, a speech act theory based hermeneutic that acknowledges the dual authorship of Scripture will not in itself answer the question "what is God like?" or "what is God saying?" Rather, it provides the boundaries and resources for

---

98. Assuming of course that God wants to be known and knows how to effectively communicate to His creatures. For a discussion of Scripture, particularly the gospels, as an "identity narrative" and its relationship to the presence of Christ see H. W. Frei, *The Identity of Jesus Christ: The Hermeneutical Bases of Dogmatic Theology* (Philadelphia: Fortress Press, 1975).

99. Contrast the Gospel of John with the book of Esther, for example.

the discussion to take place.[100] "What God is like" and "what God is saying" becomes a textual and canonical investigation[101] where interpreters must demonstrate that the supervening illocutions, both canonical and central, support their interpretation of any individual text.

---

100. Briggs, "Speech-Act Theory," 98.
101. Vanhoozer describes it as a "canonical linguistic" model.

# Part II

# Theological Interpretation and the Psalter

The goal of Part II is to demonstrate the usefulness of the hermeneutic developed in Part I and offer a level of exegetical detail currently lacking in the discussion of speech act theory and dual authorship. In Part I, the resources of speech act theory were used to clarify the discussion of dual authorship, specify the goals of theological interpretation and provide an outline of a theological hermeneutic. In Part II, I will further the discussion by applying the hermeneutic to the Psalter and to specific psalms within it. The theological interpretation of the Psalter will begin by first examining how it functioned as divine discourse in its original setting. Subsequent chapters will then complete the task of theological interpretation by demonstrating how the hermeneutic applies in general to psalms of imprecation, offering a solution to how these psalms continue to function as divine discourse. Finally, the hermeneutic will be applied to particular imprecatory psalms in order to allow for a more detailed discussion and to demonstrate the usefulness of the hermeneutic at an exegetical level.

# Chapter 4

# The Divine Illocutions of the Psalter in Its Old Testament Context

## Introduction

To explicate the way in which the psalms can be counted as divine discourse, the discussion will begin by examining how the Psalter functioned as divine discourse in its Old Testament context. The resources of speech act theory will be applied in order to discuss the function of the Psalter at various literary levels, including both generic and whole-text levels. Having outlined the human illocutionary acts within the Psalter, I will then propose the ways in which Psalter functioned as divine discourse.

### The Primary Illocutions of the Psalter

The purpose of this section is to discuss the function of the Psalter in its Old Testament context, or, in speech act categories, to discuss its primary and whole-text illocutions.[1] I do not intend in this chapter to present a comprehensive taxonomy of the illocutions of the Psalter. The focus, rather, will be on those deemed to be primary illocutions and those that may prove useful in the subsequent discussion regarding the "fit" of the imprecatory psalms within the Psalter. To this end, the discussion will focus on three ways in which the Psalter performs its primary illocutions: canonical inclusion, canonical shaping and particular literary devices.

---

1. This section will not include a discussion of lower-level illocutions (i.e., illocutions performed at various levels within a psalm) as they will be addressed in detail with respect to individual psalms in the next chapter.

*Speech Act Theory and the Psalter*
Several scholars have utilized speech act theory in their discussions of the Psalms.[2] However, many of their approaches can be clearly defined as examples of speech act criticism.[3] As such, they are not concerned with the development of a broader theological hermeneutic based upon speech act theory, rather they have analysed various psalms in terms of the speech acts contained therein.[4] Others, like Firth, helpfully note that the psalms themselves not only contain speech acts, but are, themselves, speech acts:

> In speech act terms, we can say that each of these psalms is a locution, but the teaching method adopted represents a different illocutionary force, and that the perlocution will thus vary ... Speech act theory, with its emphasis on illocutionary force and perlocutions, is a valuable aid to understanding the teaching intent of individual psalms.[5]

This observation offers an important way forward in understanding the illocutionary force of the Psalter. Not only do psalms contain speech acts, but psalms themselves are speech acts having been intentionally constructed using conventional patterns in order to accomplish a number of public actions. Understanding that the speech acts of the Psalter occur, in part, at the literary level of the psalm is critical for theological interpretation, as will be demonstrated below.

Until recently, neither the illocutionary force of the Psalter nor the ways in which it might function as divine discourse were considered appropriate lines of inquiry. The legacy of form criticism resulted in a view of the Psalter that considered it merely human words that were inextricably tied to their *Sitz im Leben*. Thankfully, the discussion has progressed in recognition that the Psalter was intentionally shaped (at least to some degree) with the intention of not merely preserving a record of worship, but of instructing future communities. This is not to deny that form criticism can offer useful observations which

---

2. See Briggs, "The Uses of Speech Act Theory," 263.
3. This was defined in Chapter 1.
4. See A. Warren, "Modality, Reference and Speech Acts in the Psalms" (Ph.D., Cambridge, 1998); Wolterstorff, *Divine Discourse*. David Cohen advances this idea by noting that the psalms contain a number of speech acts which allow the reader access to their action, "As highlighted above, each discrete type of speech act identified by Searle can be seen in the psalms of distress. From a speech act theory perspective then, their presence suggests that the function of these words, at least in their original context, was to *do something*. This idea of words *doing something* is in sharp contrast to viewing words simply as a record, informing a reader of events in the past and reflections on those events. It also suggests that a person praying the psalms of distress, and by it verbalizing their 'inner voice' as speech acts, can find a ready-made entry point for engagement with personal distress." (D. J. Cohen, *Why O Lord?* (Milton Keyes: Paternoster, 2013), 41.)
5. Firth, "The Teaching of the Psalms," 164. See also G. Wenham, *The Psalter Reclaimed: Praying and Praising with the Psalms* (Wheaton: Crossway, 2013).

enable the speech acts of a psalm to be identified. Any methodology is of benefit if it assists the reader in understanding the linguistic conventions and cultural settings within which a text is generated.⁶

*Canonical Inclusion and Primary Illocution*
That the Psalter has been intentionally shaped is widely accepted, though the degree of shaping continues to be a contested issue.⁷ The presence of such shaping suggests that the psalms within it have, at the very least, been intentionally included in the corpus. In the absence of any clear literary markers indicating that certain psalms or sections of the Psalter are to be understood as counter examples (i.e., as examples of an unrighteous response to life or foolish teaching), it can be assumed that the psalms presented are commensurate with (and comprise) the illocutionary stance of the Psalter. To suggest otherwise would incur the burden of proof.

As noted in the discussion above, the use of speech act terminology with respect to the psalms is limited, with the main exceptions being Firth and Wolterstorff.⁸ While Wolterstorff offers the most hermeneutic detail, he neglects a discussion of higher-level illocutions (i.e., at the level of the Psalter and canon). Firth, on the other hand, helpfully notes how the canonical inclusion of the Psalter has resulted in a number of illocutions. As his discussion is clearly influenced by speech act theory, it warrants a more detailed treatment.

Firth argues that the canonical presence and shaping of the Psalter both indicate a didactic function:

> Their place within the canon also means that they have a further role beyond the issues studied by the form-critical approach. That is, their very status as scripture means that they now have a teaching role. Even if it is not possible to recover the editorial process in full, it can still be argued that the psalms are indeed intended to teach.⁹

---

6. For a discussion of the canonical form of the Psalter, see Gerald Wilson's seminal work: G. H. Wilson, *The Editing of the Hebrew Psalter* (no 76; Chico: Scholars Press, 1985). For a collection of essays that demonstrate recent moves in Psalter scholarship see P. S. Johnston and D. G. Firth, *Interpreting the Psalms: Issues and Approaches* (Leicester: Apollos, 2005).

7. See D. M. J. Howard, "The Psalms and Current Study," in *Interpreting the Psalms: Issues and Approaches* (ed. D. G. Firth and P. S. Johnston; Downers Grove: IVP, 2005); G. H. Wilson, "The Structure of the Psalter," in *Interpreting the Psalms: Issues and Approaches* (ed. D. G. Firth and P. S. Johnston; Leicester: Apollos, 2005); See also J. C. McCann, *The Shape and Shaping of the Psalter* (159; Sheffield: JSOT, 1993); J. L. Mays, *The Lord Reigns: A Theological Handbook to the Psalms* (1st ed.; Louisville: Westminister John Knox Press, 1994); N. Whybray, *Reading the Psalms as a Book* (Sheffield: Sheffield Academic Press, 1996).

8. While Brueggemann does not employ speech act theory in his discussion, his understanding of the power of speech is similar when he notes the ability of the psalms to change reality. (W. Brueggemann, "Psalms and the Life of Faith: A Suggested Typology of Function," *JSOT* 17 (1980): 16.)

9. Firth, "The Teaching of the Psalms," 162.

He suggests two strategies at this canonical level: "thematic modelling through the accumulation of psalms on a given topic, and the creation of an intratextual dialogue within the book."[10] The strategy of thematic modelling requires a repetition of similar patterns of prayer in related contexts. Firth comments that there is no clearly presented rationale for such modelling and this is consistent, given their initial composition as prayers. However, the canonical portrayal of such responses in the Psalter provides an overall consistency and so models the kinds of responses that are appropriate for their corresponding circumstances.[11] The strategy of intratextual dialogue, in Firth's estimation, aids the interpretation of particular psalms. He suggests that the Psalter enacts this strategy through Brueggemann's well known classification of orientation, disorientation and reorientation, with Psalms 1, 3, and 18 being demonstrative of this.[12]

Furthermore, Firth notes that this teaching function needs to be considered with respect to "didactic levels":

> Each Psalm has a primary teaching role of its own, though it is also possible to investigate the ways in which this didactic function might contribute to the larger message of the Psalms. Such a function is not necessarily ascertained through a structured reading strategy (though it may be), but can be achieved by recognizing elements of theological consistency across a range of issues. That is to say, the editorial process may have ensured that only psalms that operated within a given set of theological assumptions remained within the collection, whilst those variations that remain are themselves an intentional element within the instruction of the book. This second-level instructional function within the book as a whole would not be in contradiction to the primary teaching of the individual psalm, but it can provide a nuanced interpretation of it. The instruction of any given psalm is thus shaped by its place within the larger book.[13]

Firth's observations are important for a number of reasons. Firstly, they call for a thematic approach to the Psalter in order to identify consistent theological stances, or in speech act terminology, the primary illocutionary stances of the Psalter. Secondly, they justify investigation at both the level of the individual psalm and the wider level of the Psalter, noting that there is a natural interplay between the two. The illocutionary force of any particular psalm will be affected by its inclusion within the Psalter. However, and most importantly, the default stance of the Psalter is that those psalms within it are not at odds with its primary illocutions. Rather, as Firth suggests, a "nuanced" interpretation of a particular psalm may be required when considered within the context

---

10. Firth, "The Teaching of the Psalms," 171.
11. Firth, "The Teaching of the Psalms," 171-172.
12. Firth, "The Teaching of the Psalms," 173.
13. Firth, "The Teaching of the Psalms," 162.

of the Psalter. Psalm 1 is an obvious example of this requirement as its portrayal of the righteous as prospering is questioned throughout the Psalter.

In terms of primary illocutions, Firth suggests that "through the compilation of the canon every psalm is in some sense mimetic, in that it has an underlying truth or insight that it seeks to communicate. At the most basic level, the majority of the psalms offer instruction on how to pray, simply because they are examples of prayer in action."[14]

Firth's proposal offers some helpful lines of inquiry in the search for understanding the illocutionary stance of the Psalter and of the individual psalms within it. He presents a cogent argument for the intentional thematic modelling of the psalms and that the inclusion of any particular psalm within the Psalter is indicative of its consistency with the teaching strategy of the Psalter. In speech act terms, *the illocutionary stance of each individual psalm is consistent with the illocutionary stance of the Psalter.*

*Canonical Shaping and Primary Illocution*
While current literature lacks a specific discussion of the primary illocutions of the Psalter, the discussion of the Psalter's shape and function is vast.[15] This shaping is one way that the Psalter performs its primary illocutions. While there is little agreement regarding the exact details and significance of the shaping, a number of structural features may assist in understanding the self-presentation of the Psalter.

As mentioned in the discussion above, it is widely accepted that the content of the Psalter was shaped, in part, to inform the worship of Israel. Significant features of this shaping include the introduction of Psalms 1 and 2, the division into five books and the corresponding "seams" between them, the flow or rhythm of the macrostructure, and the conclusion of Psalms 146 to 150.

*The Psalter as "Fashioned for the Worship of Yawheh"*[16] It is clear that some of the psalms were initially formed in relation to the cult, even if the specific details of their formation remain uncertain.[17] Various evidences, both internal

---

14. Firth, "The Teaching of the Psalms," 163. Again, Firth does not use the terms *generic or whole-text illocutions* but the concepts are clearly implied. One of Firth's significant contributions to the discussion is his explanation of how the imprecatory psalms functioned in the context of the final editing of the Psalter. However, Firth is not explicit regarding their function in the Christian canon. In an earlier work, Firth concludes that the prayers are appropriate, and implicitly endorses their continued appropriation. He concludes, "But what these psalms seek to do is to encourage an attitude that rejects the right to human violence. It encourages a position of powerlessness among the faithful so that they may trust instead in the power of Yahweh." (D. G. Firth, *Surrendering Retribution in the Psalms: Responses to Violence in the Individual Complaints* (Milton Keynes: Authentic Media, 2005), 141.)

15. As I discussed above.

16. J. Day, *Crying for Justice: What the Psalms Teach Us About Mercy and Vengeance in an Age of Terrorism* (Grand Rapids: Kregel, 2005), 22-24.

17. H. Gunkel and J. Begrich, *Introduction to Psalms: The Genres of the Religious Lyric*

and external, suggest this function: examples throughout the Old Testament of psalms being used in cultic practice; the superscriptions of the psalms; the mention of ritual activities within the psalms themselves and the antiphonal quality of many of the psalms.[18] As Firth has mentioned, the very presence of the psalms in the Psalter is evidence of their communal significance. A primary illocution of the Psalter with respect to this particular feature, is the *invitation* to "pray like this."[19] In the course of the discussion I will argue that the Psalter presents itself as something more than a collection of prayers intended to shape worship, but that it does present itself in at least that way. Wilson comments:

> The psalms are no longer just songs to be sung in worship or even heartfelt prayers with which we resonate emotionally in our own heart. Even more, they are a source of God's word to us—a word that must be considered carefully and incorporated daily into the very fabric of our lives. Beyond being models for our own prayers to God, the psalms, when meditated upon, become texts in which God speaks to us in all parts of our being . . .[20]

It is commonly suggested that Psalms 1 and 2 form an introduction to the Psalter and, as such, are intended to inform its reading strategy.[21] Childs argues that this redactional move presents the psalms both as God's word and as a medium through which God's people can respond to him:

> A clear hermeneutical guideline has been offered to the canonical function of the Psalter by the role assigned to Ps. 1 as an introduction to the corpus. The editorial positioning of this original Torah psalm has provided the psalm with a new interpretative function. As an introduction it designates those prayers which follow as the medium through which Israel now responds to the divine word. Because

---

*of Israel* (Macon: Mercer University Press, 1998). See also Mowinckle who argues for an exclusively cultic generative context (S. Mowinckel, *The Psalms in Israel's Worship* (Grand Rapids: Eerdmans 2004).

18. See J. F. D. Creach, "The Psalms and the Cult," in *Interpreting the Psalms: Issues and Approaches* (ed. P. S. Johnston and D. G. Firth; Leicester: Apollos, 2005).

19. See Barker, "Divine Illocutions," 14.

20. G. H. Wilson, *Psalms* (Grand Rapids: Zondervan, 2002), 100. Demonstrating this duality is the burden of Wallace's work in, Wallace, *Words to God*. See also B. S. Childs, *Old Testament Theology in a Canonical Context* (Philadelphia: Fortress Press, 1986), 209-210.

21. See D. M. J. Howard, "Recent Trends in Psalms Study," in *The Face of Old Testament Studies: A Survey of Contemporary Approaches* (ed. D. W. Baker and B. T. Arnold; Grand Rapids: Baker, 1999). P. D. Miller, *Interpreting the Psalms* (Philadelphia: Fortress Press, 1986). Wilson, however, has famously rejected this proposal for including Psalm 2 as part of the introduction to the Psalter, arguing that it originally functioned as the introduction to books I-III which "sought to establish a strong messianic reading" of them. (Wilson, "The Structure of the Psalter," 232-233.) For a response to Wilson, see D. M. Howard, *The Structure of Psalms 93-100* (Winona Lake: Eisenbrauns, 1997); D. C. Mitchell, *The Message of the Psalter: An Eschatological Programme in the Books of Psalms* (Sheffield: Sheffield Press, 1997).

Israel continues to hear God's word through the voice of the psalmist's response, these prayers now function as the divine word itself. Israel's prayers are not simply spontaneous musings or uncontrolled aspirations, but an answer to God's prior speaking which continues to address Israel in the Torah. The redactional position of Ps. 1 testifies that a hermeneutical shift has taken place and that the prayers of Israel which are directed to God have themselves become identified with God's fresh word to his people. The prayers are indeed the response of Israel, but offered in a continuous conversation with God through the use of this tradition.[22]

Childs' comments regarding the position of Psalm 1 supports the above observation that the Psalter is "fashioned for worship" or in his words, that the Psalter presents itself as "the medium through which Israel now responds to the divine word." Additionally, the introductory function of Psalms 1 and 2 present the Psalms themselves as *torah*.[23] Brueggemann suggests that the Psalter thus presents itself as a book to be read "through the prism of *torah* obedience."[24] The shaping of the Psalter into five books, the repeated presence of *"torah"* psalms and the introduction of the Psalms 1 and 2 are evidence that the Psalter is to be read as divine instruction.[25] Mays concurs:

> As introduction to the book, Psalm 1 invites us to expect and receive *torah* from the psalms, that is, to read them as Scripture. The reader will come upon two other great witnesses to *torah* piety in Psalms 19 and 119 . . .. Indeed, Psalm 1 wants the whole to be read as instruction—instruction in prayer, in praise, in God's way with us and our way under God.[26]

Psalm 1 with its invitation to blessing and life through a meditation on *torah* is implicitly an invitation to mediate on the contents of the Psalter. It is here that blessing will be found through an engagement with God and his instruction. Through its connection to Psalm 2, the invitation to righteousness and blessing in Psalm 1 becomes an invitation to loyalty to the king and an invitation to take refuge in him. The Psalter thus begins with an eschatological and existential focus reminding the reader of Yahweh's sovereignty, the reality of

---

22. Childs, *Old Testament Theology*, 207-208.
23. Cf. Ps. 1:2; See M. LeFebvre, "Torah Meditation in the Psalms," in *Interpreting the Psalms: Issues and Approaches* (ed. P. S. Johnston and D. G. Firth; Leicester: Apollos, 2005), 225. LeFebvre also argues that genres of wisdom and *torah* are inappropriate because hope, rather than obedience, is the primary point. He also wants to argue that *torah* is a strict reference to the Mosaic Law and does not justify Psalm 1 or the Psalter being classified as "instruction." As demonstrated above, I find this conclusion unconvincing.
24. W. Brueggemann, "Bounded by Obedience and Praise: The Psalms as Canon," *JSOT* 50 (1991).
25. The presence of divine illocutions at the generic level will be addressed in later discussion.
26. J. L. Mays, *Psalms* (Louisville: John Knox Press, 1994), 42.

divine judgment and the question of whether the readers will find themselves "standing" at the end. It is a reminder of the ever-present conflict in Yahweh's kingdom due to the presence of rebellious subjects and that Yahweh will, inevitably, vindicate His king. Miller comments on Psalm 2:

> In a marvellous piece of anthropomorphic imagery the narrator speaks of the loud and derisive laughter of God challenging the pretensions of human power (v. 4). The divine laughter is a vivid pointer to the sovereignty of God and the Lord's invulnerability to all human machinations, even those of the most powerful. In a strange way it is one of the most assuring sounds of the whole Psalter as it relativises even the largest of human claims for ultimate control over the affairs of peoples and nations. The fiercest terror is made the object of laughter and derision and thus is rendered impotent to frighten those who hear the laughter of God in the background.[27]

Therefore, Psalms 1 and 2 offer a reading strategy for the Psalter by providing a number of its primary illocutions.[28] Firstly, as mentioned above, the Psalter *invites*. It is an invitation to meditation, to blessing, to life, to submission to Yahweh and his king,[29] and to refuge.[30] The fact that most of the Psalter is then comprised of prayers and songs that are directed to Yahweh indicates that it *invites imitation*. It *offers these responses* as appropriate, even "righteous",[31] in similar situations.[32]

Secondly, the Psalter *warns*. It warns against surrounding oneself with foolish counsel, against siding with those who oppose Yahweh and his king, and warns of the temporality of human life and the certainty of judgement. It *warns* that a refuge is necessary. These illocutions of *invitation and warning* are primary illocutions of the Psalter. However, as noted above, there are other primary

---

27. Miller, *Interpreting the Psalms*, 90.

28. This list is not meant as comprehensive, rather the most significant generic illocutions are highlighted along with those important for the subsequent discussion of imprecation.

29. Note Gerald Wilson's influential claim that the Psalter both criticizes the limits of the Davidic king and at the same time affirms that only Yahweh is king. For Wilson, this assertion is the climax and centrepiece of the Psalter (Wilson, *The Editing of the Hebrew Psalter*, 215.) For additional discussion in support of this thesis see Mays, *The Lord Reigns*.Various elements of Wilson's thesis have been greatly disputed, particularly his claim that the Davidic kingship is portrayed as a failure. The presence of strongly Davidic psalms in Book V (e.g., Pss. 110, 132, and 144) largely undermines his claim. For a critique of Wilson see D. Starling, "The Messianic Hope in the Psalms," *RTR* 58, no. 3 (1999). Whybray, *Psalms*, 99. In either case, there is no dispute that one of the central claims of the Psalter is that Yahweh reigns.

30. Brueggemann, "Bounded by Obedience and Praise," 66. See also J. F. D. Creach, *Yahweh as Refuge and the Editing of the Hebrew Psalter* (Sheffield: Sheffield Press, 1996).

31. Psalm 1:5–6.

32. Implicitly and through its connection with the ensuing prayers, the introduction performs a generic illocution asserting that Yahweh will be listening.

illocutions performed by the introductory psalms. These would include the reminder that Yahweh is sovereign, that his purposes will be fulfilled and all opposition to him will be silenced. Related to this is the reminder that the world in which the readers find themselves is not the way it will always be. There will be vindication for God's people. In this way, the Psalter *offers hope*.

*The Macro-Structure of the Psalter* The introductory psalms offer a reading strategy through the performance of primary illocutions, yet this is not the only way that primary illocutions are enacted. I suggest that the internal macrostructure of the Psalter also produces illocutionary force.

While a comprehensive discussion of recent proposals regarding the shaping of the Psalter is beyond the scope of this project, of particular interest is Brueggemann's suggestion that the Psalter oscillates between orientation, disorientation and reorientation.[33] The presence of such oscillation produces a number of possible generic illocutions.

Firstly, it shapes the expectations of the readers. The wide diversity of experiences reflected in the Psalter and the content and questions of the "wisdom" psalms both contribute to this shaping. Brueggemann notes that it offers language at the limits of our common experience:

> In the Psalms, we have transmitted to us ways of speaking which are appropriate to the extremities of human experience as known concretely in Israel. Or, to use Ricoeur's language, we have "limit expressions" (laments, songs of celebration) which match "limit experiences" (disorientation, reorientation). The use of the Psalms in one's own life and in ministry depends on making a genuine and sensitive match between expression and experience. The enduring authority of this language is in the combination that it bears witness to common human experience, but it is at the same time practiced in this concrete community with specific memories and hopes. Thus the openness to the universal and the passion for the concrete come together in these poems.[34]

Similarly, it assists the reader in both understanding and accepting the reality of their current experience by "affirming" and "naming" such experience. Brueggemann comments, "the Psalms bring human experience to sufficiently vivid expression so that it may be embraced as the real situation in which persons must live."[35]

Secondly, it raises the question of whether each response is an equally "appropriate" place to be or perhaps to even remain for a time. More specifically, should the shape of our current experience always end in similar fashion to the Psalter?[36]

---

33. W. Brueggemann, *The Psalms and the Life of Faith* (Minneapolis: Fortress Press, 1995), 6-15.
34. Brueggemann, "Psalms and the Life of Faith," 16.
35. Brueggemann, "Psalms and the Life of Faith," 18.
36. This question will be discussed below with respect to Brueggemann's treatment

The function of the conclusion to the Psalter thus warrants reflection. Is the purpose of this conclusion to move the reader to this place of praise? Brueggemann suggests that a dialectical relationship is intended with Psalm 1:

> The obedience required in Psalm 1 is nowhere mentioned or on the horizon of Psalm 150. In the vision of the shapers of the Psalter, obedience has been overcome, transcended and superseded in the unfettered yielding of Psalm 150. Though obedience is the beginning point of the Psalter and insisted upon with great severity, by Psalm 150 the rigors of obedience have all been put behind the praising community. Obedience is indeed the premise and condition of praise; only the obedient can praise this God. Obedience, however, is only a beginning point beyond which the faithful characteristically move. As Israel moves from commandment to communion, the weight of duty is overridden by the delight of lyrical community with God. Obedience is a base for Israel's life with God, but those who enter into this glad communion with Yahweh are so in tune, so delighted in covenant, so in love, so eager to make response to Yahweh's sovereignty, that no explicit requirement is any longer present. The relation between the two Psalms is a dialectical one: a) only the obedient can praise; b) in praise, the community transcends obedience for the sake of joyous communion. The two propositions are in deep tension, but the second does not cancel out the first. . . . . Life lived in the context of the Psalter is the move from obedience to lyric, from response to abandonment, from duty to delight. The lyric of Psalm 150 continues to affirm and trust the moral coherence of Psalm 1, but is no longer preoccupied with that moral coherence.[37]

Brueggemann's conception of the relationship between Psalms 1 and 150 seems paradoxical. He suggests that the move is from obedience to praise and that the end of the psalm is no longer "preoccupied with that moral coherence." However, the relationship between the two displays more continuity than he allows. If the introduction invites obedience and meditation on the Psalter (and in particular, loyalty to Yahweh and his king), then Psalm 150 is a climactic expression of this obedience. Both Psalms 1 and 150 invite the reader to join with the voice of the psalmist, Psalm 1 in reference to the praise and lament contained in the Psalter and Psalm 150 as the climactic expression of the former.

The function of Psalm 150 as the conclusion to the Psalter is enhanced, as Brueggemann notes, by its unique features. Its lack of any internal reasoning and its persistent summons to all of creation (including the reader) invite reflection and response on the content and praxis of the entire Psalter. In Psalm 150 the eschatological nature of the Psalter is again in focus as it was in Psalm 1,[38] with

---

of imprecation.

37. Brueggemann, "Bounded by Obedience and Praise," 69-71.

38. For a defence of the messianic and eschatological intent of the Psalter see D. C. Mitchell, "Lord, Remember David: G H Wilson and the Message of the Psalter," *VT* 56, no. 4 (2006); Mitchell, *The Message of the Psalter*.

the expectation that this will indeed be the final result. In appropriating the words of Psalm 150, "Praise Yahweh", the reader thus enacts this psalm "early." This has the effect of *realizing that eschatological reality* in the very re-illocution of praise.[39] The oscillation of the Psalter that moves to a crescendo of praise furthermore *reminds* the reader of this imminent future and thus *creates hope*. The question of the extent to which this oscillation and final destination marginalize earlier experiences and responses will form part of the discussion below.

*The Canonical Imposition of the Psalter*  As previously suggested, the Psalter both *invites* and *confronts* the reader through its invitation to mimesis. While the reader may not be able to echo the psalmist due to the disparity in their current circumstance, the Psalter questions whether the reader has had (and will have) this response to such circumstances. It invites us to commit to its speech acts. In a section entitled "The Psalms as Speech Acts", Wenham comments on this function:

> Singing [the psalms] commits us in attitudes, speech, and actions ... Praying the psalms involves the worshipper in many commissive speech acts: the psalms as prayers are really a series of vows. This is what sets them apart from other biblical texts with an ethical dimension.[40]

On the one hand, the Psalter offers its great diversity to the reader and the community in order for them to appropriate psalms that best "fit" their circumstance, and on the other, it prepares them for new and other circumstances unlike the present. This justifies both a strategic reading of the Psalter for contextually appropriate psalms and a continuous-canonical reading that allows the Psalter to "impose" itself on the reader.[41] Furthermore, it is only by allowing such an imposition that the reader will develop a "Psalter consciousness" enabling them to read strategically when necessary. Thus, the Psalter invites both a strategic reading and a continuous-canonical reading. The latter allows the Psalter to impose itself, not only providing a level of consciousness regarding the variety of possible responses, but by also confronting the reader's praxis in whether they access the limits of appropriate (righteous) response. This "imposition" of a canonical reading (as opposed to a selective or strategic one) functions as a corrective to a truncated spirituality. Thus, the illocutionary force of the canonical shape is one of *invitation to mimesis*, which carries with it an embedded *invitation to self-reflection* if one cannot or will not echo the voice of the Psalter in the context of similar situations. Wilson states:

---

39. See J. Goldingay, *Psalms. Volume 3, Psalms 90-150* (Grand Rapids: Baker, 2008), 746-750.

40. Wenham, *The Psalter Reclaimed*, 25-28.

41. Eugene Peterson speaks of this imposition when he describes the rhythm of the psalms: ." . . we pray better, and best, when we let the rhythms of the creating word of God work themselves into the rhythms of our living, and then find expression in the psalmic rhythms of prayer." (E. H. Peterson, *Answering God: The Psalms as Tools for Prayer* (1st ed.; San Francisco: Harper & Row, 1989), 60.)

Reading the psalms from beginning to end forces us to set aside our own preconceptions and calls us to lay aside our own perceived needs as the driving force of our encounter with the psalms. Such openness allows God's freedom to challenge, confront and ultimately transform us in ways we do not control or even expect. The clear shift from dominant lament in the first half of the Psalter to predominant praise and thanksgiving in the last half indicates that we are called to live in a real world of undeniable suffering and pain. Yet lament is not God's final word. Thus it is appropriate that the Hebrew title of the Psalter is *Tehillim*, 'Praises'.[42]

Furthermore, a continuous-canonical reading confronts the reader with the communal and individual nature of the psalms. This contributes further illocutionary force to the Psalter through its invitation to the reader to reflect and respond not only on their own situation, but also on that of their community and "neighbour."

*Literary Features and Primary Illocution*
*Democratization* The democratization of the Psalter is another feature of its canonical form that produces primary illocutionary force, in many ways supporting the invitation to mimesis. This democratization is pervasive throughout the Psalter, occurring in a number of ways, one of which is its self-involving language. Readers of the Psalter have noted its invitation to appropriate the voice of the psalmist (i.e., the "I" and "we" of the Psalter).[43] More recently it has been recognized that this self-involving language has a transformative power and "fits" neatly with contemporary views of communication. Nasuti comments:

> As I have noted elsewhere, such a "sacramental" or "transformative" view of the Psalms not only fits well with Mowinckel's views of the cult; it is also very much in keeping with certain contemporary views of the way that language works, including speech-act theory and the work of such scholars as Paul Ricouer and Ludwig Wittgenstein. It also fits well with those theologians who see Scripture in general as having sacramental or transformative power, even though these scholars do not always work out the special dynamics of the Psalms."[44]

---

42. Wilson, "The Structure of the Psalter," 246.

43. Mays comments that while this language is indeed self-involving, there is perhaps a difference between contemporary appropriation of this language and the appropriation of it in ancient Israel. He notes that the "I" of ancient Israel would have been understood in the context of the group. (Mays, *The Lord Reigns*, 52.) See also K. Moller, "Reading, Singing and Praying the Law: An Exploration of the Performative, Self-Involving, Commissive Language of Psalm 101," in *Reading the Law* (New York: T&T Clark, 2007), 111-137; A. C. Cottrill, *Language, Power, and Identity in the Lament Psalms of the Individual* (London: Continuum, 2008), Chapter 1.

44. H. P. Nasuti, "God at Work in the World: A Theology of Divine-Human

Furthermore the ubiquitous and unnamed "enemies" of the psalmist and of Yahweh's king invite a "surplus of meaning." Grant comments:

> Psalms are purposefully unspecific about their historical details and setting. The psalmist may well plead his cause before God because of his enemies, but we are not told who these enemies are . . .
> Psalms were, in the main, deliberately written to be as broadly applicable as possible. The psalms are originally poetic accounts of humankind speaking to God, yet through their canonization these have become the Word of God spoken to his people. Based firmly in this idea of humanity in relationship with God, the psalms express every emotion conceivable (confidence, despair, joy, trust, etc.) and the whole point is that this expression of human emotion directed towards God is available to be adapted to a wide variety of circumstances . . . The point is that the prince and pauper have equal access to the God of creation and covenant . . . This is called democratization – the words written by a *specific* individual grounded in specific circumstances can be appropriated by *all* people in a *wide variety* of circumstances as they adopt the expression of the psalmist's thoughts and emotions to reflect their own.[45]

As Grant suggests, democratization is an important feature of the text that supports the Psalter's primary illocutions of mimesis by encouraging readers to appropriate the language as their own.

*Psalms as Poetry*   The poetic nature of the psalms also bears an inherent illocutionary force. Jeannine Brown observes that the poetry of the psalms is chosen, in part for its ability to evoke a holistic response its readers:

> Poetry is often chosen as a genre to express or evoke an emotive response. Whether expressing adoration, anger or grief, the psalmists choose poetry because it is eminently suitable for such expression. Our response then will not be adequate if we stop at a cognitive understanding of a psalm. The call is to respond holistically: emotionally, volitionally and cognitively. In the end, anticipating the kind of impact a certain genre makes should be part of our generic reading strategy.[46]

This observation reflects an ever-present tension in the engagement with the Psalter. In parallel with the prior discussion of a "strategic" versus a "continual-canonical" reading of the Psalter, there is a tension between an "emotive"

---

Encounter in the Psalms," in *Soundings in the Theology of Psalms: Perspectives and Methods in Contemporary Scholarship* (ed. R. A. Jacobson; Minneapolis: Fortress Press, 2011), 35.

45. J. A. Grant, "The Psalms and the King," in *Interpreting the Psalms: Issues and Approaches* (ed. P. S. Johnston and D. G. Firth; Leicester: Apollos, 2005), 110. See also Miller, *Interpreting the Psalms*, 22-23.

46. Brown, "Genre Criticism," 143. See also P. C. Craigie, *Psalms 1-50* (Waco: Word, 1983), 35-36.

and "reasoned" engagement.⁴⁷ The strategic reading functions best when the reader automatically appropriates the words of the Psalter as an immediate response to their current circumstance. At this point, an "emotive" element to the response is rightly elevated. On the other hand, a "reasoned" and sustained engagement of the Psalter allows for a level of reflection not possible when appropriating the psalms in prayer. The self-presentation of the Psalter, encourages both forms of engagement. The emotive engagement is invited through the genre of poetry and the reasoned engagement through the presentation of these poems in a structured book. The primary illocutions formed by the choice of poetry at the very least include a warrant for a passionate dialogue with God and recognize that our ability to adequately capture this response is limited. Wallace comments in this regard:

> ... the Book of Psalms consistently presents its prayers in poetic form and the impact and importance of this should not be overlooked ... Poetry aims to go beyond the ordinary. ... Poetry transcends the bounds of this framework in order to explore more deeply the nature of reality itself. ... First, it is a transcending of outer boundaries, those which mark the limits of what we know, perceive, or experience. Secondly, it is a transcending of our inner boundaries, those which determine how we see ourselves in relation to the world and God. ... Another aspect of poetry relevant to our consideration of prayer concerns the words, phrases, and expressions used. As I noted above, poetry employs language richer in metaphor, symbol, and imagery than prose. It does not try to express wholeness by describing something completely or exhaustively. It seeks to be succinct, employing a minimum of words, to expose and explore the heart of things.⁴⁸

*Yahweh Reigns as a Primary Illocution*
As mentioned above, "Yahweh reigns" is clearly a central theme of the Psalter, occupying a significant location in its structure. The location of the מלך יהוה psalms and the inclusion of this theme throughout the Psalter at key literary moments suggests that this declaration is a primary illocution. This illocutionary stance is consistent with the primary illocution inviting mimesis, as the praxis of the Psalter presupposes that Yahweh is sovereign, that He hears the cries of His people, that He remembers His covenant promises, and that He can and will act to save His people. Through the authentic imitation of the Psalter, God's people declare that He is King.

---

47. This is not to suggest that there is ever a clear distinction between the two, it is rather a matter of an elevated engagement with respect to one element.
48. Wallace, *Words to God*, 49–50.

*Summary of Primary Illocutions of the Psalter in its Old Testament Context*
At its broadest level the Psalter invites mimesis and creates hope. Conversely, it warns against rejecting Yahweh and his king and rebukes responses at odds with those it presents. The introduction to the Psalter invites the reader to engage with it as God's instruction and to imitate the responses in similar circumstances. A psalm's invitation to mimesis is performed not only in its relation to the introduction, but by its very inclusion within the Psalter. By appropriating the responses of the Psalter in similar situations, the reader is, in turn, invited to adopt its illocutionary stances. More specifically, this mimesis invites the reader and the community to be loyal to Yahweh and his king and to proclaim that Yahweh alone is worthy to be praised. Similarly, it calls the reader to recognize that Yahweh is the only one to whom their requests for deliverance and refuge should be directed.

The movements across the macro-structure also contribute to the illocutionary force of the Psalter in that they reflect the "limits" of human experience. Consequently, the Psalter affirms these situations and responses while shaping the expectations of God's people. The broader movement from lament to praise or "reorientation" calls the reader to remember that Yahweh reigns and that his kingdom and rule will extend throughout all creation. The invitation to praise at the conclusion of the Psalter reminds the reader of this reality and creates hope.

Significant literary features of the Psalter support its primary illocutionary stances. The choice of poetic form encourages a passionate response on the one hand while recognizing its inherent limitations on the other. That the psalms employ self-involving language and display a democratization of their circumstances further supports the invitation to mimesis.

## Various Conceptions of Dual Authorship in the Psalms

I noted that historic and recent discussions of how Scripture functions as God's word lacked precision with respect to both terminology and methodology. While this continues to be the case vis-à-vis the Psalter, a few authors have raised the issue in recent years.

As discussed, Wolterstorff's work offers a level of hermeneutic detail previously lacking and his proposal makes significant improvements to the discussion.[49] He argues cogently for the appropriation of Scripture as divine discourse and his use of speech act theory to that end is illuminating. However, while he has described and clarified the issues relating to dual authorship and additionally offered helpful lines of inquiry, his proposal falls short of offering hermeneutic clarity. This is highlighted in his treatment of the psalms where he acknowledges lower-level, intratextual illocutions yet does not grapple with how the psalms might function (and so be appropriated) at higher literary

---

49. Chapter 2 offered a detailed assessment of his proposal.

levels. Consequently, the ability of his hermeneutic to assist exegesis is limited.[50] Before offering my explanation of how the psalms function as divine discourse, a brief survey of other approaches will be presented. While there has been a continual lack of clarity regarding how the psalms function as divine discourse, that they offer a place to reflect on the problem of dual authorship has long been recognised. Bonhoeffer's summation of the conundrum is well known, "The Holy Scripture is the Word of God to us. But prayers are the words of men. How do prayers then get into the Bible? . . . are these prayers to God also God's own word?"[51]

*The Words of God are the Words of the Psalmist and the Words of the Pray-er*
Wallace proposes a clarification for how the psalms are an instance of divine discourse.[52] He suggests a blurring of boundaries where the direct words of God recorded in the psalm are juxtaposed with the response and reflection of the psalmist, often without any textual markers. This has the effect of "blurring" the boundary between the two voices. The appropriation of the psalm on the lips of God's people is the final stage in this process where the distinction in voice is entirely lost and subsumed in the voice of the pray-er:

> In each set of verses there is free movement between the psalmist speaking about God and the direct quotation of God's words without indication of the change. This is in contrast to other literatures where the 'authoritative word' is set apart from the rest of the dialogue in order to maintain its authoritative and timeless nature. The blurring of the edges in the psalms between what the psalmist says and what God says thus gives authority to the psalmist's dialogue . . .
> As we take up the psalms as prayers we enter this arena of 'blurred boundaries'. We can pray with the psalmist, but the psalmist's words are blurred with God's words. Our words become blurred with the psalmist's and with God's. This gives the psalms as prayers an authority not experienced in other prayers. The pray-er takes up the words of God to pray to God. In the Christian context, it is thus easy for the pray-er to enter imaginatively into these prayers as the

---

50. This will be highlighted in the exegetical discussion of the next chapter.
51. D. Bonhoeffer, *Psalms: The Prayer Book of the Bible* (Minneapolis: Augsburg, 1970), 13-15. Of course, there are those who reject the conundrum *a priori*, yet it is my working presupposition that a theological interpretation of Scripture needs to account for how the whole of Scripture, in its various forms, functions as divine discourse. Brueggemann disagrees, "The Psalms, with a few exceptions, are not the voice of God addressing us. They are rather the voice of our own common humanity—gathered over a long period of time, but a voice that continues to have amazing authenticity and contemporaneity." (W. Brueggemann, *Praying the Psalms: Engaging the Scripture and the Life of the Spirit* (Milton Keynes: Paternoster, 2007), 2.)
52. Wallace, *Words to God*. Wallace also notes the "incarnational nature of God's word" and while this is a common parallel, it is not clear whether the incarnation of Christ is either a justified or clarifying parallel in any way.

The Divine Illocutions of the Psalter in Its Old Testament Context    123

prayers of Christ; to be able to pray them because Christ prays them and because they have been given to us to pray. We are disciplined in our prayer by the prayers of Christ.[53]

Wallace's description of voices in the Psalter requires some clarification. Although various verses within a psalm may be directly attributed to God, this is not inconsistent with the assertion that the whole of the psalm can also be attributed to God. A problematic aspect of Wallace's explanation is that it does not account for various levels of speech. In speech act terminology, the appropriation of these intratextual illocutions would vary, depending on the voice present.[54] How, for example, do the many cries to God function as God's own voice? Ultimately, while Wallace's explanation affirms the Psalter as divine discourse, it leaves open the possibility that only parts of it can be legitimately counted as such. His attempt to attribute all of the illocutions directly to God requires more explanation.

*The Words of God are No Longer the Words of the Psalmist*

Whereas most of the discussion regarding dual authorship seeks to understand how human words become the words of God, Turner believes that in the case of psalms there is license to "break" with whatever the human author meant in their production.[55] In a somewhat ironic move, Turner marginalizes the illocutions of the human author in psalms and other wisdom literature by suggesting that in the case of these genres the intention of the human author is of little value. This is in contrast to epistolary content, where he suggests that one must attend to the "context-embedded" issues:

> On any view that the letter, appropriated as canon, represents *divine* discourse, we would need to ask about the relationship between God's speaking and (say) Paul's. The major discussion of this issue by Wolterstorff does not suggest any marginalisation of authorial discourse meaning ... Either way, however, there is no reason to believe that to speak of divine discourse implies that God abstracted Paul's 'text' from his context-embedded discourse meanings in such a way that we can cheerfully refill his words with substantially different meanings, or limit the text's meaning to such as might be provided by canonical contexts alone. Had Paul written interpreter-open psalms/proverbs/wisdom-speech, designed for all to use in different ways, we could readily make a break with whatever he meant in the context in which he first coined such utterances. But divine appropriation of writings of the *letter* genre itself implies that the

---

53. Wallace, *Words to God*, 73-74.
54. This "blurring" of voices in the text is also found in the prophets. For a discussion of this feature in the book of Jeremiah see Shead, *A Mouth Full of Fire*, 107-146.
55. Turner appears to have little concern for creating what Wolterstorff described as a "wax nose" of Scripture.

context-embedded issues remain relevant to discourse meaning (for that is the very nature of letters).[56]

While it is certainly the case that the psalms are designed to be appropriated by future generations in varied contexts, this does not justify an indifference to the speech acts that they are performing. Unless there is no possibility of misappropriation, then attending to how the human authors (here I include the editors of the psalter) envisaged the psalm to function is a critical step in the hermeneutic.

*The Words of God in the Presentation of the Psalms*

Zenger and Childs both suggest that a consideration of way the psalms are presented is indispensable for a theological interpretation. Although they do not employ speech act theory, they focus on what are effectively higher-level, generic illocutions. Consequently, their work both contributes to and is clarified by a speech act hermeneutic. Zenger comments:

> [imprecatory] psalms confront us with the reality of violence and, especially, with the problem of the perpetrators of this suffering and their condemnation by the judgment of God. In the process, they very often compel us to confess that *we ourselves* are violent, and belong among the *perpetrators* of the violence lamented in these psalms. *In that way*, these psalms are God's revelation, because in them, in a certain sense, God in person confronts us with the fact that there are situations of suffering in this world of ours in which such psalms are the last thing left to suffering human beings—as protest, accusation, and cry for help.[57]

Zenger notes that the psalms, and in this case the imprecatory psalms, are God's revelation in that he uses them to challenge the reader or pray-er to consider their own complicity in the violence that surrounds them. They also function at this level as God's reminder to the reader that these psalms are a "legitimate" last resort.

In a similar manner, Childs has noted that the presentation of the Psalter in its canonical form should effect our understanding of its function in ancient Israel, and so form the basis for a theological interpretation of the psalms:

> At times the attempt to recover a modern theological dimension has been fairly successful (cf. Barth). At other times one has the impression that the real exegetical and hermeneutical problems raised by the historical critical method have been glossed over. At least the suggestion is not too helpful that one seek to discover the

---

56. M. Turner, "Historical Criticism and Theological Hermeneutics of the New Testament," in *Between Two Horizons: Spanning New Testament Studies and Systematic Theology* (ed. J. B. Green and M. Turner; Grand Rapids: Eerdmans, 2000), 55-56.

57. E. Zenger, *A God of Vengeance? Understanding the Psalms of Divine Wrath* (Louisville: Westminster, 1996), 85, emphasis original.

spiritual meaning which is 'buried under the surface meaning of the text' (Drijvers, 12). In my judgment, the theological response to the challenge raised by Gunkel and his followers must be offered in a far more rigorous manner. It must be pursued from a very different vantage point, rather than seeking an easy compromise. Again it is my thesis that modern interpretation of the Psalter suffers from not dealing seriously with the role of the canon as it has shaped this religious literature.[58]

Childs calls for a rigorous response to the questions raised by both historical criticism and those proposing a theological interpretation of the Psalter. He suggests that the way forward in this discussion needs to consider the canonical shape of the Psalter which both justifies the project of theological interpretation and will provide a level of engagement previously lacking by those who offer "spiritual" interpretations of the text. While supporting a theological interpretation of the Psalter, Childs does not, however, offer much detail on how the Psalter functions as divine discourse, but notes that it is presented as God's law.[59]

The peculiar nature of the psalms as words from God in the form of words to God has not gone unnoticed. However, a clear understanding of how these two voices coincide is largely undeveloped. Utilizing speech act theory to this end will provide the discussion with a level of clarity and detail previously lacking. In particular, the categories of generic and whole-text illocutions will prove helpful in accounting for divine illocutions in the Psalter.

## Conclusion: Divine Illocutions and the Psalter

For individual psalms and the Psalter to be an instance of God's word means that God performs illocutions through them. Identifying these illocutions is therefore critical to offering a theological interpretation of the Psalter. Understanding how the Psalter initially functioned as divine discourse will enable discussion in subsequent chapters of how the Psalter might continue to function as divine discourse.

The previous discussion has focused on illocutions that occur at the whole-text levels of psalm and Psalter. The reason for this emphasis was twofold. Firstly, understanding the function of psalm (i.e., its overall meaning) is directly related to the whole-text illocutions in play at the level of the Psalter. Any lower-level illocutions are formed in this context. Consequently, an understanding of the Psalter's primary illocutions is fundamental to interpretation. While this is, in part, a circular relationship,[60] the illocutionary stance of the

---

58. Childs, *Introduction*, 511.
59. Childs argues that the function of Psalm 1 presents the Psalter as the words of God to his people (Childs, *Introduction*, 513).
60. This "circularity" is common to all interpretive endeavours as an understanding of the parts contribute to an understanding of the whole. Cf. G. R. Osborne, *The*

Psalter is a key to understanding the illocutions in play at the level of a psalm. Secondly, I suggest that the clearest way in which the psalms function as divine discourse is through the divine appropriation of the psalms at the whole-text level. How lower-level illocutions (i.e., those occurring within a psalm) count as God's illocutions is, in large part, more indirect and variable. At the very least, the relationship between whole-text and intratextual illocutions is one of affirmation. That is, God affirms the illocutionary stances of the psalmists within the psalms.

The self-presentation of the Psalter suggests that the reader engage it as God's word. A speech act theory based hermeneutic has demonstrated that this occurs most clearly in its whole-text illocutions. That is, *the illocutionary stance of the Psalter can be counted as the illocutionary stance of God.* At this level, there is less confusion about how God might appropriate the illocutions of the Psalter. Earlier I concluded that the human and editorial illocutions of the Psalter included the invitation to mimesis and the instillation of hope. At the same time, the Psalter warns those who would rebel against Yahweh's reign. More specifically, this mimesis invites the reader and the community to be loyal to Yahweh and his king and to proclaim that Yahweh alone is worthy to be praised. Similarly, it calls the reader to recognize that Yahweh is the only one to whom their requests for deliverance and refuge should be directed. In all of these cases, God directly appropriates the human illocutions. Furthermore, God affirms the scope of experiences and corresponding responses, using the Psalter to shape the expectation of His people.

God's appropriation of lower-level, intratextual illocutions is more nuanced. A detailed discussion of this level of illocution will be offered in subsequent chapters, but at the very least, *God affirms the illocutionary stances of the psalmist within the psalm.*

---

*Hermeneutical Spiral: A Comprehensive Introduction to Biblical Interpretation* (Downers Grove: IVP, 2006).

# Chapter 5

# The Theological Interpretation of Imprecatory Psalms

## Introduction

The goal of Part II is to demonstrate the utility of the hermeneutic developed in Part I. The previous chapter explained how the hermeneutic could be applied to the Psalter in order to uncover the divine illocutions in play in the context of the Hebrew Bible. In order to complete the demonstration and offer a contemporary theological interpretation, this chapter will focus on a particular group of psalms and discuss how they function as divine discourse in the context of the Christian canon. The final chapters will then offer detailed exegetical discussions of selected imprecatory psalms in order to prove the usefulness of the proposed hermeneutic at this level.

While any book or genre could have been chosen as the focus of Part II, the imprecatory psalms were selected for a number of reasons. Firstly, the decision to focus on the psalms was a natural one as they offer unique challenges in the discussion of divine discourse. Secondly, the imprecatory psalms feature significantly in the small volume of literature dealing with speech act theory and theological interpretation. Thirdly, as discussed below, the church has often struggled with how the imprecatory psalms function as God's word.

Therefore, it is the burden of this chapter to offer a theological interpretation of the imprecatory psalms by offering an explanation of how these psalms continue to function as divine discourse. It will be concluded that such a theological interpretation supports their continuing use and demonstrates that an *a priori* rejection of imprecation is unjustified.[1] The hermeneutic employed will proceed along the following lines of inquiry:

---

1. Parts of this chapter appear in, K. Barker, "Psalms of the Powerless: A Theological Interpretation of Imprecation," in *Stirred by a Noble Theme: The Book of Psalms in the Life of the Church* (ed. A. G. Shead; Nottingham: IVP, 2013) 205-229.

1. I will examine the "fit" of the imprecatory psalms within the illocutionary stance of the Psalter.[2] The question at this point is how the imprecatory psalms are presented in the Psalter. It will be argued that the illocutionary stance of the Psalter is both consistent with the illocutions of the imprecatory psalms, and is, in fact, formed by them. Furthermore, it will be demonstrated that the Psalter endorses their appropriation.
2. I will then discuss how the illocutionary stance of the Psalter "fits" with that of the New Testament. Particular attention will be given to possible central (supervening) illocutions that could change the conditions in which the Psalter now functions.
3. Finally, I will propose ways in which the imprecatory psalms can currently be counted as the illocutions of God.

## Various Approaches to the Imprecatory Psalms

The various approaches to the imprecatory psalms have been outlined many times and do not require a detailed presentation at this point.[3] While there are numerous treatments of imprecation, the presence of such violent language in the psalms has not received the attention it deserves. Writing in 2005, Firth notes:

> In terms of the biblical research carried out on the theme of violence to date, there has been a serious lacuna in the study of the book [of] Psalms and its perspectives on violence. The major monographs on the subject of violence within the Old Testament by Lohfink and Noort have both concentrated on narrative texts that reflect violent actions. The research of Snyman has been limited to the word חמס, specifically in terms of its use within prophetic pronouncements.

---

2. The "fit" of the imprecatory psalms within the rest of the Old Testament lies outside the scope of this book and does not offer significant advancement. While intertextual and thematic discussions can occur between the Psalter and the remainder of the OT, the OT stance towards the Psalter is found within the Psalter itself. In order to sustain my thesis, the validation of imprecation within the Psalter and within the New Testament is all that is necessary. It will be noted in the discussion below, however, that the imprecatory psalms find their basis in the covenantal promises of God found elsewhere in the OT. For example, the seemingly extreme request for the destruction of Babylonian children in Psalm 137: is based on God's own promise to do so in Isaiah 13:16. For a discussion of imprecation elsewhere in the Old Testament see P. Gilbert, "The Function of Imprecation in Israel's Eighth-Century Prophets," *Dir* 35, no. 1 (2006). Unfortunately, Gilbert's definition of imprecation is inaccurate and his overall thesis suffers as a result.

3. See Day, *Crying for Justice*, 9-35. See also Zenger, *A God of Vengeance?* J. M. LeMon, "Saying Amen to Violent Psalms: Patterns of Prayer, Belief, and Action in the Psalter," in *Soundings in the Theology of Psalms: Perspectives and Methods in Contemporary Scholarship* (ed. R. A. Jacobson; Minneapolis: Fortress Press, 2011).

Thus, although a body of research on violence within the Old Testament has been developing, no treatment of the topic has yet been presented that deals with the issue in the Psalter.[4]

This lacuna is reflected in the frequent marginalization of the imprecatory psalms within both the academy and the church, and is represented by the first approach listed below. Briefly, the various approaches can be categorized as follows:
1. Dismiss them as irrelevant. The first approach is to excise these psalms or parts thereof and ignore them completely. This move is reflected in various liturgies, yet clearly does not account for how these psalms can be considered Christian Scripture.[5]
2. Admit they are canonical, but do not accept them as appropriate for Christians. This position has three variants. First, there are those who believe imprecatory psalms to be expressions of an Old Covenant faith based on Old Covenant promises that are no longer appropriate for the people of God in the church age. In other words, they are consistent with the Psalms and the Old Testament but at odds with the teaching of the New Testament.[6] Francis Watson contends that they "incite hatred" and are never to be appropriated by Christians:

> The implied reader is expected to acquiesce in this judgment, and the text may therefore be said to perform the speech-act of inciting hatred – hatred of a particularly intense and extreme kind ... Christian victims of oppression could never legitimately appropriate this psalm in its entirety, however extreme their sufferings; and its use in Christian liturgical contexts can in no circumstances be justified. Although the psalm as a whole belongs to Christian scripture, it is not permitted to enact its total communicative intention: for all communicative actions embodied in holy scripture are subject to the criteria established by the speech-act that lies at the centre of Christian scripture, the life, death and resurrection of Jesus as the enfleshment and the enactment of the divine Word.[7]

---

4. Firth, *Surrendering Retribution*, 1.

5. The "Notes on the Pointing" which introduces the Psalms in *An Australian Prayer Book* states in note 7: "The following verses may be omitted in the public service at the discretion of the minister: 17.14; 54.5; 55.16-17; 58; 59.6,14; 68.21-23; 69.24-30; 79.10,12; 83.17; 101.6,9; 109.5-19; 137.7-9; 139.19-22; 140.9-11; 143.12." (Anglican Church of Australia, *A Prayer Book for Australia: For Use Together with the Book of Common Prayer (1662) and an Australian Prayer Book (1978)* (Alexandria: Broughton Books, 1995), 306.) For a discussion of Psalms that have been omitted by the Roman Catholic Liturgy of the Hours see W. L. Holladay, *The Psalms through Three Thousand Years: Prayerbook of a Cloud of Witnesses* (Minneapolis: Fortress Press, 1993), 304-315.

6. See D. Kidner, *Psalms 1-72: An Introduction and Commentary* (London: IVP, 1973), 249. See also J. C. Laney, "A Fresh Look at the Imprecatory Psalms," *BSac* 138, no. 549 (1981): 43-44.

7. Watson, *Text and Truth*, 120-121.

Secondly, there are those who believe that they reveal the ugly reality of sinful humanity, in any era, and are to be rejected. C. S. Lewis is famous for his numerous comments to this effect: "we must face both facts squarely. The hatred is there – festering, gloating, undisguised – and also we should be wicked if we in any way condoned or approve it or (worse still) used it to justify similar passions in ourselves."[8]

Thirdly, and in contrast to the first two, some suggest that Christians cannot appropriate these psalms for themselves as Christ is the only legitimate pray-er of these psalms.[9] These three variations recognize the canonical status of the psalms, but do not consider them to function as model prayers.

3. Accept them as a necessary but unrighteous response. Brueggemann epitomizes this more accepting position when he suggests that they are a useful and necessary way for us to engage with our rage and move our way through it.[10] Ultimately though, the prayers of these psalms are not authorized places to "remain" in Brueggemann's estimation:

> My hunch is that there is a way beyond the Psalms of vengeance, but it is a way through them and not around them. And that is because of what in fact goes on with us. Willy-nilly, we are vengeful creatures. Thus these harsh Psalms must be fully embraced as our own. Our rage and indignation must be fully owned and fully expressed. And then (only then) can our rage and indignation be yielded to the mercy of God. In taking this route through them, we take the route God 'himself' has gone. We are not permitted a cheaper, easier, more 'enlightened' way.
>
> There is no or little slippage between what is thought/felt and what is said. The Psalms are immediate.
>
> The cry for vengeance is a powerful part of disorientation . . . There is nothing pious or 'Christian' about his prayer. But (as psychotherapists know), our deep disorientation is not a time when we are able to be genuinely humane toward others because we are singularly attentive to the lack of humanness in our own life.[11]

However, while Brueggemann on the one hand argues that there "is nothing pious or Christian" about these prayers, on the other hand,

---

8. C. S. Lewis, *Reflections on the Psalms* (New York: Harcourt, 1958), 20-22. This sentiment reflects Augustine's allegorical interpretation of the Psalm, which Lewis echoes in his comments on Psalm 137 (Augustine, "Exposition on the Psalms," n.p. [cited February 29 2012]. Online: http://www.newadvent.org/fathers/1801137.htm.).

9. Waltke, "Canonical Process Approach," 13; Bonhoeffer, *Psalms*, 14.

10. Brueggemann's position will be discussed in greater detail in the later sections of this chapter. See also N. L. deClaisse-Walford, "The Theology of the Imprecatory Psalms," in *Soundings in the Theology of Psalms: Perspectives and Methods in Contemporary Scholarship* (ed. R. A. Jacobson; Minneapolis: Fortress Press, 2011), 91-92.

11. Brueggemann, *Praying the Psalms*, 34.

he recognizes the mature spirituality involved in such a response and thus displays an element of contradiction in his own thinking.¹²
4. Accept them as prayers against the sin, but not the sinner. An alternate interpretation accepts the psalms as canonical and accepts their appropriation, but does not accept that we can direct these prayers at people (i.e., "love the sinner, hate the sin"). The imprecatory Psalms are thus understood as prayers that God would judge sin or spiritual forces of evil.¹³ Since He has done so in Christ, the psalms point us to the cross and to forgiveness.¹⁴

For this position to be valid, one would need to demonstrate that it is possible to separate evil and sin from the morally capable beings that commit it. Such a demonstration is not convincing and additionally does not do justice to the specificity found in many of the psalms or in their reappropriation in the New Testament.

5. A righteous response. The imprecatory psalms are accepted as canonical and remain appropriate (even righteous) responses in similar situations. I will be defending this position in the discussion below. Day comments:

> In circumstances of sustained injustice, hardened enmity, and gross oppression, it has always been appropriate for a believer to utter imprecations against enemies or to appeal for the onslaught of divine vengeance. In certain instances today, appeals to God for his curse or vengeance are fitting.¹⁵

---

12. Brueggemann, *Praying the Psalms*, 70.

13. So J. Shepherd, "The Place of the Imprecatory Psalms in the Canon of Scripture," *Chm* 111, no. 2 (1997): 122-123, emphasis mine; D. W. Augsburger, *Hate-Work: Working Through the Pain and the Pleasures of Hate*. (Louisville: Westminster John Knox, 2004), 194; D. M. Nehrbass, *Praying Curses: The Theraputic and Preaching Value of the Imprecatory Psalms*. (Eugene: Pickwick, 2013) 162. Nehrbass suggests they sit somewhere between prescription and description. They are allowed, but not commanded. He comments, "I propose, therefore, that the psalms are a model of prayer, somewhere between prescription and description... But "allowed" is somewhere on the spectrum between descriptive and modelled. To say that something is a model means more than that it is allowed; it implies that the act is also encouraged. Unarguably, the Israelites were encouraged to sing the psalms. So within the prescription/description spectrum, I would place the psalms in the middle with the purpose of modelling prayer." (Nehrbass, *Praying Curses*, 83).

14. H. G. L. Peels, "'I Hate Them with Perfect Hatred' (Psalm 139:21-22)," *TynBul* 59, no. 1 (2008): 48.) So also Bonhoeffer, who fits both in this category and with those who argue for a Christological voice (Bonhoeffer, *Psalms*, 58-60.).

15. Day, *Crying for Justice*, 15-16. See also Zenger, *A God of Vengeance?*, 67; M. Luther, *Works* (American ed.; Saint Louis: Concordia, 1955), 1100. See also G. J. Wenham, *Psalms as Torah: Reading Biblical Song Ethically* (Grand Rapids: Baker, 2012), 167-179.

A more qualified version of this position is offered by Vos, who suggests that for the Old Testament saints, this was a matter of special revelation so that they knew for

This brief survey of responses to the imprecatory psalms will suffice for the moment. In the discussion below, those positions that are deemed most significant will be discussed in greater detail, either due to their explanation of how the Psalter functions or due to the cogency of their argument in contradiction to my own.

## Imprecation and the Illocutionary Stance of the Psalter

*Introduction*
In Chapter 4, it was argued that one of the primary illocutions of the Psalter was its invitation to mimesis with the psalms being offered as righteous responses to similar situations. Consequently, to claim that imprecation represents an inappropriate response to its circumstance one would need to demonstrate that the illocutionary stance of the Psalter vis-à-vis imprecation is distinct from its illocutionary stance vis-à-vis other types of psalms. As I discussed earlier, there is no indication that imprecation is presented in such a distinct manner; therefore, the burden of proof lies with those who make such a claim.

*Imprecation as a Righteous Response*[16]
I suggest that the Psalter offers the imprecatory psalms as righteous responses to their situations. This can be demonstrated by considering their inclusion in the Psalter, their fit with the reading strategy of the Psalter, and their fit with the theology of the Psalter. Consequently, the illocutionary stance of the Psalter should be accepted as commensurate with imprecation.

*Imprecation Fits by Inclusion* To argue that the imprecatory psalms are being presented by the Psalter in a manner different from the other kinds of psalms incurs the burden of proof. C. S. Lewis who, as has been noted, suggests these psalms are reflective of our sinful nature, concedes that imprecation "will not come away clean."[17] In the absence of literary markers or internal asser-

---

certain that the enemy was "reprobate." For Christians, we can never know for certain and therefore can never pray for the eternal judgment of particular persons as that would be both presumptuous and immoral. However, we are allowed, in fact, compelled to pray against evil people and request temporal punishment, short of death. (J. G. Vos, "The Ethical Problem of the Imprecatory Psalms," *WTJ* 4, no. 2 (1942): 138.)

David Firth argues that the imprecatory psalms both offer themselves as righteous responses and set limits for such a response. While their function in the Christian canon is beyond the scope of his work, Firth suggests that their dislocation from the cultic context indicates their instructional value for worship. (Firth, *Surrendering Retribution*, 49-50.)

16. Parts of this section appear in my recently published work, Barker, "Psalms of the Powerless."

17. Lewis, *Reflections*, 24-25.

tions to the contrary, it must be assumed that all of the psalms within the Psalter are offered to the reader in a similar manner.

Furthermore, it is tautologous to suggest that the imprecatory psalms are consistent with the illocutionary stance of the Psalter as they themselves contribute a significant percentage of its content. David Firth comments, "the editorial process may have ensured that only psalms that operated within a given set of theological assumptions remained within the collection, whilst those variations that remain are themselves an intentional element within the instruction of the book."[18] By their very presence within the Psalter, the imprecatory psalms "fit." In speech act terms, the illocutions of the Psalter are, in part, shaped by the illocutions of the imprecatory psalms. It is not surprising then, that the illocutions of the Psalter are not only consistent with imprecation but that they also encourage their appropriation.

*Imprecation as an Authorized Concession?* As mentioned above, there are those who affirm that the imprecatory psalms fit the Psalter, but that the Psalter does not present them as a "righteous" response. They are understood as a necessary way for God's people to respond to injustice, but not necessarily a righteous way. The generative processes of the psalms are used to explain why these psalms do not reflect a higher ethic or a godly response. It is suggested that the psalms are born out of fear and dissonance rather than theological or dogmatic reflection. Brueggemann comments:

> There is no or little slippage between what is thought/felt and what is said. The Psalms are immediate. There is no meditation to "clean up," censor, or filter what is going on. This directness reflects a readiness to risk in an uncalculating way with this one "from whom no secret can be hid." The Psalms dare to affirm that, as there are no secrets hid from God, so there likely is less self-deception at work in these prayers.[19]

> The cry for vengeance is a powerful part of disorientation. Such a cry blames those who have disrupted and demolished the old equilibrium. Thus in addition to the yearning to be saved from the pit, there is the counter-theme of wishing others would be sent there. There is nothing pious or "Christian" about his prayer. But (as psychotherapists know), our deep disorientation is not a time when we are able to be genuinely humane toward others because we are singularly attentive to the lack of humanness in our own life[20]

Strangely, Brueggemann does not appear to have grappled, at this point, with how the canonical formation and presentation of the Psalter affects the way that these psalms now function. The textuality of the psalms allowed the editors of the Psalter to carefully consider and reflect upon the appropriate inclusion of

---

18. Firth, "The Teaching of the Psalms," 162.
19. Brueggemann, *Praying the Psalms*, 53.
20. Brueggemann, *Praying the Psalms*, 34.

imprecation.²¹ Furthermore, their presence in the Psalter encourages a careful meditation on the one hand, and an impassioned appropriation, on the other. That these psalms represent a passionate, raw and uncensored response is not in question. However, the responses of these prayers are more powerful when it is recognized that they have subsequently been studied, authorized and utilized. Passionate response and theological depth are not mutually exclusive qualities. As I discuss below, this is demonstrated in the careful placement of Psalm 137 within the conclusion to the songs of ascent.

*Imprecation Fits the Reading Strategy of the Psalter.* The imprecatory psalms not only fit by inclusion, but they also fit the reading strategy of the Psalter which presents them in a manner similar to other psalms. The previous chapter discussed the illocutions performed in Psalms 1 and 2, which contribute to this reading strategy. Specifically, they present the Psalter as *torah*, divine instruction. I commented earlier that this introduction provides a reading strategy by performing a number of primary illocutions: the invitation to mimesis, to meditation, to life and blessing, and to refuge through a submission to Yahweh as king.²² These primary illocutions performed in the introduction are consistent with the illocutions of imprecation. I have argued elsewhere for this consistency:

> ... all of the imprecatory psalms are consistent with the themes found in Psalm 2, particularly the warning to 'Kiss the Son' or suffer his wrath. As Psalm 2 arguably functions as a type of introduction to the Psalter, the presence of the imprecatory psalms is hardly surprising.²³

The reading strategy of the Psalter presented in Psalms 1 and 2 anticipates contexts of conflict. Those who remain loyal to Yahweh will be at odds with the wicked and with the kings of the earth. Those who remain loyal will need a refuge. Both the invitation to righteousness through meditation on *torah* and the presentation of opposition to Yahweh prepare the reader for the journey of the Psalter. The imprecatory psalms are not unexpected, nor are they left behind along the way, as the "two edged sword" of Psalm 149 indicates. Rather, they serve as reminders of this opposition and as righteous responses to it.

*Imprecation Fits Theologically.* While the imprecatory psalms can be defended on the basis of their very presence within the Psalter, further support for their appropriation is found in their fit within the broader themes or primary illocutions of the Psalter. A number of these primary illocutions were just mentioned vis-à-vis the introduction of the Psalter and include the *declaration* that Yahweh is King and the corresponding *invitation* to remain loyal to him and his anointed. As I stated earlier, the location of the יהוה מלך psalms

---

21. By "textuality" I am referring to their being written rather than solely oral.
22. Chapter 4.
23. Barker, "Divine Illocutions," 11.

and the inclusion of this theme throughout the Psalter at key literary moments, suggests that this declaration be categorized as a primary illocution. This primary illocution is consistent with the illocutions of imprecation in the following ways. Firstly, imprecation is directed to Yahweh, acknowledging him as ruler and rightful judge over all creation. In so doing, it "surrenders retribution" to Yahweh and precludes any acts of personal vengeance.[24] Secondly, imprecation is based upon a desire for Yahweh to be glorified, recognizing that His reputation is at stake if injustice remains unpunished.[25] Thirdly, imprecation recognizes Yahweh's status as covenant Lord and cries out on the basis of His covenant promises. Lastly, imprecation is an act of loyalty as the psalmists seek refuge in Yahweh and distance themselves from the wicked.

The imprecatory psalms are thus offered to the reader as righteous responses to such situations. They are consistent with the Psalter's primary illocutions regarding the reign of Yahweh and model a response that honours Him as King in the midst of violent oppression.

*Summary of Imprecatory Illocutions.* While it is not my purpose in this section to provide an exhaustive taxonomy of the illocutionary acts of imprecation,[26] a number of their generic illocutions match those of the Psalter. The call to righteousness in Psalms 1 and 2 is a call to meditation on *torah* and submission to Yahweh's anointed. This reminds the reader that those who submit to Yahweh will be at odds with the "rulers of the world." It is also a reminder that the judgment of Yahweh's enemies and the vindication of His people are certain. The call to covenant loyalty within the Psalter is reflected in many of the imprecatory psalms, which explicitly name the enemies of the psalmist as the enemies of Yahweh.[27] Wenham summarizes this succinctly: "From the perspective of speech-act theory, we could describe these psalms as commissive,

---

24. Firth argues that there is an inherent consistency to the imprecatory psalms, not because they were individually constructed with such intertextuality in mind, but by their very inclusion in the Psalter. This consistency, he believes, is reflected in a number of common illocutionary stances: the offering of these psalms as right responses to violence; the condemning of any human retaliation; the assertion that judgment upon such violence is fair in its limitation to the *lex talionis;* and the "inculcation" of an attitude of dependence upon Yahweh. (Firth, *Surrendering Retribution*, 3-4.) See also Wenham, *Psalms as Torah*, 170-171.

25. John Day offers the following ways in which the imprecatory psalms reflect purposes and themes of the "highest ethical plane": "a concern for the honor of God (e.g., Ps. 74:22); a concern for the realization of justice amid rampant injustice (e.g., Ps. 58:11); a concern for the public recognition of the sovereignty of God (e.g., Ps. 59:13); a hope that divine retribution will cause the enemies to seek Yahweh (e.g., Ps. 83:17); an abhorrence of sin (e.g., Ps. 139:21); a concern for the preservation of the righteous (e.g., Ps. 143:11-12)." (Day, *Crying for Justice*, 23.)

26. In Chapters 6 and 7 I will provide a more detailed discussion of these illocutions in the context of offering a theological interpretation.

27. E.g., Ps. 139:19-22.

probably the most intensely commisive in the Psalter, as they identify their speaker so totally with the interests of God."[28]

As noted above, that the imprecations are directed to Yahweh is an affirmation of one of the Psalter's primary illocutions: the assertion that Yahweh reigns. That the psalmist cries out to Yahweh for justice to be done is not only consistent with the primary illocutions of the Psalter, but represents a righteous response to violence and oppression in Yahweh's kingdom.

*Conclusion: The Divine Illocutions of the Imprecatory Psalms in Old Testament Context*
The illocutions of the imprecatory psalms are both consistent with and, in fact, partly comprise the primary illocutions of the Psalter. This enables a clarification of how they functioned as divine discourse in their original context. The clearest level of divine appropriation is at the level of genre and psalm.[29] Examples of such illocutions are as follows: the invitation to mimesis; the affirmation of the stance(s) of the psalmist within the psalm; the promise of vindication; and the inciting of hatred towards all those who stand against Yahweh's anointed and His people.

## Imprecation and the Illocutionary Stance of the New Testament: Forgive, Bless and Love Your Enemies

*Introduction*
The previous section outlined the illocutions of imprecation and argued that they both support and are supported by the primary illocutions of the Psalter. This section will focus the discussion on whether these illocutions remain in play within the context of the Christian canon. This question was framed earlier where the notion of central illocutions was introduced. The New Testament undoubtedly performs central illocutions that, by definition, change the conditions in which the earlier locutions of the Psalter now function. As I mentioned in Chapter 3:

> Canonical and central illocutions provide boundaries within which the discussion of divine illocutions may occur. Any suggestion that God is using a text to perform illocutions other than those of the human author, requires that the related, supervening illocutions be identified and the manner of their supervention explained.

The question at hand is whether these central illocutions change the conditions in such a way that the previous illocutions of the Psalter can no longer be

---

28. Wenham, *Psalms as Torah*, 177.
29. As mentioned, there are a number of literary levels that could be investigated in this regard. However, at this stage in the discussion, the level of detail necessary in order to describe the lower-level illocutions (i.e., those within the psalms) will be reserved for the next chapter.

performed. It will be argued that this is not, in fact, the case and that the central illocutions of the New Testament are not incommensurate with the Psalter's illocutions of imprecation. Moreover, it will be argued that the illocutionary stance of the New Testament reveals its own attitude toward imprecation, supporting that of the Psalter.

The choice of which central illocutions to include in this discussion was obvious. There are a few New Testament illocutions that seem, at first glance, to be at odds with the illocutionary stance of the Psalter. Of particular note are the calls to love enemies, to bless and not curse, and to forgive. Of the three calls mentioned above, the call to forgive one's enemies will receive the most detailed treatment in the discussion below. Again, this seems like a natural choice as it offers a seemingly contrasting response to situations of injustice, oppression and violence. If the call to forgive is unqualified then the Psalter's original illocutionary stance inviting the reader to imitate imprecation becomes infelicitous. The two calls are incompatible. However, if it can be demonstrated that the New Testament call to forgive one's enemies is qualified in some way, then it may be possible that illocutionary force of the Psalter regarding imprecation and the illocutionary force of the New Testament regarding forgiveness are concurrently in play.

I will argue that the New Testament illocutions regarding forgiveness, the love of enemies and the corresponding injunction against cursing are compatible with the illocutionary stance of the Psalter with respect to imprecation. Furthermore, I will demonstrate that the New Testament itself calls for a response to injustice and oppression that imitates the Psalter's call to imprecation.

*Forgiveness and Imprecation*

*Defining Forgiveness.* Forgiveness as a topic has not been adequately explored in theological contexts.[30] Yet, as Briggs suggests, discussing forgiveness outside of a biblical and theological framework often leads to reductionistic accounts. Briggs notes, "discussions of forgiveness divorced from any theological moorings have a propensity to drift into an unbalanced focus on psychological effects alone."[31] A Christian understanding of forgiveness, however, acknowledges that it is a complex, interpersonal action that does more than effect healing in those who have been wronged. While forgiveness has been defined in many ways,[32] the definition offered here and explicated below

---

30. For a recent survey of forgiveness in theology and philosophy see Briggs, *Words in Action*, 217-255. Briggs notes, however, that "Forgiveness is a subject which, rather surprisingly, has suffered from considerable neglect in philosophical and theological reflection." (Briggs, *Words in Action*, 217.)

31. Briggs, *Words in Action*, 227-228.

32. For a review of the various conceptions of forgiveness over the last century see N. Biggar, "Forgiveness in the Twentieth Century," in *Forgiveness and Truth: Explorations in Contemporary Theology* (ed. A. McFayden and M. Sarot; Edinburgh: T&T Clark, 2001). For recent discussions on forgiveness within a theological framework see M. Volf, *Exclusion*

is as follows: *to forgive is to declare that the offender no longer owes you a debt with respect to the offence in question.* In forgiving, you perform the following actions:
1. Count the actions of another as wrongdoing.
2. Recognize that their wrongdoing has produced a debt that outweighs complete restitution.
3. Accept their apology. Which means that, at cost to yourself, you decide to treat the wrongdoer as though they owe you nothing more in this regard.

*Forgiveness is a Strong Speech Act*[33]. My argument is that forgiveness is an example of a strong speech act (i.e., strong illocution) that requires a context of penitence for it to be enacted. Strong illocutions differ in a number of ways from standard illocutions such as the declaration "It's after 10 o'clock" or the request "please pass the salt." Standard illocutions require little context and do not significantly change the world of those persons involved (e.g., In the case above you simply need "out of reach" salt and another person). Conversely, strong illocutions require both a high level of established context and have a significant effect on lives of those involved. For example, a declaration by a judge that a defendant is "guilty" requires at the very least a judicial system, an offending party and a judge who has been granted the authority to make such declarations. Most importantly, standard illocutions may or may not result in the desired perlocution (e.g., You may refuse to pass the salt); whereas, strong illocutions are so rule governed that they ensure the perlocution[34] (e.g., Once

---

*and Embrace: A Theological Exploration of Identity, Otherness, and Reconciliation* (Nashville: Abingdon, 1996); M. Volf, *Free of Charge: Giving and Forgiving in a Culture Stripped of Grace* (Grand Rapids: Zondervan, 2005); M. Volf, *The End of Memory: Remembering Rightly in a Violent World* (Grand Rapids: Eerdmans, 2006); N. Wolterstorff, *Justice in Love* (Grand Rapids: Eerdmans, 2011); L. G. Jones, *Embodying Forgiveness: A Theological Analysis* (Grand Rapids: Eerdmans, 1995); R. A. Nelson, "Exegeting Forgiveness," *ATJ* (2012). For a discussion of forgiveness within a biblical and psychological framework see F. L. Shults and S. J. Sandage, *The Faces of Forgiveness: Searching for Wholeness and Salvation* (Grand Rapids: Baker, 2003); D. A. Carson, *Love in Hard Places* (Wheaton: Crossway Books, 2002).

33. Portions of this discussion are replicated from my previous work, Barker, "Psalms of the Powerless." For a discussion of forgiveness as a speech act see T. Trzyna, "The Social Construction of Forgiveness," *CSR* 27, no. 2 (1997). Tryzna is concerned with corporate instances of forgiveness and what this indicates about membership within such "groups."

34. Austin did not employ the category of "strong" speech act, though he wrestled with a distinction between constatives and performatives where he was concerned to differentiate between simply stating something (or 'describe' or 'report') and the doing of an action (Austin, *How to Do Things*, 5-8). However, this attempt was not successful as Austin himself recognized. He concludes: "What then finally is left of the distinction of the performative and constative utterance? Really we may say that what we had in mind here was this: (a) with the constative utterance, we abstract from the illocutionary (let alone the perlocutionary) aspects of the speech act, and we concentrate on the locutionary: moreover, we use an over-simplified notion of correspondence with the

declared guilty by the judge, you become guilty, irrespective of your desire or response). The relationship is consequential so that once the illocution is uttered, a change occurs in the reality of the persons involved. In other words, because the requisite, high level of context has been established, a "strong" illocutionary act automatically results in the desired perlocution.

Forgiveness is a strong speech act. It requires a complex context and, when performed, automatically occurs, resulting in a significant change to the reality of those involved.[35] While one can utter the words, "I forgive you", unless a number of other conditions are already satisfied then the action is at best ineffective and at worst offensive. In the absence of these conditions, it misfires. It has not worked. The locution "I forgive you" has not performed the illocution of forgiveness.[36] This is obvious in various instances like a declaration of for-

---

facts – over-simplified because essentially it brings in the illocutionary aspect. This is the ideal of what would be right to say in all circumstances, for any purpose, to any audience, &c. Perhaps it is sometimes realized. (b) With the performative utterance, we attend as much as possible to the illocutionary force of the utterance, and abstract from the dimension of correspondence with facts." (Austin, *How to Do Things*, 145-146.)

Unfortunately, this conclusion proved largely unhelpful as both "performatives" and "constantives" can be subsumed in the category of illocution. In light of this confusion, Briggs notes the need to clarify the category of "strong" speech acts and suggests they be defined as those illocutions reliant on "non-linguistic convention." He comments, ." . . I shall call a strong illocution one which relies on a non-linguistic convention. This class, following Warnock, overlaps with but is not identical to Austin's explicit performative, and will include the Queen's saying 'I name this ship' not because it is an explicit performative, although it is, but because the conventions in place are not simply linguistic ones. I shall call weak illocution one where the linguistic meaning itself is the only or only significant convention in view . . . Austin's performative-constative distinction is thus retained on one level (strong against weak illocutions) while collapsed in Austin's own manner on another lever (both are illocutions)" (Briggs, *Words in Action*, 64-65.)

I have suggested in the discussion above that "strong" speech acts require both the establishment of a high level of non-linguistic context and, because of this, they are self-fulfilling. That is, the performance of the illocution ensures the perlocution. The two actions are consequential. In the example given by Briggs, the declaration of the Queen, "I name this ship" results in the ship being so named. The illocution automatically results in the perlocution since the requisite context has been established. I believe this to be a helpful clarification of the nature of "strong" speech acts as it identifies their defining feature.

35. Briggs, although not referring to the illocution as "strong" notes that forgiveness alters the reality (institutional facts) of both the wrongdoer and the injured party, "one might say that 'I forgive your debt (to me)' is the speech act of 'overcoming resentment' in the particular sense that the expectation of repayment is abandoned: the speech act alters the institutional fact which is part of the social reality of the forgiver and the forgiven." (Briggs, *Words in Action*, 242.)

36. Of course, the utterance may achieve other things, but it has "misfired" in that the intended illocution has not been performed.

giveness to a stranger, or perhaps the person uttering the words is doing so to provoke the other person, who in reality has not committed any wrong against them.

In order for forgiveness to be performed, the context must be established. It requires a context of interpersonal communication where the offender has both acknowledged their wrongdoing and repented of it. Wolterstorff asks the question:

> Can I forgive Hubert if I believe that he is not contrite? . . . I doubt it. I can be *willing* to forgive him – when he repents. I can have a forgiving disposition toward him. But it appears to me that no longer to hold against someone the wrong he did one while believing that he himself continues to stand behind the deed, requires not treating the deed or its doer with the moral seriousness required for forgiveness; it is to downplay rather than to forgive. "I suppose he did wrong me; but it's not worth making anything of it."[37]

The speech act of forgiveness requires a context of penitence.[38] In a context of impenitence, the illocution of forgiveness misfires. A Japanese proverb captures the impotence of such an act, "Forgiving the unrepentant is like drawing pictures in water."[39]

*Unconditional Forgiveness?* That forgiveness is dependent upon a context of repentance is not widely accepted. Worthington, Sharp, Learner and Sharp present a standard position on forgiveness:

> Interpersonal forgiveness is meant to be unilateral, not contingent on or waiting for the offender to accept responsibility, confess, apologize, make restitution, ask for forgiveness, and completely turn

---

37. Wolterstorff, *Justice in Love*, 173. So also D. McLellan, "Justice, Forgiveness, and Reconciliation: Essential Elements in Atonement Theology," *ERT* 29, no. 1 (2005): 13.

38. For a defense of forgiveness requiring a context of penitence, see D. W. Augsburger, *Helping People Forgive* (1st ed.; Louisville: Westminster John Knox Press, 1996); C. Brauns, *Unpacking Forgiveness: Biblical Answers for Complex Questions and Deep Wounds* (Wheaton: Crossway Books, 2008); McLellan, "Justice, Forgiveness, and Reconciliation; Wolterstorff, *Justice in Love*; C. L. Blomberg, "On Building and Breaking Barriers: Forgiveness, Salvation and Christian Counseling with Special Reference to Matthew 18:15-35," 25, no. 2 (2006); R. Swinburne, *Responsibility and Atonement* (Oxford: Clarendon, 1989).

39. Augsburger, *Helping People Forgive*, 29. Elsewhere, Augsburger defines forgiveness in the following manner, "Forgiveness is the mutual recognition that repentance of either or both parties in genuine and that right relationships have been restored or achieved." (D. W. Augsburger, "Forgiveness," in *New Dictionary of Christian Ethics & Pastoral Theology* (ed. D. J. Atkinson, et al.; Downers Grove: IVP, 1995), 389.) While I agree that repentance is required in order for forgiveness to be possible, it is perhaps overstating the nature of the action to state that "right relationships have been restored or achieved." Carson notes correctly that reconciliation does not always occur in the context of forgiveness, though it certainly cannot occur in its absence. (Carson, *Love in Hard Places*, 73.)

from the sinful and harmful acts Divine forgiveness is linked to human repentance but interpersonal forgiveness is not.[40]

These authors argue that forgiveness is always required, irrespective of the attitude of the offender. However, they recognize that this is not the case when God forgives. Divine forgiveness happens in the context of penitence. It is "linked to human repentance." Worthington states elsewhere:

> Interpersonal forgiveness, within the Scriptures, is unconditional, whereas Divine forgiveness is conditional. Divine forgiveness is based on Divine truth, justice, mercy, and love, which are granted from an omniscient, merciful, and just God. Because God knows people's hearts, God can condition forgiveness on peoples' repentance. Non-omniscient humans are called to forgive unconditionally.[41]

There seems to be little justification for drawing such a sharp distinction between divine and human forgiveness. Worthington suggests that God can conditionally forgive because He alone knows if the offender is truly repentant, whereas we are always called to forgive because we cannot be sure if the offender is ever truly repentant. However, it would seem obvious that if someone is impenitent, then it is hardly necessary to second-guess their stance towards the wrongdoing. Alternatively, if they claim penitence, then granting them the "benefit of the doubt" would be the appropriate response. (So the command to forgive seventy times seven times.)[42] Worthington's position, however, is a common understanding of Christian responsibility: God forgives only when we repent, yet we are called to forgive unconditionally, irrespective of repentance and even in the face of continued oppression.

---

40. E. L. Worthington et al., "Interpersonal Forgiveness as an Example of Loving One's Enemies," *JPT* 34, no. 1 (2006): 32. Further proponents of forgiveness not requiring repentance include: A. Bash, *Just Forgiveness: Exploring the Bible, Weighing the Issues* (London: SPCK, 2011); Nelson, "Exegeting Forgiveness; L. B. Smedes, *Forgive and Forget: Healing the Hurts We Don't Deserve* (1st ed.; San Francisco: Harper & Row, 1984); Jones, *Embodying Forgiveness*. Smedes represents a therapeutic understanding of forgiveness in his emphasis on what happens within the forgiver when they forgive (Smedes, *Forgive and Forget*, 49.)

Another example of unconditional forgiveness is offered by Cheong who offers little distinction between forgiveness and love. (F. A. DiBlasio and R. K. Cheong, "Christ-Like Love and Forgiveness: A Biblical Foundation for Counseling Practice," *JPC* 26, no. 1 (2007): 22.)

Carson also suggests that it is possible for forgiveness to occur in the absence of penitence. He comments, "It is possible for one party to forgive another from the heart while the other party remains hardened in self-righteous bitterness" and in the footnote below he continues, "there are some kinds of forgiveness in which there is neither repentance nor mutual recognition of repentance." (Carson, *Love in Hard Places*, 73.)

41. E. L. Worthington, "Just Forgiving: How the Psychology and Theology of Forgiveness and Justice Inter-Relate," *JPC* 25, no. 2 (2006).

42. Matt. 18:22.

Rather than argue that human forgiveness differs from divine forgiveness vis-à-vis a context of penitence, others argue neither human nor divine forgiveness necessarily requires penitence.[43] Carson, for example, states that the New Testament presentation of forgiveness sometimes "presupposes repentance on the part of the offender and sometimes not."[44] He offers Col. 3:12–14 and Acts 7:60 as evidence that the New Testament connects forgiveness with forbearance rather than penitence. However, Carson's appeal to Col. 3:12–14 is not convincing. There are a variety of commands simply listed in this passage and it is unreasonable to expect Paul to provide a detailed explanation of each individual command. That love, forbearance and forgiveness are all related is certainly true, but that Paul is speaking in this instance of "unconditional forgiveness" must be demonstrated. Forgiveness in the context of penitence still displays forbearance as the injured party agrees to absorb the pain and cost of the offence. Perhaps more compelling is Carson's appeal to Stephen's dying prayer in Acts 7:60 which he notes "certainly is not offered in the wake of any observable repentance!"[45] Yet even in this case, Stephen's prayer is *offered* to God. It is not formally an act of forgiveness, but demonstrates a willingness to forgive and commits the judgment to God. As Carson himself notes in relation to Jesus' similar request during the crucifixion, the prayer primarily "discloses" the heart of the pray-er, rather than saying anything clear about the nature of the forgiveness requested.[46]

Both of the above approaches fail in different ways to account for the nature of forgiveness and its presentation in Scripture. Those who suggest that human and divine forgiveness require different contexts have failed to demonstrate that this is, in fact, the teaching of the New Testament. Those who suggest that neither divine nor human forgiveness requires a context of penitence have not sufficiently explained why God continues to judge and punish the impenitent. Furthermore, the evidence provided to support human forgiveness in the absence of penitence is unconvincing. None of the examples given clearly portray forgiveness occurring in either the absence of penitence or a context of impenitence.

---

43. See Carson, *Love in Hard Places*; Jones, *Embodying Forgiveness*.

44. Carson, *Love in Hard Places*, 81. The extent of Carson's agreement is limited to his recognition that the New Testament occasionally supports unconditional repentance (i.e., repentance in the absence of penitence). Carson is critical, however, of some psychological accounts of forgiveness that focus on the personal affects of forgiving. He observes that the biblical portrayal of forgiveness offers a wide variety of motivations to forgive, and that *"psychological* benefits do not receive primary stress in Scripture" (Carson, *Love in Hard Places*, 80.) See also Anthony Bash, *Just Forgiveness*, 38-39. Bash speaks of different kids of forgiveness ("forgivenesses" is his term) and suggests that while repentance is ideal, it is not necessary for all kinds of forgiveness.

45. Carson, *Love in Hard Places*, 82.

46. Carson, *Love in Hard Places*, 78. The cry of Jesus in Luke 23 will be addressed separately in the discussion below.

A logical solution, avoided by the authors above, is to claim that God ultimately forgives everyone. This is the creative approach of Miroslav Volf. Unlike the above explanations which differentiate the requisite context of divine and human forgiveness, Volf argues that human and divine forgiveness are, in fact, the same kind of action, with neither requiring a context of penitence. He likens forgiveness to a gift that is given and sits there waiting to be "unwrapped":

> God's gift [of forgiveness] was given, it was sent. But that's not enough. We need to receive it . . . Without faith and repentance, we are not forgiven – God having done the forgiving notwithstanding. God has given, but we haven't received. Forgiveness is then stuck in the middle between the God who forgives and humans who don't receive.[47]
>
> Now apply the same analogy of a gift stuck in the middle to human forgiveness. Repentance is important, even indispensable, and it is indispensable because forgiveness is an event *between* people, not just an individual's change of feelings, attitudes, or actions. Instead of being a *condition* of forgiveness, however, repentance is its necessary *consequence*.
>
> If they imitate the forgiving God, forgivers will keep forgiving, whether the offenders repent or not. Forgivers' forgiving is not conditioned by repentance. The offenders' being forgiven, however, is conditioned by repentance—just as being given a box of chocolate is conditioned by receiving that box of chocolate. Without repentance, the forgivers will keep forgiving but the offenders will remain unforgiven, in that they are untouched by that forgiveness.[48]

To summarize Volf's position, divine and human forgiveness is the same kind of action. We are called to imitate God's forgiveness by continually and unconditionally forgiving. However, despite our forgiveness, the offender may not actually be forgiven. This will only happen if the offender truly repents. If they remain impenitent, the "gift" of forgiveness remains unopened, and they are not forgiven. Forgiveness, in this case, is "stuck in the middle."

There are a number of problems with Volf's description. First, it is terminologically confusing for Volf to suggest that one can forgive the wrongdoer but that the wrongdoer is not forgiven unless they repent and accept forgiveness. How is the first act of forgiveness actually forgiveness? While the locution "I forgive you" can be uttered in this context, if it is uttered with the intention of forgiving then it has "misfired." This is the flaw in the metaphor of the gift. One can deliver a gift and one has performed the action of gifting. That is a unilateral act. Forgiveness, on the other hand is a more complex interpersonal activity. As Volf himself maintains, forgiveness is interpersonal, "an event *between* people." It does not occur when only one party desires it or offers it. While an offended party can unilaterally *offer* forgiveness, calling the act of offering forgiveness

---

47. Volf, *Free of Charge*, 182-183.
48. Volf, *Free of Charge*, 183, emphasis orignal.

"the act of forgiving" is inaccurate and confusing.[49] Volf's explanation reveals this tension when he states, "the offenders' being forgiven, however, is conditioned by repentance."

The second problem with Volf's description is that he wants to affirm forgiveness as interpersonal, yet his explanation divorces the activity of the participants. In other words, the offended party can state, "I forgive you" and the offender can reply "I don't want your forgiveness." In this situation, has forgiveness occurred? If it has, then it is not an act between people. If it has not, then the forgiver's words are void and forgiveness has not actually occurred. Volf expresses this contradiction in the last sentence of the above quotation: "Without repentance, the forgivers will keep forgiving but the offenders will remain unforgiven, in that they are untouched by that forgiveness."[50]

The fundamental problem is that while Volf correctly states that human forgiveness reflects divine forgiveness, he also argues that God continually forgives all people despite their impenitence. This makes God's forgiveness either impotent or coercive. Either it is largely meaningless as the unrepentant remain unforgiven, or it is coercive, the unrepentant will be forgiven despite their wilful rebellion. Volf's explanation indicates the former, God's forgiveness does not actually effect forgiveness.[51] Volf concedes that repentance is necessary for the offender to actually be forgiven, so in what sense has God's forgiveness worked in the absence of such repentance?[52] Can God forgive the unrepentant

---

49. This is represented in Volf's comment quoted above, "If they imitate the forgiving God, forgivers will keep forgiving, whether the offenders repent or not." (Volf, *Free of Charge*, 183.)

50. Volf, *Free of Charge*, 183.)

51. Volf comments, "Should we forgive even those who refuse to repent? Consider once again God's forgiveness, which serves as the model for ours. There are people who think that in relation to God, repentance comes before forgiveness. But that can't be right. God doesn't angrily refuse forgiveness until we show ourselves worthy of it by repentance. Instead, God loves us and forgives us before we repent. Indeed, before we even sinned, Jesus Christ died for our sins. God's forgiveness is not reactive – dependent on our repentance. It's original, preceded and conditioned by absolutely nothing on our part. We can do nothing to become worthy of it for the same reason we can do nothing to earn any of God's gifts. Before we do anything, before we even exist, God's giving and God's forgiving are already there, free of charge. God's giving and forgiving are as unconditional as the sun's rays and as indiscriminate as raindrops. One died for *all*. Absolutely no one is excluded." (Volf, *Free of Charge*, 179–180.)

52. In a more recent work he continues with the same line of reasoning yet concedes that wrongdoers remain unforgiven if unrepentant. Volf states, "It is true that repentance—the recognition that the deed committed was evil coupled with the willingness to mend one's ways—is not so much a prerequisite of forgiveness as, more profoundly, its possible result. Yet repentance is the kind of result of forgiveness whose absence would amount to refusal to see oneself as guilty and therefore a refusal to receive forgiveness as forgiveness. Hence an unrepentant wrongdoer must in the end remain an unforgiven wrongdoer—the unconditionality of the first step in the process of forgiveness notwithstanding" (Volf, "Forgiveness, Reconciliation, and Justice," 284.) In

and still keep them under judgement? It is clear that God *loves the world* despite its rebellion, but it is far from clear that God *forgives the world* despite its impenitence. It seems that Volf and others are confusing the act of forgiveness, which requires repentance, with the *offer* of forgiveness (an act of unconditional love), which is the gospel message. The offer and the act are not identical.

In the end we are left with a number of alternatives. Either human forgiveness is different from divine forgiveness, (the former being unconditional and the latter being conditioned upon repentance) or, human forgiveness is similar to divine forgiveness with both either conditioned by repentance or entirely unconditional.

The biblical portrayal of forgiveness is that there is only one kind of forgiveness and that it is conditioned by repentance. Unconditional forgiveness is not supported in Scripture. There is no explicit command to forgive offenders who remain unrepentant. There are many commands to forgive, but they either mention repentance explicitly as a condition, or require that it be implied on the basis of (1) those passages where it is explicit and (2) divine forgiveness, where we see the mechanism of forgiveness more clearly.[53]

*Key Texts: Matthew 18 & Luke 23.* Two biblical texts are often used to defend unconditional forgiveness. The first is Matthew 18, where repentance is not mentioned explicitly with the call to forgive:

> Then Peter came to Jesus and asked, "Lord, how many times shall I forgive my brother when he sins against me? Up to seven times? Jesus answered, "I tell you, not seven times, but seventy-seven times (Matt 18:21-22).

In isolation, these verses appear to command unconditional forgiveness. However, the preceding verses (Matt 18:15-19) explain how one is to deal with a brother who is repeatedly unrepentant with respect to a matter serious enough to be brought before the whole community. The end result of his stubborn impenitence is exclusion, not forgiveness.[54] Where Matthew's account implies a penitent offender, Luke's account of the same situation makes it explicit:

> If your brother or sister sins against you, rebuke them; and if they repent, forgive them. Even if they sin against you seven times in a

---

this description, God's offer of forgiveness is "the first step" and requires the wrongdoer to repent in order for forgiveness to be completed. This is a better explanation, but is at odds with his earlier work where he states, "forgiveness is not conditioned by prior repentance." (Volf, *Free of Charge*, 183.)

53. See Blomberg, "On Building and Breaking Barriers: Forgiveness, Salvation and Christian Counseling with Special Reference to Matthew 18:15-35," 144-145.

54. Matt. 18:15-18. Blomberg also argues that the loosing and binding of v. 18 are actually references to forgiveness and the denial of forgiveness respectively and so summarize the previous teaching on community discipline. Blomberg, "On Building and Breaking Barriers: Forgiveness, Salvation and Christian Counseling with Special Reference to Matthew 18:15-35," 139.

day and seven times come back to you saying "I repent," you must forgive them' (Luke 17:3-4).[55]

In addition to Matthew 18, Jesus' prayer on the cross in Luke 23, "Father forgive them.", is often referred to as an example of divine (and human) forgiveness that is performed in the absence of penitence. However, a number of features suggest that this text does not promote unconditional forgiveness:[56] Firstly, Jesus does not pronounce forgiveness. While this is something that he often did, in this case, he requests that God forgive the offenders. Secondly, Jesus' request is quite specific. He asks that they not be held accountable for the gravity of the offence, as there was no way they could comprehend this.[57] Rather than understanding this as a request that they be forgiven of all wrongdoing connected to his execution, Jesus appears to be requesting that their culpability be limited to what they thought they were doing.[58] In light of the above, it seems unlikely that one can build a theology of forgiveness upon this text which describes such a unique event and does not present forgiveness as formally occurring.[59] The crucifixion and resurrection make forgiveness and reconciliation with God possible, not automatic.

---

55. This text should also provide the context for reading the story in Luke 5:17–26 of the paralyzed man who comes to Jesus for physical healing. Jesus both heals the man and pronounces his sins forgiven to the disgust of the Pharisees. The narrative does not directly address the penitence of the paralyzed man. Yet, the text does portray Jesus as knowing the thoughts of those present (5:22) and the paralyzed man and his friends as displaying great faith. Where the narrative explicitly portrays faith and the wider text of Luke provides the mechanism for forgiveness (17:3–4), it seems likely that the penitence is implied.

56. The originality of this logion is strongly contested as it largely occurs in the Western witnesses and does not occur in consistently reliable early manuscripts. While there continues to be some doubt about the authenticity of the logion, I have presupposed its reliability in order to address the apparent contradiction to my thesis.

For a summary of positions and a compelling defence of its authenticity, see J. R. Harrison, "Jesus and the Grace of the Cross: Luke 23:34a and the Politics of 'Forgiveness' in Antiquity," (New Orleans: SBL Annual Meeting, 2009). See also N. Eubank, "A Disconcerting Prayer: On the Originality of Luke 23:34a," *JBL* 129, no. 3 (2010); T. M. Bolin, "A Reassessment of the Textual Problem of Luke 23:34a," *Proceedings: Eastern Great Lakes and Midwest Biblical Societies* 12 (1992); J. M. Strahan, *The Limits of a Text: Luke 23:34a as a Case Study in Theological Interpretation* (5; Winona Lake: Eisenbrauns, 2012); See also Nolland who concludes, "The prayer for the cross has good claim to being based upon historical reminiscence. It offers a distinctive and poignant embodiment of Jesus' teaching on love of enemies." (J. Nolland, *Luke 18:35–24:53* (vol. 35C; Dallas: Word, 1993), 1144.)

57. For a defence of a context of "misunderstanding" leading to "unintentional sin" see Strahan, *The Limits of a Text*.

58. This understanding also informs the interpretation of Stephen's prayer discussed above. Since Stephen modelled his prayer on that of Jesus, similar conclusions can be made regarding its contribution to a theology of forgiveness.

59. Nelson states that this is an example of unconditional forgiveness but limited to the wrongdoing committed in ignorance. Specifically, he thinks that Jesus is requesting

For the purposes of my argument, it is also important to consider how this scene contributes to an understanding of imprecation. After all, Jesus requested forgiveness, not judgment. It may be helpful at this point to reflect upon the uniqueness of Christ's crucifixion. In the moment of crucifixion, Jesus did not imprecate but requested a limited culpability. Furthermore, he did not ask for deliverance, but willingly suffered the punishment of all humanity. In this climactic moment, when the triune God accomplished his eternal purposes for creation, Christ's death was not primarily the fault of the Roman soldiers or the Jewish Sanhedrin, but of all sinful humanity. Christ willingly took the place of all humanity in their rebellion against God. To imprecate against the soldiers involved would firstly trivialize the scope of its significance and wrongly attribute guilt to a select few. To imprecate in this moment would have also overplayed the significance of the suffering the soldiers inflicted. Christ willingly submitted Himself to the wrath of the Father, a fate far worse than the soldiers could inflict.[60]

---

that they not be held accountable for killing "an innocent man." He claims that Jesus had already forgiven the Roman soldiers and was now "pleading for their vertical [divine] forgiveness." (Nelson, "Exegeting Forgiveness," 51-52.) In the end, Nelson's entire argument rests on the fact that Jesus forgave human sin against God on two occasions without "any evidence of repentance", citing Mk. 2:5 and Lk. 7:48. However, as I mention above, both of these narrative accounts clearly portray the sinners as demonstrating great faith in Jesus. Any suggestion that these people were impenitent lacks substantive evidence.

Carson, who affirms unconditional forgiveness, warns against developing a theory of forgiveness based on Luke 23:34 when he notes that the text cannot be used to "overthrow other things Jesus said or did." He also agrees that we cannot know how God answered the prayer of Jesus in this regard so that the most important feature of this text is that it "discloses Jesus' heart." (Carson, *Love in Hard Places*, 77-78.)

Matthews reads this prayer in the context of Roman clemency and concludes that the "discourse of clemency is not a precise analogue" as both Jesus and Stephen appeal to "a deity" to forgive. Nevertheless, Matthews argues that in this context of Roman clemency the prayers should not be seen as acts of submission or humility but as demonstrations of power over the persecutors. (S. Matthews, "Clemency as Cruelty: Forgiveness and Force in the Dying Prayers of Jesus and Stephen," *BibInt* 17, no. 1-2 (2009): 144-145.)

60. I realize that the comment engages with a highly disputed area of atonement theory, with both the reality and extent of penal substitution being strongly contested. Irrespective of one's view on the matter, Jesus' suffering on the cross is portrayed as more than physical as his cry in Matthew 27:46 indicates.

For a recent defence of a non-violent atonement see the collection of essays in B. Jersak and M. Hardin, *Stricken by God?: Nonviolent Identification and the Victory of Christ* (Grand Rapids: Eerdmans, 2007). See also D. W. S. Belousek, *Atonement, Justice, and Peace: The Message of the Cross and the Mission of the Church* (Grand Rapids: Eerdmans 2012); J. Beilby and P. R. Eddy, *The Nature of the Atonement: Four Views* (Downers Grove: InterVarsity, 2006).

For a selection of essays in defence of penal substitution see R. R. Nicole, C. E. Hill, and F. A. James, *The Glory of the Atonement: Biblical, Historical & Practical Perspectives: Essays*

Furthermore, because of his atoning work, Christ himself would see that justice is done for all those present. He knew that all things would be placed in his hands and that He would be the one to ultimately bring justice.[61] In light of these unique features, we would not expect a response of imprecation on the lips of Christ. Nor would we expect to find a theology of unconditional forgiveness that precluded penitence. Christ will punish those who reject His kingship and atoning work and remain impenitent. The crucifixion and resurrection make forgiveness and reconciliation with God possible, not automatic. It is here we discover the basis for forgiveness, which requires all people to respond in faith and penitence.

*Forgiveness and Justice.* The proper enactment of forgiveness is significant in that it promotes and sustains justice and compassion in a number of ways. Firstly, to demand victims to forgive impenitent offenders is to force them to forgo what little justice they can receive in this life and trivializes the offence. The proper enactment of forgiveness justly labels the offence as such and is predicated by the offender having done the same. When forgiveness is declared in a context where an offender has admitted their offence against the victim and repented, forgiveness not only works, but it also grants the victim the minimum degree of justice in the offence being named and owned by the offender.

That forgiveness is an act of justice is also demonstrated in its honouring of the moral stance that the offender has taken with respect to their wrongdoing. Forgiving the penitent acknowledges this new stance of the offender towards their offence. However, enacting unconditional forgiveness rejects the wrongdoer's desire to remain unforgiven. It does not take seriously their stance toward the situation. Forgiveness cannot and should not be imposed upon the impenitent. Nicholas Wolterstorff concurs, "in the absence of repentance, to enact the resolution not to hold the deed against the wrongdoer is to insult him and to demean oneself, thereby wronging both alike."[62]

Furthermore, since unconditional forgiveness is often done in private it can circumvent justice for the accused, since to forgive someone is, first of all, to judge them. As Volf rightly states, "to forgive is to name the wrongdoing and to condemn it."[63] In this case the forgiver acts as jury and judge without allowing the alleged offender the opportunity to respond to or even be aware of the charges. In cases where the "offender" has been misjudged, forgiveness would be entirely inappropriate and the alleged offender would never know that they have been unfairly treated.[64] In cases where the offender had actually commit-

---

in Honor of Roger Nicole (Downers Grove: IVP, 2004); D. Peterson, *Where Wrath and Mercy Meet: Proclaiming the Atonement Today* (Carlisle: Paternoster, 2001).

61. That Jesus is both the model of a righteous sufferer and the one to whom the righteous sufferer commits themselves represents one of the many mysteries of the incarnation.

62. Wolterstorff, *Justice in Love*, 173.

63. Volf, *Free of Charge*, 129.

64. While the alleged "offender" is ignorant of the charges and has not been

ted an offence, "forgiving" them in private does not confront them with their wrongdoing. It does not encourage repentance or reconciliation.

The enactment of forgiveness by a Christian could demonstrate justice in additional ways. If one understands the atoning work of Christ to include the act of propitiation where God's righteous punishment of (all) sin is accomplished, then any Christian enactment of forgiveness is performed with the belief that all wrongdoing has been justly punished in the death of Christ. The result of this belief is that the act of forgiveness is always performed with the knowledge that the wrongdoer can be forgiven because God will ensure that all sin is justly punished. The victim who forgives is convinced that God will hold the wrongdoer accountable for their sins. God will either count Christ's death as sufficient payment for the sin (if the wrongdoer repents and accepts Christ's death as their own) or, in the absence of penitence, the wrongdoer will, one day, be held accountable for their sin against God. Thus, in either case, justice is maintained.

Christians also acknowledge that any wrongdoing is also, and ultimately, against God who will require justice to be done. Forgiving the wrongdoer names their actions as "wrong" and declares that their act deserves just punishment. Furthermore, in forgiving the wrongdoer, the Christian also asserts that the wrongdoing they are forgiving is also considered by God as a sin that requires punishment. To avoid this judgment, the wrongdoer must not only be penitent towards the human victim but also to God. In this way, Christian forgiveness is an additional act of judgment and justice in that it prefigures the forgiveness of God requisite for the wrongdoer to avoid eschatological judgment.

*Conclusion.* Forgiveness is a strong speech act requiring the specific context of wrongdoing and penitence in order for its performance. This is the consistent portrayal across the Christian canon with respect to both human and divine action.[65] Both the Hebrew Bible and the New Testament portray God as willing to forgive, but who only does so in the context of penitence.[66] The absence of penitence brings His judgment.[67] This picture of divine forgiveness is determinative. It should shape our understanding of its nature and provide a model for us to imitate.[68]

---

harmed, they have been wronged by the "forgiver" who has unfairly judged them.

65. For a discussion of the topic of forgiveness throughout the Protestant canon see L. Morris, *The Apostolic Preaching of the Cross* (1st ed.; Grand Rapids: Eerdmans, 1955), 144-213.

66. This portrayal of divine forgiveness is consistent throughout the Christian canon. The following texts are representative and span both genre and testament: 2 Samuel 12:13-14; Psalm 51:16-17; Ezekiel 18:30-32; Hosea 14; Mark 1:15; Luke 13:1-9; 17:3-4; Acts 2:38; 2 Corinthians 7:10; 1 John 1:9.

67. E.g., Matthew 11:20-24.

68. C.f. Matthew 18:21-25. I am not suggesting that human forgiveness is congruent with divine forgiveness in every way, for divine forgiveness 'saves' the wrongdoer from eschatological judgement. Human forgiveness foreshadows this event, but does not effect salvation. What I am suggesting, rather, is that both human and divine forgiveness

Forgiveness is a complex interpersonal activity that requires the offending party to set the context in which it can occur. This does not preclude the victim *offering* forgiveness, which is the biblical mandate, but the actual act of forgiveness is only possible in the presence of penitence.

When forgiveness is properly offered in an interpersonal setting it promotes justice. It names the wrongdoing, allows the wrongdoer a recourse for defence or the opportunity for penitence and, in a Christian context, warns of the necessity of divine forgiveness if one is to avoid eschatological judgment. If the accused is innocent, they have the opportunity to defend themselves. If they are guilty, the act has been exposed for what it is and they have the opportunity to repent. In the absence of penitence, forgiveness is not possible. In this circumstance, the willingness to forgive should be present and the offer of forgiveness can be made, but the speech act of forgiveness cannot be performed. If it is "enacted" in that context it undermines the stance of the wrongdoer and subverts justice.

*The Possibility of Imprecation.* Forgiveness is a complex interpersonal activity that requires the offending party to set the context in which it can occur. In particular, it is a strong speech act that requires a context of penitence for it to be performed. This does not preclude the victim *offering* forgiveness, but the actual act of forgiveness is only possible in the presence of penitence. Forgiveness, therefore, is one response to wrongdoers, but it is not the only possible response. The reality of impenitence and impossibility of forgiveness in this context makes it possible for the offended party to respond in other ways.

While the willingness to forgive and the corresponding offer of forgiveness are clearly modelled and commanded throughout the Scriptures, this does not discount the possibility of imprecation. This possibility occurs because forgiveness and imprecation are mutually exclusive actions with different contextual requirements. In the context of a penitent wrongdoer, imprecation is clearly inappropriate and forgiveness is demanded.[69] Alternatively, in a context of impenitence, forgiveness is an inappropriate response and, in fact, an impossible one. Furthermore, in this same context of impenitence, imprecation, though not a necessary response, could be warranted.

*Blessing, Love and Imprecation*
While it has been demonstrated that the New Testament call to forgive one's enemies is not incompatible with the Psalter's invitation to imprecate, there are other New Testament illocutions that may have changed the conditions within which the Psalter now functions. Such illocutions include the calls to both love

---

are the same kind of action requiring the same context. The interpersonal nature of forgiveness and the difference between God and humanity as "forgivers" means that their corresponding actions will differ in the scope of their significance.

69. This process may be complicated and lengthy, yet the call to forgive is clear in this circumstance.

and bless one's enemies. While the above discussion of forgiveness warranted a more detailed discussion due to both its scarcity of treatment in theological contexts and its apparent opposition to imprecation, the following discussions can be more concise as they have been dealt with elsewhere.

"*Bless and Do Not Curse*" Several authors have noted that the prohibition against cursing should not be understood as a prohibition against imprecation as the two actions are significantly different.[70] A fundamental difference is that cursing is generally directed at the enemy or wrongdoer while imprecation is always directed to God. Once again, speech act theory aids in clarifying the kind of action being performed, and in this case enables a differentiation between the act of cursing and imprecation. Cursing can be described as a strong speech act in that the uttering of the curse is self-fulfilling.[71] The utterance of the speech act is a sufficient action for the desired outcome to be achieved. Imprecation, on the other hand, being directed to God, leaves the request for judgment at His discretion and ensures that it only happens according to His will and not only the will of the oppressed. As such, it does not fit the category of a strong speech act because the perlocution is not automatic. Broadhurst helpfully draws this distinction, though he does not employ speech act theory in his discussion:

> Furthermore, even referring to these few [65 verses out of 368 in the Psalter] as "curses" may be inadequate. Anderson and Ringgren both agree that curses in the ancient Near East were believed to go instantly and automatically against the recipient and not to "go through" God. Africans also often seem to prefer a direct connection between the words spoken and the effect. While this may be true of some African belief and some ANE beliefs, I cannot bring myself to agree with this automatic retribution theory in the Hebrew culture; rather I maintain that the retribution of the Bible is intrinsic retribution. Intrinsic retribution is God, the righteous judge, punishing or rewarding people based on their actions. It is not simply automatic consequences based on actions. Yahweh himself actively bestows what comes to pass as the result of human action. Just as in other ancient Near Eastern texts, the gods are concerned with keeping a cosmic order that they themselves have usually initiated. Although many texts can be interpreted to intimately link the results with the action, it would be better understood as Yahweh himself making this close connection. He is the one who rewards and the one who punishes human action. The Israelites believed that God's

---

70. For a more detailed discussion of topic of cursing in its ANE context and in relation to imprecation in the Old Testament see Day, *Crying for Justice*, 36-48; H. G. L. Peels, *The Vengeance of God: The Meaning of the Root Nqm and the Function of the Nqm-Texts in the Context of Divine Revelation in the Old Testament* (Leiden: Brill, 1995); J. R. Broadhurst, "Should Cursing Continue? An Argument for Imprecatory Psalms in Biblical Theology," *AJET* 23, no. 1 (2004); R. Althann, "The Psalms of Vengeance against Their Ancient near Eastern Background," *JNSL* 18 (1992).

71. See the discussion above in "Forgiveness is a Strong Speech Act."

intervention was necessary. Therefore instead of cultic curses, the Hebrew Bible records Yahwistic prayers.[72]

Day also objects to the drawing of simplistic parallels between the imprecations of the Psalter and cursing, preferring to distinguish between "legitimate" and "illegitimate" curses. He argues that legitimate curses are those that reflect the laws and promises of Yahweh. These legitimate curses are simply calling upon Him to act in ways consistent with His revelation. Day states:

> ... a "legitimate" curse was distinguished from an "illegitimate" curse. One was proper and the other reprehensible. The illegitimate curse was uttered out of malice against an innocent party to effect personal gain, or "as a private means of revenge to smite a personal enemy", often in secret and with the aid of magic. The legitimate curse was uttered to cover egregious infractions of the moral order, often in a public forum with appeal to deity. Notably, it is this legitimate kind of curse that we find uttered in the imprecatory psalms.
> Furthermore, in the community of Israel, as in the broader ancient Near East, the legitimate curse was an expression of human powerlessness. It was used when people were unable to adequately help or protect themselves. This cry was the voice of the oppressed, the victim, and the unjustly accused. It was directed against powerful or unconvictable offenders. Indeed, the legitimate curse was an act of faith that God's desire for justice, as expressed in the Law and ethical teachings of religion, would be reflected in real life. When viewed in this light, the so-called imprecatory psalms and other imprecatory texts, which seem so vicious and strange to the modern reader, are seen to be expressions of faith in the just rule of Yahweh in situations in which the covenant member or community can see no other source of help or possible means of securing just treatment.[73]

It seems preferable, for the reasons outlined by Broadhurst, to separate the language of imprecation from that of curse. Even so, Day helpfully observes that "legitimate curse" (i.e., imprecation) is both an act of faith and a desire for Yahweh's justice to be realised.

The New Testament injunction against cursing one's enemies is not incompatible with the Psalter's invitation to imprecation. Cursing in the ANE context was an act of vengeance in which the illocutions of curse were believed to be strong illocutions and so effect the judgment.[74] Conversely, imprecation pre-

---

72. Broadhurst, "Should Cursing Continue?," 67-68. See also K. Koch, "Is There a Doctrine of Retribution in the Old Testament," in *Theodicy in the Old Testament* (ed. J. L. Crenshaw; vol. 4 of *Issues in Religion and Theology*; Philadelphia: Fortress Press, 1983).

73. Day, *Crying for Justice*, 36-37.

74. A recent work by D. M. Nehrbass, *Praying Curses: The Theraputic and Preaching Value of the Imprecatory Psalms*. (Eugene: Pickwick, 2013), conflates imprecation and cursing as the title suggests. While Nehrbass notes that the psalms are directed to God, he persists in labeling them curses (Nehrbass, *Praying Curses*, 98).

cludes any possibility of personal vengeance by directing the request to Yahweh and surrendering all retribution to Him.

*"Love Your Enemies"*. The New Testament injunction against cursing is combined with the command to bless. The command to love one's enemies incorporates blessing so it is convenient to treat them both together.

One way of reconciling the call to enemy love with the possibility of imprecation is to differentiate between personal enemies and the enemies of Yahweh. Imprecation is argued by some to be appropriate toward the latter and blessing appropriate toward the former. Shepherd suggest this differentiation as a possible solution:

> The emphasis is on loving those who persecute you, your own personal enemies. It is possible to distinguish between personal enemies and those who are enemies of God. Sometimes they will overlap of course, but there are those who are persistent evil-doers, opposed to God's purposes. Hence, in Paul, we see someone who is unconcerned about his personal enemies, but very severe in his condemnation of those who corrupt the gospel, and are enemies of God. The passage in Romans makes it clear also that God will judge those who persecute, and his wrath will avenge. Do these commands from Jesus and Paul, together with other teachings about forgiveness, invalidate the place of the Imprecatory Psalms, which call down judgment upon God's enemies? The commands certainly raise major questions about praying imprecations, but they do not, we would contend, negate the desire for God's name to be honoured, for God to exercise retributive justice, or for the righteous to be vindicated.[75]

While there may be cases where the above differentiation holds true, it is often the case, as Shepherd himself notes, that there is overlap between the enemies of God and those of God's people. Alternatively, if it is the case that one's "personal enemy" is not an enemy of God, then one would have to question why this person has become one's enemy. Loving one's enemy in that case would seem to be an obvious action as your enemy is not your enemy for any warranted reason. Simply stated, Christians should have no enemies other than those who are also the enemies of God.

There are further problems with the solution offered by Shepherd. Firstly, the enemies of the psalmist are often explicitly named as the enemies of Yahweh (e.g., Ps. 139:18-22). Secondly, in the absence of such an explicit labeling, the reputation of Yahweh is clearly connected to the vindication of His people, a point that the psalmist regularly employs in his rhetoric of lament. In these cases, the psalmist assumes that his vindication necessitates the destruction of his enemies and that this is a right action and consistent with Yahweh's character and promises.

---

75. Shepherd, "The Place of Imprecatory Psalms," 121.

Another attempt at differentiating the object of imprecation so that there remains a "right" appropriation of the imprecatory psalms is to "hate the sin, but love the sinner."[76] However, while there is a very occasional differentiation in Scripture between sin and sinners (c.f. Rom 7 and Jam 3), it always remains that sinners are held accountable for the sin.

Perhaps the solution to the apparent contrast between the call to love one's enemies and the invitation to imprecation is subtler than simply differentiating between the objects of each. In the previous case of forgiveness, it is clear that one cannot both forgive a wrongdoer and imprecate against them at the same time. The two illocutions are mutually exclusive, requiring different contexts. In the case of loving one's enemies, its mutual exclusivity with respect to imprecation is not as clear. It could be possible to act in love towards one's enemy, to have shown kindness towards them and to even desire their redemption while at the same time maintain a desire for God to be glorified, for justice to be done and for personal vindication. This complexity of both desire and emotion is precisely the biblical portrayal of God's own stance towards sinners. Day comments in this regard:

> Chalmers Martin distances the Christian from imprecatory prayers when he asserts that the "distinction between the sin and the sinner was impossible to David as an Old Testament saint." He adds that this distinction must now be made. According to Martin, the progress of revelation alters the Christian's stance toward the enemies of God from one of enmity against the whole being to one of mere hatred of the governing principle of sin operating through the sinner.
> However common this sentiment may implicitly be in modern Christendom, it insufficiently characterizes the broader theology of Scripture. The position of Scripture is not only "Love the sinner but hate the sin," but also paradoxically "Love the sinner but hate the sinner." Even in the New Testament, the fullness of revelation's progress, it is *sinners*—not just sin—who will be destroyed, suffering the eternal torment of hell. McKenzie rightly observes that "sin as an abstraction has no existence. The sin which we hate has its concrete existence in human wills."[77]

Furthermore, the New Testament call to love one's enemies is not the only call to love. Fundamental to the ethics of the New Testament is the love of God and neighbour (Mark 12:30-31). To act in love towards an enemy may not be possible in contexts where the enemy is so defined because of their oppression of one's neighbour and their opposition to God's kingdom. The call to "love your enemy" cannot be held above all other calls to love.

*Summary.* The New Testament calls to love and bless one's enemies and the corresponding injunction against cursing one's enemies are not incompatible with the Psalter's invitation to imprecation. These sets of illocutions could

---

76. So Shepherd, "The Place of Imprecatory Psalms," 122-123.
77. Day, *Crying for Justice*, 28-29.

co-exist. Admittedly, if this were the only line of argument in support of a contemporary application of imprecation, the evidence would be thin. However, as the following section will demonstrate, the New Testament does not simply prohibit cursing and call for a love of enemies. The New Testament portrayal of a right Christian response to wrongdoing is more complex.

*The New Testament Invitation to Imprecation*
It is not within the scope of this work to present a New Testament theology of imprecation. It will be sufficient for my purposes here to demonstrate the possibility that the illocutions of the New Testament are not at odds with those of the Psalter and in fact support them in many ways. The burden of proof lies with those who would suggest *a priori* that the two stances are incommensurate.

The New Testament calls its readers to glorify God in loyalty to Christ. It models a zeal for His glory that calls for the just punishment of His enemies, thus imitating the response of the Psalter to similar circumstances. Examples of imprecation are found throughout the New Testament and it will suffice to simply present them here as they have been discussed at length elsewhere.[78]

Jesus himself employs imprecation on a number of occasions. Day comments:

> Certainly in extreme circumstances, Jesus did not hesitate to pronounce imprecation (e.g., Mark 11:12-14, 20-21), and he uttered excoriating woes against hardened unbelief (e.g., Matt. 11:20-24; 23:13-39). Now although woes may be generally distinguished from curses, they are closely related. They bear a large measure of similarity and partial semantic overlap.
> This does not mean that Jesus acted out of accord with his own radical dictum. By Christ's own witness and example, this enemy-love is the attitude of readiness to show sustained and indiscriminate kindness. If, however, the enemy's cup of iniquity has become full to overflowing, this love is overtaken by the demands of justice and divine vengeance. Jesus' approach in this regard is strikingly similar to that of the psalmists who penned harsh words. David, for example by his testimony in Psalms 35:11-17 and 109:4-5, demonstrated habitual kindness toward enemies, only to receive abuse in return. His was an example of extreme love-and a love that finally and fittingly met its extremity.[79]

On several occasions, Paul also expressed his imprecatory prayers to the audiences of his letters. In the letter to the Galatians, he desires that those who

---

78. Shepherd notes that this area warrants further research and argues that Luke 23:34 should not exhaust our understanding of Jesus' theology of forgiveness. (Shepherd, "The Place of Imprecatory Psalms," 121.) See also Day, *Crying for Justice*; Peels, *The Vengeance of God*; Broadhurst, "Should Cursing Continue?; R. L. Thomas, "Imprecatory Prayers of the Apocalypse," *BSac* 126, no. 502 (1969).

79. Day, *Crying for Justice*, 89-90.

preach a "false gospel" be "anathema."[80] In the same letter, he expresses his desire that those who are undermining the gospel by demanding circumcision would have an accident with the knife and emasculate themselves.[81]

Against those who would argue that the examples of Paul are all cases that exclude his personal enemies, is the imprecatory prayer of the souls of the martyred saints in Revelation 6. God's response to such a request is that they must be patient, but that He would ensure their vindication and the punishment of their oppressors.

Perhaps less obvious, yet more poignant, is the invitation to all believers to enact the Lord's Prayer.[82] This prayer begins with the declaration that God deserves honour and voices a desire that His will be done throughout the heavens and the earth. This opening declaration calls for the kingdom of God to be fully realized, for all His enemies to be shamed and for Him to be honoured. Implicit in the request for personal deliverance later in the prayer is the destruction of all opposition to God's people. This prayer is fundamentally a prayer calling for *Yom Yahweh*.[83] Broadhurst concurs:

> The martyred saints continue to cry before God's throne, "How long, O Lord, holy and true . . . (Rev 6:10). Do we not ask for the same thing? Many churches announce implicit curses on the enemies of God every Sunday in the unison statement of the Lord's Prayer. In quoting the words of Christ, "Thy kingdom come," we are asking for the consummation of an era. This consummation brings about the destruction of our enemies and God's enemies. This petition involves the complete overthrow of Satan's kingdom and all his followers. There is really no difference in praying this than there is in praying an imprecatory psalm and so I suggest we should continue singing these psalms with all the fervour of the martyred saints.[84]

It is apparent that the New Testament simultaneously maintains two sets of illocutionary acts. On the one hand there is the call to love one's enemies and on the other, there is the invitation to call for justice and for God's glory in the realization of His kingdom. The presence of imprecation throughout the New Testament, therefore, supports the illocutionary stance of the Psalter.

## Conclusion: Imprecatory Psalms and Contemporary Divine Illocution

This chapter has offered a theological interpretation of imprecation by demonstrating that the divine illocutions of the Psalter in their Old Testament context

---

80. Galatians 1:8–9.
81. Galatians 5:12.
82. Matthew 6:9–13.
83. Barker, "Divine Illocutions," 14.
84. Broadhurst, "Should Cursing Continue?," 84-85.

# The Theological Interpretation of Imprecatory Psalms 157

are maintained in the context of the Christian canon. It has been demonstrated that the imprecatory psalms are consistent with (and comprise) the illocutionary stance of the Psalter. The way in which these psalms function as divine discourse is most clearly seen in their generic and whole-text illocutions. It was then demonstrated that the illocutions of the New Testament have not altered the conditions in which the illocutions of the Psalter function to the point that the Psalter's invitation to imprecation now "misfires." In fact, the illocutionary stance of the New Testament reinforces that of the Psalter by encouraging a response to violence and oppression that cries out to God for justice. In the absence of any central illocutions that would void the invitation to mimesis, the ways in which the imprecatory psalms continue to function as divine discourse will include those divine illocutions present within the Psalter. The imprecatory psalms do function in new ways within the context of the Christian canon, yet this additional function is not at odds with their original illocutionary stances. The elucidation of such a thick description that includes the illocutions performed as a result of this intertextuality is best accomplished with respect to particular psalms and is the aim of the following chapters.

# Chapter 6

# A Theological Interpretation of Psalm 137

## Introduction

The previous chapter defended the continued appropriation of imprecatory psalms by demonstrating that the illocutionary stance of the imprecation was commensurate with the illocutionary stance of the Psalter and also compatible with that of the New Testament. Furthermore, it was also suggested that the way in which the psalms function as divine discourse is most clearly seen at the generic and whole-text levels. This chapter offers a theological interpretation of Psalm 137 in order to provide a detailed demonstration of the proposed hermeneutic and a subsequent thick description of the psalm.

The focus on the Psalter to facilitate a discussion of divine discourse was a natural one. The focus on the imprecatory psalms in this and the previous chapter was prompted by two reasons. Firstly, it enables a level of exegetical detail by narrowing the focus to one genre. Secondly, the genre of imprecation brings into sharp relief the issue of dual authorship as the church has continually struggled with how the imprecatory psalms function as God's word. As noted, the imprecatory psalms have often suffered editing for liturgical purposes with some psalms being totally removed from the liturgy. Psalm 137 has suffered a similar fate.[1] This psalm was also chosen because of its role in recent discussions of speech act theory and dual authorship.[2] Furthermore, unlike many lament psalms, Psalm 137 concludes with an imprecatory statement making it particularly offensive to some.[3]

---

1. *An Australian Prayer Book* suggests that Psalm 137:7-9, and similar verses throughout the Psalter, "may be omitted in the public service at the discretion of the minister." Anglican Church of Australia, *An Australian Prayer Book* (Sydney: Anglican Information Office Press, 1978), 306.
2. See Wolterstorff, *Divine Discourse*; Watson, *Text and Truth*, 120-121.
3. See Holladay, *The Psalms through Three Thousand Years*, 312-313.

A Theological Interpretation of Psalm 137

The theological interpretation of Psalm 137 will begin with a discussion of its historical and literary contexts. A detailed exposition of the psalm will follow, where lower-level (intratextual) illocutions will be identified. Subsequently, I will offer a thick description of the illocutionary acts of the human author in the context of the Hebrew canon. Finally, I will outline the divine illocutions of Psalm 137 in this context and then in the context of the Christian canon, thus clarifying its contemporary function.

## Translation

1 By the canals of Babylon,
    there we sat,
    more so, we wept,
        as we remembered Zion.
2 On the poplars in its midst we hung our lyres.
3 For there our captors asked us for words of song:
    our mockers,[4] (words of)[5] rejoicing:
        "Sing to us from a song of Zion."
4 How could we sing a song of Yahweh on foreign ground?

5 If I forget Jerusalem,
    may my right hand forget (how to play).
6 May my tongue stick to my palate:
    If I do not remember you,
    If I do not lift up Jerusalem above my greatest[6] joy.

7 Remember, Yahweh, the sons of Edom on the day of Jerusalem,
    those who were saying:
        "Strip (her)! Strip (her)! to her foundation."
8 Daughter of Babylon, the one who is destroyed,
    Blessed is he who pays you back[7] your reward,
        exactly as[8] you rewarded us.
9 Blessed is he who seizes and smashes your infants on the rock.

---

4. "Mockers" is a *hapax legomenon*.
5. Ellipsis assumed.
6. Lit. "head, chief"
7. There is a possible play on words with "Jerusalem." Alternate translations could include: "brings you to completion" and perhaps, ironically, "brings you peace." See L. Köhler et al., *The Hebrew and Aramaic Lexicon of the Old Testament* (Leiden: Brill, 2001), 1532-1538.
8. Cf. F. Brown et al., *The Brown-Driver-Briggs Hebrew and English Lexicon* (Peabody: Hendrickson, 2000), 980. See also *HALOT*, 1365-1366.

## Literary and Historical Contexts

*Genre*

As argued previously, the ability to ascertain the generic illocutions of the Psalter and of individual psalms is critical to interpretation. The genre of Psalm 137 is that of imprecation yet, as Allen comments, "Psalm 137 defies straightforward classification in form-critical terms."[9] Ahn agrees: "Classifying Psalm 137 is complex. The form may be a communal lament, a modified Zion psalm, or a malediction against Edom and Babylon."[10] Berlin offers a similar classification but notes that the emphasis lies on the modification, "Psalm 137 transforms the Zion-song into the Jerusalem lament."[11]

The diversity of form characteristics within this psalm is not unique and demonstrates the necessity of both a thick description and a focus on the literary nature of the psalms.[12] It will be argued that while there are several attendant illocutions[13] in Psalm 137, it is broadly a communal lament[14] and primarily a psalm of imprecation.[15] Attendant illocutions explicit in many of the impreca-

---

9. L. C. Allen, *Psalms 101-150* (vol. 21; Waco: Word, 1983), 237-238. Allen notes elements of the complaint genre that include "the description of woe 1-3, which refers both to the sufferers and to their foes, vv 5-6 can be understood as an implicit confession of trust, while v7 is a petition for punishment." In the end, Allen prefers the category of a "modified Psalm of Zion." (Allen, *Psalms 101-150*, 237-241.)

10. J. Ahn, "Psalm 137: Complex Communal Laments," *JBL* 127, no. 2 (2008): 267. Ahn notes the list of genres that have been suggested, "Scholars have suggested a lament commemorating the destruction of Jerusalem (Zech 7:3), a ballad, a song of Zion, a modified Song of Zion, a Song of Ascent, a complaint, a *mock-simha*, and an imprecation." He concludes, "Psalm 137's complexity is due to the fact that it begins as a communal lament (vv. 1-3 or 1-4), has elements of a Zion psalm (vv. 4-6), and concludes as a proscription (vv. 7-9)." (Ahn, "Psalm 137," 271-272.)

11. A. Berlin, "Psalms and the Literature of Exile: Psalms 137, 44, 69, and 78," in *Book of Psalms: Composition and Reception* (ed. P. W. Flint and P. D. Miller; Leiden: Brill, 2005), 71.

12. The approach of Firth is preferred in this regard. He comments that achieving exact form-critical classification is of less importance than attending to the final form of the psalms. (Firth, *Surrendering Retribution*, 15.)

13. These attendant illocutions are performed through the features present within the imprecation.

14. The interplay between communal and individual elements in this psalm is significant and will be addressed in the exegetical discussion below. Ahn notes that the psalm does not follow the usual structure of communal lament as described by Westermann. (C. Westermann, *The Living Psalms* (Grand Rapids: Eerdmans, 1989), 26.) Ahn provides the following outline: "Address (v. 7), Lament (vv. 1-2), Its contrasts (vv. 3-4), Petition (vv. 5-6, Double request (vv. 7-8b), and Vow of praise (vv. 8c-9). (Ahn, "Psalm 137," 267.)

15. Anderson comments, "Perhaps the best solution is to class Ps. 137 as a Communal Lament culminating in an imprecation upon the enemies." (A. A. Anderson, *The Book of Psalms: Based on the Revised Standard Version* (2vols.; Grand Rapids: Eerdmans, 1981), 137.)

A Theological Interpretation of Psalm 137 161

tory psalms include a declaration of trust and loyalty to Yahweh that distances the psalmist from the enemy and affirms Yahweh's sovereign rule. Both of these attendant illocutions also feature in the songs of Zion.

*Sitz im Leben*
Historical context is more significant in the interpretation of Psalm 137 than it is for many other psalms. However, even though this is the case, the exact time of composition is unclear. Goldingay comments, "Psalm 137 is the great exception to the rule that the psalms do not reveal their historical context, except that even it is not an exception. In the end it proves the rule in the sense that it tests it but vindicates it."[16] This "vindication" is due to the ambiguity created by the various references within the psalm. Commentators support one of two periods of composition: that of the Babylonian exile or that of the subsequent, post-exilic period.[17] The opening verses indicate that the psalmist personally experienced the exile in Babylon, yet the use of the adverb שָׁם "there" suggests a distancing from that location.[18] Furthermore, in contrast to verse 4, verses 5-6 suggest that the psalmist is now able to sing songs of Zion (and the psalm itself is an instance of such an event), which also suggests temporal and geographic distance from the exile.[19] However, the last verses of the psalm suggest that Babylon is present and able to be the object of punishment. Had this psalm been composed in a post-exilic context, then the rise of the Persian Empire should have precluded this possibility. Yet, the fact that Babylon became symbolic of all those who oppose Yahweh's reign supports the possibility of a post-exilic

---

While it is true that imprecation is a sub-category of lament, the primary illocution of the psalm needs to be identified. As suggested above, imprecation is a primary illocution of the psalm.
 16. Goldingay, *Psalms 3*, 600.
 17. For an extended discussion of the debate see Allen, *Psalms 101-150*, 238-239.
 18. Goldingay notes that the use of שָׁם does not always necessitate distance noting Pss. 48:6 and 76:3. (Goldingay, *Psalms 3*, 600.) Ahn agrees and suggests that the lexeme "poetically replaces Babylon." Ahn continues to argue for an exilic date as there is no reference to the "third wave of forced migrants, that is, the 582 B.C.E group." He suggests that verses 1-6 and 7-9 describe the experience of the first wave and second waves respectively and is "reasonably certain" that the lack of reference to threefold destruction of Jerusalem confirms a date prior to 582. (Ahn, "Psalm 137," 273.) Kellerman disagrees, "Wo hat der psalmist zum ersten Mal solche Klage und solchen Fluch angestimmt? Er berichtet in v. 1-4 in zeitlicher und raumlicher Distanz von Exilsort in der Form erklarender Ruckschau; also vird er inzwischen das babylonische Exil verlassen haben. Man mus judoch in diesen vorsichtig sein; immerhin ware es auch moglich, das er in der Redeform der q. pers. pl. Sich mit den Eindrucken der Angesprochen bzw. Zuhorer indetifiziert, selbst also gar nicht das Exil erlebt hat." (U. Kellermann, "Psalm 137," ZAW 90, no. 1 (1978): 51.)
 19. Zenger argues for Asaphite temple singer authorship in postexilic Jerusalem. (F.-L. Hossfeld et al., *Psalms 3: A Commentary on Psalms 101-150* (Minneapolis: Fortress Press), 514.)

context.[20] Goldingay concludes, "It is thus impossible to be clear whether the psalm belongs in the exile or afterward, but it is easy to imagine it being used in either context."[21] That the psalm reflects on the exilic experience is clear and this, perhaps, is more important than when that reflection took place. However, the discussion below will offer some suggestions regarding the significance of either setting. Ultimately, Goldingay's comment regarding ambiguity is important as it supports the intentional democratization[22] of the psalms. Miller concurs, "even the most apparently obvious of such psalms remain to some degree debatable. The looseness of the psalms from all that historical rootage is not a problem, but a gain and opens up interpretive possibilities."[23]

*Placement within the Psalter*
Psalm 137 occurs in the middle of Book V, following closely after the Songs of Ascents (Pss. 120-34) and reflects a number of similar features. Mays observes, "The combination of formal elements, corporate and individual styles, and concern with Zion give the psalm a resemblance to the songs of ascents. Perhaps that is why it concludes the three psalms (Psalm 135-136) attached to the collection of the songs."[24] The placement of Psalm 137 within this immediate context creates interesting possibilities. Psalms 135 and 136 are praises that focus on Yahweh's faithfulness. Psalm 138 is a thanksgiving psalm that reflects on Yahweh's חסד. Placed at the conclusion of the Songs of Ascents and embedded between praise and thanksgiving, the lament of Psalm 137 does not "come away cleanly." It appears that the editors of the Psalter believed Psalm 137 not only reflected an appropriate response to its circumstance, but also represented an appropriate response of the community in their memory of those circumstances and in future instances commensurate with those of the psalm.[25] Ahn comments:

> Yet why would Psalm 137, accentuated by laments and curses, be placed in the midst of these thanksgiving and praise psalms? This is a bold but unconventional editorial move that proposes to give thanks and praise through laments laden with honest feelings of enmity. Thanksgiving and praise arise not only from positive elements in life. Rather, the true mark of these practices is finding the courage and strength to praise and give thanks when there is nothing worthwhile

---

20. Cf. Zech. 1:15.
21. Goldingay, *Psalms 3*, 601.
22. I am using the term "democratization" to refer that feature of the psalms that encourages and anticipates their appropriation by future readers and communities in various yet similar contexts.
23. Miller, *Interpreting the Psalms*, 23.
24. Mays, *Psalms*, 422.
25. Some have suggested this cluster of psalms (135-138) were used for corporate and private prayer in the courtyard of the temple (See H.-J. Kraus, *Psalms 60-150: A Commentary* (Minneapolis: Fortress Press, 1993), 497, 502, 506.) and possibly as "Songs of Descent." (Ahn, "Psalm 137," 275.)

or praiseworthy. Brueggemann says that Psalm 137 is marked not by despair but by hope. However, we cannot move into this hopeful realm all too quickly without allowing the pathos to resound and have its rightful place. The question is, Can those in Babylon, both the first wave and second wave of forced migrants, collectively voice "Hallelujah" or "Thanks be to God" in the midst of their most difficult time? The answer seems to be complex.[26]

The complexity of a communal response to Yahweh's faithfulness and חסד is demonstrated in this "supplement to the Songs of Ascents."[27] In the context of Book V, Psalm 137 represents the kind of lament more prominent in the earlier books of the Psalter. The placement of such a passionate cry for justice so near to the closing of the Psalter reflects its placement in this "supplement to the Songs of Ascents." This dual placement suggests that in the midst of great praise and thanksgiving, a response of lament, even of imprecation, will often be appropriate.[28]

*Internal Structure*

The structure of Psalm 137 is widely debated[29] with some suggesting a division of three strophes of four lines (vv. 1-3, 4-6 and 7-9),[30] others a division of three strophes with the first being the longest (vv. 1-4, 5-6, and 7-9),[31] others a total of four strophes with a the longest occurring first (vv. 1-4, 5-6, 7, and 8-9). Much of the debate centres on verse 4. It seems clear, however, that verse 4 fits best within the first strophe for a number of reasons. Firstly, the focus of the psalmist in the first four verses is on the past. Secondly, the psalmist continues to use the first person plural ("we") until verse 5. Thirdly, there is an inclusio in verses 1 and 4 where "the canals of Babylon" is in parallel with "on foreign soil."[32]

The shift in focus from past to present in verse 5 combined with a shift in voice from first person plural to first person singular suggests a new strophe at this point. A similar shift occurs in verse 7, where Yahweh is addressed for the first time and the focus is on the future vindication of Yahweh's city and His people. Verses 8 and 9 are directly addressed to Babylon rather than to Yahweh, however it must be remembered that this is a lament, which is ultimately

---

26. Ahn, "Psalm 137," 275-276.
27. K. Seybold, *Die Wallfahrtspsalmen: Studien zur Entstehungsgeschichte von Psalm 120-134* (Neukirchen-Vluyn: Neukirchener Verlag, 1978), 74.
28. Note the themes of God's judgment in Psalms 145 and 149 within the crescendo of praise at the conclusion of the Psalter. (i.e., Pss. 145:17-21; 149:6-9).
29. For a detailed discussion of the various positions see Allen, *Psalms 101-150*, 237-241. Allen himself argues for the third position described above.
30. S. Mowinckel, *Real and Apparent Tricola in Hebrew Psalm Poetry* (Oslo: Aschehoug, 1957), 102.
31. Hossfeld et al., *Psalms 3*, 513.273; Ahn, "Psalm 137," 273; G. Savran, "'How Can We Sing a Song of the Lord?' The Strategy of Lament in Psalm 137," *ZAW* 112, no. 1 (2000).
32. Hossfeld et al., *Psalms 3*, 513.

directed to Yahweh in its entirety.³³ On thematic and illocutionary grounds it is best to treat verses 7–9 as one strophe. For these reasons a three strophe structure can be presented as follows:³⁴
  I.   Remembering Exile (vv. 1–4)
  II.  Remember Jerusalem (vv. 5–6)
  III. Remember, Yahweh (vv. 7–9)

## Exposition

I.   Remembering Exile (vv. 1–4)

על נהרות בבל שם ישבנו גם־בכינו בזכרנו את־ציון׃
על־ערבים בתוכה תלינו כנרותינו׃
כי שם שאלונו שובינו דבר־שיר ותוללינו שמחה שירו לנו משיר ציון׃
איך נשיר את־שיר־יהוה על אדמת נכר׃

1   On the canals of Babylon,
      there we sat, more so, we wept,
      as we remembered Zion.
2   On the poplars in its midst
      we hung our lyres.
3   For there our captors asked us for words of song:
      our mockers, (words of) rejoicing,
      "Sing to us from a song of Zion."
4   How could we sing a song of Yahweh
      on foreign ground?

This initial strophe reflects on the "torment" of the exile. Whether or not this reflection took place shortly after the event described and during the exile is of little importance. Robert Alter proposes a chilling possibility when he suggests that the psalm as a whole was an immediate, ironic, and "bloodcurdling" response to the request of the captors:

> The Babylonians have laid waste to Jerusalem, exiled much of its population, looted and massacred; the powerless captives, ordered—perhaps mockingly—to sing their Zion songs, respond instead with a lament that is not really a song and ends with this bloodcurdling curse pronounced on their captors, who, fortunately, do not understand the Hebrew in which it is pronounced.³⁵

---

33. The discussion below will address the possible referents of the "blessed" one of verses 8 and 9.
34. For further support of this three strophe division see Allen, *Psalms 101-150*, 240-241.
35. R. Alter, *The Book of Psalms: A Translation with Commentary* (New York: W. W. Norton, 2007), 475.

A two-stage history of composition is possible, with verses 1–4 being added in the post-exilic context.[36] These verses would then function to frame verses 5–9 in ways that would have been unnecessary in their original context as a response to the captor's request. That verses 1–4 reflect a temporal and geographic distance from the events supports the possibility. In particular, the question of verse 4 is directed at future readers. Zenger comments, "v. 4 would then, like vv. 1–4 as a whole, be a retrospective element; that is, v. 4 is a question addressed to those who hear the psalm, or to those who might pray it at a later time, and explains to them the deepest reason for refusing to sing songs of Zion in 'Babylon.'"[37] Verses 5–9 would then represent a passionate response sung in the face of the captors whose desire for a song of Zion was granted. While the compositional history of the psalm is of some interest, its final form controls its function. The backward focus of these verses now functions to remind the reader of the horror of the exile and to justify the ensuing response.[38]

The focus on the location of the events is pronounced by a number of features in this first strophe. The repetition of the lexeme שׁם in verses 1 and 3 repeatedly reminds the reader of the distance to Babylon. "On the canals of Babylon" and "on foreign ground" are in parallel and form an inclusio around the strophe. The reference to "canals"[39] and "poplars" that would have lined their banks are vivid reminders of the scene.[40]

This location was an inappropriate one in which to sing a song of Zion.[41] The "captors" or "mockers"[42] seemed well aware of this. Songs of Zion are

---

36. Others have suggested a more complex history of composition with verses 1–6 or verse 7 as the original text. See Zenger for details, though he himself finds the arguments unpersuasive (Hossfeld et al., *Psalms 3*, 514.)

37. Hossfeld et al., *Psalms 3*, 516.

38. This remembering may resonate in variegated ways. An intertextual reading with the book of Ezekiel would remind the reader that the exile was not an accident and was, in fact, the just punishment of Yahweh against a "rebellious house." This intertextual resonance is quite likely due to the reference to the Chebar canal in Ezekiel. In this context, the self-involving language of verses 5–6 inviting the readers to be loyal to Jerusalem becomes more poignant.

39. "Canals" best captures the meaning of נהרות as it reflects the system built along the Euphrates River by Nebucadnezzar. See R. Albertz, *Israel in Exile: The History and Literature of the Sixth Century B.C.E* (Atlanta: Society of Biblical Literature, 2003), 59. (cf. Ezek. 1:1; 3:15, 23 etc.)

40. For a discussion of all the possible reasons the exiles might have found themselves specifically, "on the canals of Babylon" see Ahn, "Psalm 137," 12-13. It hardly seems necessary to posit a reason for such a geographic reference. It is likely that the communities would have dwelt and/or worked near the main source of water. Moreover, the alien nature of both water and flora enhances the sense of displacement and loss. See Mays, *Psalms*, 422.

41. Due to its limited usage throughout the Old Testament, Zenger notes that the choice of נכר refers intentionally to ground "owned" by foreign gods. (Hossfeld et al., *Psalms 3*, 516.)

42. This *hapax legomenon* has generated a number of suggestions, and little

declarations of Yahweh's sovereign reign. They explicitly affirm His supremacy over all creation and all the nations of the earth. This is reflected in the psalmist's description of the request in verse 4 where the "song of Zion" becomes a "song of Yahweh." Yahweh is honoured in the relocation of such psalms.[43] "There", in captivity, such a statement of Yahweh's reign served to highlight the fact that His people had lost their land. In the ANE context, this loss of land indicated the impotence of the deity connected to it.[44] For the exiles to sing a song of Zion would affirm the taunts of their captors: Yahweh was defeated and Marduk reigned supreme.[45]

The appropriate response to exile was not "rejoicing" (v. 3) with a song of Zion but "weeping" (v. 1). Verses 1-4 are therefore, the psalmists' defence of their response to the exile. "Sitting", "weeping", and the "hanging" of lyres are offered as the right response. The "hanging" of lyres could be a cause of lament as the temple singers were forced to hang up their instruments and take up forced labour. Alternatively, it could be their response to either the exile in general as it symbolized their lament[46] or more specifically to the mocking request

---

consensus. For a description of the various alternatives, see Allen, *Psalms 101-150*, 236. Arguing from an alleged Arabic parallel, Alfred Guillaume is convinced of a translation of slave-driver or someone who mistreats animals. (A. Guillaume, "Meaning of Twll in Psalm 137:3," *JBL* 75, no. 2 (1956): 143-144.) Goldingay suggests "mockers" from *talal* (Goldingay, *Psalms 3*, 599.) as does Dahood. (M. J. Dahood, *Psalms II 51-100* (16-17A; 3 vols.; Garden City: Doubleday, 1966), 271.) Zenger opts for "tormentors" noting that "the precise meaning ... is uncertain." (Hossfeld et al., *Psalms 3*, 512.) The parallel with "captors" and the context of the request for a "song of Zion" support both "mockers" and "tormentors" as possible meanings. Overall, the interpretation of the colon does not seem significantly affected by a lack of precise identification. Ahn's suggestion that the two words refer to two distinct groups within Babylonian society appears speculative and unnecessarily specific. (Ahn, "Psalm 137," 282.)

43. E.g., Pss. 46; 48; 76; 84.

44. It could also be understood as the deity's displeasure and resulting judgment upon their own people. This is reflected in 2 Kings 18:25-35 where Sennacherib is described as being sent by Yahweh to destroy Jerusalem. Peterson has noted ANE texts where the deity's displeasure with their rebellious people has led to abandonment and exile. (B. N. Peterson, *Ezekiel in Context: Ezekiel's Message Understood in Its Historical Setting of Covenant Curses and Ancient Near Eastern Mythological Motifs* (182; Eugene: Pickwick, 2012), 156-169.)

45. The main motivation for Yahweh's deliverance of His people, as portrayed in the book of Ezekiel, is that of His Name. Ezekiel notes that even though the exile is Yahweh's just punishment of "a rebellious house", the effect of this punishment is that His Name has been disgraced among the nations. To restore honor to His Name, Yahweh will deliver His people and restore both them and His land. (Ezek. 36:20-22ff.)

46. Hays comments on the significance of such an act by temple singers, "The lyre was an instrument of joy (Isa. 24:8, Gen. 31:27), so setting it aside reinforces the image of deep sadness. The lyre is also David's instrument, and a symbol of praise throughout the Psalter. In this canonical dimension, the image is breathtaking. For the psalmist to hang up his harp is like the prophet ceasing to prophesy. It suggests a complete resignation

of their captors to sing. The concluding rhetorical question in verse 4, "How could we sing a song of Yahweh on foreign ground?", highlights the fact that there was no other recourse. The refusal to sing for their captors a "standard" song of Zion was an act of loyalty to Yahweh.

With this opening strophe, the psalmist invites the reader to remember. The use of זכר in verse 1 introduces a central action of the psalm that repeats in each strophe, albeit with a different audience. Here in the first strophe, the psalmist is on the one hand calling the reader to remember the events of exile and on the other, reminding the reader of the psalmist's own response to it. The implied answer to the rhetorical question is "How could we have done anything else?" Irrespective of when these verses were initially written, they function to justify what was initially assumed to be true: the weeping, the refusal to sing a "standard" song of Zion, the subsequent declaration of loyalty (vv. 5–6) and the corresponding imprecations (vv. 7–9) are exactly what they should have done.

II. Remember Jerusalem (vv. 5–6)

אִם־אֶשְׁכָּחֵךְ יְרוּשָׁלָ͏ִם תִּשְׁכַּח יְמִינִי׃
תִּדְבַּק־לְשׁוֹנִי לְחִכִּי אִם־לֹא אֶעֱלֶה אֶת־יְרוּשָׁלַ͏ִם עַל רֹאשׁ שִׂמְחָתִי׃

5   If I forget Jerusalem,
        may my right hand forget (how to play).
6       May my tongue stick to my palate:
    If I do not remember you,
    If I do not lift up Jerusalem above my greatest joy.

While the opening strophe invited the reader to remember the circumstances of exile and the impossibility of singing a song of Zion in captivity, these verses are themselves such a song. As noted, this strophe may mark the beginning of the original song, sung in subversive response to the request of their captors.

In verses 5 and 6 the psalmist declares loyalty to Jerusalem and warns himself against forgetting Jerusalem. Forgetting or "not remembering" is in parallel with "not lifting up Jerusalem" as the greatest joy. His loyalty is then expressed in a self-imprecation, which requests physical restrictions of his tongue and his hand if he "forgets."[47] The context may suggest a temple singer who is horrified

---

to one's function with respect to God, and a state of despair." (C. B. Hays, "How Shall We Sing? Psalm 137 in Historical and Canonical Context," *HBT* 27 (2005): 44.) Savran also notes that this is the only time that musical instruments are referred to as being set down, "let alone hung up." However, he probably goes too far in suggesting an echo with violent death by hanging (2Sam 18:9) or by having one's head impaled upon a spike. (Savran, "How Can We Sing," 45–46.)

47. Note the consequential "forgetting" of his hand if he "forgets" Jerusalem. Goldingay notes that the self-curse repeats the verb but without an object, leaving the "the curse's sanction unstated", which parallels other self-curses (e.g., 132:3-5). See Goldingay, *Psalms 3*, 606.

by the possibility of such blasphemy and would rather be stripped of his abilities than use them in a way that dishonours Yahweh.[48]

A shift in focus from Babylon in verses 1-4 to Jerusalem in verses 5-6 is accompanied by a shift in focus from the group to the individual. As mentioned in previous chapters, the use of personal pronouns in the psalms is significant as it is one of the literary devices employed by the psalmist to draw the reader into the narrative of the psalm. Not only are these verses a picture of a loyal Israelite who, amidst the horror of exile, will not forget Jerusalem but will continue to "make it his greatest joy", they are also intended to become the words of the reader as well. In the relocation of the psalm in subsequent contexts and generations, the reader or listener is invited not only to affirm the illocutionary stance of the psalmist but to adopt his stance. While the plural pronouns of the first strophe reflect on a past community in Babylon and invite the reader to reflect on that experience, the shift in verses 5-6 to both Jerusalem and to self-involving, first person pronouns express the psalmist's own sentiment and challenge the reader's loyalty.

III. Remember, Yahweh (vv. 7-8)

זכר יהוה לבני אדום את יום ירושלם האמרים ערו ערו עד היסוד בה:
בת־בבל השדודה אשרי שישלם־לך את־גמולך שגמלת לנו:
אשרי שיאחז ונפץ את־עלליך אל־הסלע:

7   Remember, Yahweh, the sons of Edom on the day of Jerusalem,
those who were saying:
"Strip (her)! Strip (her)! to her foundation."
8   Daughter of Babylon, the one who is destroyed,
Blessed is he who pays you back your reward,
exactly as you rewarded us.
9      Blessed is he who seizes and smashes your infants on the rock.

The remembering of exile and the psalmist's call to remember Jerusalem reach their climax in the call to Yahweh to remember. This imperative, requesting Yahweh to remember in verse 7, is the climactic illocution within the psalm around which all other illocutions are oriented. Zenger agrees:

---

48. Hence the phrase "how to play" has been added in the translation above. See R. Davidson, *The Vitality of Worship: A Commentary on the Book of Psalms* (Grand Rapids: Eerdmans, 1998), 440-441. See also, Kraus, *Psalms 60-150*, 503.

Zenger, however, disagrees, arguing that the self imprecation of these verses should be understood in broader terms of speech and action rather than specifically referring to the skill of a temple singer, "vv. 5b and 6a cannot be restricted to the hand that plays the lyre and the tongue that sings the song; rather, "the right hand" and "the tongue" are metonyms for action and speech as two fundamental aspects of human life ... One could paraphrase vv. 5-6 very pointedly: If I do not make Jerusalem (now and in the future!) the center of my life, I would be better off dead!" (Hossfeld et al., *Psalms 3*, 518.)

This is, on the one hand, a consistent and at the same time a climactic continuation of the poetic dramaturgy: if the Israelites have not forgotten the events that overwhelmed Zion or Jerusalem-and dare not ever forget them-YHWH as well, indeed YHWH especially, may not forget them, and he ought to respond with action.[49]

The first request is that Yahweh remembers the response of Edom to the fall of Jerusalem. In a typical personification of the city, continued in verse 8 by the psalmist himself, the Edomites cry out for Jerusalem to be "stripped naked"[50] (lit. "torn or stripped down to her foundations"). Their delight in the fall of Jerusalem and the destruction of her people is not something that Yahweh should forget.[51]

The address then shifts from Yahweh in verse 7 to the people of Babylon in verses 8 and 9 whom the psalmist refers to collectively as her "daughter." The confidence of the psalmist that Yahweh will "remember" is reflected in his reference to this daughter[52] as "the one who is destroyed", effectively stating that she is already as good as dead.[53]

To "remember" implies more than simply a cognitive action. It is an appeal for Yahweh to be Yahweh, the one who hears, remembers, sees, knows and

---

49. Hossfeld et al., *Psalms 3*, 518. As mentioned earlier, imprecations such as this are often regarded as ungodly responses to the situation. Libolt's conclusion is representative of such a view (Libolt, "God Speech," 30.) In order to remove this request from the lips of the psalmist, Achtemeier suggests that the speaker of these last verses has changed and they reflect the responses of "others" to the psalmist's song (E. R. Achtemeier, *Preaching Hard Texts of the Old Testament* (Peabody: Hendrickson, 1998), 109-110.) I will argue below that the psalmist does, in fact, have Yahweh's honor in view. Achtemeier's position is not convincing as she has not offered any evidence for it other than her conclusion that the sentiment of the previous verses is at odds with vv. 7-9.

50. This is consistent with the ANE portrayal of cities as women and appears again with reference to Babylon's daughters in verse 7. The exile is also portrayed in terms of violence and rape against the woman of Jerusalem in Ezekiel 16.

51. The focus on Edom is warranted and is reflected in other exilic and post-exilic writings where Edom, like Babylon, becomes typical of the enemies of Yahweh (cf. Ezek. 25:12-14; 35:1-36:15; Obad. 10-14; Lam. 4:21-22). Calvin comments, "Vengeance was to be executed upon the other neighbouring nations which had conspired to destroy Jerusalem, so that they are all doubtless included here under the children of Edom, who are specified, a part for the whole." (J. Calvin, *Commentary on the Book of Psalms* (vol. V; Grand Rapids: Eerdmans, 1949), 195.)

52. Here the feminine metaphor is extended to the inhabitants of Babylon and anticipates her "children" in verse 9.

53. The particle השדודה is best taken as a gerund, "one who is destroyed", rather than a perfect referring to an already completed event. (For fuller discussion see Hossfeld et al., *Psalms 3*, 519.) Allen opts for an active form, "one who destroys", arguing that the context seems to suggest it as a grounds for punishment. (Allen, *Psalms 101-150*, 237.) The passive form of the MT is retained here and seems equally likely in the context as it offers hope to future readers who can all consider "Babylon" as defeated.

delivers.[54] This call for Yahweh to remember and so act on behalf of His people strengthens its connection with the psalms in its immediate context. Psalms 135 and 136 both refer to Yahweh as the one who remembers and vindicates his people.[55] They praise Yahweh for His deliverance and the destruction of His enemies and affirm that He is able to "do whatever pleases him" and "strike down the nations."[56]

The notorious concluding lines of the psalm follow the address to Babylon's daughter as the "one who is destroyed." A double blessing is pronounced upon the one who will execute justice and bring the vindication of Yahweh's people. Translating אשרי as "happy" rather than "blessed" is less than ideal,[57] confusing the force of the declaration and reducing the outcome to an emotional response. Anderson notes that אשרי is a state to be emulated[58] and it is intrinsic to those in relationship with Yahweh, who know of His great acts of deliverance.[59] This is certainly true of the blessed person in Psalms 1 and 2, which offer an interesting context within which to read these last two verses, a point which will be discussed below.

The blessed person of Psalm 137 is the one who gives Babylon her "reward." The phrase, שישלם־לך את־גמולך שגמלת לנו, reflects the *lex talionis* as does the more specific description in verse 9 of what the psalmist counts as just recompense. The repetition of גמל and the inclusion of the ש (translated "exactly as")[60] both emphasize the commensurate nature of the desired punishment. It seems likely that the choice of שלם intentionally creates both pun and dark irony. Zenger notes that שלם is the *"terminus technicus"* for the principle of retaliation and that Jerusalem is now pictured as the "city of retaliation."[61] On the one hand, the resonance with Jerusalem is obvious, on the other, the semantic domain offers a number of possibilities. While "rewarded" or "paid back" fits the context, "completed" or better yet, "made an end of" is also implied which is ironically their "peace."[62]

A context of *lex talionis* informs the interpretation of the concluding line of the psalm. Rather than a bloodthirsty response seeking to enact the greatest possible harm upon their enemies, the "seizing" and "smashing" of infants upon the rock is a chilling reminder of what the Israelites themselves suffered

---

54. Cf. Exod. 2:23-25; 3:7-10; 6:2-8. See also, K. Barker, "I Am Who I Am," in *Dictionary of the Bible and Western Culture* (ed. M. A. Beavis and M. J. Gilmour; Sheffield: Sheffield Phoenix Press, 2012), 226.
55. Pss. 135:13-14; 136:23-24.
56. Pss. 135:8-12; 136:17-22.
57. The NIV opts for "happy" and fails to repeat it the second time, imposing its own ellipsis on the cola.
58. Anderson, *The Book of Psalms*, 737.
59. Allen, *Psalms 101-150*, 47.
60. *BDB*, 980.
61. Hossfeld et al., *Psalms 3*, 519. Cf. *BDB*, 1022.
62. *BDB*, 1022.

at the hands of the Babylonians, a practice not uncommon in the ANE.⁶³ Furthermore, this last declaration is of course exactly what Yahweh had Himself promised to enact, and does not fit the geography of Babylon where such rock formations do not feature.⁶⁴

## The Illocutionary Acts of Psalm 137

Having presented an exposition of the psalm, it is now important to consider the meaning of the psalm in its entirety. As discussed in previous chapters, this is most clearly achieved by considering the illocutionary acts performed at a number of levels and by providing a corresponding "thick description" of the psalm. These authorial and literary levels will be discussed in the following order:⁶⁵
1. Human Authorial and Editorial Illocutions
   a. Primary and Attendant Illocutions of Psalm 137
   b. Primary Illocutions of the Psalter in Psalm 137
2. Divine Illocutions in the Context of the Hebrew Bible
3. Divine Illocutions in the Context of the Christian Canon—A Thick Description

*Human Authorial and Editorial Illocutions*
Many of the illocutions of Psalm 137 were discussed in the exposition above. It is important to now recognize these as being either primary or attendant. In the first strophe (vv. 1-4) the primary illocutions of the psalm are to remind the reader of the horrors of exile, and to ask the reader to acquiesce with the response of the psalmist to the request of their captors. The rhetorical question "how could we sing . . . ?" invites the reader to agree that they could not have. In so doing, an important attendant illocution is also accomplished. By recalling the weeping, and the refusal and by asking this final rhetorical question, the psalmist invites the reader to consider their own loyalty to Yahweh.

This attendant illocution of the first strophe, inviting the reader to consider their loyalty to Yahweh, becomes the primary illocution of the second

---

63. Nah 3:10; Deut 32:25; 2 Kgs 8:12.
64. Isa 13:1, 9, 14-16 (cf. Jer 51:25, 54-58). Zenger notes the presence of "thematic words" which connect Psalm 137 to Jerermiah 50-51 suggesting intentional allusion, "The proclamations of the judgment and destruction of Babylon in Jeremiah 50-51 (especially 51:6, 20-26, 49-50, 55-56) must also be adduced in an interpretation of vv. 7-9. Psalm 137:8-9 has the "thematic words" בת בבל ("daughter of Babylon"), שדד ("devastate"), שלם ("repay"), גמל ("do"), and נפץ ("destroy") in common with this perspective. It is probable that Ps. 137:8-9 was inspired by Jeremiah 50-51" (Hossfeld et al., *Psalms 3*, 520.) More broadly, the "infants" could also be a reference to the entire population of the city as her progeny (c.f. Isa. 54:1-3, 5-6, 13).
65. At a macro-level, this structure imitates Wolterstorff's "1st and 2nd Hermeneutic" by addressing the human and divine illocutions in that order.

strophe (vv. 5-6). While on the one hand the psalmist is declaring loyalty to Jerusalem and imprecating against himself, he is also performing other illocutions by offering the psalm to the reader and the community. Use of the self-involving, first person singular pronoun draws the reader into the narrative and imposes itself upon them. The challenge to "consider Jerusalem my highest joy" also confronts the reader, reinforcing the invitation that they consider their own conviction.

The move to the third strophe is marked by a change in the direction of address. Here the call to remember is directed at Yahweh, and, as noted, is not really a call to recall something to mind but a call to act in accordance with His covenant promises, to bring justice and to vindicate His people. The address to Babylon and the declaration of blessing upon the one who will enact this punishment must be considered in light of the song being sung to Yahweh. This is also true of the first two strophes. While they have their own primary and attendant illocutions as mentioned above, in the context of the third strophe where Yahweh is revealed as the one to whom the psalm is addressed, the earlier strophes now function to perform additional illocutions vis-à-vis verses 7-9. Now the call to remember and to covenant loyalty is informed by the imprecatory call to Yahweh. The psalmist affirms his loyalty and that of the community (vv. 1-4), asserts that his greatest concern is for Yahweh's kingdom (vv. 5-6), and now calls for Yahweh himself to remember what has happened and be equally concerned (vv. 7-9).

At each stage of the psalm, the psalmist is presenting his response (and that of the exilic community and subsequent users) as one that is righteous. The effect of concluding with the imprecation against Babylon and Edom suggests that this is a climactic act of loyalty consistent with the acts of the previous strophes. Francis Watson argues that this psalm incites hatred, and so dismisses any contemporary appropriation of it.[66] He is correct in noting that it incites hatred. He is wrong, however, to dismiss this function. While the psalmist is imprecating against Edom and Babylon, he is also asserting that this response of hatred toward the enemies of Yahweh's kingdom is both justified and righteous. The use of אשׁרי in the last verses suggests that both the desiring and the enacting of the punishment are acts of righteousness as the Psalter clearly portrays אשׁרי as the state of the righteous (cf. Ps 1:1). This is further supported by the appeal to the *lex talionis* that models a just response to the oppression and violence. Therefore, the psalmist presents the closing imprecation as the product of a long-standing loyalty and an act of righteousness while at the same time appealing to Yahweh to be similarly impassioned and to act on behalf of His people.

A particular feature of this psalm is its oscillation between communal and individual lament and this movement is used to construct associated illocutionary forces. In the first and third strophes, the psalmist recalls the community's experiences of exile and calls for Yahweh's just punishment of the wicked

---

66. Watson, *Text and Truth*, 120-121.

"exactly as they rewarded us." However, in the second strophe, the psalmist personally responds to this situation with a self-imprecation and an implicit declaration of loyalty. This oscillation has a number of effects. Firstly, the context of a communal experience of oppression assists the reader in determining "similar circumstances." Secondly, the self-involving language of the second strophe encourages the reader to enter the narrative of the psalm and respond to this communal crisis. The effect of this literary movement is that it calls for the reader to consider their obligation as part of the broader community of God's people and challenges their response to communities in crises.[67]

What has been noted in the above discussion is that a number of illocutions are performed by way of the psalmist directing the psalm to Yahweh. At the same time, different illocutions are performed in the offering of the psalm (by the psalmist and editors of the Psalter) to the reader and the community.[68] Illocutions directed to Yahweh include: the declaration of loyalty to His kingdom and the request that He vindicate His people by destroying the enemy. Illocutions directed to the reader and the community include the justification of the exiles' prior actions and the challenge to the contemporary audience to acquiesce and adopt the stance of the psalmist. Likewise, the psalm also challenges the reader's loyalty to Yahweh and invites them to reflect on their own response to injustice.

As suggested in earlier chapters, using speech act theory to classify illocutions as either primary or attendant provides a valuable clarifying tool for biblical interpretation in its endeavour to discover the meaning of a text. The "meaning" of the text or the "main purpose(s)" of the psalm are those primary illocutions which the attendant illocutions then serve. In this case, the lower-level, attendant illocutions of each strophe serve the primary illocution of

---

67. The reverse situation is also present within the Psalter and this important interplay between the community and the individual is one of its significant contributions to the canonical proclamation. This reverse situation occurs through the inclusion of individual laments within the Psalter. In a community context, the psalms of the individual not only validate their utility by the individual but call for the community to recognize the importance of such a response and speak as a community on behalf of the individual. The following chapter will address this issue briefly with respect to Psalm 69, yet further work is required on how these individual psalms direct their illocutionary forces at the community in particular. On the function of individual laments within a community see Firth, *Surrendering Retribution*, 13.

68. I have intentionally avoided a discussion of canonical stages along the lines suggested by Waltke and Kaiser. (Kaiser, *Toward an Old Testament Theology*; Waltke, "Canonical Process Approach.") The speculative nature of such stages and the limited exegetical benefit of such an inquiry render the discussion unnecessary. Alternatively, I have opted to discuss these issues under human and divine illocutions and the category of "direction of address." The human and divine illocutions recognize literary levels from those internal to a psalm to those of the broader Psalter. Additionally, the "direction of address" accounts for how the psalm functions as the prayer *of* an individual or the community and how it functions as a proclamation *to* the individual and the community.

imprecation. While imprecation is a primary illocution of Psalm 137, it is not its only primary action. Additional primary illocutions are performed through the inclusion of the psalm in the Psalter and the canon.

*Primary Illocutions of the Psalter in Psalm 137*
As discussed in previous chapters, the Psalter performs a number of primary illocutions which need to be accounted for in the interpretation of any individual psalm. With respect to Psalm 137, the Psalter's invitation to mimesis (the offering of the psalms as righteous responses in similar situations) is particularly important. This primary illocution mirrors the way in which the psalmist himself has constructed Psalm 137 to engage the reader and invite them to adopt his stance. Additionally, the psalmist's declaration of loyalty and the imprecation are also consistent with the Psalter's primary illocution declaring the reign of Yahweh. I have commented elsewhere on a number of generic illocutions common to the imprecatory psalms which are applicable in the case of Psalm 137:

> More specifically, the sub-generic illocutions of the imprecatory psalms might include the following: the assertion that vengeance is the Lord's, the call to surrender retribution to him, and the implicit command not to exceed commensurate levels of judgment.[69]

*Divine Illocutions in the Context of the Hebrew Bible*
Having discussed the human illocutions performed in Psalm 137, a theological interpretation requires that the text be examined vis-à-vis its function as divine discourse. The discussion will begin with the way in which God spoke through the psalm in its Old Testament context, and subsequently consider how God continues to speak through the psalm in a canonical, new covenant context.

It was noted above that the psalm was addressed to two audiences, namely Yahweh and the Israelite community, and that these directions of address had distinct illocutions associated with them. The psalmist of Psalm 137 was conscious of both audiences as the first strophe anticipates the Israelite community and speaks of Yahweh in the third person, whereas, in the second strophe the psalmist addresses himself (and implicitly, Yahweh), and in the third he addresses Yahweh directly. Where the psalmist is addressing himself or Yahweh, the illocutions (of self-imprecation and those declaring loyalty to Yahweh and requesting Him to "remember") cannot also be understood as Yahweh's illocutions. This is the conundrum of the psalms: human words directed to God are somehow the words of God directed to humanity. At this point, God cannot be performing these particular illocutions. Again, I have summarized

---

69. Barker, "Divine Illocutions," 11. By "sub-generic" I was referring to the imprecatory psalms as a sub-genre of lament.

this elsewhere and argued that the illocutions directed to Him are not directly appropriated by Him:

> I would propose that psalms like 137 be understood as divinely sanctioned human responses. In other words, God is appropriating the generic illocutions rather than the original illocutions of the human author at the time of the prayer. In Psalm 137, God is not appropriating the illocution of self imprecation requesting that 'his hand might wither', nor is he appropriating a memory of captivity which he did not experience, nor is he appropriating the request that he himself remember the evil actions of the Edomites. Rather, God is appropriating the entire psalm as a proper response to extreme violence. This also means that he appropriates a number of secondary or ancillary illocutions along the way. Wherever the psalmist affirms something about reality, God would also affirm that same thing, etc. However, the main point that the human author of the psalm is making is also the main point that God is making: respond like this when faced with this kind of circumstance.[70]

Therefore, when the psalmist performs illocutions directed to God (i.e., the "original" illocutions of the quotation above),[71] God *affirms the stance of the psalmist but does not appropriate them*. In this way there is synchronic illocutionary divergence. God does not perform all of the illocutions of the human author at that point in time.[72] In contrast, when the psalmist is addressing the audience, God also addresses the audience by performing the same illocutions. This is an instance of synchronic illocutionary convergence. Similarly, many of the primary illocutions of the Psalter are also instances of synchronic illocutionary convergence. In particular, the invitation of the Psalter to mimesis and its affirmation of the psalms within it as righteous responses to similar situations are also divine illocutions.[73]

---

70. Barker, "Divine Illocutions," 11-12. In this reference I am using the term "generic illocutions" to refer more broadly to illocutions occuring at the level of the Psalter, rather than illocutions that are solely a product of genre. As I discussed above, this is how Vanhoozer uses the term in some cases. I have since adopted the term "primary illocutions of the Psalter" to refer to these particular actions.

71. By "original" I was distinguishing between the illocutions of the psalm in isolation (its "original" illocutions) and its illocutions performed by way of its inclusion in the Psalter. I have since clarified this terminology by referring to "direction of address." The "original" illocutions of the quotation above are best recognized as those illocutions performed in the psalm that are directed to God. This is a necessary correction of the terminology as clearly some of the "original" illocutions were also addressed to the Israelite community and the reader and in those cases do not fit the argument being presented.

72. This was the burden of Chapter 4 which sought to demonstrate that the Psalter presents itself as collection of righteous responses.

73. There is also a possibility of further divine illocutions produced through the intratextuality of the Psalter. While the level of editorial intentionality is difficult to ascertain, a presupposition of divine supervention in the Psalter's editorial process

*Divine Illocutions in the Context of the Christian Canon—A Thick Description*
The discussion has focused on the human and divine illocutions of Psalm 137 in its Old Testament contexts. What remains is an examination of how the psalm now functions as divine discourse in its canonical, new covenant context. Chapter 3 introduced the concept of central illocutions, which canonically supervene in such a way that they alter the context in which other illocutions subsequently exist. Chapter 5 discussed New Testament illocutions related to imprecation that may be considered central illocutions. These illocutions were examined in order to determine the nature of their supervention. In particular, I examined whether or not they have changed the conditions in which the illocutions of the Psalter now exist to such an extent that the invitation to imprecation is no longer in play. In other words, has the presence of any particular New Testament illocution altered the context so that there is no longer illocutionary convergence between the divine and human authors vis-à-vis the offering of the imprecatory psalms as righteous responses. I concluded that this was, in fact, not the case and that the New Testament not only affirms the stance of the Psalter but that its own stance toward imprecation is similar.

With that in mind, it remains for me to address how in fact the New Testament has altered the context and what divine illocutions are subsequently being performed through Psalm 137. Rather than resulting in a reduction of illocutionary action by the voiding of previous illocutions, the New Testament provides central illocutions that expand the illocutionary force of Psalm 137.[74]

I suggested that God appropriates the primary illocutions of the Psalter in *offering* these psalms to His people, and *inviting* their utility in similar circumstances. Moreover, God is not only appropriating the whole-text illocutions of the psalm, but is also performing attendant illocutions based upon their content. As God is offering the psalm as an example of a righteous response, He is therefore *affirming* the stance of the psalmist within the psalm. This makes sense of the difficulty in construing how the words of God's people directed to God can be counted as God's words directed to God's people. In this way the entire Psalter continues to function as divine discourse.

In the case of Psalm 137, and commonly in the imprecatory psalms, God is affirming the loyalty of the psalmist, the anger of the psalmist and the psalmist's desire that God's name and His people are vindicated. Far from being at odds with "the speech-act that lies at the centre of Christian scripture, the life, death and resurrection of Jesus as the enfleshment and the enactment of the divine Word,"[75] the illocutions of Psalm 137 gain a new focus through their rela-

---

creates the possibility for boundless intratextual intentionality and corresponding illocutionary action. In this way, the complexity of the Psalter with its multi-authored, diachronic formation mirrors that of the broader canon where the same possibility for boundless intratextual intention and corresponding divine canonical illocutions exists.

74. The next five paragraphs are drawn from my previous work, Barker, "Psalms of the Powerless."

75. Watson, *Text and Truth*, 121.

A Theological Interpretation of Psalm 137 177

tionship with the totality of the canon. The New Testament provides a vision of reality and of the future where all of God's enemies, and so the enemies of His people, will be destroyed by His Son.[76] The prayers of loyalty to Zion become prayers for God's kingdom and the rule of Christ to be fully realized. The prayer for vindication is performed with the knowledge of God's wrath being satisfied in the One to whom the prayer is now offered. This One now has the right and the role of bringing God's judgment upon all who reject Him.

It was noted earlier that some claim this psalm "incites hatred", and so can never be appropriated by Christians.[77] In contrast to this view, I suggested here that God's offering of Psalm 137 to His people is an invitation to respond likewise in similar situations. As such, He offers this psalm as a righteous response to extreme violence. However, there is important sense in which the text also "incites hatred." In offering this psalm to His people, God is inviting them to imitate its content, its pathos, its faith – its hatred. In a world where injustice, violence and oppression are rampant and God's people are being afflicted at the hands of the wicked, Psalm 137 confronts an apathetic and ambivalent people and incites them to hate, incites them to side with Yahweh, His Son and His people and hate all those who will not give Him glory. At the same time, imprecation precludes human vengeance and calls for the oppressed to surrender retribution to the God who will justly judge.

As mentioned earlier, the Psalter anticipates a surplus of meaning by intentionally not naming the enemies of God's people. While the reference to Edom and Babylon are uncommonly specific in the psalms, they were retained in this Psalm. In a post–Babylonian era, they quickly became symbolic for all those who oppose Zion. The New Testament proclamation concerning the second coming of Christ is replete with such examples,[78] thus encouraging the use of Psalm 137 in a way that the author and editors anticipated. The New Testament invitations to rejoice at the fall of Babylon and to distance oneself from her indicate that the new covenant community should consider all those who oppose the Kingdom of God and oppress His people as instances of Babylon.

The canonical context provides immeasurable possibilities for divine, intertextual intention and its corresponding illocutions.[79] The example above is perhaps one of the clearest intertextual relationships suggesting that the contemporary divine illocutions of Psalm 137 include the call to pray against the enemies of Christ's kingdom. Another example of where the canonical

---

76. Revelation 4; 5; 19. This vision coheres with that of the Psalter where the praise of Psalm 150 is preceded by the destruction of all those opposed to the reign of Yahweh (Psalm 149).

77. Watson, *Text and Truth*, 120.

78. 1 Pet. 5:13; Rev. 14:8; 16:9; 17:5; 18:2, 10, 21.

79. Consequently, it is beyond the scope of this book to discuss every possible way the canonical context shapes the illocutionary force of the psalm. Rather, the aim is to demonstrate the utility of the hermeneutic and to offer primary ways in which this occurs.

context results in an expansion of divine illocutions in Psalm 137 is in the use of אשרי. The "blessed" person in the Psalter is the one who avoids the company of the wicked, commits to Yahweh, meditates on *torah* and seeks refuge in the Son.[80] Here in Psalm 137, the blessed person is the one who will enact God's just punishment. As mentioned in the above quotation, the New Testament declares that Christ will accomplish this at his second coming. Therefore, what was originally left unspecified has been specified in the Christian canon. This specificity is an example of the expansion of divine illocutions in Psalm 137. The human authors of the psalm did not, indeed could not, name the agent of Yahweh's justice, yet by way of the canonical proclamation, God now declares that His Son is the ultimate referent of the blessed one of Psalm 137.[81]

## Conclusion

The application of the proposed hermeneutic has informed a theological interpretation of Psalm 137, clarifying the way in which it functions as divine discourse. This was accomplished first by understanding both the human and divine illocutions performed in its original context (i.e., that of the Psalter). Secondly, it needed to be determined which of these divine illocutions remain in play in the canonical, New Covenant context. In order to make such a determination it was necessary to assess the impact of any central illocutions (those that may have changed the reality in which the previous illocutions of the Psalter now exist). In particular, the New Testament illocutions regarding the atoning work of Christ, His subsequent rule, and the certainty of eschatological judgment set the context in which Psalm 137 now functions. Divine illocutions produced by this new context were then identified. Rather than reducing the range of divine illocutions in Psalm 137, the central illocutions of the New Testament support the illocutionary stance of the Psalter and, in fact, expand its illocutionary force. When read in the canonical context, the original divine illocutions of Psalm 137 remain in play. In the context of Christological proclamation, additional divine illocutions are formed that provide a level of specificity previously lacking.

---

80. Pss. 1 and 2. It is also possible that the king is the picture of the ideal Israelite who fulfills the role of the one who has chosen loyalty and life with Yahweh. See J. A. Grant, *The King as Exemplar: The Function of Deuteronomy's Kingship Law in the Shaping of the Book of Psalms* (Leiden: Brill, 2004). This, then, provides another way in which the canonical context produces divine illocutions in the Psalter by declaring Christ to be both King and Yahweh.

81. This does not exclude the existence of multiple referents prior to the enactment of *Yom Yahweh* at the return of Christ. Neither does it replace Yahweh Himself as the primary agent of the act as the psalmist, of course, directs the psalm to Yahweh and calls on Him to act. Hence, the specific nature of the referent is an "expansion" in that it does not discount other possible referents.

This theological interpretation of Psalm 137 proposes that God continues to affirm the stances of the psalmist. Furthermore, God appropriates the primary illocution of the Psalter in offering the psalm as a righteous response and inviting mimesis in similar situations. Finally, God also appropriates the attendant illocutions challenging both the reader's loyalty to His Son and their response to other communities suffering violent oppression.

I have argued that imprecation is a justified response in the face of continued violence and impenitence. However, it is not always a necessary response. Wisdom is required in judging what settings count as similar to those of the psalms and of their New Testament appropriation. A context of direct violence against God's people by an implacable enemy is an obvious candidate for imprecation. I consider the bombings of Christian churches in Pakistan, and the recent massacres of Christian communities in Syria to be examples of a such a context. However, I have intentionally used the broader language of "extreme violence." Direct attacks against God's people are not the only contexts where God's rule is rejected and His just punishment and deliverance is required. Developing a vision of the world that matches God's vision is foundational to Christian maturity and will shape our responses to injustice. As Christians, we should not only be concerned about the oppression of other Christians, but for all those who are suffering horrific oppression. Whether it is the rule of an unjust government, the rape and torture of women by military groups, or the exploitation of children at the hands of private enterprise, all evil is to be named and handed over to God. McCann states it well:

> In the face of monstrous evil, the worst possible response is to feel *nothing*. What *must* be felt is grief, rage, outrage. In their absence, evil becomes an acceptable commonplace. To forget is to submit to evil, to wither and die; to remember is to resist, be faithful, and live again.[82]

---

82. J. C. McCann, *A Theological Introduction to the Book of Psalms: The Psalms as Torah* (Nashville: Abingdon, 1993), 121, emphasis original.

# Chapter 7
# A Theological Interpretation Of Psalm 69

## Introduction

The previous chapter examined Psalm 137 as an example of a communal imprecation regarding a communal experience of exile and oppression. I concluded that the divine illocutions *point* to Christ in a variety of ways and *invite mimesis* with Him in view.[1] The purpose of this last chapter is to apply the hermeneutic to an individual psalm and to explore whether its theological interpretation reveals similar divine illocutions.

Psalm 69 was chosen as the primary text for this discussion, not only because it is an individual lament, but also because of its use in the New Testament. Its application to Christ by New Testament writers raises significant issues for theological interpretation. Following a brief survey of Christological interpretation and the psalms, I will examine Psalm 69. At this point, a detailed exegetical discussion similar to that offered for Psalm 137 would be repetitive and unnecessary. Therefore, I will present a brief exposition of Psalm 69 focusing on issues relating to imprecation and those that anticipate its use in the New Testament. Subsequent to my summary of these original illocutions, I will then discuss Psalm 69 (and, to a lesser extent, Psalm 109) in light of New Testament usage and suggest the way that this canonical context produces contemporary divine illocutions.

---

1. In Chapter 6 I suggested that the central illocutions regarding Christ formed the following divine illocutions in Psalm 137: 1) Invitations of loyalty to Zion and to Jerusalem become invitations of loyalty to Christ and His kingdom; 2) Christ is declared to be the climactic "blessed one" of the psalm as He is the one through whom God will vindicate his people and destroy "Babylon"; 3) Christ is also declared to be the one to whom and through whom the psalm is offered, being both mediator and king.

## Christological Interpretations of Psalm 69

*Christ is the Speaker of Psalm 69*
A number of interpreters suggest that the New Testament reveals Christ as the ultimate pray-er of the psalms and that Christians can only pray the psalms in the recognition that they speak of Christ and his life.² Waltke is representative of this position when he asserts that the psalms were never understood as prayers "for everyone", arguing that they were originally understood solely as prayers of the king:

> It would be utterly foreign to the culture of pre-exilic Israel to suppose that the psalms were democratized in their interpretation. Such an interpretation would be appropriate for texts in our democratic, twentieth-century Western societies, but it would be unthinkable during the monarchy in pre-exilic Israel.³

Consequently, Waltke reduces the function of the psalms to a portrayal of the prayers of Christ, which can only be appropriated by Christians if they understand they are praying with Him. He continues:

> [Christ] alone is worthy to pray the ideal vision of a king suffering for righteousness and emerging victorious over the hosts of evil. As the corporate head of the church, he represents the believers in these prayers. Moreover, Christians, as sons of God and as royal priests, can rightly pray these prayers along with their representative Head.⁴

Hays offers a more balanced position in his attending to the original meaning of the psalm. However, like Waltke, he believes an important contribution of the gospel to the reading of Psalm 69 is that it requires Jesus to be the speaker. It

---

2. D. Bonhoeffer, *Life Together: Prayerbook of the Bible* (trans. D. W. Bloesch and J. H. Burtness; Minneapolis: Fortress Press, 1996), 46. 402-18; R. B. Hays, "Can the Gospels Teach Us How to Read the Old Testament?," *ProEccl* 11, no. 4 (2002); D. Kidner, *Psalms 1-72: An Introduction and Commentary* (Nottingham IVP, 2008); Kraus, *Psalms 60-150*; Waltke, "Canonical Process Approach," 13.

3. Waltke, "Canonical Process Approach," 13. He suggests that the intertestamental period might be responsible for the loss of a messianic interpretation and that this required rectification. (Waltke, "Canonical Process Approach," 15-16.) For a defence of democratization as a primary function of the Psalter see Grant, *The King as Exemplar*, 22-23.

4. Waltke, "Canonical Process Approach," 16. See also Kraus who concludes, "From the NT perspective, only through the suffering of Jesus as the servant of God has the mystery of the message of Psalm 69 been revealed. For Christians, the essential content of *this psalm will henceforth be accessible in no other way*. The fulfilment "fills" the kerygma of this OT psalm that transcends all individualism; it enters the inexhaustible profundity of the expressions of suffering of a song which, in its powerful proclamation, stands beside Isaiah 53 and Psalm 22 and 118." (Kraus, *Psalms 60-150*, 65, emphasis not original.)

remains unclear whether Hays believes this Christological fulfillment precludes any further appropriation by the followers of Jesus.

> What does a reading of Psalm 69 in light of the Gospel story disclose? In what sense can the disciples be said to have believed this Scripture in a new way as a result of the resurrection?
> The most important clue lies in the fact that the post-resurrection reading sketched in John 2 requires us to understand Jesus as the *speaker*, the praying voice of the Psalm. Notice that the Psalm is formulated in the first person: "Zeal for your house will consume *me*." This interpretation opens up the entire Psalm, not just one half-verse of it, as a proleptic disclosure of the mystery of Jesus' identity. Indeed, from a range of other evidence we know that the early church did read Psalm 69 in precisely this way, as a passion psalm portraying Jesus as the righteous sufferer.[5]

Hays wonders whether the above interpretation suggests that not only this psalm but the entire Psalter be read as the prayers of Christ, "From this perspective to "believe the Scripture" would mean to understand that Jesus is the speaker of the Psalm taken as whole — or perhaps even of the Psalter as a whole?"[6] His explanation of the relationship between the original context and the New Testament context is that David's voice had "anticipated" Christ's, "Thus, a reading of Psalm 69 after the passion and resurrection of Jesus would disclose that the Psalm is to be read as a poetic depiction of the suffering and vindication of Jesus the Messiah, whose voice "David" had anticipated."[7]

This "figural" reading does not, in Hay's estimation, negate the previous function of the psalm in its earlier context of the Psalter. Rather, he argues that both contexts support and inform one another:

> Such retrospective reading neither denies nor invalidates the meaning that the OT text might have had in its original historical setting. Psalm 69 is fully comprehensible as an expression of Israelite piety: it is a prayer for deliverance in a time of trouble and suffering. When it is reread, however, in light of the NT's story of Jesus' passion and resurrection, it takes on additional resonances beyond those perceptible to its earlier readers. The figural correlation between the psalmist's prayer and the story of Jesus illuminates both in unexpected ways.[8]

Hays helpfully notes the mutual illumination of the psalm and the gospel, and that the psalm takes on "additional resonances." However, his explanation of the continuing function of Psalm 69 remains unclear. His affirmation of the

---

5. Hays, "Can the Gospels Teach Us," 13.
6. Hays, "Can the Gospels Teach Us," 414. I will argue below that the New Testament does indeed cast Jesus in the role of the psalmist due to its multiple and various references to the Psalm.
7. Hays, "Can the Gospels Teach Us," 413-414.
8. Hays, "Can the Gospels Teach Us," 414-415.

past function does not automatically affirm this function in the canonical context. Have these new "resonances" changed the context of the psalm so that it no longer functions as a model of a righteous response to suffering? Hays continues his explanation in a footnote:

> This example illustrates what is meant by "figural reading." The retrospective interpretation of an OT text as a typological prefiguration of a subsequent person or event does not in any way annihilate the historical reality of the precursor. Both type and antitype are embraced together as concrete disclosures of God's activity in the world. Therefore, the hermeneutical current flows in both directions, as the "meaning" of each pole in the typological correlation is enhanced by its relation to the other.[9]

Again, this explanation of a "figural reading" affirms the past function of the text or its "historical reality" as a "disclosure of God's activity." He affirms the original context and the function of the psalm as a disclosure of God's action, but does not discuss the other functions of the psalm or whether they are similarly affected. This lack of clarity highlights the need for a speech act theory based hermeneutic which recognizes a variety of actions performed in the text and the necessity for determining which actions remain in play in new contexts. While Hays has affirmed the previous context, it is unclear how the original context continues to function in light of the New Testament.

I will argue that the canonical context requires the psalms to be read with a Christological focus. However, this Christological focus is more nuanced than simply identifying Jesus as the prayer of the psalm. The above discussion of Psalm 137 demonstrated that the central illocutions of the canon have created a number of different illocutions vis-à-vis the Psalter. Rather than reduce all of the psalms to the prayers of Christ, it has revealed that Christ is also a referent within the psalms, the one to whom the psalms are addressed, and the exemplar whom we are to imitate.

Those, like Waltke and Hays, who suggest a reduction of function have not clearly demonstrated why this reduction has occurred. I have argued that an understanding of the contemporary function of the psalms requires the following methodology: determining the original illocutions in the context of the Psalter, determining the effects of the central illocutions of the New Testament upon the Psalter, determining the effects of the particular stance of the New Testament towards the psalm in question, and finally, determining the divine illocutions of the Psalter produced by this new context. Neither Waltke nor Hays have demonstrated how the stance of the New Testament has affected the function of the psalms other than to affirm Christ as the speaker in a select number of cases. This demonstrates the need for greater precision in assessing the psalms' function across the various canonical horizons. I suggest that a dual agency, speech act account is better equipped for this task.

---

9. Hays, "Can the Gospels Teach Us," 415.

### Christ is the "Consummate Example" of Psalm 69

Other interpreters understand the New Testament proclamation to affect the psalms in a different manner. They suggest that the canonical function of the psalms is not limited to either a proclamation about Christ or a presentation of his voice, but exhibits a more complex function.[10] Grant follows Moller's three "strands" to describe the New Testament appropriation of the Psalms:

> ... first, the evangelists present Jesus adopting the psalms as his own prayers; secondly, the psalmic references to YHWH, and his works, are presented as being equally applicable to Jesus himself; and thirdly, the psalms are presented as having a prophetic role, predicting especially the trials and sufferings of Christ.[11]

Futato agrees and notes further that the function of the psalms as Christ's prayers does not preclude them being our prayers as well. He suggests that the interpretation of the psalms as the prayers of Christ strengthens their earlier invitation to mimesis since Christ has offered them "for us." Appealing to Colossians 3:16 he comments:

> When reading a psalm, it is helpful to read that psalm both as being spoken by Christ and as speaking about Christ. Each of these perspectives will yield different insights into any given psalm. Both perspectives can be used for the simple reason that Christ is the Lord of the covenant and the Servant of the covenant. As the Lord of the covenant, Christ is the one to whom the psalms are addressed *by us*; and as the Servant of the covenant, Christ is the one by whom the psalms are voiced for us.[12]

Futato has correctly identified a number of ways in which the psalms function (or, in speech act terminology, a variety of illocutions performed by them). He suggests that they make assertions about Christ, are offered to us as words we can speak to Christ and finally that they are offered to us by way of Christ speaking them before us and on our behalf, "So, when we read the laments, we are singing and reading about Christ, who has gone before us and sung the laments for us."[13]

---

10. M. D. Futato and D. M. Howard, *Interpreting the Psalms: An Exegetical Handbook* (Grand Rapids: Kregel, 2007); J. L. Mays, *Psalms* (Louisville: John Knox Press, 2011); Miller, *Interpreting the Psalms*; J. A. Grant, "Singing the Cover Versions: Psalms, Reinterpretation and Biblical Theology in Acts 1-4," *SBET* 25, no. 1 (2007); F. G. Villaneuva, "Preaching Lament," in *Reclaiming the Old Testament for Christian Preaching* (ed. G. J. R. Kent, P. J. Kissling, and L. A. Turner; Downers Grove: IVP 2010); Nasuti, "God at Work."; R. P. Belcher, *The Messiah and the Psalms: Preaching Christ from All the Psalms* (Fearn: Mentor, 2006).

11. Grant, "Singing the Cover Versions," 29.

12. Futato and Howard, *Interpreting the Psalms*, 174.

13. Futato also provides a brief yet helpful explanation of how a Christological reading of the psalm is affected by the genre of the psalm. (Futato and Howard, *Interpreting the Psalms*, 176-182.)

Similarly, Mays prioritizes the original function of the psalms and argues that their use by New Testament authors does not determine the totality of their function:

> Psalm 69 cannot be read directly as the prayer of Jesus or as an intentional prophecy of his suffering. But it does provide a context for reflection on the passion of one who bore reproach for the sake of his God and by the way he bore it and by the vindication of his resurrection gave hope to the lowly and promise that God's saving will for his servants will be completed. Jesus is the consummate and correcting example of the kind of person for whom the psalm was composed.[14]

Mays' comments on the Christological use of Psalm 22 further clarifies his understanding of how the New Testament usage of the psalms affects their continuing function. He argues that Jesus was doing exactly what the psalm intended of its audience, and that in doing so, Jesus validated the original function of the psalm:

> Psalm 22 was composed for liturgical use. What one hears through it is not the voice of a particular historical person at a certain time but one individual case of the typical. Its language was designed to give individuals a poetic and liturgical location, to provide a prayer that is paradigmatic for particular suffering and needs. To use it was to set oneself in its paradigm.
>
> That is first of all what Jesus does in his anguished cry to God when he begins to recite the psalm. He joins the multitudinous company of the afflicted and becomes one with them in their suffering. In praying as they do, he expounds his total identification with them. He gives all his followers who are afflicted permission and encouragement to pray for help. He shows that faith includes holding the worst of life up to God."[15]

If we adopt speech act terminology to explain such a position, then the appropriation of Psalm 22 by Jesus is a "correct" perlocution, a response that is consistent with the illocutions of the psalm. In appropriating the psalm, Jesus

---

14. Mays, *Psalms*, 232-233.

15. Mays, *Psalms*, 106. It is curious that Mays then appears to contradict himself a few pages later in support of a position similar to that of Bonhoeffer where Christ is the true pray-er of the psalm. He argues that Psalm 22 is unlike many other psalms which do invite mimesis, "The use of Psalm 22 in the New Testament and in the liturgy of Holy Week gives hermeneutical directions about the way believers are to understand it. We are given a role in the scenario of the psalm. We do not identify, either as individual or community, with the person who prays and praises, as in the use of many other psalms. That role is claimed for and explicated by Jesus alone. We are, rather, the congregation on Passion Sunday and Good Friday who listen to the psalm as hearing the words of our Lord and strain to understand what his performance of his psalm means." (Mays, *Psalms*, 113.)

both affirms His status as the exemplar of the psalm and validates its continued appropriation. The fulfilment of the psalm in the life of Jesus does not preclude further appropriation by His followers. On the contrary, Jesus stands in solidarity with the psalmist and those who suffer like Him, both vindicating their past responses and providing a model for the future.[16]

*Conclusion*
It is clear that the New Testament portrays the psalms as fulfilled in Christ. Those who suggest that this fulfilment precludes any continuing invitation to mimesis have unnecessarily reduced the canonical function of the psalms and have not appreciated the various illocutions currently in play. They have failed to account for how the psalms continue to function as divine discourse other than God's declaration that that the psalms speak of Christ and that Christ is the speaker in the psalms. This conclusion ignores the original function of the psalms and drastically reduces their relevance for contemporary readers.

In the subsequent discussion, I will argue that the New Testament stance towards the psalms does not reduce their function in a way that limits it to declarations about Christ. Rather, this new understanding adds to the "thickness" of the psalm and reinforces the previous editorial and divine illocutions.

## Exposition of Psalm 69

*Translation of Psalm 69*
1   For the director, upon the *Shoshanim*. Of David.

2   Save me, O God,
        for waters have reached my throat.[17]
3   I have sunk in muddy depths:
        and there is no foothold.
    I have entered deep waters:
        and the flood has engulfed me.
4   I am exhausted with calling:
        and my throat is dry.

---

16. Villaneuva offers a similar explanation, "Now, on the cross, Jesus continues to teach them how to pray. By praying the Psalms, and especially the lament psalms, Jesus points the way further into the heart of God where all our sufferings are validated, accepted and embraced. Praying the lament psalms makes us one with Jesus in taking the sufferings and brokenness of our world." (Villaneuva, "Preaching Lament," 80.)

17. A possible translation of נפש. For a discussion of this translation see O. Sander, "Leib-Seele-Dualismus Im Alten Testament," ZAW 77, no. 3 (1965). The imagery of this strophe supports such an understanding as the threat of drowning appears imminent. In Psalm 57:7, the reference to "noose" and the parallel with "feet" also support this translation. (Dahood, *Psalms II 51–100*, 53.)

My eyes have failed:
   waiting for my God.
5   More numerous than the hairs on my head are those who
   hate me without cause.
   Those who destroy me grow strong,
       my lying enemies.
   What I did not steal, I now restore.

6   O God, you know my foolishness:
       and my guilt is not hidden from you.
7   Let not those who hope in you be shamed because of me,
       O Lord Yahweh of hosts:
   Let not those who seek you be disgraced because of me, O God of Israel.
8       For it is for your sake I have borne reproach:
       and disgrace covers my face.
9       I have become a stranger to my brother:
       and an alien to my mother's sons.
10      For jealousy for your house has consumed me:
       and the reproaches of those who reproach you have
       fallen upon me.
11      When I wept and my throat/life fasted:
       it became a reproach to me.
12      When I made sackcloth my clothing:
       I became a byword to them.
13      Those who sit at the gate speak of me:
       (as do)[18] the taunting songs of drunkards.
14  But as for me, my prayer comes to you,
       O Yahweh, (in a / may it be a) time of favour.

   O God in your great loyal love, answer me,
       in the faithfulness of your salvation.
15      Rescue me from the mire,
       so that I do not sink:
   So I am rescued from those who hate me,
       and from the deep waters.
16      Let not the flood waters engulf me:
       Let not the depths swallow me:
       Let not the pit close its mouth over me.
17  Answer me, O Yahweh, for Your loyal love is good:
       on account of your great compassion, turn to me.
18  And do not conceal your face from your servant:
       for I am in distress, answer me quickly.

---

18. Alt. "with."

19 Draw near to my life[19] and redeem it:
   on account of my enemies, redeem me.

20 You know my reproach and my shame and my disgrace:
   before you are all my adversaries.
21 Reproach has broken my heart,
   I hoped for sympathy but there was none:
   for comforters, but I could not find them.
22 They put poison in my food:
   and for my thirst they made me drink vinegar.
23    May their table be a trap before them:
      and their prosperity[20] a snare.
24    May their eyes grow too dark to see:
      and their loins constantly tremble.
25    Pour out your wrath upon them:
      and your fiery anger overtake them.
26    May their camp become desolate:
      and in their tents may no one dwell.
27    For you – whom You struck, they pursued:
      and the pain of your slain they recounted.
28    Place guilt upon guilt:
      and do not let them come into your righteousness.
29    Let them be wiped from the book of life:
      and with the righteous may they not be written.
30 But as for me, I am afflicted and in pain:
   May Your salvation, O God, lift me up.

31 I will praise God's name in song:
   and will extol Him with thanksgiving.
32 May it be better to Yahweh than an ox:
   a bull with horns and split hooves.
33 The afflicted see and rejoice:
   those who seek God, may their hearts live.
34 For Yahweh listens to the needy:
   and does not despise his captives.
35 The heavens and earth will praise Him:
   the seas and all that moves in them.
36 For God will save Zion:
   and build[21] the cities of Judah:
   and they will dwell there and possess it.
37 And the seed of His servants will inherit it:

---

19. Cf. v2.
20. LXX suggests an emendation to "recompense."
21. Or "rebuild."

A Theological Interpretation of Psalm 69          189

and those who love His name will dwell in it.

*Literary and Historical Contexts*
*Genre* Psalm 69 is an individual lament where the psalmist portrays his situation as one of unjust accusation and physical threat.[22] The psalmist imprecates against this unnamed enemy in a sustained plea to Yahweh for salvation. He cries out to God for deliverance, appeals on the basis of his innocence, acknowledges his guilt in other areas,[23] calls for God to act justly and in accordance with His character, and concludes with a declaration of hope that God will in fact vindicate His servants. Zenger comments:

> In its overall movement from appeal to God (invocation), to lament with dramatic depiction of the crisis, to petition for an end to the crisis through rescue/destruction of the enemies, to vow of praise with hymnic preparation, the psalm presents itself as a richly faceted prayer of lament or petition by an individual person, an "I."[24]

Wilson argues that the ending of the psalm suggests its initial individual nature has been applied in the post-exilic community and that the enemies in this final form are those captives who mock the faith of the remnant:

> It is clear from the concluding verses (69:33-36) that this individual lament has been reinterpreted to speak to the exilic community. In this later context the rejection the psalmist experiences should perhaps be understood as scorn from those cynical captives who pour out contempt on his expressions of zeal for the Jerusalem temple (69:9) and on his contrition for the communal sins that brought the nation to this pass.[25]

---

22. Various commentators contest the individual nature of the psalm. (See C. A. Briggs and E. G. Briggs, *A Critical and Exegetical Commentary on the Book of Psalms* (New York: C. Scribner's Sons, 1906); Mowinckel, *The Psalms in Israel's Worship*.)
  However, a majority view understands the psalm to speak plainly of an individual's suffering. For a fuller discussion see Firth who also categorizes the psalm as one of the "Psalms of Sickness" rather than a "Psalm of False Accusation." (Firth, *Surrendering Retribution*, 126-129.) He notes that the classification of Psalm 69 is notoriously difficult due to the complex nature of its content. See also Kraus, *Psalms 60-150*, 60.
23. For a defense of the "guilt" in v. 6 constituting a coherent picture of the psalmist and not as mutually exclusive to claims of righteousness see C. de Vos and G. Kwakkel, "Psalms 69: The Petitioner's Understanding of Himself, His God, and His Enemies," in *Psalms and Prayers: Papers Read at the Joint Meeting of the Society of Old Testament Study and Het Oudtestamentische Werkgezelschap in Nederland En België, Apeldoorn August 2006* (ed. B. Becking and E. Peels; vol. 55 of *Oudtestamentische Studiën*; Leiden: Brill, 2007).
24. F-L. Hossfeld et al., *Psalms 2: A Commentary on Psalms 51-100* (Minneapolis: Fortress Press, 2005), 172.
25. Wilson, *Psalms*, 949.

Yet, Goldingay has probably captured the evidence best when he notes that it is the psalm of an individual, but that this individual has a representative role in the community:

> In vv. 1–5 one might reckon that the suppliant is a private individual speaking of the acts of other elements within the community, in the manner of many psalms. But vv. 7–12 suggest someone with a distinctive religious commitment, suggesting that the attackers are people with other forms of religious commitment, whom God should remove from the community, the psalm urges. Further, v. 6 already suggests that the suppliant is not merely a private individual but someone who in some sense represents a community. The protests and pleas thus concern the destiny of this community as well as that of this individual, and the confession of trust looks forward to a restoring of Jerusalem and Judah.[26]

*Sitz im Leben* The exact setting of the psalm is heavily debated with many commentators proposing a multi-stage development as in the case of Wilson.[27] The final stanza suggests either an exilic or post-exilic setting with its references to both "captives" and the rebuilding of Judah (vv. 31–37). It is also uncertain whether the psalm emphasizes an individual or communal application. Tate concludes, "The determination of the exact context intended for the suppliant in the psalm is very elusive."[28] While questions of composition and provenance are important and can aid in understanding the function of the psalm, I suggest that a "text imminent" approach is preferred where final form is given priority.[29] That the psalm remains a lament of the individual is clear, yet the circumstances of the lament could be expanded to include those of the community.

*Placement within the Psalter* Psalm 69 represents the ubiquitous oscillation between praise and lament in the Psalter. Psalms 65–68 are psalms of praise and reflect on Yahweh's great power and acts of salvation. Psalms 69–72 represent the conclusion to a Davidic Psalter with Psalms 69–71 forming a final plea for

---

26. J. Goldingay, *Psalms. Volume 2, Psalms 42-89* (Grand Rapids: Baker, 2007), 338.

27. For a good summary of the debate see Hossfeld et al., *Psalms 2*, 174-176. Zenger himself argues for a multi-stage development, positing that the psalm of an individual has been expanded at every level "The primary psalm was *continued by expansion* of each of the three structural elements (lament, petition, vow of praise) by vv. 6–14b (lament), vv. 20-30 (petition), and vv. 32-34 (vow of praise). The immediate, mortal conflict between the petitioner and his enemies is given a complex theological depth dimension. The root of the conflict is revealed: it is the petitioner's passionate advocacy of right worship in the Temple; this is a matter of a publically enacted group conflict." (Hossfeld et al., *Psalms 2*, 176.).

28. M. E. Tate, *Psalms 51-100* (vol. 20; Dallas: Word, 1990), 192. Goldingay concurs, "As usual we cannot infer the precise nature of an individual suppliant's experience from the details of the language used to describe it, not least its hyperbole." (Goldingay, *Psalms 2*, 339.)

29. The illocutions of the psalm are only accessible in this final form, though an understanding of how the psalmist shaped the material will assist in this determination.

deliverance and vindication. While these psalms are clearly linked by theme and genre, their connection is further strengthened by shared vocabulary. Throughout this group the psalmist associates himself with the עני ("poor")[30] and אביונים ("needy")[31], and calls for Yahweh to act חושה ("quickly").[32] The psalmist is also concerned that those who hope in Yahweh not יכלמו ("be disgraced") but that those who seek his life be disgraced.[33] A repeated word-group in Psalms 69-71 describes this "disgrace." In addition to כלם, the psalmist describes their situation as one of בוש and חרפה ("shame and reproach"). The use of חרפה a total of five times in Psalm 69[34] connects the psalm to Psalm 71:13. Outside of these occurrences, the word last occurs in Psalm 44, which makes its appearance in these two psalms more pronounced. Following Psalm 71, the word is used nine times in the remainder of the Psalter. Similarly, the presence of בשת in Psalm 69 also marks the first occurrence of this noun since Psalm 44 and it too occurs in Psalm 70 and then not again until Psalm 109. The verbal form בוש last occurs in Psalm 53 and reoccurs in Psalms 69, 70 and 71.[35]

Much of the above mentioned vocabulary continues in Psalm 72 where the Davidic king is portrayed as protecting the עני "poor"[36] and אביונים "needy."[37] He is the one who will נצל "save" and ישע "deliver" them.[38] Although this language "save and deliver" is common in the Psalter, there is a concentration in Psalms 69-72.[39] These characteristics of the king in Psalm 72 form the content of the pleas in Psalms 69-71. This intertextuality provides interesting rhetorical possibilities. The king is portrayed as one who will "save" and "deliver" the "afflicted" and "needy", yet this is not the king's experience of Yahweh in Psalms 69-71. His plea is that Yahweh would act in accordance with His character and consistent with His previous actions (Pss 65-68). In this context, Psalm 72 functions as a further reminder that God has given this role to the king. By implication, this rule of the king should be one that is first modelled by Yahweh, thus adding force to the pleas of the previous three psalms.

Zenger notes that Psalm 69 fits neatly within this group as a conclusion to the David collection for three reasons:

> Psalm 69 was apparently chosen for this concluding composition for three reasons: (a) because of the multiple perspectives in its

---

30. Pss. 69:30; 70:6
31. Pss. 69:34; 70:6
32. Pss. 70:2, 6; 71:12. Ps. 69:18 also calls for Yahweh to act quickly but uses the synonym מהר.
33. Ps. 69:7 and Ps. 70:3 respectively.
34. Ps. 69:8, 10, 11, 20, 21.
35. Ps. 69:7, 70:3; 71:1, 13, 24.
36. Ps. 72:2, 4, 12.
37. Ps. 72:4, 13, 14.
38. Ps. 72:12.
39. Seven occurrences of ישע and five occurrences of נצל are found in Pss. 69-72. The last occurrences of ישע and נצל are found in Pss. 65 and 59 respectively.

depiction of the crisis it can function as a summary of the psalms of lament collected in Psalms 51ff.; (b) because of its relation to Psalm 40, the penulitmate psalm in the first Davidic collection (Psalms 3-41), it underscores the intended parallel between the two Davidic Psalters (cf. also, correspondingly, the paralleling of Psalm 70 and 40:14-18); (c) because of its interest in the Temple, or right worship in the Temple, this psalm is suited to make "David" a zealot for the true cult of the Temple and thus to create a bridge to the following Asaph composition in Psalms 73-83.[40]

The above parallels noted by Zenger suggest that the portrayal of David in the collection and in Psalm 69 is that of a righteous responder who both represents the people and leads the people in their response to Yahweh.[41]

*Internal Structure* The psalm can be divided into two stanzas (vv. 2-30 and vv. 31-37).[42] This division is clearly marked by a transition in language, genre and direction of address. In the first stanza the psalmist addresses Yahweh and pleas with him for deliverance in typical lament form. Support for this division is also found in the repetition of the vocative אלהים and the plea to ישׁע which form an inclusio.[43]

Verses 2-30 can be divided further into four strophes as follows: verses 2-5 form the initial plea for salvation followed by the complaint which employs imagery of chaos and drowning; verses 6-14b is another plea followed by a defence of innocence and loyalty to Yahweh; verses 14c-19 return to the imagery of chaos in verses 2-5 and ask for a quick answer from Yahweh; verses 20-30 return to the defence of innocence and include an imprecation against those who are against the psalmist. The second stanza (vv. 31-37) reflects the confidence of the psalmist that Yahweh will hear and act. It contains a declaration of praise and a shift in address to the reader or community. The structure is thus:

I.  Cry for Salvation (vv. 2-30)
    a.  Cry and Complaint (vv. 2-5)
    b.  Cry and Defence (vv. 6-14a)
    c.  Cry for Quick Rescue (vv. 14b-19)
    d.  Defence and Imprecation (vv. 20-30)
II. Declaration of Confidence (vv. 31-37)

---

40. Hossfeld et al., *Psalms 2*, 176.

41. See also Wenham who, in discussing Psalms 35, 69 and 109, suggests that on the one hand, the indefiniteness of the psalms encourages identification with them in a range of experiences, and on the other hand, the ascription to David encourages imitation by presenting him as the ideal responder. (Wenham, *Psalms as Torah*, 168.)

42. See L. C. Allen, "The Value of Rhetorical Criticism in Psalm 69," *JBL* 105, no. 4 (1986). So also Tate, *Psalms 51-100*, 193; Hossfeld et al., *Psalms 2*, 172-173.

43. The inclusio is strengthened by the fact that there it represents the only two occurrences of ישׁע.

*Textual Observations*
I. Cry for Salvation (vv. 2-30)
This first stanza of the psalm divides into four strophes, which oscillate between imagery and reality. The first and third strophes are connected by their imagery of chaos and drowning and by their plea for God to save and rescue. The second and fourth strophes are a complaint marked by language of "disgrace, reproach and shame", identifying both God and human enemies as the source of trouble.

I. a. Cry and Complaint (vv. 2-5)
A desperate plea opens the psalm, the vocative אלהים beginning this and following two strophes. Images of deep water and flood are employed by the psalmist to express his feeling of immanent death as the ancient Near Eastern concepts of chaos and destruction are represented.[44] Helpless to act or move, the psalmist pictures these waters at his neck and his feet so that he cannot find solid ground.

Plea turns to complaint as the psalmist points out that his continual cry has gone unanswered leaving him exhausted and parched. Dahood notes the irony portrayed by the flood of waters reaching the neck of the psalmist, yet "the poet's throat burns and is hoarse from crying to God for help."[45]

While God is directly addressed, the psalmist employs the third person "my God" in order to both emphasize their intimate relationship and to picture the futility of the plea by creating a sense of distance. In this opening strophe, the use of self-involving language draws the reader into the narrative of the psalm as readers (and reciters) are invited to consider their own relationship with God.

Imagery gives way to reality as the psalmist identifies the nature of the threat as enemies who hate him without cause. The hopelessness and injustice of his situation is expressed in the overpowering strength of his enemies and their unjust and likely impossible request that he return that which he did not steal.[46]

I. b. Cry and Defence (vv. 6-14a)

---

44. L. Ryken et al., "Water," in *Dictionary of Biblical Imagery* (Downers Grove: IVP, 1998), 929-932. See also McCarter who discusses Psalm 69 and other representative texts to argue for an allusion to Mesopotamian mythology where a "*cosmic* river ordeal" represented legal proceedings and judgment. (P. K. McCarter, "River Ordeal in Israelite Literature," *HTR* 66, no. 4 (1973).) See also H. G. May, "Some Cosmic Connotations of Mayim Rabbim, "Many Waters"," *JBL* 74, no. 1 (1955).

45. Dahood, *Psalms II 51-100*, 156.

46. Cohen notes that this ambiguity is a typical feature of lament and has an intentional function, "These psalms, used as part of liturgical ritual, recognize the presence of some kind of enemy for all people in distress. However, the enemy being anonymous allows for their identity to be metaphorical or real; oneself, God, someone or something else." (Cohen, *Why O Lord?*, 68.) Zenger also notes that the ambiguous nature of the demand is intentional as it allows the situation to function paradigmatically (Hossfeld et al., *Psalms 2*, 178.), a feature typical of lament.

The cry to God is repeated in verse 6 where the psalmist acknowledges his folly and his sinfulness. At the same time he asserts his blamelessness with respect to the accusations directed at him by his enemies.[47] The psalmist argues for his vindication on the basis that its denial will be to the detriment of those who have committed themselves to Yahweh. The psalmist is therefore portrayed as one who represents the people of God. His life will be evaluated in light of God's promises and is paradigmatic for how the people will view the validity of their own faith.

Three Hebrew words בוֹשׁ, כְּלֹא, חֶרְפָּה (shame, disgrace, and reproach) are employed to describe both the current situation of the psalmist and the corresponding situation of God's people should He not act in deliverance.[48] This combination is repeated at the beginning of the fourth strophe where God is said to not only "know" the folly and guilt of the psalmist, but he also "knows" the "shame, disgrace, and reproach" that the psalmist unjustly suffers. As Wilson notes, these descriptors are not merely feelings of the psalmist but represent "visible actions of communal rejection and detraction."[49]

The psalmist then reminds God that the cause of his suffering is his loyalty to Him. He bears "reproach" for God's sake and reminds Him of the fact by repeating the word four times in quick succession. The specifics of the "zeal" or "jealousy" he has for the house of Yahweh are unclear from the text but indicate that such "jealousy" is at odds with the majority.[50] The lament of the psalmist brings "reproach" from everyone in society, including his immediate family. The references to those in power ("at the gate") and to the drunkards form a merism, implying everyone in the community is against him.[51]

The closing lines of the strophe confront Yahweh directly and return to the theme of verses 1-5 where the psalmist challenges Yahweh's apparent absence. The psalmist contrasts himself with Yahweh as he continues to pray, "But as for me, my prayer comes to you." The psalmist knows that Yahweh has made promises, Yahweh should listen, and Yahweh should deliver. Verse 14 is echoed in Isaiah 49:8-9, "In a time of favour I have answered you, on a day of salvation I have helped you."

---

47. Goldingay concurs noting the inconsistency if understood as admission of guilt with respect to the charges in view. (Goldingay, *Psalms 2*, 341.) See also Tate, *Psalms 51-100*, 196.

48. For a discussion of the cultural linguistic context of "shame" in the Psalter see Tucker who notes that unlike narrative and prophetic texts in the Old Testament where shame is often associated with gender, the Psalter appears to operate with a different background, specifically that of the patron–client relationship. (W. D. Tucker, "Is Shame a Matter of Patronage in the Communal Laments?," *JSOT* 31, no. 4 (2007). 470-471.)

49. Wilson, *Psalms*, 952.

50. Kraus believes that the psalmist is writing in a post-exilic context, urging the community to rebuild the temple. (Kraus, *Psalms 60-150*, 62.)

51. Alternatively, as I noted in my translation, those at the gate could be mocking him "with" the songs of drunkards.

I. a'.  Cry for Quick Rescue (vv. 14b–19)
The psalmist continues his plea and emphasizes the desperation of his situation by requesting three times that God "answer" him. The imagery of chaos once again slips into reality where "deep waters" are in parallel with "those who hate me." His life is in imminent danger as the depths are about to "swallow him" and the "pit close its mouth" over him.[52]

In this strophe the distance of Yahweh is emphasized with the psalmist requesting that Yahweh "turn to me" and "draw near to my life."[53] The psalmist reminds God of God's own character, invoking the covenant name, and appealing to His qualities of חסד, אמת, and רחם (loyal love, faithfulness, and compassion). This antimony forms the crux of the psalmist's argument.

I. b'.  Defence and Imprecation (vv. 20–30)
In this fourth strophe the psalmist returns to the themes found in the second where he described his situation as one of בוש, כלמ, חרפה (shame, disgrace, and reproach). The psalmist states that he knows that God knows the details of his oppression as all his enemies are "before" God (v. 20). Even though God knows his situation, the psalmist still experiences total abandonment and life threatening danger (vv. 21–22).[54] In response to this situation he imprecates against his adversaries in a succession of requests that picture a reversal of the "good things of life."[55] The imprecation climaxes in verse 29, "Let them be wiped from the book of life, and with the righteous may they not be written."[56] That

---

52. The personification of death in verse 16 parallels the Canaanite portrayals of Mot, god of death who "devours" his prey. (V. H. Matthews and D. C. Benjamin, *Old Testament Parallels: Laws and Stories from the Ancient near East* (Fully rev. and expanded 3rd ed.; New York: Paulist Press, 2006), 157-168.)

53. Note the play on words between פנה and פניך in vv. 17 and 18. For God to "conceal" his face from His people is considered an act of judgment. (cf. Deut. 31:17, 18; 32:20; Pss. 13:2; 30:7-8; 88:15 etc.) Groenewald notes that combination of פנים and סתר is a fixed collocation and means "that God refuses to hear and answer his prayers, which is tantamount to cutting off all contact with him. The actual distress of this servant is thus not so much the threat posed by the enemies, but the absence of Yahweh's face, i.e., his attentive countenance." (A. Groenewald, *Psalm 69: Its Structure, Redaction and Composition* (Munster: LIT Verlag, 2003), 90-91.)

54. Zenger notes that both the food and the drink are poisonous, the latter being pure vinegar in contrast to thirst-quenching water mixed with vinegar. (cf. Ruth 2:9, 14; Hossfeld et al., *Psalms 2*, 182.)

55. Tate, *Psalms 51-100*, 199.

56. The portrayal of God having such a book occurs throughout the Psalter and the canon (Psa. 139:16; Exod. 32:32-33; cf. Ezek. 9 and Rev. 20:11-15). Broadhurst notes that to attempt to change these verses into a statement of fact rather than desire in order to "soften" their tone is not justified by the syntax. He states, "This syntactical relationship (imperative-imperfect) usually results in the imperfects being translated as jussives. A jussive is generally translated as a want or desire. Therefore, the imprecation in these verses is not simply a statement of fact; rather it is a wish or desire of the psalmist. This makes this particular solution improbable." (Broadhurst, "Should Cursing Continue?,"

his requests are justified is clear from the earlier strophe where these adversaries are persecuting the psalmist for his loyalty to Yahweh (v. 10). In this strophe, once again, the guilt of the enemies is clear (v. 28) with the contrast between the "guilty" and the "righteous" concluding the imprecation. The difference between the psalmist and his enemies is reflected in their respective destinies as it is in Psalm 1. The psalmist pleads for salvation and knows that the righteous will live in the presence of God. At the same time, he asks that the right judgment of his enemies will be swift and that they experience their rightful destiny, exclusion from God's presence.

Verse 30 contrasts the psalmist's situation of "affliction" with that of the enemies' "prosperity" stating, "But as for me, I am afflicted and in pain."[57] The contrast may also be with Yahweh who in verse 20, "knows" the reproach, disgrace and shame of the psalmist yet the psalmist is still "afflicted and in pain." This is heightened by the reference to Yahweh's actions in verse 27 where the psalmist acknowledges that Yahweh is sovereign over the enemies, "For you – who You struck . . ." This appears to indicate that the affliction of the psalmist is at the hand of Yahweh. By invoking the descriptor עני "afflicted", the psalmist is aligning himself with those who are faithful and righteous throughout the Psalter, whom God has promised to deliver.

The psalmist concludes this strophe and stanza with an appeal for "God" to "save" (forming the inclusion with verse 1). He reminds God of several facts pertinent to his plea: that he is afflicted, that he knows God knows he is afflicted, that God himself has brought the affliction, that the psalmist is "righteous" and does not deserve the affliction, and that God has promised to deliver him from it.

The deliverance of the psalmist is dependent upon the removal of the enemies and the psalmist appeals to God to judge them according to their guilt. De Vos and Kwakkel suggest that the imprecation is not an act of "devotional humility," arguing that if the psalmist were in a position of power, he would have taken vengeance himself:

> It is, indeed, remarkable that the petitioner leaves all the vengeance to God. Just this point seems to comfort some commentators. It seems to alleviate the harshness of the imprecations. However, the reason for leaving the revenge to God apparently is not devotional humility, but rather a lack of strength. One should recall the expressions of misery at the beginning of the psalm. The petitioner wants God to do what he himself is not able to do. [fn 53. Possibly these imprecations must be seen in the light of curses someone could express to repay aggression, e.g., Lev. 5:1; Judg. 17:3; Prov. 29:24 . . . ] He does not have enough power to destroy the tents of the adversaries and he is not in the position to hold them off from God's righteousness. Since the suffering petitioner himself wants to experience God's דקה again,

---

73.)

57. Note the similar contrast in Psalm 73.

the people who are a threat to this relationship to God have to be annihilated.[58]

The suggestion that the psalmist would have taken vengeance if it were in his power to do so is purely speculative. That the psalmists are in a position of weakness is often the case, but it is not necessarily the case in every psalm. Psalm 139 is an example where the psalmist (possibly David) is not obviously in a position of weakness and arguably in a position where he could (even rightly) take action against the wicked. In this case, the psalmist recognizes his own culpability and desires transformation. His imprecation is an act of loyalty to Yahweh in both the desire that those who defame Yahweh be punished and in the desire that the psalmist himself be kept from becoming like them. Many of the imprecatory psalms are spoken by or, at the very least attributed to, the king and this is possibly the case in Psalm 69, as I discussed earlier.[59] In Psalm 69, the "poverty, affliction, and neediness" of the psalmist is a product of their zeal for Yahweh and not clearly a socio-economic description. Even though the threat of danger is acute and pictured as life threatening, it is not certain that the psalmist was impotent to act against his afflicters. The suggestion that imprecation is necessarily borne out of powerlessness and that the psalmist would have taken vengeance if they had sufficient power and opportunity is speculative.[60]

---

58. de Vos and Kwakkel, "Psalm 69," 171.
59. This issue was not highlighted in the previous discussion of Psalm 137 where the psalmist is clearly not in a position to enact judgment. In that context, the scope of the wrongdoing is, on the one hand, well beyond the psalmist's influence and on the other hand, it is possible that the original referent, Babylon, had already met its end at the hand of the Persians. Thus, the psalmist commits judgment to Yahweh and anticipates a future when Yahweh will need to act once again on behalf of his people.
60. For example, the superscription of Psalm 57 encourages a reading of the psalm in light of the narrative of Samuel where David, though fleeing for his life, did possess the power and opportunity to destroy his enemy Saul. Rather than act in vengeance, David allows Saul to live and commits his cause to Yahweh.
For a discussion of the various uses of the term "poor" in the Psalter see S. Croft, *The Identity of the Individual in the Psalms* (Sheffield: Sheffield Academic, 1987), 49-72. For a discussion of the rhetoric of powerlessness in the Psalms see Cottrill, *Language, Power, and Identity*. Cottrill argues that the self-representation of the psalmist as powerlessness is a way of persuading himself and others that his desire for violence is "unproblematic, uncomplicated, and ultimately positive." (Cottrill, *Language, Power, and Identity*, 155.) She comments, "language of powerlessness enables the psalmist to claim authority according to different relational frameworks that co-exist in the psalmist's imagination and mingle in the construction of the psalm itself . . . [and] organizes others' responses to his suffering, providing those addressed a culturally valued way of responding to his pain." (Cottrill, *Language, Power, and Identity*, 151.)
While I am not convinced by Cottrill's conclusions regarding the value (or lack thereof) of such prayers and the violence that they request, I agree that the psalmist is casting themselves in the role of one who is totally dependent upon God and offers their prayer as a model response. Cottrill notes helpfully, "Though the dominant

II. Declaration of Confidence (vv. 31-37)
The psalmist concludes with a shorter stanza expressing his confidence in God's salvation and recognizing that God delights in the praises of his people more than sacrifices (vv. 31-32).[61] This praise is anticipated as psalmist awaits the moment when his faith will be vindicated, thus the anticipation of praise anticipates deliverance. Perhaps further anticipation of deliverance is indicated by the psalmist's use of the covenant name, יהוה, which evokes the memory of Yahweh as one who is faithful to His covenant promises.[62] The expectation of vindication is enhanced by his repetition of עני "afflicted", here paired with אביון "needy" as is common through the Psalter. As mentioned above, this combination occurs again in Psalm 72 where it is a mark of the Davidic king that he saves the עני and the אביון.[63] In fact, this is not just the quality of the Davidic king but something that is declared true of Yahweh throughout the Psalter.[64]

The final verses anticipate the vindication not only of the psalmist but, more broadly, of all of God's people,[65] "His captives." Those who "seek God" will live and all the earth will recognize His kingship and praise Him.[66] The subtlety of the self-involving language of the first stanza is now replaced with a more explicit invitation to be those who both seek God and bring him delight in praise. Because "Yahweh listens", the reader is invited to speak, to cry out in their "affliction" and "need" and find deliverance.

*Summary of Illocutions in the Old Testament Context*
Psalm 69 provides a portrait of a righteous sufferer who joins with the weak and afflicted in a desperate plea to God for deliverance. This portrait is then used to invite the audience to be like the psalmist and to respond in like manner to

---

representation of the self is as endangered, this language is simultaneously a means of claiming authority and making demands, both modes of empowerment for the psalmist. Further, it organizes the psalmist's experience of suffering for others, casting his plight in a culturally valued discourse that also offers a recognized mode of response to witnesses. As the psalmist inhabits the role of the sufferer in the language of the laments, he also makes claims about how others-the hearing audience and God-should respond to his pain by assuming the role of the sympathetic protector." (Cottrill, *Language, Power, and Identity*, 157-158.)

61. Note the wordplay between song (שיר) and ox (שור) in verses 31 and 32 respectively.

62. This is an unusual designation within the so-called Elohistic Psalter. Prior to its increased usage in Pss. 68-71, יהוה occurs only once in the previous ten psalms (64:11).

63. Ps. 72:12-14.

64. Pss. 9:10-14; 10:12; 12:6 (MT); 14:6; 18:27; 22:24; 34:6; 35:10; 40:17; 68:10; 86:1; 107:41; 140:12. See also Croft, *The Identity of the Individual*, 49-72.

65. Goldingay notes this is the first time that the heavens and the earth are involved in praise, a picture that will feature throughout the Psalter from this point forward. (Goldingay, *Psalms 2*, 354.)

66. Cf. Ps. 9:9-12.

similar circumstances.⁶⁷ The loyalty of the psalmist challenges their own loyalty, reminds them of its cost, and offers them hope in the God who is faithful to His promises. As is common throughout the Psalter, the self-involving nature of the language invites and imposes imitation. The first person references of the first stanza draw the reader into the narrative of the psalm and invite reflection on how their own life and voice compare to that of the psalmist.

The portrait of the psalmist is one who suffers "without cause" for the sake of Yahweh. His suffering is a consequence of his loyalty to Yahweh as the "reproaches" directed at Yahweh also fall upon him. A zeal for Yahweh's honour characterises the life of the psalmist and creates conflict with the wicked. This part of the portrait reminds the audience that they too should willingly suffer "without cause" at the hands of the wicked and questions the nature of their own "zeal." At the same time, the psalmist's recognition of guilt reminds the reader that this is not a claim of sinless perfection and invites reflection on the nature of their own sin and whether they suffer as a righteous follower of Yahweh or as the wicked. The employment of key descriptors strengthens the portrait of the sufferer as he describes himself as "weak" and "afflicted", those whom Yahweh watches over and delivers. The imprecatory verses form part of this portrait and are, in this context, offered to the reader as righteous response to unjust suffering.

In his cry for deliverance, the psalmist displays a boldness that challenges Yahweh's apparent absence, affirms Yahweh's character and reminds Him of "how he is supposed to act." Yahweh is reminded of His loyal love, faithfulness, and compassion as the psalmist makes his appeal and questions the dissonance between his faith and his experience.

The movement in the second stanza from plea to praise, or perhaps, to wisdom, is marked by a change in person and direction of address. The psalmist now explicitly includes himself in a long and perpetual tradition of those who are "weak" and "afflicted" and "seek God." He addresses the audience indirectly in the third person, reminding them that a response of praise is one that brings Yahweh delight and that loyalty to Yahweh will be vindicated.

As I have argued in earlier chapters, the divine illocutions of the psalm occur most clearly at the generic and whole-text levels. In this case, God is offering the psalm as a righteous response to unjust suffering. He *affirms* the stance of the psalmist throughout the psalm: his voice, his boldness, his innocence, his

---

67. deClaisse/-Walford notes that this dual function of both addressing God and the people is an inherent quality of the psalms. In discussing the purpose of Psalm 44 she concludes, "And so the people cry out. To what end? What do they hope to accomplish with their words, with their rhetoric? To whom are they speaking? A God who seems to have forgotten the covenant promises ... Or do they speak to themselves as encouragement not to lose heart ... The answer to both questions is a resounding 'yes.' The people are speaking to God *and* themselves." (N. L. deClaisse/-Walford, "O God, Why Do You Hide Your Face?," in *My Words Are Lovely* (ed. R. L. Foster and D. M. Howard; vol. 467 of *The Library of Hebrew Bible/Old Testament Studies*; New York: T&T Clark, 2008), 129.)

zeal, his loyalty and his desire for justice and deliverance. God also reminds the reader of His loyal love, faithfulness, and compassion, even when circumstances suggest the contrary.

Primary divine illocutions of the psalm are the invitations to "suffer without cause" and to "seek God" in times of oppression. The psalmist is portrayed as desperate. His loyalty to Yahweh has brought conflict and suffering, and his life is under threat. This psalm represents his "last breath" as the waters rise "to his neck." Even now, he will not give up on Yahweh. He knows that Yahweh "knows" and that Yahweh has promises He will keep. The psalmist has not renounced his faith or sided with wicked. He has committed himself to Yahweh and, consequently, to a course of the suffering reproach with Him. Therefore, God uses this psalm to *question* the reader: "Are you zealous for My Name? Are you suffering without cause? Are you committed to a course that may bring suffering? Will you remain loyal and seek Me to the very end."

## New Testament Illocutions Regarding Psalm 69

*Introduction*
A theological interpretation of Psalm 69 must move beyond the discussion of divine illocutions in the original context of the Hebrew canon to how the text continues to function as divine discourse. As mentioned in previous chapters, discovering the contemporary divine illocutions requires an understanding of how central illocutions have affected the context within which the locutions of the Psalter now exist. This was the burden of Chapter 5 and its conclusions form the background to this discussion. One of the reasons that Psalm 69 was selected was its usage in the New Testament. Not only do the central illocutions of the New Testament affect the context of the psalm, the New Testament authors quote directly from Psalm 69, adopting particular stances toward it. Therefore it is necessary to consider not only the central illocutions, but also the particular stances of the New Testament toward Psalm 69 and assess their contribution to its interpretation in the canonical context.

As noted above, the New Testament proclamation refers to Psalm 69 on a number of occasions and portrays the events of Jesus' betrayal and crucifixion as its fulfillment. The purpose of this section, therefore, is to evaluate the stance of the New Testament towards Psalm 69, assess the impact of this stance upon the original illocutions of Psalm 69, and so provide a thick description of the psalm.

*Psalm 69 in John*
John portrays Jesus typologically as the righteous sufferer.[68] In Chapter 2 of his gospel account, John states that the disciples realized the fulfillment of Psalm

---

68. Kostenberger notes that this is part of John's larger pattern "of aligning Jesus

69:9a in Jesus' clearing of the temple.⁶⁹ Obermann correctly notes that John's use of Psalm 69:9 was intended to evoke the entire psalm and anticipates the suffering of Jesus at the hands of the wicked:

> Through the words of the psalm, the Temple action becomes an indication that Jesus' zeal will lead to his future death. The psalm's words reveal Jesus as someone alienated from his relatives and (representatively) suffering disgrace for God's sake.⁷⁰

It has also been noted that John's use of a future tense, καταφάγεταί, is a departure from both the MT and the LXX, κατέφαγεν, and enhances the reference to the crucifixion.⁷¹

This initial association of Jesus with the psalmist is sustained throughout John's gospel.⁷² In 15:25 Jesus declares that the hatred directed at him is a fulfillment of Ps. 69:4 since, like the psalmist, he will suffer unjustly.⁷³ With his reference to Psalm 69, Jesus places both himself and his disciples within the narrative of the psalmist. In this pericope, Jesus prepares his disciples for the conflict and suffering ensured by their faithfulness to him (15:18; 16:1-4). Their suffering is to be expected because the world hated both him and the Father (15:18, 23). Therefore, rather than present Psalm 69 as solely fulfilled in the suffering of

---

and his ministry with the experience of a king and/or prophet who is zealous for God and as a result suffers humiliation by God's own people–a pattern that encompasses the use of Ps. 69 both here and in 12:25 and extends also to the use of Ps. 22 in 12:24 and the possible allusion to Ps. 69:21 in 19:28-30 (see also Paul's use of Ps. 69:9b in Rom 15:3). The mention of Jesus's brothers immediately prior to the present pericope in 2:12 (cf. 2:1-2) in conjunction with the reference to their unbelief in 7:5 may further accentuate the evangelist's depiction of Jesus in terms of the psalmist's lament that he has become a stranger to his brothers." (A. Kostenberger, "John," in *Commentary on the New Testament Use of the Old Testament* (ed. G. K. Beale and D. A. Carson; Grand Rapids: Baker 2007), 434.)

69. John 2:17; Bryan argues unconvincingly that the "zeal" being referred to in the gospel is that of the Jewish zeal for Herod's temple rather than Jesus' zeal for His Father's house (S. M. Bryan, "Consumed by Zeal: John's Use of Psalm 69:9 and the Action in the Temple," *BBR* 21, no. 4 (2011).)

70. A. Obermann, *Die Christologische Erfüllung der Schrift im Johannesevangelium: Eine Untersuchung zur Johannieschen Hermeneutik Anhand der Schriftzitate* (Tübingen with umlaut: Mohr (Siebeck), 1996), 126. See also Beasley-Murray who suggests a more overt translation of John 2:17, "Zeal for your house will destroy me." (G. R. Beasley-Murray, *John* (Dallas: Word, 1989), 39.)

71. D. A. Brueggemann, "The Evangelists and the Psalms," in *Interpreting the Psalms: Issues and Approaches* (ed. D. G. Firth and P. S. Johnston; Downers Grove: IVP, 2005), 273.

72. Goldingay suggests a further Johannine usage in Revelation 21 where he hears echoes of the desire that the names of the enemy be "blotted out of the book of life and not be listed with the righteous" (Goldingay, *Psalms 2*, 356. Cf. Rev. 21:27).

73. Kostenberger notes four possible entailments supplied by the context of the psalm: "(1) the large number of the sufferer's enemies; (2) the great power of those enemies; (3) the false charges levelled by the enemies; (4) the righteous sufferer's prayerful trust in God." (Kostenberger, "John," 494.)

Jesus, John is affirming that those disciples who faithfully follow Jesus also enter the paradigm of the psalm.

Brawley appears conflicted vis-à-vis the impact of John on the function of Psalm 69. On the one hand he concludes that the psalm is no longer about God's people and solely refers to the Messiah, "Viewed through John 19, Psalm 69 no longer expresses the common lot of righteous people who suffer for God's sake but exclusively the lot of the messianic righteous one who suffers for God's sake."[74] On the other hand he affirms that the enemies of God and God's people in the psalm continue as referents:

> If John 19:28-29 tropes Psalm 69 to interpret the opposition to Jesus in his crucifixion, then the trope also interprets opposition to Jesus contemporaneous with the authorial audience. From this point of view, Psalm 69 becomes a proleptic anticipation far beyond the limits of the life of the psalmist. But the transumption of it in John 19 is also a prolepsis of a divine triumph over enemies. Thus the trope takes on the capacity to interpret resistance to Jesus for readers of a future beyond Jesus and to place that resistance in the context of the universal salvific reality of God (Ps. 69:32-33).[75]

This second statement suggests that the psalm still speaks of the vindication of God and His people by warning future enemies that their destruction is certain. Surely this interpretation, which appears cogent, suggests that not only the Messiah, but all of those who suffer for Him can pray the psalm with the same expectation, and in fact, with greater certainty than that of the psalmist.

As mentioned above, direct reference to Psalm 69 occurs a third time during the account of the crucifixion (19:28-37).[76] The connection to Psalm 69

---

74. R. L. Brawley, "An Absent Complement and Intertextuality in John 19:28-29," *JBL* 112, no. 3 (1993): 440.

75. Brawley, "An Absent Complement," 443.

76. While some have suggested Ps. 22 as the referred text (R. E. Brown, *The Gospel According to John (XIII-XXI)* (Garden City: Doubleday, 1970), 929.), Brawley argues convincingly that the surrounding context supports intertextuality with Ps. 69. He suggests that the context is marked by methexis ("the mutual participation between subsidiary and primary meanings of metaphors", see P. E. Wheelwright, *The Burning Fountain: A Study in the Language of Symbolism* (Bloomington: Indiana University Press, 1968), 76-77.) He notes that on either side of the offer of vinegar are images used in the fulfilment of scripture. In these cases, it is not the act of Jesus that is the focus, but the actions of his persecutors. Therefore, the fulfilment of scripture in 19:28 is not the declaration of "thirst" but the action of the soldiers in giving Jesus a drink. Furthermore, he argues according to Hays's criteria for intertextuality that "Nevertheless, recurrence and thematic coherence indicate that the route to Psalm 69 is circuitous. Allusions to Psalm 69 elsewhere in John and previous appearances of the theme of thirst make intertextual references complex ... Because John 19:28-29 makes an allusion without a specific citation, the text leaves it up to the reader to recall the psalm. But the text induces the reader to recall more than simply thirst and vinegar. A part of the larger dimension of the allusion is the citation of the psalm in John 2:17. Even though the cleansing of the

is strengthened by verse 28, where Jesus is conscious that he is fulfilling scripture. His request for a drink is both precipitated by his real thirst and also by his knowledge that the reception of a drink will evoke the narrative of the psalm.⁷⁷ John records that Jesus is given "wine vinegar" to drink. The word used to describe the drink in all four gospel accounts is ὄξος, which refers to either "sour wine" or "vinegar"⁷⁸ and is the word used to translate חמץ in the LXX (68:22; MT 69:22). This drink, rather than acting as a sedative, "prolonged life and therefore pain" and should be understood as an act of sadism rather than compassion.⁷⁹

John's use of Psalm 69 places Jesus in the paradigm of the psalmist. It functions in the early chapters to prepare the reader for the unjust suffering that Jesus will experience. In the upper room discourse, it functions as reminder to His disciples (and the reader) that this kind of opposition is normative for those who seek and side with Yahweh. Finally, in the passion narrative it portrays those involved in his death as the enemies of God who are certain to face judgment. The evoking of Psalm 69 juxtaposes the entirety of the psalm with life and death of Jesus.⁸⁰ The final verses of the psalm, therefore, function as a reminder

---

Temple occurs at the beginning of Jesus' ministry, the narrator's commentary connects it and the citation of Psalm 69 with Jesus' death. Jesus confronts his opponents in the Temple with a saying that the narrator links to the death and resurrection of Jesus. After the resurrection – after a divine salvific act echoing the restoration of God's servants in Zion (Ps. 69:35) – the disciples recalled Ps. 69:9 to explain his innocence in spite of opposition (John 15:24). Thus, the larger context of John proleptically correlates Psalm 69 with the death of Jesus at the hands of opponents, and the appeal to the wider aspects of the psalm elsewhere in John imply reminiscence of the psalm as a whole. Vinegar for a thirsty Jesus, then, is a synecdochical allusion to the suffering for God's sake that Psalm 69 reflects." (Brawley, "An Absent Complement," 438-439.)

77. Carson concludes, "John wants to make his readers understand that every part of Jesus' passion was not only in the Father's plan of redemption but a consequence of the Son's direct obedience to it . . . And either way, the hermeneutical assumption is that David and his experiences constitute a prophetic model, a 'type', of 'great David's great son'." (D. A. Carson, *The Gospel According to John* (Leicester: IVP, 1991), 619-20. So also A. J. Köstenberger, *John* (Grand Rapids: Baker 2004), 550; H. N. Ridderbos and J. Vriend, *The Gospel According to John: A Theological Commentary* (Grand Rapids: Eerdmans, 1997), 616.)

78. BAGD suggests that this cheaper version of wine was popular among soldiers because it more effectively quenched thirst, however, its usage in this scene indicates malice (F. W. Danker, W. Bauer, and W. Arndt, *A Greek-English Lexicon of the New Testament and Other Early Christian Literature* (3rd ed.; Chicago: University of Chicago Press, 2000), 574.) Carson notes that this drink should not be confused with the earlier drink offered to Jesus while on his way to be crucified as Mark refers to this drink as ἐσμυρνισμένον οἶνον (wine mixed with myrrh). (Carson, *The Gospel According to John*, 620.)

79. Köstenberger, *John*, 550. See also Wilson, *Psalms*, 955. Brawley notes the different uses of this drink across the four gospel accounts. While Matthew and Mark both view the drink as an act of compassion, Luke portrays it as an act of mockery. (Brawley, "An Absent Complement," 436.)

80. So Zenger, "It is crucial here that the *whole psalm* be heard as context if one is

of the vindication of Jesus in His resurrection and consequent vindication of all who "seek" God.

*Psalms 69 and 109 in Acts*

In Acts 1, Peter quotes from Psalms 69 and 109 to explain the death of Judas and justify his replacement.[81] This use of the two psalms by Peter is perhaps the most confronting in the New Testament as he directly references their imprecatory components.

Authors disagree regarding the particulars of how Peter employs Psalm 69 with some suggesting a reference to the vacant field and others the vacant office. Novick offers a mediating position, suggesting that the use of Psalm 69:25 functions as a concrete reference to both the field where he died and, symbolically, to the vacancy of his office.[82] This distinction, however, does not affect the Christological interpretation of the psalm. In either case, and in both psalms, it is clear that the reference places Judas in the category of enemy and implies that Jesus becomes its supplicant.

This typological interpretation of the psalms was not uncommon.[83] Marshall suggests that while a typological function is not the only way Luke employs the Old Testament, in this case the "Pattern and Type" function is likely:

> In some cases the Scripture may establish a pattern that could recur but that fitted (supremely) the life of Jesus or the early church. This may be the case with the citations in Acts 1:20, which could be

---

to understand the function of the pericope on the cleansing of the Temple within the whole scope of John's Gospel ... if we consider ... the entire psalm as the fundamental interpretive key (perhaps, because v. 10, even more important than Psalm 22) for Jesus' suffering, death *and* resurrection ("rescue from the power of death." ...) and that of the community constituted by him in the horizon of 69:33-34. Indeed, in light of 69:35-37 the Christ-event achieves altogether cosmic dimensions." (Hossfeld et al., *Psalms 2*, 185, emphasis original.)

81. Acts 1:16, 20a. Marshall notes that while this is the only direct quotation of Psalm 109 in the New Testament, there are "coincidences of language between 108:16 LXX and Acts 2:37 and between 108:25 LXX and Mark 15:29" which demonstrate the psalm was familiar to early Christians. Possible echoes of the psalm also occur in Matt. 5:43-44 and Luke 6:27-28. (I. H. Marshall, "Acts," in *Commentary on the New Testament Use of the Old Testament* (ed. G. K. Beale and D. A. Carson; Grand Rapids: Baker 2007), 530.)

82. T. Novick, "Succeeding Judas: Exegesis in Acts 1:15-26," *JBL* 129, no. 4 (2010): 795-799.

83. Marshall offers six different ways that Luke makes use of the Old Testament: 1) History, 2) Promise and Fulfilment, 3) Pattern and Type, 4) Principles, 5) Characterisation, 6) Allegorization, though he notes that allegorization is not a characteristic in Acts. (Marshall, "Acts," 519-520.) Bock agrees, noting that Peter uses both Psalms 69 and 109 "typologically-prophetically to declare Judas as judged." This use of the psalm, in Bock's opinion, is not at odds with its original context in the Psalter as the psalm functioned to encourage God's people to reflect "upon the way God acts and cares for the righteous who cry out to God." (D. L. Bock, *Acts* (Grand Rapids: Baker, 2007), 86-87.)

interpreted as examples of what should happen to the psalmist's enemies and therefore to Judas in particular rather than as specific predictions relating to Judas.[84]

Building upon Longenecker's categories of "corporate solidarity" and "correspondences in history", Grant also suggests that the reinterpretation of Psalms 69 and 109 in Acts is not unexpected. He argues that the community understood the individual psalmists as their representatives and expected that the events of the psalms would find fulfillment in future generations:

> This is a prime example of reinterpretation/recontextualization: the early Christians saw the David of Psalms 69 and 109 as a representative figure and, therefore, the events that took place in the psalmist's historical reality as 'furthering the redemptive message' of their present day. David's imprecation on his enemies (Ps. 69:25), therefore, can be seen as appropriate explanation of the events surrounding the death of Judas although the two are, prima facie, separated by a millennium. Similarly, the prayerful plea that an enemy be removed from his office and replaced by another (Ps. 109:8) was read as divine counsel for the apostles' day and situation despite the separation of time and setting.[85]

This portrayal of Judas as the enemy implies that Jesus is the supplicant of both psalms. The direct reference to the imprecation reminds the reader of the language the supplicant employed in their desperate plea. While the imprecation of verse 8 is significant, "May his days be few; may another take his place of leadership", it is the following verses that are particularly confronting:

> May his descendants be cut off, their names blotted out from the next generation.
> May the iniquity of his fathers be remembered before the LORD; may the sin of his mother never be blotted out.
> May their sins always remain before the LORD, that he may cut off the memory of them from the earth.[86]

---

84. Marshall, "Acts," 520.

85. Grant, "Singing the Cover Versions," 41-42. See also S. Moyise, *The Old Testament in the New: An Introduction* (London: Continuum, 2001), 7. Keener notes that Peter's quotation from these two Psalms is not surprising as there was a long tradition of associating the psalms with the Davidic King, "Jewish interpreters frequently applied the psalms to King David, it made sense to early Christians to apply them to the Davidic king par excellence (cf. Acts 2:30, 34); depictions of the psalmist's enemies thus become appropriate for the enemies of the Messiah and his people (Acts 4:25-27). If these verses applied to oppressors of the righteous generally, then "how much more" (*qal vaomer*, a "light to heavy" argument) ought they apply to Judas, betrayer of the righteous one" (C. S. Keener, *Acts: An Exegetical Commentary* (Grand Rapids: Baker 2012), 765.)

86. Ps. 109:13-15. This extreme language is echoed in Psalm 69:22-28 as discussed above.

The extreme nature of these imprecations has caused many authors to reject their exemplary function and any association with Jesus. The following comments are representative:

> In speaking about the Imprecatory Psalms C. S. Lewis describes Psalm 109 as 'perhaps the worst'. McCann refers to the Psalm as 'the worst case scenario', and Bruggemann describes the central section as a 'song of hate', in which there is 'free, unrestrained speech of rage seeking vengeance'.[87]

> ...we certainly cannot square them with the ethics of Jesus. No amount of apologetic straining can make the following passage (Ps 109:6–12) an expression of the Spirit of God.[88]

> Thus Psalm 109 surely engages in "overkill" in its wishes and prayers against the "wicked." The words pile up like our nuclear stockpiles, without recognizing that nobody needs to be or could possibly be violated in that many ways. But this is not action. It is words, a flight of passion in imagination.[89]

Psalm 109 is confronting in its extreme language and because the imprecation is directed at personal enemies, even if they are, by implication, the enemies of God. Yet, the stance of both Luke and Peter towards this psalm and Psalm 69 is that they find fulfilment in the suffering of Jesus. Rather than reject Psalm 109 as too vindictive and too consumed with personal vengeance, the New Testament stance towards the psalm portrays Judas' death as justified and Jesus as the righteous supplicant. Goldingay comments:

> There is some irony in the fact that the point where the NT concentrates most of its use of the psalm is where commentators see it as unworthy of the NT. (Kidner, *Psalms*, 1:248). Apparently it was fine for the suppliant to pray the prayers in vv. 22–29. The NT implies that they fit into God's purpose that wrongdoing should receive its reward and that people who are unjustly attacked should be delivered.[90]

As Marshall and Grant have suggested, recognition of the fulfilment of these psalms in the life of Jesus does not preclude other instances of fulfilment. It is, in part, because these psalms were assumed to "fit" the circumstances of the contemporary generation that the early Christians were confident in their application of the psalms in this case. Psalms 69 and 109 were not considered to be solely "about" Judas. Rather, Judas fits the paradigm of the enemy and Jesus that of the afflicted one *par excellence*.

---

87. Shepherd, "The Place of the Imprecatory Psalms," 30.
88. R. H. Walker, *The Modern Message of the Psalms* (New York: Abingdon Press, 1938), 183.
89. Brueggemann, *Praying the Psalms*, 65–66.
90. Goldingay, *Psalms 2*, 356.

The usage of Psalms 69 and 109 in Acts can be summarized in the following illocutions. Luke portrays Judas as the enemy of God and of the psalmist. In doing so, Luke argues that his death was appropriate and his replacement necessary. Furthermore, it is implied that Jesus is the supplicant of the psalms who suffers at the hands of the wicked because of his commitment to Yahweh. This typological interpretation of the psalms does not preclude any previous or future referents, but demonstrates that the circumstances of Jesus' suffering climacticly fulfil their paradigm.

*Psalm 69 in Romans*

Paul quotes Psalm 69 on two occasions in his letter to the Romans (11:9–10; 15:3). In Chapter 11:9–10 Paul quotes from the LXX (68:23–24; MT 69:23–24).[91] Seifrid notes that this psalm was applied to the wicked in earlier Jewish texts (*Odes Sol.* 5:5; *Midr. Esther* 7:9).[92] Here in Romans, Paul directs the imprecation at unbelieving Israel:

> The context in Romans already makes clear that it is the proclamation of the crucified and risen Christ that brings the present moment of judgment and hardening upon Israel (cf. 9:30–33; 10:3, 19–21). In appealing to the Davidic psalm, Paul makes the Christological moment central. Just as David once pronounced a curse on his enemies, so now the Son of God, of the seed of David (1:3), who, according to Paul's later citation of this very psalm, bore the reproaches of God's own enemies, pronounces a curse on unbelieving Israel ... Of course, David appears as a witness alongside the mixed citation of Deut. 29:4 and Isa. 29:10. Israel's disobedience has not been confined to a single event, but rather has been repeated in its history with God. The former judgments of God, which have repeatedly come upon his people, have been recapitulated finally in Christ.[93]

Paul's use of Psalm 69 recalls the original sense where unbelieving Israel are oppressing the one who remains loyal to Yahweh. Paul's use is consistent with Luke's as they both cast Judas and unbelieving Israel as the enemies and imply that Jesus is the supplicant of the psalm. Paul's application in Romans also

---

91. For a discussion of how the LXX differs from the MT at this point and how Paul diverges from the LXX see M. A. Seifrid, "Romans," in *Commentary on the New Testament Use of the Old Testament* (ed. G. K. Beale and D. A. Carson; Grand Rapids: Baker 2007), 670. Seifrid argues that the details of these differences are significant and that the reference to the "table" should be understood as a rebuke of Jewish Christian exclusivity (Seifrid, "Romans," 671.) Other commentators disagree, suggesting the function of the quotation should be understood in broad terms and any attempts to align its detail goes beyond what Paul intended (See T. R. Schreiner, *Romans* (Grand Rapids: Baker Books, 1998), 589; D. J. Moo, *The Epistle to the Romans* (Grand Rapids: Eerdmans, 1996), 683.) The level of detail suggested by Seifrid is clearly hard to verify and, thankfully, not critical to my argument.
92. Seifrid, "Romans," 670.
93. Seifrid, "Romans," 671.

recalls Luke's use of Psalm 109 where the imprecatory component of the psalm was used to speak of Judas and, once again, Jesus is the implied imprecator.

Schreiner notes that the New Testament writers understood this psalm to be fulfilled in Jesus but that it probably applied in a similar way to the church:

> The NT Writers perceived that the psalm was fulfilled in the life of Jesus of Nazareth, who was unjustly rejected and suffered, even though he was filled with zeal for the house of God (Ps. 69:9). We know from Rom. 15:3 that Paul also related the psalm to Jesus, and presumably the church also was the object of suffering and rejection (cf. 8:17, 36) because they had identified with Jesus as Messiah. The curse pronounced upon the psalmist's enemies, therefore, was applied to unbelieving Jews of Paul's day who rejected Jesus as their Lord and oppressed the church.[94]

This application to the church is demonstrated more clearly in Paul's second quotation of the psalm (15:3). The context of this quotation is Paul's encouragement to the "strong" that they should consider the "weak." Just as Jesus did not live to please himself, Christians should live to please their neighbour (15:1-3). Paul then quotes from Psalm 69:9 (68:10 LXX) "The insults of those who insult you have fallen on me." This quotation of Psalm 69 is significant because it accomplishes two things. Firstly, as demonstrated in the discussion above, the psalm continues to be applied to Jesus as the righteous sufferer. Secondly, the example of Jesus as the righteous sufferer is offered to the church as model for them to imitate.[95] In this way, Paul is inviting his readers to identify with both Jesus and the psalmist and place themselves in the narrative of Psalm 69. In the context of Paul's argument the suffering of the "strong" is hardly comparable to the suffering envisaged in the psalm and its fulfilment in the passion of Jesus.

Subsequent verses support the claim that Paul is invoking Psalm 69 as both an example of Jesus' suffering and as invitation to the church to consider themselves in the same narrative. In verse 4 Paul writes, "For everything that was written in the past was written to teach us, so that through endurance and the encouragement of the Scriptures we might have hope." With this verse Paul is both referring to the quotation of verse 3 and also anticipating the Old Testament quotations of verses 9-12.[96] In referring back to the quotation of Psalm 69:9, Paul suggests that the church will be encouraged and have hope in their suffering by remembering that their suffering imitates that of Jesus. It is a mark of their loyalty to God and their righteousness. Furthermore, the reference to Psalm 69 most likely evokes the entire psalm. In this case, the righteous sufferer of the psalm anticipates his vindication and that of all God's people, all who "seek Him" (69:31-37).

---

94. Schreiner, *Romans*, 588.

95. So Moo, "Paul therefore implicitly appeals to Jesus' giving of himself in service to others as a model to imitate." (Moo, *The Epistle to the Romans*, 869. See also Schreiner, *Romans*, 747. L. Morris, *The Epistle to the Romans* (Grand Rapids: Eerdmans, 1988), 499.)

96. Schreiner, *Romans*, 748.

The quotation of Psalm 69 in this context places both Jesus and the church in the pattern of the psalmist. In doing so, Paul encourages the church to suffer willingly like Jesus reminding them that the vindication the psalmist anticipated was realised by Jesus and will likewise be realised by them if they accept the invitation to mimesis.

*Summary of New Testament Illocutions Regarding Psalm 69*
The New Testament demonstrates a consistent stance towards Psalms 69 and 109. Jesus is consistently portrayed as fitting the paradigm of the psalmist. He is the righteous sufferer who suffers innocently for his dedication to God. By placing the life of Jesus in the paradigm of these psalms, the authors also present Jesus as one who will be and, in fact, has been, vindicated. Furthermore, those who reject and oppress Jesus are cast in the role of the enemies in the psalms. They are pictured as those whom God should rightly judge. Both implicitly and explicitly, *Jesus is then portrayed not only as the righteous sufferer but as the supplicant and imprecator of the psalms.*

The stance of the New Testament towards these psalms is also consistent in its portrayal of Jesus' followers. While those who reject Jesus are cast in the role of the enemy, *those who follow Jesus are encouraged to see themselves as the righteous supplicant in these psalms*. This invitation is clear on two occasions discussed above. In John 15, Jesus reminds his disciples that the opposition he encounters is not unexpected. Consequently, his disciples should not be surprised if they find themselves in the same narrative. John's use of Psalm 69 in this case invites the reader to be the righteous sufferer of the psalm and be encouraged. In Romans 15, Jesus' willingness to suffer is presented as the ultimate example for the church to imitate. The call to follow this example and to find hope in the paradigm of the psalmist is explicit.

The New Testament stance towards these psalms provides a new context in which the psalms are now interpreted. While it is clear that the New Testament proclaims Jesus as the climactic supplicant of the psalms this does not exhaust their typological fulfilment. As demonstrated, the New Testament writers also invite the followers of Jesus to enter the same paradigm in imitation of him. Furthermore, the stance of the New Testament does not condemn or abrogate the imprecations found within these psalms. On the contrary, these imprecatory prayers are implicitly cast on the lips of Jesus, validating both past and future appropriation by righteous sufferers.

## Conclusion: A "Theologically Thick" Description of Psalm 69

A "theologically thick" description of Psalm 69 will demonstrate the range of divine illocutions currently in play. This requires an assessment of the original human and divine illocutions in the Old Testament context, followed by a consideration of how central and New Testament illocutions affect the context in which the previous illocutions now function. Having assessed the New Testament stance towards imprecation in Chapter 5 and its particular stance toward Psalm 69 in the discussion above, I conclude that the canonical context of the psalm affirms its original divine illocutions. Furthermore, the canonical context supervenes upon Psalm 69 to produce new illocutions. These new illocutions are not at odds with those of its original context, nor do they change the context in such a way that the previous illocutions are no longer in play. Rather, the illocutions formed in the canonical context constitute the *sensus plenior* of Psalm 69 and are consistent with those previously performed.

As stated, the first part of the method is to determine the original illocutions of the psalm, both human and divine. As much of Psalm 69 is characteristically addressed to God, it is clear that God is not performing all of the illocutions embedded within the psalm. With respect to these particular illocutions, I conclude that God affirms the various stances of the psalmist. As I stated above, He *affirms* the stance of the psalmist throughout the psalm: his voice, his boldness, his innocence, his zeal, his loyalty and his desire for justice and deliverance. God also reminds the reader of His loyal love, faithfulness, and compassion, even when circumstances suggest the contrary.

I identified the primary divine illocutions in the Old Testament context as the invitation to "suffer without cause" and to "seek God" in such a context. Another way of construing these illocutions is in the form of a series of questions where God challenges the reader by asking: "Are you zealous for My Name? Are you committed to a course that may bring suffering? Are you suffering without cause? Will you remain loyal and seek Me to the very end."

In Chapter 5, I argued that various New Testament illocutions that may, at first glance, appear to be at odds with the invitation to imprecation are not inconsistent with such a call. In fact, the stance of the New Testament confirms a place for imprecation as a response to extreme violence and oppression. The discussion above, regarding the New Testament stance towards Psalm 69 also supports a consistent function throughout the canon. These texts present Jesus as the supplicant, while Judas, unbelieving Jews, and those opposing the church are cast in the role of the enemy. This portrayal of Jesus as the supplicant of the psalm does not, however, exhaust its reference. Rather, the New Testament writers present Jesus as a climactic fulfilment of the righteous sufferer of Psalm 69 and offer Him as the exemplar. This portrayal of Jesus both expands the referent of the psalm and supports its original illocutions inviting mimesis. Two passages in particular make this invitation explicit. Both John 15 and Romans 15 present Jesus as the exemplar of the righteous sufferer and invite the reader to follow Him in the course of suffering.

Perhaps most confronting is the implication that Jesus is the supplicant of Psalm 69 who imprecates to the Father, requesting deliverance and justice. The New Testament stance toward imprecation is therefore not one of abrogation, but of affirmation. Furthermore, the vindication that the psalmist anticipates is realised in the life of Jesus. In this way, the hope that is offered in the final verses of Psalm 69 is strengthened by the vindication of Jesus who completes the paradigmatic portrait of the righteous sufferer.

In the previous chapter I offered brief examples of what I considered "similar situations" to that of Psalm 137. In Psalm 137, the suffering of a community was in view. Here in Psalm 69, it is the individual who is oppressed and their sense of isolation is acute. As I have argued, Jesus has validated the suffering and the response of the psalmist so that this psalm continues to be offered to the reader and the community. Examples of such individual oppression include those who have suffered malicious slander or marginalization for their faith, or even had their life threatened because of their loyalty to Christ. Yet, the ambiguity of the violence and oppression presented in the psalm encourages reflection on other possible situations. Perhaps the revolting abuse of children by those who would claim to be God's servants is another situation where the imprecation of this psalm could be appropriated. That the psalm reflects the situation of an individual but is then presented to the community for appropriation suggests that a primary illocution of psalms like Psalm 69 is the invitation to the community to cry out with, and on behalf of, those who think they cry alone.

# Conclusion

My goal was to provide an outline of a theological hermeneutic and demonstrate its utility in a particular set of Old Testament texts. To this end, the focus of Part I was to define the goals of theological interpretation and develop the requisite hermeneutic. Part II applied the hermeneutic to the Psalms in general and the imprecatory psalms in particular. A detailed exegesis and corresponding theological interpretation of select psalms was then offered in order to demonstrate the utility of the hermeneutic. Psalm 137 was chosen as a communal lament and in light of its common rejection as divine discourse. Psalm 69 was similarly discussed with a particular focus on Christological interpretation of individual psalms and its use in the New Testament.

Part I introduced speech act theory as a way of clarifying the nature of communication and defining what it means for a text to have meaning. I agreed with those who prioritize the illocutionary act as the locus of meaning. This understanding of meaning was consistent with my realist presuppositions, as meaning is understood to be a product of convention where an author adopts a particular stance in the public domain. I also sided with those calling for a reformulation of theological hermeneutics using the resources of speech act theory, thus rejecting suggestions that the theory had a very limited application. While it is true that speech act theory cannot in itself overcome all the challenges of theological interpretation, at the very least it provides a level of clarity previously lacking in the discussion. In particular, it clarifies what it means for Scripture to function as the word of God and consequently shapes the nature of a theological hermeneutic.

With the aid of speech act theory, I discussed the category of *sensus plenior*. I concluded that approaches affirming single determinate meaning, where the human and divine illocutions are coterminous, have not accounted for how Old Testament texts continue to function as God's word without resulting in a reductionism at odds with their presuppositions vis-à-vis inspiration. On the other hand, I noted that descriptions of *sensus plenior* were largely limited to discussions of prophetic texts and did not account for the wide range of genres where the divine illocutions must necessarily be divergent in the canonical context. Of the few writers who have noted this lacuna, their responses have been largely suggestive and have not provided a clear hermeneutic or a detailed exegetical application. I concluded that there remained a need for a speech act theory based hermeneutic that accounted for *sensus plenior*, both clarifying its goals and controls, and offering a detailed application to a particular genre.

I provided an outline of such a theological hermeneutic in Chapter 3. Here I argued that theological interpretation requires a thick description of a text. This necessity is a product of the inherent complexity of textual communication where illocutions are performed at a number of literary levels from sub-sentential to the level of an entire book or collection. This complexity is exaggerated in the case of Scripture where I argued that illocutions occur uniquely at the level of canon. Adding to this complexity is the conviction that Scripture is used to perform both human and divine illocutions and that illocutionary divergence between the two is relatively common, as human authors could not anticipate all the ways a text would function in the finalised canon. Recognition of illocutionary divergence raises the question of how to uncover divine illocutions and whether we are not simply adjusting the "wax nose." As I noted elsewhere:

> It needs to be recognized that across genres and within genres God's illocutions might be identical with the human author's, yet they might be necessarily different. It is not a simple divine appropriation of every human speech act and it is not a simple appropriation of only higher-level speech acts. Each genre and text requires individual analysis to determine exactly how God is speaking through it. Again, a sensus plenior approach that utilizes speech act theory recognizes the complexity of God's speech in Scripture and allows for greater precision in discussing how and, in particular, at what level, God is communicating.[1]

In keeping with my presuppositions regarding inspiration, I argued that the first step in determining the divine illocutions should be to count them as congruous with the human illocutions wherever this "made sense." This decision is not theological in the sense that the illocutions are assessed against God's character. Rather, the question is whether God *could* logically take the stance of the human author. I suggested that such divergence occasionally occurs at lower literary levels, but that illocutionary convergence is clearly found at the generic and whole-text levels.

The identification of human illocutions and their appropriation by God is one way that Scripture functions as divine discourse. However, this does not exhaust the divine illocutions of Scripture. I also suggested that God may perform illocutions beyond those of the human author, and that this should be understood as *sensus plenior*. In order to determine these distinctly divine illocutions, I argued that canonical and central illocutions must be identified. I noted that the identification of canonical and central illocutions is not a given product of my hermeneutic. Rather, this is the joint task of biblical scholars and systematic theologians. However, once such illocutions are identified and the level of their supervention established, these illocutions become the basis for determining the divine illocutions. The canonical and central illocutions have, by definition, changed the reality in which all the locutions of the Scripture now

---

1. Barker, "Speech Act Theory," 235.

exist. This enables an assessment of which previous illocutions remain in play. It also enables the assessment of how this contextual change produces new, divine illocutions. In this way, the boundaries of a *sensus plenior* are established and any suggestion that God is using a text to perform illocutions other than those of the human author now requires that the supervening illocutions be identified and the manner of their supervention explained.

Part II sought to offer an application of the theological hermeneutic to a particular book and particular texts in order to demonstrate its effectiveness for theological interpretation. Application to the Psalter highlighted the necessity of such a hermeneutic. It was clear that God does not directly perform many of the intratextual, lower-level illocutions of the psalms. However, I argued that a theological hermeneutic of the Old Testament must begin by uncovering the human and divine illocutions in this context. Only then is it possible to assess whether these illocutions remain in play and whether new illocutions are being performed.

I suggested that the clearest way that the Psalms functioned as divine discourse is at the generic and whole-text levels where God appropriates the stance of the psalmists and editors, at the level of psalm and Psalter. In short, the illocutionary stance of the Psalter should be counted as the illocutionary stance of God. This makes sense of the difficulty in construing how the words of God's people directed to God can be counted as God's words directed to God's people. The primary illocutions of the Psalter which should be counted as divine illocutions include the following: the invitation to mimesis; the declaration that Yahweh is king and the corresponding invitation to be loyal to Him and his king; the offering of hope; the warning against rebellion; the affirmation of both the experiences of the psalmists and their collective responses. At this point, I deferred a detailed explanation of how the intratextual illocutions of a psalm were related to the divine illocutions at this level. However, I noted that at the very least, God affirms the illocutionary stances of the psalmists within the psalm.

Having suggested the above ways in which the Psalter functioned as divine discourse, a theological interpretation required that canonical and central illocutions be considered in order to determine how the Psalter continues to function in this way. I chose the imprecatory psalms as the focus of this discussion in order to provide an increased level of detail and also because they are often rejected as instances of divine discourse. I demonstrated that the imprecatory psalms are, first of all, consistent with the illocutionary stance of the Psalter. Then, through a discussion of canonical and central New Testament illocutions relevant to these psalms, I established that the illocutionary stance of the New Testament is consistent with that of the imprecatory psalms. I demonstrated that these New Testament illocutions have not altered the conditions in which the illocutions of the Psalter now function to the point that the Psalter's invitation to imprecation now "misfires." In particular, I argued that the illocutions calling for forgiveness and inviting imprecation concurrently exist, as their requisite conditions are mutually exclusive.² Furthermore, I noted that the illocutionary stance of the New Testament reinforces that of the Psalter by encouraging a response to extreme violence and oppression that cries out to God for justice.

In the remaining chapters I increased the focus of the discussion to individual psalms in order to allow for a level of detail previously absent in many discussions of theological interpretation. I applied the hermeneutic first of all to Psalm 137 as representative of a communal lament. I suggested that God is both appropriating the generic and whole-text illocutions of the psalm inviting mimesis, and also performing attendant illocutions affirming the stance of the psalmist *within* the psalm. In the case of Psalm 137, and commonly in the imprecatory psalms, God is affirming the loyalty of the psalmist, the anger of the psalmist and the psalmist's desire that God's name and His people are vindicated.

When considered in light of the New Testament illocutions, I concluded that these central illocutions expand, rather than diminish, the illocutionary force of Psalm 137. For example, the prayers of loyalty to Zion become prayers for God's kingdom and the rule of Christ to be fully realized. The prayer for vindication is performed with the knowledge of God's wrath being satisfied in the One to whom the prayer is now offered. This One now has the right to bring God's judgment upon all who reject Him.

I also noted that this psalm continues to "incite hatred" while simultaneously precluding any response of human vengeance. I argued that Psalm 137 confronts an apathetic and ambivalent people and incites them to hate, incites them to side with Yahweh, His Son, His people and all those suffering at the hands of the wicked. This distancing and loyalty is supported by the New Testament use of Babylon as representative of all those opposed to God and His kingdom.

I concluded that the imprecatory psalms remain an instance of divine discourse where the original illocutions remain in play and new illocutions are formed in the context of the New Testament. With respect to imprecation, I noted that while it continues to be offered as a righteous response, it is not always a necessary response. It remains for Christians to consider what counts as a "similar situation."

Having demonstrated the utility of the hermeneutic in a theological interpretation of Psalm 137, I offered a discussion of Psalm 69 as representative of an individual imprecatory psalm and of a psalm that is directly applied to Christ in the New Testament. My conclusions, in general, were similar to those for Psalm 137 where I argued that canonical and central illocutions have not changed the context of the psalm in such a way that its original illocutions now misfire. Rather, the divine illocutions offering the psalm to the reader as an example of a righteous response remain in play. Again, in a manner similar to Psalm 137, I

---

2. At this point, the resources of speech act theory made a surprising contribution, enabling a clarification of the nature of forgiveness and its requisite context.

argued that this canonical context expands rather than diminishes the illocutionary force of the psalm and this expansion should be understood as its *sensus plenior*.

I identified the primary divine illocutions, occurring at the level of genre, as the invitations to both "suffer without cause" and "seek God" in times of oppression. I also suggested that God affirms the stance of the psalmist within the psalm: his voice, his boldness, his innocence, his zeal, his loyalty and his desire for justice and deliverance. Simultaneously, God reminds the reader of His loyal love, faithfulness, and compassion when circumstances suggest the contrary. I concluded that these original divine illocutions continue to function and that the Christological use of the New Testament supports and expands their illocutionary force. The New Testament presents Jesus as the supplicant of Psalm 69. This fulfilment of the psalm does not preclude its further appropriation or fulfilment in the life of the reader. The continued invitation to mimesis is supported by the New Testament presentation of the Jesus as the exemplar of Psalm 69 who invites the reader to follow Him in the course of suffering. The imprecatory components of the psalm are not excluded from this invitation as Jesus himself is cast in the role of the imprecator. The vindication of Jesus creates a context which enhances the hope offered by Psalm 69. Through the paradigm of Psalm 69, God continues to invite the reader to remain loyal to Him and to expect both suffering and vindication to be the result.

I have demonstrated the benefits of a speech act theory based hermeneutic for theological interpretation by providing both a detailed outline of a theological hermeneutic and its application to specific texts. Speech act theory clarifies the nature of communication, the locus of meaning, and what it means for a text to function as divine discourse. I have also demonstrated the necessity of a thick description of a text that accounts for how the canonical and central illocutions supervene by altering the context in which previous illocutions now function.

The application of the hermeneutic to the Psalter and specific imprecatory psalms allowed for a level of detail previously lacking in the discussion. I concluded that the clearest way that these psalms function as divine discourse is at the generic and whole-text levels, though this function is not limited here. Furthermore, in my discussion of New Testament illocutions I demonstrated the process required to determine how the Old Testament texts continue to function as divine discourse. My conclusions regarding the continuing function of the imprecatory psalms as examples of a righteous response were not critical to the overall thesis. If I had determined that the canonical and central illocutions of the New Testament had, in fact, altered the context of the psalms to such an extent that their original invitation to mimesis now misfires then the thesis would have been equally successful. The hermeneutic would have been utilized in such a way to explicate a theological interpretation of these psalms. However, this was not the case and my application of the hermeneutic suggests that God continues to perform similar illocutions in the canonical context, and that a Christological interpretation of these psalms supports and expands their illocutionary force.

I believe a number of related areas of inquiry would benefit from my conclusions. At the broadest level, more work could be done in clarifying how specific genres and texts continue to function as divine discourse. The application of the hermeneutic to the Psalter suggests the need to assess each genre and text in order to determine how it specifically functions as divine discourse. My choice of the Psalms was natural, yet arbitrary. It was natural in that the problem of dual authorship and divine discourse is obvious in this book, yet arbitrary since any Scriptural genre or book could be investigated in the same manner. As I mentioned briefly in the discussion above, the contemporary function of the Old Testament legal material is a clear candidate for such work.

Other areas where the hermeneutic may prove useful is in identifying how a number of the above themes function at the canonical level (e.g., blessing, lament, kingship, messiah and Zion). In turn, this identification of thematic function has wider implications for the nature of theology. A speech act hermeneutic that accounts for divine discourse would supplement theology's traditional systematization of propositions by recognizing that divine revelation occurs in many other illocutionary categories. A systematic theology that is supplemented by a full range of illocutions would offer an expanded understanding of divine revelation.

Similarly, the theological hermeneutic I have proposed would also benefit the task of homiletics with its desire to speak God's words to His people. Not only will the hermeneutic allow for greater clarity in understanding how particular texts function as divine discourse, but it would also aid the preacher in the tasks of contextualization and application. The identification of the divine illocutions mediated by the text will provide a clearer pathway to application as illocutions are, by nature, directed at an audience.

Lastly, I hope my discussion of the imprecatory psalms encourages the people of God to return to patterns of prayer that acknowledge God's rule over some of the worst possible experiences. In light of this, more work needs to be done to encourage the incorporation of imprecation in corporate worship, which, in turn, would both model and validate their appropriation by individuals who need them most.

# Bibliography

Anglican Church of Australia, *An Australian Prayer Book*. Sydney: Anglican Information Office Press, 1978.

———. *A Prayer Book for Australia: For Use Together with the Book of Common Prayer (1662) and an Australian Prayer Book (1978)*. Alexandria: Broughton Books, 1995.

Achtemeier, E. R. *Preaching Hard Texts of the Old Testament*. Peabody: Hendrickson, 1998.

Adam, P. *Hearing God's Words: Exploring Biblical Spirituality*. New Studies in Biblical Theology 16. Downers Grove: IVP, 2004.

Adams, J. W. *The Performative Nature and Function of Isaiah 40-55*. Library of Hebrew Bible/Old Testament Studies : 448. New York: T&T Clark, 2006.

Ahn, J. "Psalm 137: Complex Communal Laments." *Journal of Biblical Literature* 127, no. 2 (2008): 267-289.

Albertz, R. *Israel in Exile: The History and Literature of the Sixth Century B.C.E.* Atlanta: Society of Biblical Literature, 2003.

Allen, L. C. *Psalms 101-150*. Vol. 21, Word Biblical Commentary. Waco: Word, 1983.

———. "The Value of Rhetorical Criticism in Psalm 69." *Journal of Biblical Literature* 105, no. 4 (1986): 577-598.

Alston, W. P. *Illocutionary Acts and Sentence Meaning*. Ithaca: Cornell University Press, 2000.

Alter, R. *The Book of Psalms: A Translation with Commentary*. 1st ed. New York: W. W. Norton, 2007.

Althann, R. "The Psalms of Vengeance Against Their Ancient Near Eastern Background." *Journal of Northwest Semitic Languages* 18 (1992).

Anderson, A. A. *The Book of Psalms: Based on the Revised Standard Version*. 2 vols, New Century Bible Commentary. Grand Rapids: Eerdmans, 1981.

Augsburger, D. W. *Hate-Work: Working Through the Pain and the Pleasures of Hate*. Louisville: Westminster John Knox Press, 2004.

———. *Helping People Forgive*. 1st ed. Louisville: Westminster John Knox Press, 1996.

———. "Forgiveness." Page 389 in *New Dictionary of Christian Ethics & Pastoral Theology*. Edited by D. J. Atkinson, D. Field, A. F. Holmes and O. O'Donovan. Downers Grove: IVP, 1995.

Augustine. "Exposition on the Psalms." No pages. Cited February 29 2012. Online: http://www.newadvent.org/fathers/1801137.htm.

Austin, J. L. *How to Do Things with Words*. 2nd ed, The William James Lectures 1955. Oxford: Clarendon Press, 1975.

Barker, K. "Divine Illocutions in Psalm 137: A Critique of Nicholas Wolterstorff's 'Second Hermeneutic'." *Tyndale Bulletin* 60, no. 1 (2009): 1-14.

———. "Speech Act Theory, Dual Authorship, and Canonical Hermeneutics: Making Sense of Sensus Plenior." *Journal of Theological Interpretation* 3, no. 2 (2009): 227-239.

———. "I Am." Page 226 in *Dictionary of the Bible and Western Culture*. Edited by M. A. Beavis and M. J. Gilmour. Sheffield: Sheffield Phoenix Press, 2012.

———. "Psalms of the Powerless: A Theological Interpretation of Imprecation." in *Stirred by a Noble Theme: The Book of Psalms in the Life of the Church*. Edited by A. G. Shead. Nottingham: IVP, forthcoming 2013.

Bartholomew, C., S. Hahn, R. Parry, C. Seitz, and A. Wolters. *Canon and Biblical Interpretation*. Scripture and Hermeneutics Series. Grand Rapids: Zondervan, 2006.

Bartholomew, C. G. "Listening for God's Address: A Mere Trinitarian Hermeneutic for the Old Testament." Pages 3-19 in *Hearing the Old Testament: Listening for God's Address*. Edited by C. G. Bartholomew and D. J. H. Beldman. Grand Rapids: Eerdmans, 2012.

Bartholomew, C. G. and D. J. H. Beldman. *Hearing the Old Testament: Listening for God's Address*. Grand Rapids: Eerdmans, 2012.

Barton, J. *Reading the Old Testament: Method in Biblical Study*. Rev. and enlarged. ed. Louisville: Westminster John Knox, 1996.

Bash, A. *Just Forgiveness: Exploring the Bible, Weighing the Issues*. London: SPCK, 2011.

Beasley-Murray, G. R. *John*. Word Biblical Commentary. Dallas: Word, 1989.

Beilby, J. and P. R. Eddy. *The Nature of the Atonement: Four Views*. Downers Grove: InterVarsity, 2006.

Belcher, R. P. *The Messiah and the Psalms: Preaching Christ from All the Psalms*. Fearn: Mentor, 2006.

Belousek, D. W. S. *Atonement, Justice, and Peace: The Message of the Cross and the Mission of the Church*. Grand Rapids: Eerdmans, 2012.

Berlin, A. "Psalms and the Literature of Exile: Psalms 137, 44, 69, and 78." Pages 65-86 in *Book of Psalms: Composition and Reception*. Edited by P. W. Flint and P. D. Miller. Leiden: Brill, 2005.

Berry, C. E. "Speech-Act Theory as a Corollary for Describing the Communicative Dynamics of Biblical Revelation: Some Recommendations and Reservations." *Criswell Theological Review*, no. 7 (2009): 81-100.

Biggar, N. "Forgiveness in the Twentieth Century." Pages 181-219 in *Forgiveness and Truth: Explorations in Contemporary Theology*. Edited by A. McFayden and M. Sarot. Edinburgh: T&T Clark, 2001.

Blomberg, C. L. "On Building and Breaking Barriers: Forgiveness, Salvation and Christian Counseling with Special Reference to Matthew 18:15-35." *Journal of Psychology and Christianity* 25, no. 2 (2006): 137-154.

Blue, S. A. "Meaning, Intention, and Application: Speech Act Theory in the Hermeneutics of Francis Watson and Kevin J Vanhoozer." *Trinity Journal*, no. 23 (2002): 161-184.

Bock, D. L. *Acts*. Baker Exegetical Commentary on the New Testament. Grand Rapids: Baker, 2007.

———. "Evangelicals and the Use of the Old Testament in the New." *Bibliotheca sacra* 142, no. 567 (1985): 209-223.

———. "Evangelicals and the Use of the Old Testament in the New." *Bibliotheca sacra* 142, no. 568 (1985): 306-319.

Bockmuehl, M. N. A. and A. J. Torrance. *Scripture's Doctrine and Theology's Bible: How the New Testament Shapes Christian Dogmatics*. Grand Rapids: Baker 2008.

Bolin, T. M. "A Reassessment of the Textual Problem of Luke 23:34a." *Proceedings: Eastern Great Lakes and Midwest Biblical Societies* 12 (1992): 131-144.

Bonhoeffer, D. *Life Together: Prayerbook of the Bible*. Translated by D. W. Bloesch and J. H. Burtness. Minneapolis: Fortress Press, 1996.

———. *Psalms: The Prayer Book of the Bible*. Minneapolis: Augsburg, 1970.

Booth, W. C. *The Rhetoric of Fiction*. Chicago: University of Chicago Press, 1961.

Bowald, M. A. *Rendering the Word in Theological Hermeneutics: Mapping Divine and Human Agency*. Aldershot: Ashgate, 2007.

Brauns, C. *Unpacking Forgiveness: Biblical Answers for Complex Questions and Deep Wounds*. Wheaton: Crossway Books, 2008.

Brawley, R. L. "An Absent Complement and Intertextuality in John 19:28-29." *Journal of Biblical Literature* 112, no. 3 (1993): 427-443.

Brett, M. G. "Motives and Intentions in Genesis I." *Journal of Theological Studies*, no. 42 (1991): 1-16.

Briggs, C. A. and E. G. Briggs. *A Critical and Exegetical Commentary on the Book of Psalms*. The International Critical Commentary on the Holy Scriptures of the Old and New Testaments. New York: C. Scribner's Sons, 1906.

Briggs, R. S. "Scripture as Communication: Introducing Biblical Hermeneutics." *Evangelical Quarterly* 80, no. 1 (2008): 61-62.

———. "The Uses of Speech-Act Theory in Biblical Interpretation." *Currents in Research* 9 (2001): 229-276.

———. *Words in Action: Speech Act Theory and Biblical Interpretation: Toward a Hermeneutic of Self-Involvement*. Edinburgh: T&T Clark, 2001.

———. "Speech-Act Theory." Pages 75-110 in *Words and the Word: Explorations in Biblical Interpretation and Literary Theory*. Edited by D. G. Firth and J. A. Grant. Downers Grove: IVP 2008.

Broadhurst, J. R. "Should Cursing Continue? An Argument for Imprecatory Psalms in Biblical Theology." *Africa Journal of Evangelical Theology* 23, no. 1 (2004): 61-89.

Brown, F., E. Robinson, S. R. Driver, C. A. Briggs, F. Brown, and W. Gesenius. *The Brown-Driver-Briggs Hebrew and English Lexicon*. Peabody: Hendrickson, 2000.

Brown, J. K. *Scripture as Communication: Introducing Biblical Hermeneutics*. Grand Rapids: Baker, 2007.

———. "Genre Criticism and the Bible." Pages 111-150 in *Words and the Word: Explorations in Biblical Interpretation and Literary Theory*. Edited by D. G. Firth and J. A. Grant. Downers Grove: IVP 2008.

Brown, R. E. *The Gospel According to John (XIII-XXI)*. Anchor Bible 29a. Garden City: Doubleday, 1970.

———. "Sensus Plenior in the Last Ten Years." *Catholic Biblical Quarterly* 25, no. 3 (1963): 262-285.

———. *The Sensus Plenior of Sacred Scripture*. Baltimore: St. Mary's University, 1955.

Brueggemann, D. A. "The Evangelists and the Psalms." Pages 263-278 in *Interpreting the Psalms: Issues and Approaches*. Edited by D. G. Firth and P. S. Johnston. Downers Grove: IVP, 2005.

Brueggemann, W. "Bounded by Obedience and Praise: The Psalms as Canon." *Journal for the Study of the Old Testament* 50 (1991): 63-92.

———. *Praying the Psalms: Engaging the Scripture and the Life of the Spirit*. Milton Keynes: Paternoster, 2007.

———. *The Psalms and the Life of Faith*. Minneapolis: Fortress Press, 1995.

———. "Psalms and the Life of Faith: A Suggested Typology of Function." *Journal for the Study of the Old Testament* 17 (1980): 3-32.

Bryan, S. M. "Consumed by Zeal: John's Use of Psalm 69:9 and the Action in the Temple." *Bulletin for Biblical Research* 21, no. 4 (2011): 479-494.

Callahan, J. P. *The Clarity of Scripture: History, Theology & Contemporary Literary Studies*. Downers Grove: IVP, 2001.

Calvin, J. *Commentary on the Book of Psalms*. Vol. V. Grand Rapids: Eerdmans, 1949.

Caneday, A. B. "Is Theological Truth Functional or Propositional? Postconservatism's Use of Language Games and Speech-Act Theory." Page 137-160 in *Reclaiming the Center: Confronting Evangelical Accommodation in Postmodern Times*. Edited by M. J. Erickson, P. K. Helseth and J. Taylor. Wheaton: Crossway Books, 2004.

Carson, D. A. *From Sabbath to Lord's Day: A Biblical, Historical and Theological Investigation*. Grand Rapids: Zondervan, 1982.

Carson, D. A. *The Gospel According to John*. Leicester: IVP, 1991.

———. *Love in Hard Places*. Wheaton: Crossway Books, 2002.

Carson, D. A. and J. D. Woodbridge. *Hermeneutics, Authority and Canon*. Nottingham: IVP, 1986.

Childs, B. S. *Introduction to the Old Testament as Scripture*. Philadelphia: Fortress Press, 1979.

———. *Old Testament Theology in a Canonical Context*. Philadelphia: Fortress Press, 1986.

Clark, D. "Beyond Inerrancy: Speech Acts and an Evangelical View of Scripture." Pages 113-134 in *For Faith and Clarity: Philosophical Contributions to Christian Theology*. Edited by J. K. Beilby. Grand Rapids: Baker, 2006.

Cohen, D. J. *Why O Lord?* Milton Keyes: Paternoster, 2013.

Cottrill, A. C. *Language, Power, and Identity in the Lament Psalms of the Individual*. Library of Hebrew Bible/Old Testament Studies 493. London: Continuum, 2008.

Craigie, P. C. *Psalms 1-50*. Word Biblical Commentary. Waco: Word, 1983.

Craigo-Snell, S. N. "Command Performance: Rethinking Performance Interpretation in the Context of Divine Discourse." *Modern Theology* 16, no. 4 (2000): 475-494.

Creach, J. F. D. *Yahweh as Refuge and the Editing of the Hebrew Psalter*. Journal for the Study of the Old Testament Supplement Series. Sheffield: Sheffield Press, 1996.

———. "The Psalms and the Cult." Pages 119-137 in *Interpreting the Psalms: Issues and Approaches*. Edited by P. S. Johnston and D. G. Firth. Leicester: Apollos, 2005.

Croft, S. *The Identity of the Individual in the Psalms*. Journal for the Study of the Old Testament Supplement. Sheffield: Sheffield Academic, 1987.

Dahood, M. J. *Psalms II 51-100*. 1st ed. 3 vols, The Anchor Bible 16-17A. Garden City: Doubleday, 1966.

Danker, F. W., W. Bauer, and W. Arndt. *A Greek-English Lexicon of the New Testament and Other Early Christian Literature*. 3rd ed. Chicago: University of Chicago Press, 2000.

Davidson, R. *The Vitality of Worship: A Commentary on the Book of Psalms*. Grand Rapids: Eerdmans, 1998.

Davis, E. F. and R. B. Hays. *The Art of Reading Scripture*. Grand Rapids: Eerdmans, 2003.

Day, J. *Crying for Justice: What the Psalms Teach Us About Mercy and Vengeance in an Age of Terrorism*. Grand Rapids: Kregel, 2005.

de Vos, C. and G. Kwakkel. "Psalms 69: The Petitioner's Understanding of Himself, His God, and His Enemies." Pages 159-179 in *Psalms and Prayers: Papers Read at the Joint Meeting of the Society of Old Testament Study and Het Oudtestamentische Werkgezelschap in Nederland En België, Apeldoorn August 2006*. Edited by B. Becking and E. Peels. of *Oudtestamentische Studiën* 55. Leiden: Brill, 2007.

deClaissé-Walford, N. L. "O God, Why Do You Hide Your Face?" Pages 121-131 in *My Words Are Lovely*. Edited by R. L. Foster and D. M. Howard. of *The Library of Hebrew Bible/Old Testament Studies* 467. New York: T&T Clark, 2008.

———. "The Theology of the Imprecatory Psalms." in *Soundings in the Theology of Psalms: Perspectives and Methods in Contemporary Scholarship*. Edited by R. A. Jacobson. Minneapolis: Fortress Press, 2011.

Dempster, S. G. "Torah, Torah, Torah: The Emergence of the Tripartite Canon." Pages 87-127 in *Exploring the Origins of the Bible: Canon Formation in Historical, Literary, and Theological Perspective*. Edited by C. A. Evans and E. Tov. Grand Rapids: Baker 2008.

DiBlasio, F. A. and R. K. Cheong. "Christ-Like Love and Forgiveness: A Biblical Foundation for Counseling Practice." *Journal of Psychology and Christianity* 26, no. 1 (2007): 14-25.

Du Plessis, J. G. "Speech Act Theory and New Testament Interpretation with Special Reference to G.N. Leech's Pragmatic Principles." Pages 129-134 in *Text and Interpretation: New Approaches in the Criticism of the New Testament*. Edited by P. J. Hartin, J. H. Petzer and B. M. Metzger. Leiden: Brill, 1991.

Esler, P. F. *New Testament Theology: Communion and Community*. Minneapolis: Fortress Press, 2005.

Eubank, N. "A Disconcerting Prayer: On the Originality of Luke 23:34a." *Journal of Biblical Literature* 129, no. 3 (2010): 521-536.

Evans, C. A. and E. Tov. *Exploring the Origins of the Bible: Canon Formation in Historical, Literary, and Theological Perspective*. Grand Rapids: Baker, 2008.

Evans, D. D. *The Logic of Self-Involvement: A Philosophical Study of Everyday Language with Special Reference to the Christian use of Language about God as Creator*. London: SCM, 1963.

Firth, D. G. *Surrendering Retribution in the Psalms: Responses to Violence in the Individual Complaints*. Paternoster Biblical Monographs. Milton Keynes: Authentic Media, 2005.

———. "The Teaching of the Psalms." Pages 159-174 in *Interpreting the Psalms: Issues and Approaches*. Edited by P. S. Johnston and D. G. Firth. Leicester: Apollos, 2005.

Firth, D. G. and J. A. Grant. *Words and the Word: Explorations in Biblical Interpretation and Literary Theory*. Downers Grove: IVP 2008.

Fowl, S. E. *The Theological Interpretation of Scripture: Classic and Contemporary Readings*. Blackwell's Readings in Modern Theology. Cambridge: Blackwell, 1997.

———. "The Role of Authorial Intention in the Theological Interpretation of Scripture." Pages 71-87 in *Between Two Horizons: Spanning New Testament Studies and Systematic Theology*. Edited by J. B. Green and M. Turner. Grand Rapids: Eerdmans, 2000.

Frei, H. W. *The Identity of Jesus Christ: The Hermeneutical Bases of Dogmatic Theology*. Philadelphia: Fortress Press, 1975.

Futato, M. D. and D. M. Howard. *Interpreting the Psalms: An Exegetical Handbook*. Grand Rapids: Kregel, 2007.

Genette, G. *Narrative Discourse Revisited*. Ithaca: Cornell University Press, 1988.

Gibbs, R. W. *Intentions in the Experience of Meaning*. Cambridge: Cambridge University Press, 1999.

Gilbert, P. "The Function of Imprecation in Israel's Eighth-Century Prophets." *Direction* 35, no. 1 (2006): 44-58.

Goldingay, J. *Models for Interpretation of Scripture*. Grand Rapids: Eerdmans, 1995.

———. *Psalms. Volume 2, Psalms 42-89*. Baker Commentary on the Old Testament Wisdom and Psalms. Grand Rapids: Baker, 2007.

———. *Psalms. Volume 3, Psalms 90-150*. Baker Commentary on the Old Testament: Wisdom and Psalms. Grand Rapids: Baker, 2008.

Gorman, D. "The Use and Abuse of Speech-Act Theory in Criticism." *Poetics Today* 20, no. 1 (1999): 93-120.

Goswell, G. "The Order of the Books in the Greek Old Testament." *Journal of the Evangelical Theological Society* 52, no. 3 (2009): 449-466.

———. "The Order of the Books in the Hebrew Bible." *Journal of the Evangelical Theological Society* 51, no. 4 (2008): 673-688.

Grant, J. A. *The King as Exemplar: The Function of Deuteronomy's Kingship Law in the Shaping of the Book of Psalms*. Society of Biblical Literature Academia Biblica,. Leiden: Brill, 2004.

———. "Singing the Cover Versions: Psalms, Reinterpretation and Biblical Theology in Acts 1-4." *Scottish Bulletin of Evangelical Theology* 25, no. 1 (2007): 27-49.

———. "The Psalms and the King." Pages 101-118 in *Interpreting the Psalms: Issues and Approaches*. Edited by P. S. Johnston and D. G. Firth. Leicester: Apollos, 2005.

Greidanus, S. *The Modern Preacher and the Ancient Text: Interpreting and Preaching Biblical Literature*. Grand Rapids: Eerdmans, 1988.

Grenz, S. J. "The Spirit and the Word: The World-Creating Function of the Text." *Theology Today* 57, no. 3 (2000): 357-374.

Grenz, S. J. and J. R. Franke. *Beyond Foundationalism: Shaping Theology in a Postmodern Context*. Louisville: Westminster John Knox Press, 2001.

Grice, P. *Studies in the Way of Words*. Cambridge: Harvard University Press, 1989.

Groenewald, A. *Psalm 69: Its Structure, Redaction and Composition*. Altes Testament Und Moderne 18. Munster: LIT Verlag, 2003.

Guillaume, A. "Meaning of Twll in Psalm 137:3." *Journal of Biblical Literature* 75, no. 2 (1956): 143-144.

Gunkel, H. and J. Begrich. *Introduction to Psalms: The Genres of the Religious Lyric of Israel*. Mercer Library of Biblical Studies. Macon: Mercer University Press, 1998.

Hardin, M. and B. Jersak, eds. *Stricken by God?: Nonviolent Identification and the Victory of Christ*. Grand Rapids: Eerdmans, 2007.

Harrison, J. R. "Jesus and the Grace of the Cross: Luke 23:34a and the Politics of 'Forgiveness' in Antiquity." New Orleans: SBL Annual Meeting, unpublished, 2009.

Hays, C. B. "How Shall We Sing? Psalm 137 in Historical and Canonical Context." *Horizons in Biblical Theology* 27 (2005).

Hays, R. B. "Can the Gospels Teach Us How to Read the Old Testament?" *Pro Ecclesia* 11, no. 4 (2002): 402-418.

Helm, P. "Speaking and Revealing." *Religious Studies* 37, no. 3 (2001): 249-258.

Hengel, M., R. Deines, and M. E. Biddle. *The Septuagint as Christian Scripture: Its Prehistory and the Problem of Its Canon*. North American paperback ed. Grand Rapids: Baker 2004.

Holladay, W. L. *The Psalms through Three Thousand Years: Prayerbook of a Cloud of Witnesses*. Minneapolis: Fortress Press, 1993.

Horton, M. S. *Covenant and Eschatology: The Divine Drama*. Louisville: Westminster John Knox Press, 2002.

Hossfeld, F-L., E. Zenger, L. M. Maloney, and K. Baltzer. *Psalms 2: A Commentary on Psalms 51-100*. Hermeneia – A Critical and Historical Commentary on the Bible. Minneapolis: Fortress Press, 2005.

———. *Psalms 3: A Commentary on Psalms 101-150*. Hermeneia – A Critical and Historical Commentary on the Bible. Minneapolis: Fortress Press.

Houston, W. J. "What Did the Prophets Think They Were Doing? Speech Acts and Prophetic Discourse in the Old Testament." *Biblical Interpretation* 1, no. 2 (1993): 167-188.

Howard, D. M. *The Structure of Psalms 93-100*. Biblical and Judaic Studies from the University of California, San Diego. Winona Lake: Eisenbrauns, 1997.

Howard, D. M. J. "Recent Trends in Psalms Study." Pages 329-368 in *The Face of Old Testament Studies: A Survey of Contemporary Approaches*. Edited by D. W. Baker and B. T. Arnold. Grand Rapids: Baker, 1999.

———. "The Psalms and Current Study." Pages 23-40 in *Interpreting the Psalms: Issues and Approaches*. Edited by D. G. Firth and P. S. Johnston. Downers Grove: IVP, 2005.

Irsigler, H. "Psalm-Rede als Handlungs-, Wirk- und Aussageprozeß: Sprechaktanzlyse und Psalmeninterpretation am Beispiel von Psalm 13", in K. Seybold and E. Zenger, eds., *Neue Wege der PsalmenForschung: Für Walter Beyerlin* (Freiburg: Herder, 1994) 63-104.

Johnson, E. "Author's Intention and Biblical Interpretation." in *Hermeneutics, Inerrancy, and the Bible*. Edited by E. D. Radmacher and R. D. Preus. Grand Rapids: Academie Books, 1984.

Johnson, E. E. "Dual Authorship and the Single Intended Meaning of Scripture." *Bibliotheca sacra* 143, no. 571 (1986): 218-227.

Johnson, S. L. *The Old Testament in the New: An Argument for Biblical Inspiration*. Grand Rapids: Zondervan, 1980.

Johnston, P. S. and D. G. Firth, eds. *Interpreting the Psalms: Issues and Approaches*. Leicester: Apollos, 2005.

Jones, L. G. *Embodying Forgiveness: A Theological Analysis*. Grand Rapids: Eerdmans, 1995.

Kaiser, W. C. *Toward an Old Testament Theology*. Grand Rapids: Baker, 1981.

———. "Legitimate Hermeneutics." Pages 117-150 in *Inerrancy*. Edited by N. L. Geisler. Grand Rapids: Zondervan, 1980.

Keener, C. S. *Acts: An Exegetical Commentary*. Grand Rapids: Baker 2012.

Kellermann, U. "Psalm 137." *Zeitschrift für die alttestamentliche Wissenschaft* 90, no. 1 (1978): 43-58.

Kidner, D. *Psalms 1-72: An Introduction and Commentary*. Tyndale Old Testament Commentaries. Nottingham IVP, 2008.

Koch, K. "Is There a Doctrine of Retribution in the Old Testament." Pages 57-87 in *Theodicy in the Old Testament*. Edited by J. L. Crenshaw. in *Issues in Religion and Theology* 4. Philadelphia: Fortress Press, 1983.

Köhler, L., W. Baumgartner, M. E. J. Richardson, and J. J. Stamm. *The Hebrew and Aramaic Lexicon of the Old Testament*. Leiden: Brill, 2001.

Kostenberger, A. "John." Pages 415-512 in *Commentary on the New Testament Use of the Old Testament*. Edited by G. K. Beale and D. A. Carson. Grand Rapids: Baker 2007.

Köstenberger, A. J. *John*. Baker Exegetical Commentary on the New Testament. Grand Rapids: Baker 2004.

Kraus, H-J. *Psalms 60-150: A Commentary*. Minneapolis: Fortress Press, 1993.

La Sor, W. S. "Prophecy, Inspiration, and Sensus Plenior." *Tyndale Bulletin* 29 (1978): 49-60.

———. "The 'Sensus Plenior' and Biblical Interpretation." in *Scripture, Tradition, and Interpretation: Essays Presented to Everett F. Harrison*. Edited by W. W. Gasque and W. S. La Sor. Grand Rapids: Eerdmans, 1978.

Lane, W. L. *Hebrews 1-8*. Word Biblical Commentary 47a. Dallas: Word, 1991.

Laney, J. C. "A Fresh Look at the Imprecatory Psalms." *Bibliotheca sacra* 138, no. 549 (1981): 35-45.

Lanser, S. S. *The Narrative Act: Point of View in Prose Fiction*. Princeton: Princeton University Press, 1981.

Law, T. M. *When God Spoke Greek: The Septuagint and the Making of the Christian Bible*. Oxford: Oxford University Press, 2013.

LeFebvre, M. "Torah Meditation in the Psalms." Pages 213-225 in *Interpreting the Psalms: Issues and Approaches*. Edited by P. S. Johnston and D. G. Firth. Leicester: Apollos, 2005.

LeMon, J. M. "Saying Amen to Violent Psalms: Patterns of Prayer, Belief, and Action in the Psalter." Pages 93-110 in *Soundings in the Theology of Psalms: Perspectives and Methods in Contemporary Scholarship*. Edited by R. A. Jacobson. Minneapolis: Fortress Press, 2011.

Levering, M. *Participatory Biblical Exegesis: A Theology of Biblical Interpretation*. Reading the Scriptures. Notre Dame: University of Notre Dame Press, 2008.

Lewis, C. S. *Reflections on the Psalms*. New York: Harcourt, 1958.

Lewis, G. R. "The Human Authorship of Inspired Scripture." Pages 229-266 in *Inerrancy*. Edited by N. L. Geisler. Grand Rapids: Zondervan, 1980.

Libolt, C. "God Speech: A Conversation with Nicholas Wolterstorff's Divine Discourse." *Crux* 43, no. 3 (2007): 22-31.

Lindbeck, G. "Postcritical Canonical Interpretation: Three Modes of Retrieval." Pages 26-51 in *Theological Exegesis: Essays in Honor of Brevard S. Childs*. Edited by B. S. Childs, C. R. Seitz and K. Greene-McCreight. Grand Rapids: Eerdmans, 1999.

Luther, M. *Works*. American ed. Saint Louis: Concordia, 1955.

Macky, P. W. "The Multiple Purposes of Biblical Speech Acts." *Princeton Seminary Bulletin* 8, no. 2 (1987): 50-61.

Marshall, I. H. "Acts." Pages 513-606 in *Commentary on the New Testament Use of the Old Testament*. Edited by G. K. Beale and D. A. Carson. Grand Rapids: Baker 2007.

Matthews, S. "Clemency as Cruelty: Forgiveness and Force in the Dying Prayers of Jesus and Stephen." *Biblical Interpretation* 17, no. 1-2 (2009): 118-146.

Matthews, V. H. and D. C. Benjamin. *Old Testament Parallels: Laws and Stories from the Ancient Near East*. 3rd ed. New York: Paulist Press, 2006.

May, H. G. "Some Cosmic Connotations of Mayim Rabbim, "Many Waters."" *Journal of Biblical Literature* 74, no. 1 (1955): 9-21.

Mays, J. L. *The Lord Reigns: A Theological Handbook to the Psalms*. 1st ed. Louisville: Westminister John Knox Press, 1994.

———. *Psalms*. Interpretation, a Bible Commentary for Teaching and Preaching. Louisville: John Knox Press, 2011.

———. *Psalms*. Interpretation, a Bible Commentary for Teaching and Preaching. Louisville: John Knox Press, 1994.

McCann, J. C. *The Shape and Shaping of the Psalter*. Journal for the Study of the Old Testament Supplement Series 159. Sheffield: JSOT, 1993.

———. *A Theological Introduction to the Book of Psalms: The Psalms as Torah*. Nashville: Abingdon, 1993.

McCarter, P. K. "River Ordeal in Israelite Literature." *Harvard Theological Review* 66, no. 4 (1973): 403-412.

McConville, G. "Divine Speech and the Book of Jeremiah." Pages 18-38 in *The Trustworthiness of God: Perspectives on the Nature of Scripture*. Edited by P. Helm and C. R. Trueman. Grand Rapids: Eerdmans, 2002.

McKnight, E. V. *Reading the Bible Today: A 21st Century Appreciation of Scripture*. Macon: Smyth & Helwys, 2003.

McLellan, D. "Justice, Forgiveness, and Reconciliation: Essential Elements in Atonement Theology." *Evangelical Review of Theology* 29, no. 1 (2005): 4-15.

Meadowcroft, T. *Haggai*. Readings: A New Biblical Commentary. Sheffield: Sheffield Phoenix, 2006.

Miller, P. D. *Interpreting the Psalms*. Philadelphia: Fortress Press, 1986.

Mitchell, D. C. "Lord, Remember David: G H Wilson and the Message of the Psalter." *Vetus Testamentum* 56, no. 4 (2006): 526-548.

———. *The Message of the Psalter: An Eschatological Programme in the Books of Psalms*. Journal for the Study of the Old Testament Supplement Series. Sheffield: Sheffield Press, 1997.

Moberly, R. W. L. "What Is Theological Interpretation of Scripture?" *Journal of Theological Interpretation* 3, no. 2 (2009): 161-178.

Moller, K. "Reading, Singing and Praying the Law: An Exploration of the Performative, Self-Involving, Commissive Language of Psalm 101." Pages 111-137 in *Reading the Law*. New York: T&T Clark, 2007.

Moo, D. J. *The Epistle to the Romans*. The New International Commentary on the New Testament. Grand Rapids: Eerdmans, 1996.

———. "The Problem of Sensus Plenior." Pages 179-211 in *Hermeneutics, Authority, and Canon*. Edited by D. A. Carson and J. D. Woodbridge. Eugene: Wipf & Stock, 1986.

Morris, L. *The Apostolic Preaching of the Cross*. 1st ed. Grand Rapids: Eerdmans, 1955.

———. *The Epistle to the Romans*. Grand Rapids: Eerdmans, 1988.

Mowinckel, S. *The Psalms in Israel's Worship*. The Biblical Resource Series. Grand Rapids: Eerdmans 2004.

———. *Real and Apparent Tricola in Hebrew Psalm Poetry*. Oslo: Aschehoug, 1957.

Moyise, S. *The Old Testament in the New: An Introduction*. Continuum Biblical Studies Series. London: Continuum, 2001.

Murphy, N. C. "Textual Relativism, Philosophy of Language, and the Baptist Vision." Pages 245-270 in *Theology without Foundations: Religious Practice and the Future of Theological Truth*. Edited by S. Hauerwas, N. C. Murphy and M. Nation. Nashville: Abingdon Press, 1994.

Nasuti, H. P. "God at Work in the World: A Theology of Divine-Human Encounter in the Psalms." Pages 166-172 in *Soundings in the Theology of Psalms: Perspectives and Methods in Contemporary Scholarship*. Edited by R. A. Jacobson. Minneapolis: Fortress Press, 2011.

Nehrbass, D. M. *Praying Curses: The Theraputic and Preaching Value of the Imprecatory Psalms*. Eugene: Pickwick, 2013.

Nelson, R. A. "Exegeting Forgiveness." *American Theological Inquiry (Online)* (2012).

Neufeld, D. "Acts of Admonition and Rebuke: A Speech Act Approach to 1 Corinthians 6:1-11." *Biblical Interpretation* 8, no. 4 (2000): 375-399.

———. *Reconceiving Texts as Speech Acts: An Analysis of 1 John*. Vol. 7, Biblical Interpretation. Leiden: Brill, 1994.

Nicole, R. R., C. E. Hill, and F. A. James. *The Glory of the Atonement: Biblical, Historical & Practical Perspectives: Essays in Honor of Roger Nicole*. Downers Grove: IVP, 2004.

Noble, P. R. *The Canonical Approach: A Critical Reconstruction of the Hermeneutics of Brevard S. Childs*. Biblical Interpretation Series. Leiden: Brill, 1995.

Nolland, J. *Luke 18:35-24:53*. Vol. 35C, Word Biblical Commentary Dallas: Word, 1993.

Novick, T. "Succeeding Judas: Exegesis in Acts 1:15-26." *Journal of Biblical Literature* 129, no. 4 (2010): 795-799.

Obermann, A. *Die Christologische Erfüllung der Schrift im Johannesevangelium: Eine Untersuchung zur Johannieschen Hermeneutik Anhand der Schriftzitate*. Wissenschaftliche Untersuchungen zum Neuen Testament 2. Reihe 83. Tübingen with umlaut: Mohr (Siebeck), 1996.

Osborne, G. R. *The Hermeneutical Spiral: A Comprehensive Introduction to Biblical Interpretation*. Downers Grove: IVP, 2006.

---. "Literary Theory and Biblical Interpretation." Pages 17-50 in *Words and the Word: Explorations in Biblical Interpretation and Literary Theory*. Edited by D. G. Firth and J. A. Grant. Downers Grove: IVP 2008.

Peels, H. G. L. "'I Hate Them with Perfect Hatred' (Psalm 139:21-22)." *Tyndale Bulletin* 59, no. 1 (2008): 35-51.

---. *The Vengeance of God: The Meaning of the Root Nqm and the Function of the Nqm-Texts in the Context of Divine Revelation in the Old Testament*. Oudtestamentische Studiën,. Leiden: Brill, 1995.

Peterson, B. N. *Ezekiel in Context: Ezekiel's Message Understood in Its Historical Setting of Covenant Curses and Ancient near Eastern Mythological Motifs*. Princeton Theological Monograph Series 182. Eugene: Pickwick, 2012.

Peterson, D. *Where Wrath and Mercy Meet: Proclaiming the Atonement Today*. Carlisle: Paternoster, 2001.

Peterson, E. H. *Answering God: The Psalms as Tools for Prayer*. 1st ed. San Francisco: Harper & Row, 1989.

Poythress, V. S. "Canon and Speech Act: Limitations in Speech-Act Theory, with Implications for a Putative Theory of Canonical Speech Acts." *Westminster Theological Journal* 70, no. 2 (2008): 337-354.

---. "Divine Meaning of Scripture." *Westminster Theological Journal* 48, no. 2 (1986): 241-279.

Pratt, M. L. *Toward a Speech Act Theory of Literary Discourse*. Bloomington: Indiana University Press, 1977.

Quinn, P. L. "Can God Speak? Does God Speak?" *Religious Studies* 37, no. 3 (2001): 259-269.

Ricœur, P. *Interpretation Theory: Discourse and the Surplus of Meaning*. Fort Worth: Texas Christian University Press, 1976.

---. "The Model of the Text: Meaningful Action Considered as a Text." Pages 144-167 in *From Text to Action: Essays in Hermeneutics II*. Evanston: Northwestern University Press, 2007.

---. *The Rule of Metaphor: Multi-Disciplinary Studies of the Creation of Meaning in Language*. University of Toronto Romance Series 37. Toronto: University of Toronto Press, 1977.

---. "Toward a Hermeneutic of the Idea of Revelation." Pages 73-118 in *Essays on Biblical Interpretation*. Edited by P. Ricœur and L. S. Mudge. Philadelphia: Fortress Press, 1980.

Ridderbos, H. N. and J. Vriend. *The Gospel According to John: A Theological Commentary*. Grand Rapids: Eerdmans, 1997.

Ryken, L., J. Wilhoit, T. Longman, C. Duriez, D. Penney, and D. G. Reid. "Water." Pages 929-932 in *Dictionary of Biblical Imagery*. Downers Grove: IVP, 1998.

Sander, O. "Leib-Seele-Dualismus Im Alten Testament." *Zeitschrift für die alttestamentliche Wissenschaft* 77, no. 3 (1965): 329-332.

Sandy, D. B. *Plowshares & Pruning Hooks: Rethinking the Language of Biblical Prophecy and Apocalyptic*. Downers Grove: IVP, 2002.

Sarisky, D. *Scriptural Interpretation: A Theological Exploration*. Challenges in Contemporary Theology. Malden: Wiley-Blackwell, 2013.

Savran, G. ""How Can We Sing a Song of the Lord?" The Strategy of Lament in Psalm 137." *Zeitschrift für die alttestamentliche Wissenschaft* 112, no. 1 (2000): 43-58.

Scalise, C. J. *Hermeneutics as Theological Prolegomena: A Canonical Approach*. Studies in American Biblical Hermeneutics. Macon: Mercer University Press, 1994.

Schreiner, T. R. *Romans*. Baker Exegetical Commentary on the New Testament. Grand Rapids: Baker Books, 1998.

Searle, J. R. *The Construction of Social Reality*. New York: Free Press, 1995.

———. *Expression and Meaning: Studies in the Theory of Speech Acts*. Cambridge: Cambridge University Press, 1979.

———. *Intentionality, an Essay in the Philosophy of Mind*. Cambridge: Cambridge University Press, 1983.

———. *Speech Acts: An Essay in the Philosophy of Language*. London: Cambridge University Press, 1969.

Searle, J. R., F. Kiefer, and M. Bierwisch. *Speech Act Theory and Pragmatics*. Synthese Language Library 10. Dordrecht: D. Reidel, 1980.

Seifrid, M. A. "Romans." Pages 607-694 in *Commentary on the New Testament Use of the Old Testament*. Edited by G. K. Beale and D. A. Carson. Grand Rapids: Baker 2007.

Seitz, C. R. *The Goodly Fellowship of the Prophets: The Achievement of Association in Canon Formation*. Acadia Studies in Bible and Theology. Grand Rapids: Baker 2009.

———. *Prophecy and Hermeneutics: Toward a New Introduction to the Prophets*. Studies in Theological Interpretation. Grand Rapids: Baker, 2007.

———. "The Canonical Approach and Theological Interpretation." Pages 58-110 in *Canon and Biblical Interpretation*. Edited by C. Bartholomew, S. Hahn, R. Parry, C. Seitz and A. Wolters. Vol. 7. Grand Rapids: Zondervan, 2006.

Seybold, K. *Die Wallfahrtspsalmen: Studien zur Entstehungsgeschichte von Psalm 120-134*. Biblisch-Theologische Studien 3. Neukirchen-Vluyn: Neukirchener Verlag, 1978.

Shead, A. G. *A Mouth Full of Fire: The Word of God in the Words of Jeremiah*. New Studies in Biblical Theology. Nottingham: Apollos, 2012.

Shepherd, J. "The Place of the Imprecatory Psalms in the Canon of Scripture." *Churchman* 111, no. 1 (1997): 27-47.

———. "The Place of the Imprecatory Psalms in the Canon of Scripture." *Churchman* 111, no. 2 (1997): 110-126.

Shults, F. L. and S. J. Sandage. *The Faces of Forgiveness: Searching for Wholeness and Salvation*. Grand Rapids: Baker, 2003.

Sloane, A. *At Home in a Strange Land: Using the Old Testament in Christian Ethics*. Peabody: Hendrickson, 2008.

———. *On Being a Christian in the Academy: Nicholas Wolterstorff and the Practice of Christian Scholarship*. Paternoster Biblical and Theological Monographs. Carlisle: Paternoster, 2003.

Smedes, L. B. *Forgive and Forget: Healing the Hurts We Don't Deserve*. 1st ed. San Francisco: Harper & Row, 1984.

Smith, B. "Towards a History of Speech Act Theory." Pages 26-61 in *Speech Acts, Meaning, and Intentions: Critical Approaches to the Philosophy of John R. Searle*. Edited by A. Burkhardt. Berlin: de Gruyter, 1990.

Starling, D. "The Messianic Hope in the Psalms." *Reformed Theological Review* 58, no. 3 (1999): 121-134.

Stein, R. H. "The Benefits of an Author-Oriented Approach to Hermeneutics." *Journal of the Evangelical Theological Society* 44, no. 3 (2001): 451-466.

Strahan, J. M. *The Limits of a Text: Luke 23:34a as a Case Study in Theological Interpretation*. Journal of Theological Interpretation Supplements 5. Winona Lake: Eisenbrauns, 2012.

Swinburne, R. *Responsibility and Atonement*. Oxford: Clarendon, 1989.

Tate, M. E. *Psalms 51-100*. Vol. 20, Word Biblical Commentary. Dallas: Word, 1990.

Thiselton, A. C. *The First Epistle to the Corinthians*. New International Greek Testament Commentary. Grand Rapids: Eerdmans, 2000.

———. *New Horizons in Hermeneutics: The Theory and Practice of Transforming Biblical Reading*. Grand Rapids: Zondervan, 1992.

———. "Speech-Act Theory and the Claim That God Speaks: Nicholas Wolterstorff's Divine Discourse." *Scottish Journal of Theology* 50, no. 1 (1997): 97-110.

———. "Communicative Action and Promise in Hermeneutics." Pages 133-239 in *The Promise of Hermeneutics*. Edited by R. Lundin, A. C. Thiselton and C. Walhout. Grand Rapids: Eerdmans, 1999.

———. "Reader-Response Hermeneutics, Action Models, and the Parables of Jesus." Pages 79-113 in *The Responsibility of Hermeneutics*. Edited by R. Lundin, A. C. Thiselton and C. Walhout. Grand Rapids: Eerdmans, 1985.

———. "Authority and Hermeneutics: Some Proposals for a More Creative Agenda." Pages 107-141 in *A Pathway into the Holy Scripture*. Edited by P. E. Satterthwaite and D. F. Wright. Grand Rapids: Eerdmans, 1994.

———. "Hermeneutics." Pages 283-287 in *Dictionary for Theological Interpretation of the Bible*. Edited by K. J. Vanhoozer, C. G. Bartholomew, D. J. Treier and N. T. Wright. London: SPCK, 2005.

Thomas, R. L. "Imprecatory Prayers of the Apocalypse." *Bibliotheca sacra* 126, no. 502 (1969): 123-131.

Thompson, M. *A Clear and Present Word: The Clarity of Scripture*. New Studies in Biblical Theology. Nottingham: Apollos, 2006.

Tilley, T. W. *The Evils of Theodicy*. Washington: Georgetown University Press, 1991.

Treier, D. J. *Introducing Theological Interpretation of Scripture: Recovering a Christian Practice*. Grand Rapids: Baker, 2008.

———. *Virtue and the Voice of God: Toward Theology as Wisdom*. Grand Rapids: Eerdmans, 2006.

———. "Canonical Unit and Commensurable Language: On Divine Action and Doctrine." Pages 211-228 in *Evangelicals & Scripture: Tradition, Authority, and Hermeneutics*. Edited by V. Bacote, L. C. Miguélez and D. L. Okholm. Downers Grove: IVP, 2004.

Trzyna, T. "The Social Construction of Forgiveness." *Christian Scholar's Review* 27, no. 2 (1997): 226-241.

Tsohatzidis, S. L. "Ways of Doing Things with Words." Pages 1-25 in *Foundations of Speech Act Theory: Philosophical and Linguistic Perspectives*. Edited by S. L. Tsohatzidis. London: Routledge, 1994.

Tucker, W. D. "Is Shame a Matter of Patronage in the Communal Laments?" *Journal for the Study of the Old Testament* 31, no. 4 (2007): 465-480.

Turner, M. "Historical Criticism and Theological Hermeneutics of the New Testament." in *Between Two Horizons: Spanning New Testament Studies and Systematic Theology*. Edited by J. B. Green and M. Turner. Grand Rapids: Eerdmans, 2000.

Vanhoozer, K. J. *The Drama of Doctrine: A Canonical-Linguistic Approach to Christian Theology*. 1st ed. Louisville: Westminster John Knox Press, 2005.

———. *First Theology: God, Scripture & Hermeneutics*. Downers Grove: IVP, 2002.

———. *Is There a Meaning in This Text?: The Bible, the Reader, and the Morality of Literary Knowledge*. Grand Rapids: Zondervan, 1998.

———. "The Semantics of Biblical Literature: Truth and Scripture's Diverse Literary Forms." Pages 53-104 in *Hermeneutics, Authority and Canon*. Edited by D. A. Carson and J. D. Woodbridge. Nottingham: IVP, 1986.

———. "From Speech Acts to Scripture Acts: The Covenant of Discourse & the Discourse of Covenant." Page 159-203 in *First Theology: God, Scripture & Hermeneutics*. Edited by K. J. Vanhoozer. Downers Grove: IVP, 2002.

———. "Imprisoned or Free? Text, Status, and Theological Interpretation in the Master/Slave Discourse of Philemon." Page 51-93 in *Reading Scripture with the Church: Toward a Hermeneutic for Theological Interpretation*. A.K.M. Adam, Stephen E. Fowl, Kevin J. Vanhoozer, and Francis Watson. Grand Rapids: Baker, 2006.

Vanhoozer, K. J., C. G. Bartholomew, D. J. Treier, and N. T. Wright. *Dictionary for Theological Interpretation of the Bible*. London: SPCK, 2005.

Villaneuva, F. G. "Preaching Lament." Pages 64-84 in *Reclaiming the Old Testament for Christian Preaching*. Edited by G. J. R. Kent, P. J. Kissling and L. A. Turner. Downers Grove: IVP, 2010.

Volf, M. *The End of Memory: Remembering Rightly in a Violent World*. Grand Rapids: Eerdmans, 2006.

———. *Exclusion and Embrace: A Theological Exploration of Identity, Otherness, and Reconciliation*. Nashville: Abingdon, 1996.

———. *Free of Charge: Giving and Forgiving in a Culture Stripped of Grace*. Grand Rapids: Zondervan, 2005.

———. "Forgiveness, Reconciliation, and Justice." Pages 268-287 in *Stricken by God?: Nonviolent Identification and the Victory of Christ*. Edited by B. Jersak and M. Hardin. Grand Rapids: Eerdmans, 2007.

Vos, J. G. "The Ethical Problem of the Imprecatory Psalms." *Westminster Theological Journal* 4, no. 2 (1942): 123-138.

Walker, R. H. *The Modern Message of the Psalms*. New York: Abingdon Press, 1938.

Wallace, H. N. *Words to God, Word from God: The Psalms in the Prayer and Preaching of the Church*. Aldershot: Ashgate, 2005.

Wallace, M. I. "Divine Discourse: Philosophical Reflections on the Claim That God Speaks." *Pro Ecclesia* 7, no. 2 (1998): 242-244.

Waltke, B. K. "Canonical Process Approach to the Psalms." Pages 5-15 in *Tradition and Testament: Essays in Honor of Charles Lee Feinberg*. Edited by C. L. Feinberg, J. S. Feinberg and P. D. Feinberg. Chicago: Moody Press, 1981.

Ward, T. *Word and Supplement: Speech Acts, Biblical Texts, and the Sufficiency of Scripture*. Oxford: Oxford University Press, 2002.

Wardlaw, T. R. J. "Discourse Analysis." Pages 266-317 in *Words and the Word: Explorations in Biblical Interpretation and Literary Theory*. Edited by D. G. Firth and J. A. Grant. Downers Grove: IVP 2008.

Warren, A. "Modality, Reference and Speech Acts in the Psalms." Ph.D., Cambridge, 1998.

Watson, F. *Text and Truth: Redefining Biblical Theology*. Grand Rapids: Eerdmans, 1997.

Wenham, G. J. *The Psalter Reclaimed: Praying and Praising with the Psalms*. Wheaton: Crossway, 2013.

_____. *Psalms as Torah: Reading Biblical Song Ethically*. Grand Rapids: Baker, 2012.

———. "Towards a Canonical Reading of the Psalms." Pages 333-351 in *Canon and Biblical Interpretation*. Edited by C. Bartholomew, S. Hahn, R. Parry, C. Seitz and A. Wolters. Grand Rapids: Zondervan, 2006.

Westermann, C. *The Living Psalms*. Grand Rapids: Eerdmans, 1989.

Westphal, M. "On Reading God the Author." *Religious Studies* 37, no. 3 (2001): 271-291.

Wheelwright, P. E. *The Burning Fountain: A Study in the Language of Symbolism*. New and rev. ed. Bloomington: Indiana University Press, 1968.

White, H. C. "The Value of Speech Act Theory for Old Testament Hermeneutics." *Semeia* 41 (1988): 41-63.

Whybray, N. *Reading the Psalms as a Book*. Sheffield: Sheffield Academic Press, 1996.

Wilson, G. H. *The Editing of the Hebrew Psalter*. Dissertation Series / Society of Biblical Literature no 76. Chico: Scholars Press, 1985.

———. *Psalms*. The NIV Application Commentary. Grand Rapids: Zondervan, 2002.

———. "The Structure of the Psalter." Pages 229-246 in *Interpreting the Psalms: Issues and Approaches*. Edited by D. G. Firth and P. S. Johnston. Leicester: Apollos, 2005.

Wisse, M. "From Cover to Cover? A Critique of Wolterstorff's Theory of the Bible as Divine Discourse." *International Journal for Philosophy of Religion* 52, no. 3 (2002): 159-173.

Wittgenstein, L. *Philosophical Investigations*. 3rd ed. New York: Macmillan, 1968.

Wolterstorff, N. *Divine Discourse: Philosophical Reflections on the Claim That God Speaks*. Cambridge: Cambridge University Press, 1995.

———. *Justice in Love*. Emory University Studies in Law and Religion. Grand Rapids: Eerdmans, 2011.

———. "The Promise of Speech-Act Theory for Biblical Interpretation." Pages 73-90 in *After Pentecost: Language and Biblical Interpretation*. Edited by C. G. Bartholomew, C. J. D. Greene and K. Möller. Carlisle: Paternoster Press, 2001.

Worthington, E. L. "Just Forgiving: How the Psychology and Theology of Forgiveness and Justice Inter-Relate." *Journal of Psychology and Christianity* 25, no. 2 (2006): 155-168.

Worthington, E. L., C. B. Sharp, A. J. Lerner, and J. R. Sharp. "Interpersonal Forgiveness as an Example of Loving One's Enemies." *Journal of Psychology & Theology* 34, no. 1 (2006): 32-42.

Wright, C. J. H. *Old Testament Ethics for the People of God*. Downers Grove: IVP, 2004.

Wright, N. T. *The New Testament and the People of God*. Christian Origins and the Question of God. Minneapolis: Fortress Press, 1992.

Zenger, E. *A God of Vengeance? Understanding the Psalms of Divine Wrath*. Louisville: Westminster, 1996.

Zimmermann, J. *Recovering Theological Hermeneutics: An Incarnational-Trinitarian Theory of Interpretation*. Grand Rapids: Baker, 2004.

# Index of Authors and Subject

**A**
allegorical  42, 61, 130
Altson, William P.  74
Alter, Robert  164
Austin, John L.  15–16, 24, 26, 30, 66, 69, 76, 138–139
authorial discourse  21–23, 26, 32, 35, 63, 80, 123
authorial intention  29, 35, 41–42, 45–47, 53, 61, 70

**B**
Babylon  170–172, 177, 180, 197, 215
background  13, 56, 71, 87, 98, 100, 194
Barker, Kit  66, 93, 112, 127, 132, 134, 138, 156, 170, 174, 176, 213
Bartholomew, Craig  1–3, 5, 6, 41
bless, blessed, blessing  154, 159, 164, 168, 170, 172, 178, 180, 217
Briggs, Richard S.  2, 4–6, 12, 15–17, 20, 21, 53, 68, 70, 104, 108, 137, 139
Brown, Jeannine K.  15, 47–53, 55, 73, 74, 86, 119
Brown, Raymond E.  37–38, 202
Brueggemann, Walter  51, 109–110, 113–116, 122, 130–131, 133, 163, 206

**C**
canonical
  canonical illocution  4, 30, 34, 50, 56–58, 95–98, 100, 102, 176
  canonical inclusion  107, 109
  canonical genre  96–97, 102
  canonical context  8, 40, 53, 91, 103, 124, 177–178, 180, 183, 200, 210, 212, 216
  canonical shaping  41, 107, 111
Carson, D. A.  5–6, 21, 38, 45, 138, 140–142, 147, 201, 203–204, 207
central illocution  72, 98–101, 103, 136–137, 157, 176, 180, 183, 200, 213–216
Childs, Brevard S.  2, 44, 64, 81, 112–113, 124–125
Christological  8, 131, 178, 180–185, 204, 207, 212
communal  1, 8, 18, 34, 112, 118, 160, 163, 173, 189–190, 194, 212, 215
communicative
  act, action  7, 17–19, 21–23, 26–29, 32, 34–36, 47, 50–53, 57, 63, 65, 69–70, 73, 75, 82, 90, 92, 94, 96, 129
  intention  26–28, 47–49, 53, 57, 71–72, 90, 96, 129
contextualization  49–51, 217
continuous-canonical reading  117–118
covenant  34, 45, 48, 52, 65, 90, 94, 99, 120, 129, 135, 152, 172, 174, 176–178, 184, 198
Creach, Jerome F. D.  112, 114
cult  111, 118, 192
curse, cursing  17, 131, 137, 151–153, 155–156, 162, 164, 167, 195–196, 207–208

**D**
Day, John  111, 128, 131, 135, 151–152, 154–155

democratization 118–119, 121, 162, 181
deputation 33, 58
diachronic illocutionary
  divergence 91, 93–95, 99, 101–102, 176
direction of address 172–173, 175, 192, 199
discourse
  authorial 21–23, 26, 32, 35, 63, 80, 123
  human 20, 58–59, 60
divine discourse 1, 3–5, 7–8, 36–39, 51–52, 56, 58–62, 64–65, 90, 92, 95, 103, 105, 107–108, 121–123, 125–127, 136, 157–158, 174, 176, 178, 186, 200, 212–217
dual authorship 3, 7–8, 22, 36–37, 47, 55–56, 58–59, 62–66, 103, 105, 121–123, 158, 217

E
eschatological 45, 113, 116–117, 149–150, 178
Evangelical 40, 43–44
extra-linguistic 98–100

F
Firth, David G. 2, 28, 33–34, 67, 70, 85–86, 88, 108–113, 119, 128–129, 132–133, 135, 160, 173, 189, 201
forgiveness 131, 137–155, 214–215
form criticism 108

G
generic illocution 86, 88, 114
Goldingay, John 38, 117, 16–162, 166–167, 190, 194, 198, 201
Grant, Jaime A. 2, 67, 70, 85–86, 119, 178, 181, 184, 205–206

H
hermeneutic
  non-realist 11, 21–22, 24, 27–28, 70, 73
  realist 29, 70, 73, 212
  reconceptualising 33

Romantic 32, 70, 75, 79
theological 1–7, 16–17, 20–21, 29, 35–36, 55, 65–66, 88, 98, 105, 108, 212–214, 216–217
Holy Spirit 52–53

I
illocution(s)
  "in play" 45, 53, 61, 65, 81–82, 90, 95, 99, 125–127, 136–137, 176, 178, 183, 186, 209–210, 214–215
  attendant (or secondary) 14, 63, 79, 83, 88–89, 94–95, 99–100, 160–161, 171–173, 176, 179, 215
  canonical 4
  central 89, 98–103, 136–137, 157, 176, 178, 180, 183, 200, 213–216
  divine 56–57, 60, 64, 90–93, 95–96, 101–103, 107, 109, 111–113, 115, 117, 119, 121, 123, 125, 127, 134, 136, 156–157, 159, 171, 173–178, 180, 183, 186, 199–200, 209–210, 212–217
  higher-level 79, 84, 87, 92–93, 97, 101, 109, 124, 213
  human 58, 91–92, 94, 96, 101–102, 107, 126, 174, 213
  lower-level 77, 79, 83, 86–88, 92, 96–98, 102, 107, 121, 125, 126, 136, 159, 173, 214
  primary 44, 63, 83, 88–89, 94, 99–100, 107, 109–111, 112, 114–115, 118–121, 125, 132, 134–136, 161, 171, 173–176, 179, 211, 214
  sentential 83, 84, 89, 93, 96, 98, 100
  strong 19, 21, 74, 98, 138–139, 152
  sub-sentential 83, 99–101, 103, 213

super-sentential 83, 84, 99–100
supervening 98, 103–104, 128, 136, 214
sum of 57, 64, 83, 90, 96
whole-text 88–89, 100, 107, 111, 125–126, 157–158, 176, 199, 213–216
illocutionary
convergence 175–176, 213
divergence (see diachronic illocutionary divergence and synchronic illocutionary divergence
level(s) 84, 99–101
stance 7, 62, 65, 78, 101–102, 109–111, 120–121, 125–126, 128, 132–133, 135–137, 156–158, 168, 178, 214–215
intentional fallacy 70–72, 74, 76

**L**
lament 8, 34, 88, 115–116, 118, 121, 124, 153, 158, 160–164, 166, 172–174, 180, 184, 186, 189–190, 192–194, 198, 201, 212, 215, 217
language games 15, 22, 69, 80
*lex talionis* 125, 170, 172

**M**
Mays, James L. 109, 113–114, 118, 162, 165, 184–185
McCann, John C. 109, 179, 206
meaning, (see also thick description, sum of illocutions)
determinate 22, 23, 52, 53, 69
single determinate 45, 53, 212
surplus of 119, 177
metaphor, metaphorical 21, 55, 59–61, 74, 76–77, 120, 143, 169, 193, 202
Miller, Patrick D. 112, 114, 119, 160, 162, 184
mimesis, mimetic 111, 117–121, 126, 132, 134, 136, 157, 174, 175, 179–180, 184–186, 189, 209–210, 214–216

misfire 25, 74, 80, 139, 140, 143, 157, 214, 215, 216

**N**
New Criticism 76, 79
noematic 23, 74, 76–79, 93

**P**
penitence, penitent 138, 140–150, 179
performative 12, 13, 18, 21, 50, 67, 69, 138, 139
perlocution, perlocutionary act 12, 14, 17, 19, 22–27, 30, 33, 51–52, 64, 67, 72–75, 108, 138–139, 151, 185
perlocutionary intent, intention 49, 51, 72–75
Psalter, primary illocutions of 107, 109–112, 114–115, 118–121, 125, 132, 134–136, 171, 174–176, 179, 211, 214
Poythress, Vern S. 7, 21, 38–40, 55, 67, 82–85
public action 30, 32, 70, 79, 108

**R**
reader response 22, 25
relocution 166, 168
rhetorical 59–60, 84, 167, 171, 191
Ricoeur, Paul 11, 17, 21, 23, 26, 41, 76–78, 84, 115
rule-governed 16, 82

**S**
Searle, John R. 6, 12–17, 19, 26–27, 30, 67–68, 76, 82, 85–86, 108
Seitz, Christopher R. 1, 6, 19, 20, 41, 56, 64
self-involving 20, 118, 121, 165, 168, 172–173, 193, 198–199
sense and reference 12–13, 45–46
*sensus plenior* 7, 37–38, 40–48, 52–57, 61, 65–66, 90–91, 93–94, 96, 99, 101, 210, 212–214, 216
speech act criticism 16–18, 20, 34–35, 67, 108

strong speech act, (see illocution, strong)   24, 72, 138–139, 149–151
structuralist, structuralism   11, 70, 76, 79–82, 103
supervention, supervening   98, 103–104, 128, 136, 175–176, 213–214
synchronic illocutionary convergence   175
synchronic illocutionary divergence   91–92, 96, 101–102, 175

**T**
text imminent   190
thick description   29, 35, 63, 82–85, 89–90, 94, 101, 157–160, 171, 200, 209, 213, 216
Thiselton, Anthony C.   2, 4, 11, 18–19, 21, 23, 26, 36
*torah*   113, 134–135, 178
transhistorial intention   48, 65
Treier, Daniel J.   1, 4, 6,–7, 28, 55, 64, 82, 86–87

**V**
Vanhoozer, Kevin J.   1–6, 13, 15, 17, 21–22, 26, 28–30, 34–36, 39, 48, 52, 55–56, 58, 60, 64, 70–71, 75, 78–79, 81–82, 86–89, 95–98, 104, 175
Volf, Miroslav   137–138, 143–145, 148

**W**
Wenham, Gordan J.   41, 108, 117, 131, 135–136, 192
Wilson, Gerald H.   109, 112, 114, 116–118, 189–190, 194, 203
Wolterstorff, Nicholas   2–6, 15, 17–18, 21, 27–28, 30–32, 34, 39, 41, 44, 55–56, 58–64, 67, 70, 73, 76–80, 92–93, 96, 101, 108–109, 121, 123, 138, 140, 148, 158, 171

**Y**
Yahweh reigns   114, 120–121, 136
*Yom Yahweh*   156, 178

# Index of Scripture

Genesis
  31:27   166

Exodus
  2:23–25   170
  3:7–10   170
  6:2–8   170
  15:22–27   85
  20:2   91
  32:32–33   195

Leviticus
  5:1   196

Deuteronomy
  29:4   207
  31:17–18   195
  32:20   195
  32:25   171

Judges
  17:3   196

Ruth
  2:9, 14   195

2 Samuel
  12:13–14   149
  18:9   167

2 Kings
  8:12   171
  18:25–35   166

Esther
  7:9   207

Psalms
  1   89, 110–114, 116, 125, 134–135, 196
  1:1   172
  1:2   113
  1:5–6   114
  1–2   170, 178
  2   89, 111–114, 134–135
  3   110
  3–41   192
  9:10–14   198
  9:9–12   198
  10:12   198
  12:6   198
  13:2   195
  14:6   198
  17:14   129
  18   110
  18:27   198
  19   113
  22   181, 185, 201–202, 204
  22:24   198
  30:7–8   195
  34:6   198
  35   192
  35:10   198
  35:11–17   155
  40   192
  40:14–18   192
  40:17   198
  44   191, 199
  45:17–21   163
  46   166
  48   166
  48:6   161
  51   92, 192

51:16–17   149
53   191
54:5   129
55:16–17   129
57   197
57:7   186
58   129
58:11   135
59   191
59:6, 14   129
65   191
65–68   190–191
68–71   198
68:10   198
68:21–23   129
69   1, 8, 173, 180–182, 184–186, 189–192, 197–198, 200–212, 215–216
69–71   190–191
69–72   190–191
69:10   191
69:10   196
69:11   191
69:14b–19   192, 195
69:17–18   195
69:18   191
69:2–30   192–193
69:2–5   192–193
69:20   191, 195–196
69:20–30   192, 195
69:21   191, 201
69:21–22   195
69:22–28   205
69:24–30   129
69:25   204–205
69:27   196
69:28   196
69:29   195
69:30   191, 196
69:31–32   198
69:31–37   190, 192, 208
69:32–33   202
69:33–34   204
69:33–36   189
69:34   191

69:35   203
69:35–37   204
69:4   201
69:6–14a   192–193
69:7   191
69:8   191
69:9   189
69:9   203, 208
69:9a   201
69:9b   201
70   191–192
70:2   191
70:3   191
70:6   191
71   191
71:1   191
71:12   191
71:13   191
71:24   191
72   191, 198
72:12   191
72:12–14   198
72:13   191
72:14   191
72:2   191
72:4   191
73   196
73–83   192
74:22   135
76   166
76:3   161
79:10, 12   129
83:17   129, 135
84   166
86:1   198
88:15   195
93   59, 62
101:6, 9   129
107:41   198
109   180, 191–192, 204–208
109:13–15   205
109:4–5   155
109:5–19   129
109:6–12   206
109:8   205

110    114
118    181
119    113
120–134    162
132    114
132:3–5    167
135    170
135–137    162
135:13–14    170
135:8–12    170
136    170
136:17–22    170
136:23–24    170
137    1, 8, 59, 128, 130, 134, 158,
       160–163, 170–171, 174–180,
       183, 197, 211–212, 215
137:1–4    163, 166, 171
137:1–9    159
137:5–6    163, 167
137:7–9    129, 158, 168
137:8–9    171
137:9    170
138    162
139    197
139:18–122    153
139:19–22    129, 135
139:21    135
140:12    198
140:9–11    129
143:11–12    135
143:12    129
144    114
146–150    111
149    134, 177
149:6–9    163
150    116–117

Proverbs
29:24    196

Isaiah
13:1    171
13:14–16    171
13:16    128
13:9    171

24:8    166
29:10    207
40–55    89
49:8–9    194
53    181
54:1–3    171
54:13    171
54:5–6    171

Jeremiah
50–51    171
51:25    171
54:58    171

Ezekiel
1:1    165
9    195
16    169
3:15    165
3:23    165
18:30–32    149
25:12–14    165
35:1–36:15    169
36:20–22ff    166

Hosea
14    149

Amos
1–9    56

Obadiah
10–14    169

Jonah
1–4    3, 56, 88, 95–96

Nahum
3:10    171

Zechariah
1:15    162
7:3    160

# Index of Scripture

Matthew
- 5:43–44   204
- 6:9–13   156
- 11:20–24   149, 155
- 18   146
- 18:15–19   145
- 18:21–22   145
- 18:21–25   149
- 18:22   141
- 19:4–5   36
- 23:13–39   155
- 27:46   147

Mark
- 1–16   25, 203
- 1:15   149
- 11:12–14   155
- 11:20–21   155
- 12:30–31   154
- 15:29   204

Luke
- 5:17–26   146
- 6:27–28   204
- 13:1–9   149
- 17:3–4   146
- 23   142
- 23:23–34   155
- 23:34a   146, 147

John
- 2   182, 200
- 2:17   201–202
- 15   209–210
- 15:24   203
- 19   202
- 19:28–29   202

Acts
- 1   204
- 1:16   204
- 1:20   204
- 2:30   205
- 2:34   205
- 2:37   204
- 4:25–27   205

Romans
- 1:9   93
- 7   154
- 11:9–10   207
- 12   153
- 15   209–210
- 15:3   201, 207–208

1 Corinthians
- 6:1–11   18
- 6:5   18

2 Corinthians
- 7:10   149

Galatians
- 1:8–9   156
- 5:12   156

Colossians
- 3:12–14   142
- 3:16   184

2 Timothy
- 3:16   36, 97

Philemon
- 1–25   3

Hebrews
- 1–13   81
- 4   45

1 Peter
- 5:13   177

2 Peter
- 3:16   36

James
- 3   154

1 John
  1:9   149

Revelation
  2:11   25
  4   177
  5   177
  6   156
  6:10   156
  14:8   177
  16:9   177
  17:5   177
  18:2   177
  18:10   177
  18:21   177
  19   177
  20:11–15   195
  21   201
  21:27   201

www.ingramcontent.com/pod-product-compliance
Lightning Source LLC
Chambersburg PA
CBHW030515080526
44586CB00011B/200